THE CONCEPT OF THE BUDDHA

This book presents an analysis of one of the fundamental Mahāyāna Buddhist teachings, namely the three bodies of the Buddha (the *trikāya* theory), which is considered the foundation of Mahāyāna philosophy. The author traces the development of the concept of the Buddha from the historical human teacher in early Buddhism to the philosophical concept of three bodies, particularly the *saṃbhogakāya*, which is the Buddha endowed with supernatural attributes and qualities. The author's translations from early and middle Mahāyāna *sūtras* and *śāstras* make newly accessible a wealth of material. This work is an outstanding research text for students and scholars of Mahāyāna Buddhism and anyone interested in Buddhist philosophy.

Guang Xing obtained his Ph.D. from the School of Oriental and African Studies, the University of London, in 2003. He is a research assistant professor at the Centre of Buddhist Studies, the University of Hong Kong. His research interests are Chinese and Mahāyāna Buddhist studies, particularly the origin of Mahāyāna.

ROUTLEDGECURZON CRITICAL STUDIES IN BUDDHISM

General Editors: Charles S. Prebish and Damien Keown

RoutledgeCurzon Critical Studies in Buddhism is a comprehensive study of the Buddhist tradition. The series explores this complex and extensive tradition from a variety of perspectives, using a range of different methodologies.

The series is diverse in its focus, including historical studies, textual translations and commentaries, sociological investigations, bibliographic studies, and considerations of religious practice as an expression of Buddhism's integral religiosity. It also presents materials on modern intellectual historical studies, including the role of Buddhist thought and scholarship in a contemporary, critical context and in the light of current social issues. The series is expansive and imaginative in scope, spanning more than two and a half millennia of Buddhist history. It is receptive to all research works that inform and advance our knowledge and understanding of the Buddhist tradition.

THE REFLEXIVE NATURE OF AWARENESS
Paul Williams

ALTRUISM AND REALITY
Paul Williams

BUDDHISM AND HUMAN RIGHTS
Edited by Damien Keown, Charles Prebish and Wayne Husted

WOMEN IN THE FOOTSTEPS OF THE BUDDHA
Kathryn R. Blackstone

THE RESONANCE OF EMPTINESS
Gay Watson

AMERICAN BUDDHISM
Edited by Duncan Ryuken Williams and Christopher Queen

IMAGING WISDOM
Jacob N. Kinnard

PAIN AND ITS ENDING
Carol S. Anderson

EMPTINESS APPRAISED
David F. Burton

THE SOUND OF LIBERATING TRUTH
Edited by Sallie B. King and Paul O. Ingram

BUDDHIST THEOLOGY
Edited by Roger R. Jackson and John J. Makransky

THE GLORIOUS DEEDS OF PURNA
Joel Tatelman

EARLY BUDDHISM – A NEW APPROACH
Sue Hamilton

CONTEMPORARY BUDDHIST ETHICS
Edited by Damien Keown

INNOVATIVE BUDDHIST WOMEN
Edited by Karma Lekshe Tsomo

TEACHING BUDDHISM IN THE WEST
Edited by V. S. Hori, R. P. Hayes and J. M. Shields

EMPTY VISION
David L. McMahan

SELF, REALITY AND REASON IN TIBETAN PHILOSOPHY
Thupten Jinpa

IN DEFENSE OF DHARMA
Tessa J. Bartholomeusz

BUDDHIST PHENOMENOLOGY
Dan Lusthaus

RELIGIOUS MOTIVATION AND THE ORIGINS OF BUDDHISM
Torkel Brekke

DEVELOPMENTS IN AUSTRALIAN BUDDHISM
Michelle Spuler

ZEN WAR STORIES
Brian Victoria

THE BUDDHIST UNCONSCIOUS
William S. Waldron

INDIAN BUDDHIST THEORIES OF PERSONS
James Duerlinger

ACTION DHARMA
Edited by Christopher Queen, Charles Prebish and Damien Keown

TIBETAN AND ZEN BUDDHISM IN BRITAIN
David N. Kay

THE CONCEPT OF THE BUDDHA
Guang Xing

THE CONCEPT OF THE BUDDHA

Its evolution from early Buddhism to the *trikāya* theory

Guang Xing

RoutledgeCurzon
Taylor & Francis Group
LONDON AND NEW YORK

Transferred to digital printing 2010

First published 2005
by RoutledgeCurzon
2 Park Square, Milton Park,
Abingdon, Oxon, OX14 4RN

Simultaneously published in the USA and Canada
by RoutledgeCurzon
270 Madison Ave, New York, NY 10016

RoutledgeCurzon is an imprint of the Taylor & Francis Group

Typeset in 10/12pt Times by Graphicraft Limited, Hong Kong

British Library Cataloguing in Publication Data
A catalogue record for this book is available
from the British Library

Library of Congress Cataloging in Publication Data
A catalog record for this book has been requested

ISBN 0–415–33344–X (hbk)
ISBN 978–0–415–33344–3 (hbk)

ISBN 0–415–60002–2 (pbk)
ISBN 978–0–415–60002–6 (pbk)

This book is dedicated to all the teachers who have helped and guided me, and to Po Lin Monastery, which has generously supported me in my studies

CONTENTS

ACKNOWLEDGEMENTS

This book is a revised version of my Ph.D. dissertation. I am most deeply indebted to many people who have advised, assisted and supported me in the process of writing and revising it. First and foremost, I am very grateful to Professor Tadeusz Skorupski and Professor Timothy Barrett, for their guidance and the numerous improvements they made to my work. I am also indebted to Professor Brian Bocking, Professor Paul Harrison and Dr K. Anuruddha, my friends Dr Jing Yin, Dr Simu W. D. Kim and Dr Yao Zhihua, for their valuable suggestions and critical analysis which helped me to formulate my ideas for this book. My special thanks also go to Professor Damien Keown, Dr Andrew Skilton and Professor John Makransky for their critical suggestions and responses when I revised it. I must express my special gratitude to Mr Zhao Puchu for his continuous support and encouragement which have sustained me through my years of study at SOAS.

Dr Toshiichi Endo and Mr Pathompong Bodhiprasiddhinand kindly furnished me with many useful books and articles for my references and Ms Francesca Tarocco helped me with some French passages. The free CDs of the Taisho Tripiṭaka provided by the Chinese Buddhist Electronic Text Association in Taiwan were very useful in my research. To all of them I am most thankful. My thanks also go to Ms Ho Wai Yee and Ms Jan Nicol for their tireless efforts in reading all my draft chapters, Mr Gianpaolo Vetturini, Ven. Weizhong and Dr Sun Shuyun for proofreading the final work and Ms Wu Xiujne for preparing the index. Thanks are also due to Mr and Mrs Wong Guotian, Mr and Mrs Li Guocheng, Mr and Mrs Hongyun Mok, Ken and Anita Hudson, Tu Jian and Li Yiren, to mention but a few, who have helped me in various ways.

Thanks also go to the *Buddhist Studies Review* and the *World Hongming Philosophical Quarterly* for their permission to reprint papers published in their journals.

My studies at SOAS were made possible by the scholarship generously offered by Po Lin Monastery, Hong Kong, which also agreed to support me financially so that I could complete my thesis after my three-year scholarship. In the final year of my study, I also received a Sutasoma scholarship to revise my thesis.

ABBREVIATIONS

*	Indication of a reconstructed Sanskrit title from an ancient Chinese translation of Buddhist text whenever the original Sanskrit is lost.
A	*Aṅguttaranikāya*
Aṣṭa	*Aṣṭasāhasrikā Prajñāpāramitāsūtra*
attrib.	attributed to
Avataṃsaka	*Buddhāvataṃsaka-mahāvaipulya-sūtra*
BCE	Before Common Era
CE	Common Era
D	*Dīghanikāya*
Dhp.	*Dhammapada*
DPPN	*Dictionary of Pāli Proper Names*, edited by Malalasekera
Kośa	*Abhidharmakośabhāṣya* of Vasubandhu
M	*Majjhimanikāya*
Miln.	*Milindapañha*
MMPS	Mahāyāna *Mahāparinirvāṇasūtra*
MPPŚ	**Mahāprajñāpāramitāśāstra* attributed to Nāgārjuna
MS	*Mahāyānasaṃgraha* of Asaṅga
MSA	*Mahāyānasūtrālaṃkāra* of Asaṅga
Pts.	*Paṭisambhidāmagga*
PTS	The Pali Text Society
S	*Saṃyuttanikāya*
T	*Taisho Shinshu Daizokyo*
tr.	translation
Vibhāṣā	**Mahāvibhāṣāśāstra*
Vsm.	*Visuddhimagga*

GLOSSARY

Āśrava Taints, or activity which is based on ignorance and is therefore saṃsāric, defiled, contaminated.

Bhavāgra The highest heaven of form, the ninth and the last of the fourth dhyāna heavens.

Bodhyaṅgāni The seven characteristics of bodhi or seven factors of enlightenment.

Buddhadhātu The Buddha-nature.

Buddhakṣetra The Buddha land or field.

Gotra Clan.

Hīnayāna Small vehicle, a term denotes all the eighteen or twenty sectarian schools arose after the passing away of Gautama Buddha and before the common era. It is a term given by the Mahāyānists.

Indriya Faculty.

Kaniṣka A king of India, a renowned patron of Buddhism, the date is not certain but around 1st BCE to 1st CE.

Kātyāyanīputra A teacher of the Sarvāstivāda school and the attributed author of the *Mahāvibhāṣāśāstra*.

Kleśa Defilement, all of the thoughts, words, actions and emotions which arise and cease based on ignorance and desire which keep human beings trapped in the cycle of birth and death, and which result in suffering.

Kṣaṇa A moment, an instant.

Mahāpuruṣa A great man who is endowed with the thirty-two major and eighty minor physical marks. The destination for such a person is either to become a full enlightened Buddha or an universal monarch.

Manomayakāya A body made of mind.

Pañca-kaṣāya Five turbidities: (1) 劫濁 *kalpakaṣāya*, the defilement of the trends of the present age; (2) 見濁 *dṛṣṭikaṣāya*, the defilement of mistaken views; (3) 煩惱濁 *kleśakaṣāya*, the defilement of afflictions; (4) 眾生濁 *sattvakaṣāya*, the defilement of being a sentient being; (5) 命濁 *āyuḥkaṣāya*, the defilement of having a lifetime.

Paracittajñāna The knowledge of other people's thinking.

Prahāṇāni Eliminate (permanently); to cut off, to sever, to destroy, to end.

Praṇidhāna The great vow, of a Buddha, or a bodhisattva, to save all the living and bring them to Buddhahood.

Prapañca Conceptual elaboration; idle discourse; frivolous talk; intellectual play; ideational proliferation. According to Nāgārjuna, it means words that conceal and cover reality, which are nothing but subjective counterfeits, and lead further into ignorance and affliction.

Pratisaṃvid The unhindered powers of interpretation.

Prayoga Making great endeavour.

Pṛthagjana Ordinary people without any spiritual attainment.

Ṛddhipādās The psychical power.

Rūpakāya The physical body. In the text, it is the physical body of the Buddha.

Saṃvṛtijñāna Ordinary or worldly knowledge or wisdom.

Śaikṣa Those who are still learning before attaining arahatship, the opposite is *aśaikṣa*, those who are beyond learning.

Śūnyatā Literally means emptiness, philosophically it means non-substantiality or non-self nature.

Tathāgatagarbha The womb of the tathāgata, or the matrix of the Thus Come One(s).

Tathatā Suchness, the nature of both conditioned and unconditioned things.

Trisāhasra Three thousand.

Upāyakauśalya Skill in means, a method employed by bodhisattvas to save sentient beings.

Vicāra Inquire, investigative thought.

Vikalpa To discriminate, distinguish.

Vimukti Liberation, salvation, deliverance.

Vimukti-jñāna-darśana The knowledge-and-vision of liberation, the knowledge and experience of *nirvāṇa*.

Vitarka Discursive thought.

INTRODUCTION

The purpose of the research

The *trikāya* theory is one of the most important and fundamental doctrinal developments of Mahāyāna Buddhism. The concepts of the *dharmakāya* and the *nirmāṇakāya* were already present in early Buddhism although the latter concept was expounded in the different form of *rūpakāya* that carries different implications. The concept of the *saṃbhogakāya*, however, appeared much later. The Buddha worshipped by Mahāyānist followers is an omnipotent divinity endowed with numerous supernatural attributes and qualities. This Buddha is none other than the *saṃbhogakāya*. How and why the concept of the *saṃbhogakāya* came into being is of great interest to the present writer because it is only with the advent of this concept that the *trikāya* theory came into existence. Besides, this question is closely related to a number of others. What position does the historical Buddha hold in Mahāyāna if its followers worship an almighty Buddha? How is this historical Buddha related to the *dharmakāya*?

Despite the importance of the *trikāya* theory, there is no comprehensive study of how the concept of the Buddha developed from early Buddhism to the formulation of this theory. Systematic research on the issue began in the early twentieth century with de La Vallée Poussin and Chizen Akanuma, who were the first to deal with this complex subject.[1] Their studies contributed significantly to knowledge about the most important features of this doctrine. However, these are primarily surveys that merely provide a picture of the final form of the doctrine, but do not trace the development of the notion of the Buddha in any detail.

Nagao Gadjin made an excellent study of the subject and noted several important points.[2] According to him, the *saṃbhogakāya* has a twofold character: in one aspect, it transcends the human Buddha (the theory of the *nirmāṇakāya*); in the other, it concretizes the absolute (the theory of the *dharmakāya*). Thus the *saṃbhogakāya* occupies a central position in the *trikāya* doctrine. The soteriological power of the Buddha is developed in conjunction with this double character. It was beyond the scope of Nagao's research, however, to trace the origin and development of the *trikāya* theory.

N. Dutt devotes a chapter of his work *Mahāyāna Buddhism* to the conception of *kāya*.[3] Unlike the scholars mentioned above, Dutt's discussion of the concept of *kāya* covers studies of the *Nikāyas* and the early Indian Buddhist schools. His discussion of the *kāya* concept in the *Nikāyas* is significant in that it collects and analyses all relevant passages on the subject. He points out that the conception of *kāya* in the *Nikāyas* has no metaphysical or doctrinal implications, but pertains, rather, to a realistic concept of the Buddha. His discussion on the concept of the Buddha in the early Indian Buddhist schools and the three bodies of Mahāyāna Buddhism still largely remains a survey.

S. Takeuchi's study of the bodies of the Buddha focuses primarily on Mahāyāna *sūtras*, particularly Yogācāra works.[4] Besides outlining the importance of the concept of the *saṃbhogakāya*, he dedicates a section of his article to a discussion of its origin. Takeuchi asserts that the *saṃbhogakāya* is closely connected with the bodhisattva ideal. Its key aspect is the vow that a bodhisattva takes at the beginning of spiritual training, which remains in force until the attainment of Buddhahood. In this connection, the *Sukhāvatīvyūhasūtra*, one of the earliest Mahāyāna texts, plays an important role as Amitābha Buddha is generally considered a *saṃbhogakāya*. However, the actual origin and development of the concept remain unexplained.

A recent study on the three bodies was conducted by John Makransky, who concentrates primarily on a discussion of the controversies over interpretation of the bodies of the Buddha in India and Tibet.[5] Although he also devotes two chapters to the concept of the Buddha in the Sarvāstivādin *Abhidharma* and the *Prajñāpāramitāsūtras*, these merely constitute a survey. It was beyond the scope of Makransky's research to trace the development of the theory of the three bodies prior to its formulation since his concern is the controversy over the *Abhisamayālaṃkāra* on Buddhahood, which is a piece of work written after the formulation of the *trikāya* theory.

With the exception of Makransky, who conducted a book-length study on the three bodies, the other scholars mentioned above have only written either articles or single chapters on this topic. There is no comprehensive study explaining how, why and when the three-body theory was formulated. The present study is an attempt to trace the development of the concept of the Buddha as a human teacher and guide in early Buddhism, up to the formulation of the three-body theory. Special emphasis will be extended to the following issues. First, how and why did the Mahāsāṃghikas conceive of a transcendental Buddha and what were the doctrinal foundations for the concept? Second, the origin of the notion of the *dharmakāya* and its development in Mahāyāna thought will be discussed, by extension showing how and when it became an ontological truth and cosmic body. Third, the origin of the *saṃbhogakāya* will be studied, along with a discussion on what problems, if any, such a concept was intended to solve.

The method of the research

In this study the present writer will rely chiefly on primary sources such as the early and middle Mahāyāna *sūtras* and *śāstras* in Chinese translation, for most original Sanskrit texts are lost. The development of the concept of the Buddha will be traced from a historical perspective, and translations and interpretations of the relevant passages in these *sūtras* are also provided. Furthermore, an attempt will be made at an interpretation of the hermeneutics the Mahāyāna authors intended to convey.

First of all, the term 'the early and middle Mahāyāna *sūtras* and *śāstras*' requires explanation. As a working premise, the history of Mahāyāna can be divided into three periods. The first runs from the first century CE, or even the first century BCE, to the fourth century CE, before the time of Asaṅga and Vasubandhu. This is considered the period of the rise and formation of Mahāyāna Buddhism, because Mahāyāna *sūtras* were already in existence in the first century CE, as indicated by the translation of the *Aṣṭa* into Chinese in the second century CE.[6] Scholars such as Conze think that the basic *Prajñāpāramitā* probably dates back to the first century BCE.[7] It seems that by the fourth century, Mahāyāna Buddhism was already a prominent school since at this time eminent personages such as Asaṅga and Vasubandhu were converted into the new faith from the Sarvāstivāda school. This is discussed in Chapter 5 below. Moreover, Kumārajīva (active in China between 402 and 413) translated a lot of Mahāyāna *sūtras* and *śāstras* at the beginning of fifth century, such as **Pañcaviṃśatisāhasrikā* and *Mādhyamikaśāstra*.

The second period is from the fourth century CE, the time of Asaṅga and Vasubandhu, to the sixth century CE. During this period Mahāyāna developed, as different schools, such as the Mādhyamika and the Yogācāra, as well as the concept of *tathāgatagarbha*, emerged and matured.

The third period is from the seventh century onwards, from the beginning of Tantrayāna to the disappearance of Buddhism in India.

The present research mainly focuses on the first and second periods of Mahāyāna Buddhism, with the emphasis on the first. It is a well-known fact that the Mahāyāna *sūtras* are almost impossible to date. Hence, the dates of the Chinese translations are used as a working hypothesis except in cases where there are already scholarly established dates but these are extremely rare.[8] There are two reasons for employing this method. First, it is obvious that the dates of the Chinese translations of the Mahāyāna *sūtras* are the only dates we know for historical research. Second, the dates of the Chinese translations of these *sūtras* and *śāstras* give us an order to follow, and roughly correspond to the development of the Mahāyāna *sūtras* in India. An analysis of the Chinese translations of the Mahāyāna *sūtras* and *śāstras* used in the present book supports this assertion. In this analysis, representative translators and their translations have been chosen. See the Appendix for a brief outline of the chronology of the Chinese translations of the Mahāyāna *sūtras* and *śāstras*.

We start with Lokakṣema (active in China in 178–189 CE) who is one of the earliest translators. His translations are mostly of early Mahāyāna *sūtras* such as the *Daoxingbanruojing* (the oldest extant version of the *Aṣṭa*) and the **Akṣobhyatathāgatasyavyūhasūtra*. He is followed by Zhi Qian (222–280) whose translations are also of early Mahāyāna *sūtras* such as the *Damingdujing* (another translation of the *Aṣṭa*) and the **Vimalakīrtinirdeśasūtra*, as well as Avadāna literature. Then, with the translations of Dharmarakṣa (266–313), the emphasis changes and the soteriology of the Buddha is stressed and praised. These include the **Pañcaviṃśatisāhasrikā*, the *Dushipin-jing* and the *Rulaixingxian-jing*. They are discussed in Chapter 4 below. Mokṣala's translation of another version of the **Pañcaviṃśatisāhasrikā* in 291 aroused great interest in the study of the *Prajñāpāramitāsūtras* in China, and subsequently different groups came into existence known as the Six Houses and Seven Schools.[9] This period is called 'the ancient translation' in China and corresponds to the first period of Mahāyāna Buddhism.

Kumārajīva (402–413) is a prominent person in Chinese Buddhism because his translations are lucid and easy to read and also because he translated a large number of Indian works. Most of his translations belong to the Mādhyamika school, especially the works of Nāgārjuna such as the controversial **Mahāprajñāpāramitāśāstra*, the **Daśabhūmikavibhāṣāśāstra* and the *Prajñāpāramitāsūtras*, as a result of which the Mādhyamika school was introduced into China. At the same time, Buddhabhadra (410–421), a contemporary of Kumārajīva, translated *sūtras* including the **Avataṃsaka* which, like Dharmarakṣa's translations, praises the powers and qualities of the Buddhas, and the **Mahāvaipulyatathāgatagarbhasūtra* which introduces a new branch of learning, the *tathāgatagarbha*. But it is the **Sandhinirmocanasūtra* in the translations of Bodhiruci (508–535) that marks the appearance of Yogācāra thought in China. From then on, more works on Yogācāra thought were translated by Paramārtha (546–569), such as the *Mahāyānasaṃgraha* and the **Buddhagotraśāstra*. This shows that Yogācāra as a school was already established in India at this time. This corresponds to the second period of Mahāyāna Buddhism.

Xuanzang (645–664), another major figure in Chinese Buddhism, translated volumes of works, mainly Yogācāra treatises such as the **Mahāyānasaṃgrahabhāśya*, the **Yogācārabhūmiśāstra* and the **Vijñāptimātratāsiddhiśāstra*, as well as the seven *Abhidharma* works of the Sarvāstivāda. The Yogācāra school was thus introduced and established in China. A little later, Yijing (695–713) translated many vinaya works of the Mūlasarvāstivāda. This probably indicates that the Sarvāstivāda still existed in India at this time and it split again, giving rise to a new school, the Mūlasarvāstivāda. This brief analysis of the history of Chinese translations suggests that it roughly reflects the development of Indian Buddhist thought.

A second problem concerning Mahāyāna *sūtras* is that they are constantly subject to growth and additions. It is interesting to note that the later Chinese translations of a *sūtra* or a *śāstra* are usually longer than the early translations of the same text. The *Vibhāṣā* is a very good example. There are three Chinese translations of this text: the first, by Saṅghabhūti, is much shorter than Xuanzang's, the third. This is discussed in detail in Chapter 2 below. However, in the present study of the early Indian Buddhist schools, Xuanzang's translation of the *Vibhāṣā* is used for the following two reasons. First, the two earliest surviving translations are only partial versions of the original text. According to the preface written by Daoan (312–385 CE), a contemporary of Saṅghabhūti, the treatise was originally much longer, but the oral transmitter of the text forgot parts of it so that only forty discussions were translated.[10] The second extant translation by Buddhavarma is also partial. It originally comprised one hundred fascicles, but due to unrest in the area where the translation was being carried out, forty fascicles were lost and only sixty have survived. But Xuanzang's translation, though very late, is a complete text. Second, the early Indian Buddhist schools, mainly the Sarvāstivāda and the Mahāsāṃghika, did not disappear after the rise of Mahāyāna Buddhism. On the contrary, they survived for several centuries and the Theravāda still exists today. In fact, the Sarvāstivāda developed even further and gave rise to the Mūlasarvāstivāda. The evidence is that Yijing translated a large number of Vinaya texts of the Mūlasarvāstivāda, as discussed above. Furthermore, these schools, especially the Sarvāstivādins, debated with the Mahāyānists and even rejected their concept of the Buddha. This is discussed in Chapter 5 below. Thus it is only Xuanzang's complete translation of the *Vibhāṣā* that provides a full picture of the concept of the Buddha of the Sarvāstivāda.

Third, in the analysis of some philosophical passages in the ancient texts, later translations are used where they shed light on the earlier ones. This is particularly useful in the case of Lokakṣema's translation of the *Aṣṭa*, because some passages in it are not intelligible while the corresponding passages in Kumārajīva's translation of this text are clear. This method helps us to understand and interpret the corrupted passages in the ancient texts which are important for our research on the development of Mahāyāna ideas and thoughts although they may have slightly changed over time. However, this method is adopted to interpret only passages that are found in both translations, not the passages that have been added and considerably revised in later translations as misinterpretation might result.

Fourth, since the emphasis of this book is on the Mahāyāna development of the concept of the Buddha and the sources utilized are mainly Mahāyāna *sūtras*, the *Nikāya* and the *Āgama* sources are taken as the earliest Buddhist literature without detailed analysis of their substrata. However, the Pāli

Nikāyas are always used as the prime source in discussions of early Buddhism. The Chinese *Āgamas* are only used as supporting evidence because they have been revised and changed over time by the early Indian Buddhist schools and even the early Mahāyānists. This point is discussed in further detail in Chapter 2 below. Thus, the Pāli *Nikāya* sources are cited as primary evidence, then followed by the Chinese *Āgama* sources.

The Pāli *Nikāyas* might also be thought to belong to a particular school, namely the Theravāda, and as such perhaps not representative of the earliest strata in the Buddhist literature. Although this may be true, when compared with the Chinese *Āgamas*, the Pāli *Nikāyas* are still the less corrupted. Moreover, the latter are in their original language while the former are in a translated form. The Chinese *Āgamas*, according to scholars, were translated from Sanskrit, not Pāli. Gautama Buddha very explicitly told his disciples that they should learn his teaching in their own language, and not translate it into refined Sanskrit.[11] Therefore, the original Sanskrit *Āgamas* from which the Chinese translations were made were initially translated texts, while the Pāli *Nikāyas* are in their original language, notwithstanding controversies as to whether Pāli was the language of the original proto-canon. It is therefore justifiable to use the Pāli *Nikāyas* as a prime source for the study of early Buddhism.[12]

Since both the Pāli *Nikāyas* and the Chinese *Āgamas* are used in the present book as primary sources, Pāli terminologies are used when Pāli sources are consulted. Otherwise, Sanskrit terminologies are used throughout because the main sources are Mahāyāna *sūtras* in Chinese translations of the Sanskrit originals. Almost all the English translations of passages taken from the Chinese sources and used as evidence for discussion are mine unless otherwise stated.

Lastly, some of my friends oppose the use of the term Hīnayāna in the text since it is biased. However, no other term can be used in its place to cover all early Indian Buddhist schools before the rise of Mahāyāna.

1

THE CONCEPT OF THE BUDDHA IN EARLY BUDDHISM[1]

In the earliest Buddhist literature, namely the Pāli *Nikāyas* and the Chinese *Āgamas*, the Buddha is portrayed in two aspects: the human and the superhuman or supernormal. In the first aspect the Buddha is seen to have constantly interacted with his disciples as well as with other religious groups of his time. In the second aspect, the Buddha is seen as an object of religious worship for his followers, a saviour of the world.[2] These two aspects intermingle to such an extent that it is extremely difficult to separate one from the other without doing injustice to the concept as a whole. The more rationalist Buddhist scholars attempt to minimize the 'irrational' by claiming that the occurrence of miracles in Buddhist literature was due to apocryphal accretion and interpolation. At the same time, some early Western Buddhist scholars may have overstated the superhuman character of the Buddha, asserting that it was simply a solar myth.[3] After vigorous research into both literary and archaeological sources, most Buddhist scholars today accept the historicity of Gautama Buddha. However, the superhuman and supernormal elements of the Buddha may have coexisted from the very beginning of Buddhist literature or even during Gautama's lifetime. It is problematic thus simply to dismiss any of those elements outright, because all the miracles performed by Gautama according to the *sūtras* are within the six modes of higher knowledge which, according to early Buddhism, can be attained through meditation. According to the *sūtras*, Gautama confidently believed this to be so. Even some modern scholars such as Gokhale assert that such miracles are possible when the mind becomes concentrated and clear through the practice of meditation.[4] These two aspects of the Buddha may have existed side by side from the inception of Buddhism, and may have served as a foundation for the later development of the concept of the Buddha. These two aspects form the subject of inquiry of this chapter.

The human Buddha

The human identity of the Buddha is manifested in the difficulties that he encountered during his lifetime, although they are deeply embedded in legends and mythology. Such difficulties are his illnesses, his emotions, the troubles within his own community of monks, and his being assaulted and slandered by his enemies. These accounts clearly point to a vivid historical personage who walked on Indian soil as the leader of a religious tradition.

Human and physiological elements

The Buddha was physically like any other human being, subject to the laws of nature which made him vulnerable to fatigue, illness, ageing, decay and death, as described in the *sūtras*. Instances of the Buddha's illnesses are not rare in the *sūtras*, which describe him as suffering constantly from back pain and stomach troubles.[5] Both the Pāli and the Chinese versions of the *Mahāparinirvāṇasūtra* mention two typical examples of the Buddha's illness which eventually led to his death.[6] The Pāli commentaries explain that the Buddha suffered backache in old age owing to the severe austerities he practised during the six years preceding his enlightenment,[7] and the unsuitable meals taken during that period were responsible for the dyspepsia that persisted throughout his life, culminating in his last serious illness of dysentery.[8] It was because of all these physical troubles that the Buddha had to consult Jīvaka, the royal physician of King Bimbisāra.[9] This also is referred to in the *Milindapañha*.[10]

The Buddha, like any other human being, slept during the night and ate in the day. This is mentioned in many places in the canon. To illustrate this point, we shall cite one example from the *Udāna*.[11] A Bhikkhu named Soṇa, who had never seen the Buddha, once came to visit him and spent a night in his company. This monk witnessed what the Buddha did during that night. The Buddha is described as having spent much of the night in the open meditating and to have washed his feet before retiring; at dawn the following morning, he got up and meditated again.[12] This sort of ablution, a very common practice in the life of an ordinary human being in those times, shows the human side of Gautama Buddha.

The *Saṃyuttanikāya* relates that when the Buddha was old, Ānanda noticed a great change in his physique. His limbs had become slack and wrinkled, his body bent forward, and a change was also apparent in his sense faculties.[13] In the *Mahāparinibbānasutta*, the Buddha told Ānanda:

> I too, Ānanda, am now old, and full of years, my journey is drawing to its close, I have reached my sum of days, I am turning eighty years of age; and just as a worn-out cart, Ānanda, can be kept going only with the help of thongs, so methinks, the body of the Tathāgata can only be kept going by repairs.[14]

So the body of the Buddha, just like that of any other human being, became weak when he grew old. It was due to all these factors that in his old age Gautama Buddha had to ask Ānanda to become his permanent attendant, and take on the duties which he performed with a loving heart and strong faith for twenty-five years.[15] In his last days, the Buddha's strength quickly ebbed away after his last meal, and according to the Pāli commentary, he had to stop twenty-five times while travelling three *gāvutas* (approximately eight to twelve miles) from Pāvā to Kusināra where he finally passed away.[16]

Troubles confronted by the Buddha

No matter how great a religious founder and teacher Gautama Buddha was, as described in Buddhist literature, he was not able to completely influence every single individual he conversed with. He had opponents within his own community of monks, such as the well-known Devadatta who even challenged his authority as the leader of the Saṃgha and plotted against his life.[17]

The *vinaya* frequently mentions a group of monks called Chabbaggiyas[18] as being guilty of various *vinaya* offences. They were known to have attempted to exploit loopholes in the community regulations.[19] They had persuaded the Buddha to institutionalize many rules concerning the life of a recluse. Assaji, Punabbasu, Paṇḍuka, Lohitaka, Mettiya and Bhummaja were the leaders of the Chabbaggiyas, and are sometimes referred to in the scriptures as 'the six groups' notorious for their misconduct. There were also nuns among their followers, such as Mettiyā,[20] who likewise violated the *vinaya* rules in various ways.[21] A serious dispute on *vinaya* rules among the Kauśāmbī (Pāli: Kosambī) monks is also related: this incident could not be solved even by the Buddha, who could only go away.[22] Thus, during the Buddha's old age, Kāśyapa complained that it was difficult to speak to the monks for they were intractable and heedless of instructions.[23] He told the Buddha that 'formerly there were both fewer precepts and more bhikkhus established as *arhats* [Pāli: *arahat*], but now there are more precepts and fewer bhikkhus established as *arhats*.'[24] Even the Buddha could not do anything to prevent it but said that his teaching would disappear from the world one day in the future.

Some of the Buddha's disciples were dissatisfied with either his teaching or the Buddha himself and left his Order, some returning to lay life and others joining other *śrāmaṇa* groups.[25] Phagguna Bhikkhu, for example, was dissatisfied when the Buddha admonished him for misconduct. On another occasion, he put a series of questions to the Buddha who rejected them as wrongly formulated.[26] Later it was reported that Phagguna returned to lay life.[27] In a similar case, Ariṭṭha was reported to have held a pernicious view for which the Buddha rebuked him. As he did not want to give up his view, he returned to lay life when an act of suspension was imposed on him.[28] Sunakkhatta, who once was a personal attendant of the Buddha, became dissatisfied and left the Order because the Buddha did not perform any miracles for him or explain the beginning of the world to him.[29]

Some people were attracted by Gautama Buddha and had interesting conversations with him, yet were not converted because they were suspicious of his claim to enlightenment. On his way to Benares immediately after his enlightenment, Gautama Buddha met the Ājīvaka Upaka, who inquired about his teacher and his Dharma. Gautama Buddha then told him that he had no teacher and that he himself was the supreme teacher, the Fully Enlightened One. However, Upaka, the very first person the Buddha met after his enlightenment, went away shaking his head, without being converted.[30] Doṇa, the Brahmin, asked Gautama whether he was a *deva*, a *gandharva*, a *yakṣa* or a human being. Gautama declared that he was none other than the Buddha because he had destroyed the *kleśas* which cause one to be born as all those kinds of beings. Doṇa, however, was not convinced and went away.[31] Thus both Upaka and Doṇa exhibited a thoroughly sceptical attitude towards Gautama's claim to full enlightenment as they both went off without being converted. As Naughton states, this reaction seems a very natural one.[32] The fact that the Pāli *suttas* portray Gautama Buddha directly after his enlightenment in such an uncomplimentary way is probably good evidence for the authenticity of these attitudes. No later redactor would be likely to fabricate such stories. Similar incidents are also mentioned in the *Majjhimanikāya* where it is said that although the wanderer Udāyin conversed with Gautama Buddha on several occasions, he was still not converted.[33] Daṇḍapāṇi, a Śākya who met the Buddha at Kapilavastu, was also not converted despite the fact that they had an interesting conversation.[34] According to the *Majjhimanikāya* commentary, Daṇḍapāṇi sided with Devadatta, the Buddha's arch foe, and his manner of asking questions was therefore arrogant and deliberately provocative.[35]

According to the *Saṃyuttanikāya*, Gautama Buddha encountered other troubles in addition to the incidents mentioned above. He was once refused alms food and had to return with an empty bowl when he went to the Brahmin village, Pañcasālā.[36] The *Dhammapada* commentary explains that he actually starved for a day at this village, because none of the inhabitants was willing to offer him alms.[37] The *Vinaya* mentions that Gautama was even criticized by the people of Rājagṛha for making women childless widows as a result of men renouncing the world.[38] Most of the discourses delivered by the Buddha were received by the audience with delight, evidenced by the statement at the end of many *sūtras* that 'the bhikṣus are delighted at and accept the Buddha's discourse'. However, not all the discourses delivered by Gautama Buddha were happily received by his disciples, one example being the Pāli *Mūlapariyāyasutta*: when Gautama Buddha delivered this discourse, 'the Bhikkhus did not delight in the Blessed One's words'.[39] All these incidents show that the Buddha was not divine but a human being who had to face all the troubles that may beset a leader.

The emotions of the Buddha

Only on rare occasions in the canon did Gautama Buddha show emotions. But a few cases suggest that Gautama Buddha felt uneasy and reproached his disciples when they misunderstood and wrongly interpreted his teachings. As the Dharma was his great discovery, his life's work and his message to the suffering world, he would not tolerate his own monks who misrepresented it through carelessness or ill will, particularly when their task was to pass the message down to future generations. Sāti, a fisherman's son, is a good example. He wrongly understood the master's teaching that consciousness survives the body and takes another form in the new life. Upon hearing this, Gautama cried out:

> Foolish man, to whom have you ever known me to teach the Dhamma in that way? Foolish man, in many discourses have I not stated consciousness to be dependently arisen, since without a condition there is no origination of consciousness? But you, foolish man, have misrepresented us by your wrong grasp and injured yourself and stored up much demerit.[40]

Ariṭṭha, a former vulture trainer, was another monk who was reproached by the Buddha in a similar manner for his misunderstanding of the Dharma. The Buddha blamed him for being a foolish and misguided man.[41] The commentary explains that while reflecting in seclusion, Ariṭṭha came to the conclusion that there would be no harm for bhikṣus to engage in sexual relations with women, and he therefore maintained that these should not be prohibited by monastic rules.[42] In both cases the monks were of humble origins and probably had no education of any kind, and so had difficulty in understanding the Buddha's teaching in its philosophical dimensions. But the two topics – one concerning a fundamental doctrine, the other a fundamental practice – are crucial to an understanding of the Buddha's teachings. It therefore appears that the Buddha reproached them with personal feeling.

In these two cases, it could perhaps be argued that the Buddha was not angry. However, in another case, what he said concerning Devadatta suggests that he was angry, at least in the literal sense of the word. Devadatta intrigued for the leadership of the Saṃgha and asked the Buddha to hand it over to him. The Buddha said: 'Not even to Sāriputta and Moggallāna would I hand over the Order, and would I to thee, vile one, to be vomited like spittle?'[43] In the *Aṅguttaranikāya*, we find the following saying of Gautama Buddha when Ānanda made inquiries about Devadatta:

> And so long as, Ānanda, I saw a bright spot in Devadatta, even the prick-end of a horse-hair in size, I declared not: 'Devadatta is wayward gone, hell-bound for a *kalpa*, unpardonable' – but it was when I saw none, that I declared thus . . .[44]

The same comment is also found in the Chinese counterpart, the **Ekottarāgama*.[45] It is not unlike a curse, and arguably motivated by anger. The incident was a bitter experience in the life of Gautama Buddha because Devadatta, a monk and disciple in his own community, had tried with some success to split the Order he had established with much effort. Therefore whenever Devadatta was mentioned, Gautama Buddha would speak of him as a bad person of evil intention.

The Saṃgha was the disseminator of the Buddha's message to the world. Gautama was very concerned about the split in the Saṃgha for in the last few years of his life he saw what had happened to Jain monks.[46] The **Mahāvibhāṣāśastra*, referring to Devadatta, mentions that the bad *karma* entailed by the destruction of the Saṃgha is graver or heavier than that caused by shedding the blood of the Buddha. The split in the Saṃgha was explained as the destruction of the *dharmakāya* while shedding the blood of the Buddha harms the *rūpakāya*.[47]

Apart from these, there are at least two passages in the *Mahāparinibbānasutta* that illustrate the Buddha displaying emotion, this consisting in feeling appreciation for beautiful things. The first incident was when the Licchavis of Vesālī (Skt: Vaiśāli), wearing clothes of different colours and various kinds of ornaments, approached the Buddha in carriages. Gautama said to his disciples:

> O brethren, let those of the brethren who have never seen the Tāvatiṃsa gods, gaze upon this company of the Licchavis, behold this company of the Licchavis, compare this company of the Licchavis, for they are even as a company of Tāvatiṃsa gods.[48]

The second incident occurred after the Buddha and Ānanda had returned from begging in Vesālī. The Buddha addressed Ānanda: 'How delightful a spot, Ānanda, is Vesālī, and how charming the Udena Shrine, and the Gotamaka Shrine . . .'[49] These two incidents are also mentioned in the Chinese translations of the *Mahāparinirvāṇasūtra*.[50] These pieces of literature suggest that the Buddha had emotions which he manifested in different ways. If his sense of appreciation shows the compassion of Gautama Buddha, then anger definitely shows his human side because a Buddha, at least by definition, is a person who has eliminated the three evils: greed, hatred and ignorance. These incidents therefore reveal the human aspect of the Buddha.

Slander and assaults from enemies

Early Buddhist literature describes two incidents in which the Buddha is slandered by his opponents and they are referred to in the *Pubbakammapiloti* of the *Apadāna* as the remaining effects of the bad *karma* done by the Buddha in his previous lives.[51] In the first, Ciñcāmānavikā, a beautiful female ascetic (*parivrājaka*) from another Order, was persuaded by her fellow ascetics to discredit the Buddha because they found that the contributions they received had diminished due to his popularity. She pretended to have become pregnant by the Buddha and, with a wooden disc tied round her body, came to where he was addressing a large congregation. Her accusation was soon found to be false and she was chased away by the audience.[52] The second story, recorded in the *Udāna*, is about Sundarī, also a female ascetic from another Order, who was persuaded by her fellow ascetics to insult the Buddha and his disciples. She visited Jetavana where the Buddha was residing and pretended to have stayed the night with him and to have left in the morning. After some days, the heretic ascetics hired some villains to kill Sundarī and hide her body under a heap of rubbish near Jetavana. When her disappearance was reported to the king, a search was carried out and her body was found. Her fellow ascetics then went about the streets of the city crying: 'Behold the deeds of the Śākya monks.'[53]

This analysis of the Buddha's physical illness, troubles in life, emotions and assaults from enemies suggests that he was a human teacher and guide who suffered the full range of difficulties liable to afflict a great man within his own community as well as in encounters with his opponents. It is from this human aspect of the great teacher as described in early Buddhist literature that the Sarvāstivāda and other Hīnayāna schools formulated their concept of a human Buddha.

The superhuman Buddha

In the descriptions of the same early Buddhist literature, Gautama Buddha is also associated with various kinds of miracles, which were either performed by him or occurred naturally to mark special events in his life. Apart from these miracles, his physical body is described as having the thirty-two marks of a great man. This superhuman character plays a special and important role in the life of Gautama Buddha as a religious leader and founder. It is possibly due to the tendency to idealize the Buddha that these superhuman characteristics were ascribed to him, probably as early as during the lifetime of Gautama.

The physical marks

The *Lakkhaṇasutta* of the *Dīghanikāya* and the *Brahmāyusutta* of the *Majjhimanikāya* state that the Buddha had the thirty-two physical marks of a great man (*mahāpurisa*), and this is also confirmed by the Chinese *Āgamas*.[54] Scholars are of the opinion that the concept of a great man is pre-Buddhistic and that the tradition was adapted from Brahmanical tradition and applied to the Buddha when he was idealized.[55] There are two reasons for this assertion. First, the Buddhist concept of a great man has a spiritual rather than a physical sense because the Buddha reinterpreted the concept of the *mahāpurisa* and gave it a new meaning, as he did with other concepts such as *karma*. Scholars have collected the passages concerning the term *mahāpurisa* in the Pāli canon and pointed out that it was used in an ethical sense to mean one who possessed an emancipated mind (*vimuttacitta*), and one who had destroyed all defilements.[56] In the *Aṅguttaranikāya*, the definition of a *mahāpurisa* is as follows: one who is concerned with the welfare of the great mass of people, who has mastery of thought and the ability to experience the four ecstasies that are beyond thought yet pertain to the present life, and who has discarded intoxication arising from lust, as well as becomings from speculation and ignorance.[57] In this sense, an *arhat* could also be called a *mahāpurisa*.[58] However, the faithful followers seem to have forgotten or rather ignored this fact, and to have attributed to the Buddha the list of thirty-two physical marks.[59] Second, the *Brahmāyusutta* of the *Majjhimanikāya* states that it was the Brahmin Brahmāyu, learned in the three Vedas and versed in the knowledge of the marks of a great man, who sent his pupil Uttara to examine the Buddha about his physical marks.[60] The *Selasutta* of the *Suttanipāta* states that the tradition of the marks of a great man had been handed down in the Brahmin hymns.[61] This is a direct reference to the concept of a great man in the Brahmanical tradition.

In addition to the thirty-two marks, Gautama Buddha is described as having an attractive and penetrating voice with eight qualities: it was distinct, intelligible, melodious, audible, ringing, euphonious, deep and sonorous.[62] Perhaps the Mahāsāṃghikas interpreted this to mean that the Buddha spoke in only one voice but sentient beings understood it according to their inclinations.[63] In the *Mahāparinibbānasutta*, the hue of the Buddha's skin the night before he passed away is described as exceedingly bright, so bright that even the burnished cloth of gold lost its splendour when he wore it.[64] This has been taken up by the Mahāyānists as an important topic and developed to mean the light radiated from the Buddha's body.

Although it is stated in the *sūtras* that the Buddha had all these distinguishing bodily features, he was not necessarily recognized by ordinary people when he walked about on the road.[65] The *Dhātuvibhaṅgasutta* of the *Majjhimanikāya* mentions that Pukkusāti renounced the world in the name of the Buddha without ever having seen him. He did not recognize the

Buddha when they met in a potter's hut and apologized for calling him *āvuso* (Skt: *āvusa*, brother), a term used for addressing an equal.[66] According to Walpola Rahula, in early Buddhism a disciple usually addressed his master by the term *bhante*, which approximately means 'Sir' or 'Lord'.[67] The *Upakkilesasutta* of the same *Nikāya* mentions another example of the Buddha being indistinguishable from other monks in physical appearance. Gautama Buddha, after having left the Kosambī monks, came to the park where venerable Anuruddha and two other fellow monks were staying. The park keeper did not recognize the Buddha by his physical appearance and asked him not to enter the park because three mendicants were practising seriously there.[68] The same incident is also found in the Chinese **Ekottarāgama*.[69] In these two instances, had the Buddha possessed the thirty-two bodily marks of a great man, he would certainly have been recognized at a glance. Having long arms that could reach to his knees without him bending, for instance, would have constituted a visible sign. This suggests that the faithful followers must have endowed the Buddha with these physical attributes over time in order to glorify him. But as W. Pachow indicates, these marks do not actually enhance the real importance of the Buddha as an enlightened teacher.[70]

Miracles

The miracles associated with Gautama Buddha are traditionally reckoned as belonging to the *adbhuta-dharma* of the nine or twelve divisions (*navāṅga* or *dvādaśāṅga*) of the Buddhist scripture.[71] They are described in various passages in the early scriptures.

1 The *Aṅguttaranikāya* mentions an immense light that appeared on four occasions in the life of the Buddha: his descent from Tuṣita heaven, his birth, his enlightenment and his first public preaching.[72]
2 The *Acchariyābbhūtasutta* of the *Majjhimanikāya* is an account of twenty miracles that occurred at the time of the Buddha's birth, according to Ānanda, such as an earthquake, two streams of water, one cool and one warm, pouring down from heaven to bathe him, and infinite light.[73]
3 Both the *Aṅguttaranikāya* and the Chinese *Madhyamāgama* mention an earthquake before the Buddha's passing away, and this is also mentioned in all the versions of the *Mahāparinirvāṇasūtra*.[74]
4 The *Iddhipāda-Saṃyutta* mentions six modes of supernatural power (*abhijñā*) of the Buddha which he gained through meditation.[75]

The fact that the miracles of the Buddha are reckoned as *adbhuta-dharma* by the early compilers of Buddhist scriptures suggests that from the very beginning these wondrous things were looked upon as special events. These miracles can be divided into two groups: (1) the supernormal events that occurred in nature to mark special occasions in the life of the Buddha such as his birth, enlightenment and death; (2) the supernormal acts performed by Gautama Buddha himself.

The first group of supernatural events occurred on many important occasions in the life of Gautama Buddha, namely his birth, his enlightenment, his first sermon and his death. The *Acchariyābbhūtasutta* of the *Majjhimanikāya* describes a series of miracles that occurred to mark the birth of the Buddha. Perhaps, for the faithful devotees, the birth of the Buddha on earth was the most marvellous event in living memory. Other supernatural events fall primarily into two categories: those involving light and those involving earthquakes. Gokhale remarks that these events can be explained as the result of *dharmatā*, the nature of things, implying that they were not causally connected with the Buddha but occurred in the natural course of events.[76] The special events in the life of Gautama Buddha were certainly extraordinary occasions for his faithful followers and even for his immediate disciples, who most likely were convinced that these should be marked by extraordinary occurrences in nature. However, these events do not affect the attainments and achievements of the Buddha but only suggest that he was not an ordinary being.

The second kind of miracle is important to our study. It falls within the six modes of higher knowledge (*abhijñā*) and could be performed not only by the Buddha but by anyone who had attained the higher concentration or the four *dhyānas*, such as an *arhat*.[77] This is described in detail in the *Sāmaññaphalasutta* as the fruit of the *samaṇa*'s life.[78] The six modes of higher knowledge are: (1) supernatural power (*iddhi-vidhā*); (2) the divine ear (*dibba-sota*); (3) penetration of the minds of others (*ceto-pariya-ñāṇa*); (4) memory of former existences (*pubbe-nivāsānussati*); (5) the divine eye (*dibba-cakkhu*); (6) extinction of all cankers (*āsavakkhaya*). According to the *Sāmaññaphalasutta*, these six modes of knowledge are in ascending order; the knowledge of the extinction of all cankers is the highest and can be attained only by a Buddha, a *pratyekabuddha* and an *arhat*. The first five are mundane and the last is supramundane; thus it is only through acquiring the sixth knowledge that one becomes liberated.

The Buddha, according to the *Mahāsaccakasutta*, had attained three kinds of knowledge on the night of his enlightenment: he perceived his own past lives, he saw the past lives of other beings, and he knew that his cankers were destroyed.[79] These three knowledges correspond to the fourth, the fifth and the sixth of the six modes of higher knowledge.

Most of the miracles performed by the Buddha according to the *sūtras* and *vinaya* belong to the first category, that of supernatural power (*ṛddhi*).[80] The *vinaya* describes many miracles performed by the Buddha immediately after his enlightenment: the miracle of hiding Yaśa so that his father could not see him, and the series of miracles performed to convert the three Kāśyapa brothers.[81] The *Mahāparinirvāṇasūtra* cites three miracles performed by Gautama Buddha through the use of his supernatural power (*ṛddhi*): the crossing of the Ganges River as fast as a strong man could stretch forth his arm;[82] extending his life-span to a *kalpa* or to the end of the *kalpa* if desired;[83] and making turbid water clear.[84] The *Majjhimanikāya* also cites three miracles performed by the Buddha: vanishing without a trace in front of Brahmā;[85] walking at his normal pace while Aṅgulimāla could not catch up even by running at full speed;[86] and showing his male organ by a supernatural feat.[87] There are more examples in the canon but it is unnecessary to mention them all. According to the *Sampasādanīyasutta* of the *Dīghanikāya*, supernatural power is ignoble if used for worldly aims and purposes, but it is noble if used for a higher and virtuous aim.[88] These powers had little or nothing to do with the realization of the highest goal of *nirvāṇa*, and it is for this very reason that Gautama imposed monastic rules prohibiting any display of miracles. He considered such displays to be similar to a respectable woman flaunting her womanly tokens in public.[89] When converting individuals, Gautama Buddha always enjoyed using rational persuasion, which is called *anuśāsanī prātihārya*, the miracle of education or instruction. The conversion of the three Kāśyapa brothers is perhaps the only example recorded in the entire Pāli canon of Gautama's used of supernatural power. It happened at the very beginning of his public ministry when he had no influence at all in religious circles. Hence, it might have been for pragmatic reasons that Gautama resorted to *ṛddhi*, if he possessed any, to convert these three renowned hair-matted ascetics. Even so, it was difficult to convert them, as described in the text.

That Gautama Buddha possessed those six modes of higher knowledge was most probably genuinely believed during his lifetime, and all his *arhat* disciples were also believed to have such knowledge. Maudgalyāyana, who was renowned for his *ṛddhi*, is a good example. Gokhale comments:

> There is reason to believe that Gotama, in the context of his times, accepted without demur, the validity of knowledge gained by extrasensory perception and the ability of a human being to exercise supernatural and supernormal powers by the strength of his will cultivated to an extraordinary extent.[90]

Although this may be difficult to accept from a modern academic perspective, it is not simply refutable. It is more acceptable and relevant that these six modes of higher knowledge distinguish Gautama Buddha from others. However, he did not claim a monopoly of them, but stated that anyone could achieve them by means of earnest practice. This suggests that the superhuman character of the Buddha was believed to exist side by side with his human aspect in early Buddhism.

In addition to the six modes of higher knowledge, both the *Nikāyas* and the *Āgamas* state that the Buddha had ten powers (*bala*) and four kinds of intrepidity (*vaiśāradya*).[91] The Sarvāstivādins asserted that these are qualities exclusive to the Buddha, not shared by *arhats* who are, however, equal in terms of liberation. However, as the term 'exclusive' is not used in the relevant *sūtras*, the compiler of the **Mahāprajñāpāramitāśāstra* states that these qualities are in fact shared by *arhats*. We will return to this topic in Chapter 2 below. Therefore, in the process of idealization of the Buddha, these qualities, along with great compassion (*mahākaruṇa*) and the three bases of mindfulness, were termed 'the eighteen exclusive qualities' of the Buddha. The 'eighteen exclusive qualities' are likely to have had an apocryphal function to distinguish the Buddha from other liberated individuals although they are found individually in the early scriptures.

It is clear from this analysis that the concept of the Buddha in early Buddhism holds two aspects: the human identity and the superhuman character. It is more than probable that on the basis of the human elements of the Buddha, the Sarvāstivādins formulated their concept of the Buddha as a human being. On the other hand, the Mahāsāṃghikas conceived their transcendental Buddha on the basis of the superhuman or divine powers, because they were the faithful and accepted whatever was said in the *sūtras* as truth (this will be discussed in Chapter 3 below). This does not necessarily imply that the Sarvāstivādins did not accept the superhuman aspects of the Buddha, but that they regarded them with greater caution. Vasumitra's treatise states that they did not take every word of the Buddha as the teaching of Dharma.

2

THE CONCEPT OF THE BUDDHA IN THE EARLY INDIAN BUDDHIST SCHOOLS

(I) The Sarvāstivāda

The concept of the Buddha was significantly advanced at the time of the early Indian Buddhist schools, especially the Sarvāstivāda and the Mahāsāṃghika.[1] The Sarvāstivādins were more empirical in their approach. They summarized and synthesized the attributes and qualities of the Buddha as described in the early *sūtras* before formulating, for the first time, the two-body theory: that of the *rūpakāya* and the *dharmakāya*.[2] The *rūpakāya*, according to the Sarvāstivādins, although impure, is endowed with the thirty-two major and eighty minor marks as well as a one-fathom halo. The *dharmakāya* is endowed with the eighteen exclusive attributes: the ten powers, the four kinds of intrepidity, the three foundations of mindfulness and great compassion. None of the constituents of either the *rūpakāya* or the *dharmakāya* are innovative; rather, they consist of the qualities of the Buddha which were already present in early Buddhism. Some of them, such as the ten powers and the thirty-two major marks were simply taken from the *Nikāyas* and the *Āgamas* with further explanations. Other qualities, for instance the eighty minor marks and the one-fathom halo, were taken after careful synthesis. This will become clear as we proceed to analyse the Sarvāstivāda concept of the Buddha step by step.

The two-body theory

Scholars such as Yinshun postulate that the two-body theory, the *rūpakāya* and the *dharmakāya* of the Buddha: is formulated for the first time by Nāgārjuna in his **Mahāprajñāpāramitāśāstra* (MPPŚ) in order to solve the complex problem concerning the *rūpakāya* of the Buddha: this is the issue of his superhuman attributes, a subject of debate between the Sarvāstivādins and the Mahāsāṃghikas for several centuries.[3] However, early Buddhist schools such as the Sarvāstivāda had already formulated this theory to explain their concept of the Buddha in the *Vibhāṣā*. The latter predates the composition of the MPPŚ.[4] There are three Chinese translations of the *Vibhāṣā*, and the two-body theory is found in all of them.

In order to have a clear understanding of this two-body theory, let us first examine the three different Chinese translations of the *Vibhāṣā*. The earliest translation by Saṅghabhūti in 383 CE is entitled the **Vibhāṣāśāstra* and is comprised of fourteen fascicles. According to the preface written by Daoan (312–385 CE), a contemporary of Saṅghabhūti, the treatise was originally much longer, but the oral transmitter of the text forgot parts of it so that only forty discussions were translated.[5] The second translation by Buddhavarma in 437–439 CE is entitled **Abhidharmavibhāṣāśāstra*. It was originally in one hundred fascicles, but due to unrest in the area where the translation was being carried out, forty fascicles were lost and only sixty are extant. The longest and latest recension is the **Mahāvibhāṣāśāstra* (*Vibhāṣā*) in two hundred fascicles, translated by Xuanzang in 656–659 CE. According to Yinshun's study on the Sarvāstivāda teachers and treatises, since its first compilation the *Vibhāṣā* has been rearranged, revised and enlarged over the course of time. Even the earliest Chinese translation by Saṅghabhūti was not rendered from the first original version, but from the medium-length and revised version. Buddhavarma's is a revised and also enlarged version while Xuanzang's is the longest and latest.[6]

Let us now return to the discussion of the two-body theory in the three versions. The *Vibhāṣā* mentions the two-body theory in the context of the purity of the Buddha's *rūpakāya*. The Mahāsāṃghikas asserted that the *rūpakāya* is pure due to the following statement found in collections of early *sūtras* such as the **Saṃyuktāgama*: 'The Tathāgata was born in the world, abided in the world, and yet was not defiled by the worldly *dharmas*.'[7] But the Sarvāstivādins differed from the Mahāsāṃghikas by using the two-body theory to reinterpret the same quotation.

According to the earliest translation of the *Vibhāṣā*, the Sarvāstivādins stated:

> It is on account of the *dharmakāya* that the *sūtra* states thus. However, it also refers to the *rūpakāya* when it says: 'the Tathāgata was born in the world and abided in the world.' While the *sūtra* refers to the *dharmakāya* when it says: 'yet he was not defiled by [literally: attached to] the worldly *dharmas* and attached to nothing [because he] attained *sambodhi* so he transcended the world.'[8]

The second translation contains a similar statement.

> The *sūtra* refers to the *rūpakāya* when it says: 'the Tathāgata was born in the world and abided in the world', but it refers to the *dharmakāya* when it says: 'appearing in the world but was not defiled by the worldly *dharmas*'.[9]

The third translation of the *Vibhāṣā* concurs by stating:

> The *sūtra* speaks secretly concerning the *dharmakāya*. It refers to the Buddha's *rūpakāya* appearing in the world when it says: 'the Tathāgata was born in the world and abided in the world', but it refers to the *dharmakāya* when it says: 'yet it was not defiled by the worldly *dharmas*'.[10]

It is evident here that the concept of the Buddha of the Sarvāstivāda school includes two bodies: the physical body and the spiritual body. There exists evidence that strongly supports the assertion that the two-body theory was formulated earlier than the MPPŚ. First, according to Yinshun, the original version of the *Vibhāṣā* may have been composed in the second century CE after King Kaniṣka's rule and before the composition of the MPPŚ.[11] The evidence for this is that the MPPŚ mentions the title of the *Vibhāṣā* ten times: five times as *Apitanpiposa* (*Abhidharmavibhāṣā*) and five times just as *piposa* (*Vibhāṣā*) or *piposalun* (*Vibhāṣāśāstra*).[12] Apart from this, it also mentions 'the disciples of Kātyāyanīputra' or simply 'Kātyāyanīputra' seven times, twice in association with the *Abhidharmavibhāṣā* and three times in association with the *Abhidharma*.[13] The author even quotes the *Vibhāṣā* many times, mostly in the context of criticism. The following are three places in which the title of the *Vibhāṣā* is mentioned in the MPPŚ, two of them in association with Kātyāyanīputra:[14]

> The disciples of Kātyāyanīputra said: 'although in the *Tripiṭaka* the Buddha did not say it, logically, it should be so. It is said so in the chapter on the bodhisattva in the *Abhidharmavibhāṣā*.'[15]
>
> It is stated in the *Abhidharmavibhāṣā* of Kātyāyanīputra thus: 'it is not mentioned in the *Tripiṭaka*.'[16]

When discussing the bad *karma* of the Buddha, it is stated in the MPPŚ:

> The Buddha did not say so, it is said by the *Abhidharmavibhāṣāśāstra* teachers. Answer: the *Abhidharma* was preached by the Buddha, and you, *śrāvakas*, composed the *Vibhāṣā* on the basis of the *Abhidharma*, and thus this should not be wrong. Again, Vakula did not fall into the evil realms for ninety-one *kalpas* as a result of offering to the Saṅgha a *haritakī* [Pāli: *harītaka*] fruit. How could the Bodhisattva fall into hell on account of some insignificant *karma* since he had obtained much merit by making offerings with his own body in numerous lives? Thus the *Vibhāṣā* could not be wrong. The Hīnayānists, therefore, do not understand the *upāyakauśalya* of the Bodhisattva.[17]

These quotations show that the author of the MPPŚ not only knew the *Vibhāṣā* itself but was also well acquainted with the background of its composition. He knew that the great Sarvāstivāda teacher Kātyāyanīputra and his disciples were closely related to the *Vibhāṣā*. Lamotte is of the opinion that the author of the MPPŚ was an expert on the *Abhidharma* of the Sarvāstivāda and might even have taught the six *Abhidharmas* and the *Vibhāṣā* in either Kashmir or Gandhāra before he was converted to the Mahāyāna.[18] The author frequently quotes from the *Abhidharma* works of the Sarvāstivāda school both to substantiate his opinions and to make criticisms. Lamotte suggests that the author may even have had a copy of the *Vibhāṣā* at hand when he composed the MPPŚ. It is fairly certain that the two-body theory had already been formulated and used by different schools, in particular the Sarvāstivāda, prior to the composition of the MPPŚ. The author of the MPPŚ simply adopted the two-body theory from the *Vibhāṣā* to explain the complex problem concerning the *rūpakāya* of the Buddha since it was the most sophisticated theory concerning the concept of the Buddha at the time.

It could be argued that although the composition of the earliest version of the *Vibhāṣā* is attributed to an earlier date than that of the MPPŚ, the former text may still have been influenced by or have actually adopted the two-body theory from the latter. The *Vibhāṣā* had been revised and enlarged time and again in the course of transmission before it was translated. However, this argument does not hold since the two-body theory is found in all three Chinese translations, as discussed above. Moreover, the earliest translation of the *Vibhāṣā* certainly predates Kumārajīva's translation of the MPPŚ in 402–406 CE. This does not, however, absolutely guarantee that the MPPŚ was drafted later.

Thus we can see that the *rūpakāya* and the *dharmakāya* had already been formulated as a theory by the Sarvāstivādins prior to the composition or translation of the MPPŚ. Its first appearance can be dated at the latest to the second century when the *Vibhāṣā* was composed.

Reynolds has shown that descriptions of several bodies of the Buddha can be found in early Buddhism, namely the *dhammakāya*, the *rūpakāya* and the *manomayakāya*.[19] It seems, however, that these terms encapsulate only simplistic ideas and concepts which cannot be regarded as a theory when compared to the *Abhidharma* works of the Sarvāstivāda school. Four passages in the Pāli *Nikāyas* use the term *dhammakāya*, and these have been collected and analysed by N. Dutt.[20] In these passages, the term *dhammakāya* simply denotes the teaching of the Buddha and has no philosophical connotations whatsoever. We will return to this topic in Chapter 4 below. The only instance where both the physical body (*pūtikāya*) and the *dhammakāya* are mentioned is in the *Saṃyuttanikāya* where Vakkali wished to see the Buddha in person. The *sūtra* explicitly emphasizes that the Buddha advised Vakkali to learn and practise the Dharma rather than to see his physical body. It was the Sarvāstivādins who first formulated the two-body theory to explain the concept of the Buddha.

The *rūpakāya*

The Sarvāstivāda school's concept of the *rūpakāya* comprises two aspects: its nature and its physical attributes. According to the Sarvāstivādins, the nature of the *rūpakāya* is impure (*āśrava*); the physical attributes are best described in a stock passage which frequently appears in the *Vibhāṣā*: 'The Buddha has thirty-two major marks as physical adornment and eighty minor marks as ornaments, his body is golden in colour with a one-fathom halo radiating from it.'[21] Thus, in addition to the thirty-two major marks and the golden complexion found in early Buddhist *sūtras*, the Sarvāstivādins formulated two more sets of qualities and added them to the *rūpakāya* of the Buddha: the eighty minor marks and one-fathom rays.

On the nature of the rūpakāya

The Sarvāstivādins asserted the impurity of the Buddha's *rūpakāya* although they attributed a lot of physical qualities to him. According to the *Vibhāṣā*, they asserted it for two reasons. 'The *rūpakāya* of the Buddha was born from *āśrava*, it is therefore said to be impure, and as it can also cause *āśrava* in others, it is not pure.'[22] In order to support their assertion, the Sarvāstivādins argued:

> It is against the *sūtras* that the *rūpakāya* is considered to be pure (*anāśrava*). It is stated in the *sūtras* that 'the fool as well as the wise one obtains the physical body with consciousness due to ignorance and attachment.'[23] The Buddha was considered as one of the wise so his body was a result of ignorance and attachment. Consequently his body was not pure. If the physical body of the Buddha was pure, without defilement, then women would not love, Aṅgulimālya would not hate, the Uruvilva Kāśyapa brothers would not be ignorant of, and the proud Brahman would not look down upon the Buddha. The *rūpakāya* must be impure since it causes greed, hatred, illusion and pride.[24]

It is clear from this argument that the two reasons given by the Sarvāstivādins in support of their concept of the impure *rūpakāya* are: (1) it is born of *āśrava*, the result of ignorance and attachment; (2) it causes *āśrava* in others. In the context of the first reason, the following problem arises. If the *rūpakāya* of the Buddha was not pure and was the result of ignorance and attachment, then was the consciousness of the Bodhisattva not pure when he descended from Tuṣita heaven and entered the womb of his mother? In the same *Vibhāṣā*, however, it is said that the Bodhisattva entered his mother's womb during his last birth with correct thought, without inverted thought, and he likewise abided in the womb and was born.[25] The Sarvāstivādins put forward the following explanation to reconcile this contradiction. They stated:

> Right thought only means without inverted (*viparīta*) thought and without inverted recognition (*adhimokṣa*), not the absence of ignorance. The Bodhisattva also had love towards both his body and his parents when he took birth. Question: if so, what is the difference between a Buddha and a sentient being? Answer: an ordinary sentient being, when he obtains birth, does not think of father as father and mother as mother. Therefore, the male hates his father while he breeds love towards his mother. In other words, there arises inverted thought in the male to meet the mother and in the female to meet the father. The Bodhisattva was different in that he thought of father as father and mother as mother. (The Bodhisattva thought thus:) 'depending on them I will get a body, will obtain the superior reward in Jambudvīpa and then attain *anuttara-samyak-saṃbodhi* by which I will benefit sentient beings.' When this thought arose, he bred love towards his parents and thus was born. Therefore, right thought means without inverted thought, not the absence of *kleśa*.[26]

Thus the Sarvāstivādins solved the problem in a logical manner.

With regard to the second reason, that the *rūpakāya* of the Buddha could cause *āśrava* in others since it was not pure, the other schools asked just how the Tathāgata had eliminated all the *kleśas* and habitual forces (*vāsanā*) while still impure.[27] The Sarvāstivādins explained that though the Buddha had eliminated all *āśravas* in himself, he could still cause *āśravas* in others.[28] Although the Buddha could live without quarrelling (*araṇā*) with others, it was for the sake of sentient beings that he did not do so. He either consoled or praised or even scolded his disciples according to their temperaments in order to guide them in the Dharma. They might nourish hatred, pride or greed as a result of the rebuke or praise, but they would have the good seed planted within them.[29] The argument put forward by the Sarvāstivādins is that the Buddha 'quarrelled' with others out of compassion in order to save them. As discussed in Chapter 1 above, the Buddha probably showed some kinds of indignation and appreciation during his lifetime. If this were the case, the Sarvāstivāda argument would indeed be forceful.

Physical attributes of the rūpakāya

The physical attributes of the Buddha, as mentioned above, are comprised of four categories: (1) the thirty-two major marks; (2) the eighty minor marks; (3) a golden complexion; (4) a one-fathom halo. These four categories are mentioned with some variation in both the *Milindapañha* and its counterpart, the Chinese translation of the **Nāgasena Bhikṣu Sūtra*.[30] The latter is very short compared with the former; it corresponds only to the first part of the *Milindapañha*, from pp. 1–89.[31] Scholars are of the opinion that the original first part was compiled in the first century CE.[32] This would indicate that these physical attributes of the Buddha had already been formulated by the first century CE.

In order to trace the development of these four categories of physical attributes of the Buddha, we must analyse the *avadāna* literature which forms a special group of texts narrating the past lives of the Buddha and his disciples. The Chinese translation of the *avadāna* texts can be divided into the following three groups, according to the categories of attributes mentioned above. The first group includes the *sūtras* that mention only the first two categories, namely the thirty-two major and eighty minor marks. They are the **Madhyametyuktasūtra*, the *Dafangbianfobaoenjing*, the **Atītapratyutpannahetuphalasūtra*, the **Mahālaṅkārasūtraśāstra* attributed to Aśvaghoṣa, and the **Abhiniṣkramaṇasūtra*.[33] Of these five texts, the first two were translated around the end of the second and the beginning of the third centuries CE.[34] The second group includes *sūtras* that mention three categories of attributes: the first two plus the fourth, that of the light. They are the **Caryānidānasūtra*, the **Pūrṇamukhāvadānaśataka*, the **Dharmapadāvadānasūtra*, the **Karuṇāpuṇḍarīkasūtra*, the **Mūlajātahṛdayabhūmidhyānasūtra* and the **Samadattamahārājasūtra*.[35] The first two were translated between the end of the second and the end of the third centuries CE. The only *sūtra* that mentions the first two and the golden complexion is the **Samantaprabhāsasūtra*, a version of the *Lalitavistara*, which was translated by Dharmarakṣa in 308.[36] The third group, comprising ten texts in all, includes *sūtras* that mention all four categories of attributes. The **Nidānacaryāsūtra* was the first to be translated at the end of the second century CE. The majority of the pertinent texts were translated between the third and fourth centuries.[37]

This brief survey suggests that these four categories of physical attributes of the Buddha developed in at least three stages. The first stage is the appearance of the thirty-two marks in the late strata of the *Nikāyas* and the *Āgamas*. The second stage is the addition of the eighty minor marks to the list of the Buddha's physical attributes when the *avadāna* literature began to develop. The Pāli *Apadāna*, which belongs to the *Khuddakanikāya*, the latest of the five *Nikāyas*, already uses the term 'eighty minor marks'.[38] It was during the third and last stage that the golden complexion and one-fathom halo were added to the list, by thc first century CE at the latest. With the appearance of the *Milindapañha*, the formulation of the four categories of physical attributes of the Buddha was complete.

The four categories of physical attributes of the Buddha were likely to have first been formulated by, or at least in close association with, the Sarvāstivāda school. After all, the **Nāgasena Bhikṣu Sūtra* is closely associated with, if not a direct product of, this school. Several points support this assertion. First, the birthplace of Nāgasena was Kashmir, where the main centre of the Sarvāstivāda was located according to the Chinese translation mentioned above.[39] Second, according to N. Dutt, Nāgasena is referred to in the **Abhidharmakośavyākhya* as *pūrvaka sthavira*, a teacher of the Sarvāstivāda school.[40] Third, Dutt thinks that the original text was most probably in Sanskrit. Other scholars such as Rhys Davids are also of a similar opinion that the *Milindapañha* was a translation either from Sanskrit or from some North Indian Prakrit.[41] The Sarvāstivādins were known to have used Sanskrit as their literary language. Fourth, the place names mentioned in the **Nāgasena Bhikṣu Sūtra* suggest that the original text was probably compiled in Northwest India, the stronghold of the Sarvāstivāda school. For instance, Sāgala, or Se-jian in Chinese, has been identified as Sialkot in West India.[42] Fifth, King Milinda/Menander, the main interlocutor of the dialogues, flourished in Northwest India. One may thus conclude that it was the Sarvāstivādins who first formulated these four categories of attributes as the physical marks of the Buddha. The four categories became a codified list, formulated in stock phrases, of the physical qualities of the Buddha that is used in many later works such as the *Vibhāṣā*. Even the Mahāyānists adopted them in their literature. The following is an analysis of these physical attributes of the Buddha.

The Sarvāstivādins developed the idea of the thirty-two marks in early Buddhism, making the *rūpakāya* physically perfect in every aspect. For instance, the description of the Buddha's body as being the colour of gold, given in the *Dīghanikāya*, is not in itself novel. But the Sarvāstivādins interpreted it as a superhuman quality. For them the glory of the golden rays from the Buddha's body exceeded all worldly golden light and surpassed even the light of the Paranirmitavaśavartin, the highest heaven in the world of desire. The skin of the Buddha is said to be so delicately smooth that no dusty cleaves to his body. This is further interpreted to imply that even if the Buddha walks on a dusty mountain with a strong wind blowing, no dust cleaves to his body or feet. The Sarvāstivādins explained that the Buddha's superior and supremely keen sense of taste was a result of the purity of his tongue, so that all kinds of food became delicious when they came into contact with it. The mark of Brahmā's voice, which is described in the *sūtras* as corresponding to the voice of the *karaviṅka* bird, is attributed to a wonderful element in the throat of the Buddha that makes him speak with a pleasant, elegant and harmonious voice.[43] These examples show that although the Sarvāstivādins insisted on the impurity of the *rūpakāya*, they developed the thirty-two major marks, attributing superhuman qualities to the Buddha that are not found in early Buddhist literature.

According to the *Vibhāṣā*, the Sarvāstivādins even attempted to explain the merits required for the achievement of the thirty-two major marks, although they had different opinions among themselves.[44] Some said that they are caused by one thought but can only be completed by many thoughts. Others said that each of the thirty-two marks is caused by a related thought, for example one causing the soles of his feet to be flat and another causing a protuberance to appear on top of the head. Thus the thirty-two major marks are caused by thirty-two thoughts and the completion of each mark requires a substantial accumulation of virtuous *karma*. Opinions differ as to which of the thirty-two major marks was first manifested on Śākyamuni. Some were of the opinion that the mark of the flat soles appeared first, and the other marks followed. Others thought that the mark of blue eyes came first because the Buddha observed the world with blue eyes. As we have already noticed, in most *sūtras* the lists of thirty-two marks begin with 'the flat soles'; only in a few biographical *sūtras* such as the **Kumārakuśalaphalanidāna-sūtra*, the **Vaipulyamahāvyūhasūtra* and the Chinese translation of the *Lalitavistara* do the lists start with the protuberance of the crown. The theory that the flat soles came first is likely to have been based on the early *sūtras* that usually begin their list with this mark.

The Sarvāstivādins further explained that each of the thirty-two major marks is the outcome of one hundred merits, which is the same as one hundred thoughts.[45] The Bodhisattva would initially have had fifty thoughts to make the physical body pure, providing the conditions for a *mahāpuruṣa* mark to develop. Then he would need one thought to initiate the process, and a further fifty thoughts to complete the first mark. The same process would then be repeated for the other thirty-one marks. Thus each of the Buddha's bodily marks was founded on one hundred merits.

With regard to the fifty thoughts, opinions were again divided among the Sarvāstivādins. Some explained that there are five thoughts for each of the ten *kuśalakarmas*: (1) the thought not to kill; (2) the thought of exhortation; (3) the thought of praise; (4) the thought of enjoyment of other people's good deeds; (5) the thought of one's good deeds for *bodhi*. But others interpreted the five thoughts for each of the ten *kuśalakarmas* differently, as lower, medium, upper, superior and highest thoughts. Still others interpreted them in the following way: (1) the thought of purity by *prayoga*; (2) the thought of fundamental purity; (3) the thought of purity arising subsequently; (4) the thought not harmed by investigation (*vitarka*); (5) the thought associated with mindfulness.

With regard to the quantity of one's merit, the authors of the *Vibhāṣā*, after a review of various opinions, explain that the merit of the Buddha is immeasurable. This is due to the fact as a bodhisattva he practised the *pāramitās* for three *asaṃkhyeyakalpas*. It is only Buddhas who acquire the one hundred merits required for gaining one *mahāpuruṣa* mark. Thus each of the thirty-two major marks is endowed with one hundred merits.

It is interesting to note that in their commentaries, the Theravādins maintain that the Buddha's mark of one hundred merits (*satapuññalakkhaṇa*) was a separate issue.[46] It is explained in the commentary on the *Buddhavaṃsa*:

> The mark of a hundred merits means that if all beings in the endless *Cakkavālas* were each to perform one meritorious deed a hundred times, the Bodhisatta was born, having by himself performed a hundredfold all the deeds done by all these beings. Therefore, he is referred to as having the mark of a hundred merits. But 'some' say that each mark is produced for every hundred meritorious deeds. Considering that 'anyone may become a Buddha' [this interpretation] is rejected in the commentaries.[47]

Here, the mark of a hundred merits means countless merits performed by the Buddha in the past as a Bodhisattva. However, the sentence '"some" say that each mark is produced for every hundred meritorious deeds' coincides with the Sarvāstivāda explanation with which the Theravādins appear to disagree. If the two explanations given by the two schools on the one hundred merits are compared, that of the Theravāda is not clear because it is ambiguous as to whether the mark of a hundred merits refers to all the merits done by the Buddha as a Bodhisattva or only some of them. The Sarvāstivāda explanation appears more logical and intuitive, since for each mark the Buddha performed one hundred merits. It may be possible that the Theravādins were heavily influenced by the Sarvāstivāda interpretation.

The merits required for these marks, according to the Sarvāstivāda, are completed in the last hundred *mahākalpas*. It is stated in the *Vibhāṣā*: 'How long does it take to complete the maturation of the marks? Answer: it usually takes one hundred *mahākalpas*, but Śākyamuni Bodhisattva took only ninety-one due to his industrious work.'[48] These one hundred *mahākalpas* came after the completion of the third *asaṃkhyeyakalpa*, when the Bodhisattva was destined to become a Buddha, and during this period of time the Bodhisattva practised only in order to acquire the marks.[49]

According to tradition, the Cakravartin king also has the thirty-two major marks on his body. Then what is the difference between the Buddha's marks and those of the Cakravartin? The Sarvāstivādins explained that the marks of the Buddha are superior in the six ways of being: (1) magnificent; (2) distinct; (3) complete; (4) in the proper place; (5) in accordance with superior wisdom; (6) in accordance with the destruction of *kleśa*.[50]

The eighty minor marks (*aśīti-anuvyañjanāni*) of the Buddha, which are not found in early Buddhism, are probably another development by the Sarvāstivādins. A careful analysis of the eighty items shows that they are not new creations, but a much more detailed physical description of the Buddha on the basis of the thirty-two major marks. Table 2.1 provides a concordance of the similarities between the *mahāpuruṣalakṣaṇa* and the *aśīti-anuvyañjanāni*.

Table 2.1 Comparison of the *mahāpuruṣalakṣaṇa* and the *aśīti-anuvyañjanāni* *

Mahāpurisalakkhaṇa	*Aśīti-anuvyañjanāni*
1 he has well-planted feet (*suppatitthipāda*)	10 even feet
2 his palms and soles are marked with wheels (*hetthāpadatalesu cakkāni jātāni*)	43 fine hand lines 44 deep hand lines 45 long hand lines 80 the palms and soles marked with *śrīvatsa*, *svastika*, *nadyāvarta* and *lalita* symbols
3 he has projecting heels (*āyatapaṇhi*)	
4 he has long fingers and toes (*dīghaṅgulī*)	1 fingernails of copper colour 2 smooth fingernails 3 prominent fingernails 4 rounded fingernails 5 slender fingers 6 well developed fingers
5 he has soft and tender hands and feet (*mudutalunahatthapāda*)	42 delicate hands like cotton
6 he has webbed hands and feet (*jālāhatthapāda*)	
7 he has prominent ankles (*ussanpāda*)	7 concealed veins 8 unknotted veins 9 concealed ankles
8 his legs are like an antelope's (*enijaṅghā*)	
9 standing and without bending he can touch his knees with either hand (*thatakova anonamanto ubhohi hattehi jaṇṇukāni parimasati*)	
10 his male organ is concealed in a sheath (*kosohitavatthaguhya*)	24 sex organ complete
11 his complexion is the colour of gold (*suvaṇṇavaṇṇa*)	
12 his skin is so delicately smooth that no dust cleaves to his body (*sukhumachavi*)	
13 the hairs of his body grow singly, one to each pore (*ekekalomā*)	
14 the hairs of his body turn upwards, curling to the right (*uddhaggaloma*)	
15 his body grows straight (*brahmujjugatta*)	18 rounded body 19 smooth body 20 regular body

Table 2.1 (*cont'd*)

Mahāpurisalakkhaṇa	*Aśīti-anuvyañjanāni*
	21 pure body 22 tender body 23 stainless body
16 he has seven protuberances (*sattussada*)	41 body free from freckles and black spots
17 the upper part of his body is like that of a lion (*sīhapubbaddhakāya*)	27 youthful body 28 energetic body 29 lofty body 30 well-composed body
18 there is no indentation between his shoulders (*citantaramsa*)	25 body has broad and graceful limbs,
19 his proportions have the symmetry of the banyan tree (*nigrodhaparimaṇḍala*)	31 well-proportioned limbs and parts thereof
20 his bust is equally rounded (*samavattakkhandha*)	33 rounded sides of the body 34 smooth sides of the body 35 not bulging sides of the body
21 his sense of taste is supremely acute (*rasagghasaggi*)	
22 his jaw is like a lion's (*sīhahanu*)	
23 he has forty teeth (*cattālīsadanta*)	
24 his teeth are equal (*samadanta*)	53 rounded canine teeth 54 sharp canine teeth 57 regular canine teeth
25 his teeth are closely set (*avivaradanta*)	56 even canine teeth
26 his white teeth are lustrous (*susukkadāṭha*)	55 white canine teeth
27 his tongue is long and slender (*pahūta-jivhā*)	46 not too enlongated mouth 47 the mouth resembling the *bimba* (fruit) 48 pliable tongue 49 slender tongue 50 red tongue
28 he has a divine voice like the *karaviṅka* bird (*brahmasvara*)	51 voice of a roaring elephant or thundering clouds 52 articulate, attractive and gentle speech
29 his eyes are blue-black (*abhinīlanetta*)	32 clear and pure sight
30 he has eyelashes like those of a cow (*gopakhuma*)	60 clear eyes 61 large eyes 62 thick eyelashes

Table 2.1 (cont'd)

Mahāpurisalakkhaṇa	*Aśīti-anuvyañjanāni*
	63 [the white and dark section of] the eyes beautifully [contrast] like the petals of a white and dark lotus 64 long eyebrows 65 soft eyebrows 66 even eyebrows 67 smooth eyebrows
31 between the eyebrows is a hairy mole, white and like soft cotton down (*uṇṇā*)	
32 there is a protuberance on his head (*unhīsasīsa*)	
	11 gait of a lion 12 gait of an elephant 13 gait of a swan 14 gait of a bull 15 gait of swaying towards the right 16 pleasing gait 17 steady gait
	36 slim abdomen 37 deep navel 38 clockwise coiled navel
	58 prominent nose 59 Neat nose
	68 thick and long ears 69 even ears 70 unimpaired hearing
	71 well-formed forehead 72 broad forehead 73 well-developed head 77 undishevelled/untousled head
	74 black hair like that of the black bee 75 thick hair 76 soft hair 78 pliable hair 79 fragrant hair
	26 even pace 39 agreeable in all respects 40 pure conduct

* The list of the thirty-two marks is taken from the *Mahāpadānasutta* (D ii, 16–18) while the eighty minor marks are taken from the **Mahāprajñāpāramitāsūtra*, T6, 968a–969a. Therefore, in the description of the thirty-two marks, Pāli terminology is used while in the description of the eighty minor marks, Sanskrit terminology is used since these two *sūtras* are in Pāli and Sanskrit respectively. These *sūtras* have been chosen to show how many items have been added to make list of eighty marks compared with the earliest list of the thirty-two marks.

From Table 2.1 it is clear that most of the eighty minor marks are related to the thirty-two major marks. Thus the eighty minor marks are merely a detailed description of the Buddha's bodily features. The question is posed in the *Vibhāṣā* of where the eighty minor marks are to be found.[51] The Sarvāstivādins explained that they are among the major marks, but not mixed with them, just as the flowers in the forest make the trees distinctive. This argument also suggests that other schools did not agree with the Sarvāstivādins on the eighty minor marks. However, these attributes became significant at a later period and were accepted by the remaining Buddhist traditions such as Mahāyāna and Theravāda.

The list of eighty minor marks is found neither in the *Nikāyas* nor in the *Āgamas*. However, the term 'eighty minor marks' is mentioned in the Chinese translation of the *Mahāparinirvāṇasūtra* of the **Dīrghāgama*, and the **Aśokasūtra* of the **Saṃyuktāgama*.[52] It is clear that the term 'eighty minor marks' is a later interpolation in the *Mahāparinirvāṇasūtra* in the **Dīrghāgama*, because it is not mentioned in either the Pāli version or the other three independent Chinese translations of the *sūtra*.[53] The **Aśokasūtra* was obviously a later insertion into the **Saṃyuktāgama* because, first, the entire *sūtra* is about King Aśoka, and second, there are two similar independent works in the Taisho *Tripiṭaka* which are later works: the **Aśokasūtra* and the *Biography of Aśoka*. Therefore, the eighty minor marks were not originally in either the **Dīrghāgama* or the **Saṃyuktāgama*, but were added later in the course of transmission. There is no mention of the term in the **Madhyamāgama*. Of the four *Āgamas*, only the *Ekottara* contains the term 'eighty minor marks', using it thirteen times but without enumerating the eighty items.[54] In some places, the *Ekottara* also mentions the golden complexion and the light separately from the terms 'thirty-two major' and 'eighty minor marks'.[55] This text had been revised by the early schools and, according to some scholars such as Yinshun, was even influenced by Mahāyāna teachings.[56] Yinshun provides us with two pieces of textual evidence. First, in the introductory chapter of the Chinese **Ekottarāgama*, it is stated: 'The Bhagavan delivered the Dharma in various ways, while the bodhisattvas made up their minds to learn the Mahāyāna.'[57] Second, Chapter XVIII states: 'Śāriputra, the Tathāgata says that there are four unfathomable things which the Hīnayānists do not understand.'[58] The term 'eighty minor marks', therefore, was probably interpolated into the original version of the *Ekottara* by the transmitters according to the teaching of their own school after Buddhism had split into different schools. As evidence, the term 'eighty minor marks' is not found in the four Pāli *Nikāyas*.

The earliest use of the term 'eighty minor marks' is in the Pāli *Apadāna* and the first part of the *Milindapañha* discussed above.[59] The term appears more frequently in biographical *sūtras* of the Buddha as well as in the Mahāyāna *sūtras* and treatises. The first complete list of the eighty minor marks is found in two biographical *sūtras* of the Buddha. They are the

**Abhiniṣkramaṇasūtra*, which was translated into Chinese by Jñānagupta in 587 CE, and the **Vaipulyamahāvyūhasūtra*, which is a translation of the *Lalitavistara* made by Divākara in 683 CE.[60] Although the term 'eighty minor marks' is mentioned once in another early Chinese translation of the *Lalitavistara*, entitled the **Samantaprabhāṣa-sūtra*, made by Dharmarakṣa in 308 CE, the eighty items are not given.[61] The list of eighty items is also found in the Sanskrit version of the *Lalitavistara*. It is possible that the list was inserted at a later date into both the **Vaipulyamahāvyūhasūtra* and the Sanskrit version of the *Lalitavistara*, which had perhaps been revised by the Mahāyānists since the title includes the word *vaipulya*.

The **Abhiniṣkramaṇasūtra* is the most comprehensive biography of the Buddha available to us. H. Nakamura is of the opinion that this work was transmitted by the Dharmaguptaka school.[62] However, at the end of the text it is said that the Mahāsāṃghikas named it the 'Great Matter' (*Mahāvastu*); the Sarvāstivādins called it the 'Great Adornment' (*Mahāvyūha* or *Lalitavistara*); the Kāśyapiyas entitled it the 'Buddha's Former Nidāna or Avadāna'; the Dharmaguptakas called it 'Śākyamuni's Former Practice' (*Buddhacarita*) and the Mahīśāsakas named it the 'Root of Vinayapiṭaka' (*Vinayapiṭakamūla*).[63] The text itself also mentions the opinions of different schools on certain issues. So it seems that this work did not belong to any particular school mentioned in the *sūtra* but was shared by all, in spite of some variations on minor points. Apart from this, the **Abhiniṣkramaṇasūtra* displays many Mahāyānistic elements. First, it mentions Vairocana Buddha at the beginning.[64] It further advocates skilful means (*upāyakauśalya*) as a method of teaching sentient beings, such as appearing in respect-inspiring forms – which could vary according to pupils' inclinations – and so bringing them to the Dharma of all Buddhas.[65] We are inclined to think that this work was shared by most early Indian Buddhist schools and was later revised by the Mahāyānists or the Mahāsāṃghika-Mahāyānists.

In the Theravāda tradition, the list of eighty items is found only in the sub-commentaries such as the *Milindapañhaṭīkā* and the *Jinālaṅkāraṭīkā* (or *Jinālaṅkāravaṇṇanā*).[66] T. Endo, who has made a study of the concept of the Buddha in the Pāli commentaries, is of the opinion that the Theravādins adopted the concept of *asīti-anuvyañjanāni* from another early Buddhist school and later adopted the list in its entirety.[67] This Buddhist school is perhaps none other than the Sarvāstivāda.

From the above investigation of the eighty minor marks, it seems that the term appears in the Buddhist literature quite early, but the list of eighty items is frequently mentioned in biographical *sūtras* of the Buddha which display certain Mahāyāna elements. The MPPŚ records that the Sarvāstivādins believed in the eighty minor marks.[68] If the eighty minor marks had been originated by the Mahāyānists, then the Sarvāstivādins would probably not have accepted them as they completely repudiated the Mahāyāna teachings.[69] The eighty minor marks must be closely associated with the

Sarvāstivāda school. This is borne out by our analysis of the **Nāgasena Bhikṣu Sūtra*, as discussed above. It was probably the Sarvāstivādins who created the eighty minor marks on the basis of the thirty-two major marks, and subsequently they became very significant. The Mahāyānists and the Theravādins then incorporated them into their attributes of the Buddha.

The golden complexion is one of the thirty-two major marks. From our examination of the *sūtras* and commentaries, we have no clue as to why this particular mark is taken out and listed separately as one of the four categories of the physical attributes of the Buddha. Perhaps we may surmise that it was singled out from the thirty-two marks as a very easily visible sign. As we have seen, much importance was attached to it: the golden rays radiating from his complexion exceeded any other golden light and the skin of the Buddha was so smooth that no dust cleaved to his body.

The earliest occurrence of the term 'one-fathom halo' is in the *Buddhavaṃsa* and the *Vimānavatthu* of the *Khuddakanikāya*.[70] However, the term is considered post-canonical.[71] According to the *Vibhāṣā*, the Sarvāstivādins called the one-fathom halo 'superior light',[72] for the following reasons. First, the light radiates perpetually from the Buddha's body. Unlike other kinds of light that are not constant, this light is always there, so it is called 'superior light'. Second, a one-fathom halo surrounds the body of the Buddha, so no dust or insects can come near him. Third, the Buddha has three kinds of light that outshine all other kinds of light. They are: (1) the golden light from his body which outshines mountains of gold; (2) the white light from the Buddha's teeth which outshines mountains of snow; (3) the all-pervading pure light of the Buddha's wisdom which destroys all heretical theories. All other kinds of light disappear when they encounter these three kinds of light. It is therefore called superior light.[73]

This attribute is not given in the original list of the thirty-two marks in the *Nikāyas* and the *Āgamas*, but it appears among them later in the biographical *sūtras* such as the **Atītapratyutpannahetuphalasūtra*, and the **Samadattamahārājasūtra*.[74] It is also found in the list in the **Saṅghabhedavastu* of the **Mūlasarvāstivāda Vinaya* and many Mahāyāna *sūtras* such as the **Prajñāpāramitā*.[75] However, according to the *Vibhāṣā*, the Sarvāstivāda regarded this attribute as a separate quality of the Buddha. The compilers of the *Vibhāṣā* commented on the issue to the effect that although it is not one of the thirty-two marks, all the Buddhas have a superior light with a one-fathom halo that radiates from their bodies at all times.[76]

Apart from the one-fathom halo, the *Buddhavaṃsa* also states that the Buddha had a hundred rays (*śataraśmi*) of six colours radiating from his body.[77] Commentaries such as the *Sāratthappakāsinī* give a more detailed explanation of the rays of the Buddha, saying that they emanate from six parts of the Buddha's body: the front, the back, the right and left hands, the hairs of his head, and the soles of his feet.[78] However, this attribute is not included in the list of the thirty-two major marks in the Theravāda tradition.

It is significant that the authors of the **Prajñāpāramitāsūtras* further developed this mark as a supreme attribute of the Buddha. According to the **Prajñāpāramitāsūtras*, before the Buddha started to preach he first emitted rays from all parts of his body, including the pores on his head, this was the supreme light, which illuminated three thousand great world systems. Those who encountered such light would attain full enlightenment.[79] Then the Mahāyānists made the supreme light a special attribute of the Buddha. This will be discussed in Chapter 7 below.

Adorned with all these attributes and qualities, the physical body of the Buddha is perfect, according to the Sarvāstivādins. No one could have meditated upon the uncleanness of the human body when observing the physical body of the Buddha, because the external appearance of the *rūpakāya* of the Buddha was so clear, bright and subtle that no one could be disgusted by it.[80] There was no scar on the *rūpakāya* even after Devadatta injured the Buddha's feet, because of the merit accumulated in numerous *kalpas* of the past.[81]

In spite of their view that the Buddha was a human being, the Sarvāstivādins also maintained that he had immeasurable physical strength, like Nārāyana, the hero of divine power.[82] After quoting contending opinions, the *Vibhāṣā* characterizes the strength of Nārāyana as limitless like mental strength. However, the Buddha reached his fall physical strength at the age of twenty-five and retained it until the age of fifty, after which it gradually declined. The *Āgamas* contain an independent *sūtra* entitled the '*Sūtra* on the Wrestlers Who Were Trying to Move a Mountain', which describes the Buddha's physical strength as immeasurable, just as it is described in the *Vibhāṣā*.[83] Though this *sūtra* may have been compiled quite late, it nevertheless suggests that the Sarvāstivādins had made their statement on the basis of the *sūtras*. However, other schools such as the Mahāsāṃghikas maintained that the physical strength of the Buddha, like his mental strength, never decreased. According to the Sarvāstivādins, only the strength of the *dharmakāya* does not decrease, whereas the physical strength of the *rūpakāya* does decrease because the heterogeneous effects produced by heterogeneous causes (*vipāka-phala*) of *karma* decrease. The *rūpakāya* will come to an end when the *vipāka-phala* are exhausted.[84] The Sarvāstivādins therefore considered harming the physical body of the Buddha to be only the second among the five grave sins whereas splitting the Saṃgha was regarded as the first because all Buddhas respect the *dharmakāya*. Shedding the blood of the Buddha only harms the *rūpakāya* whereas causing a schism within the Saṃgha is seen as destroying the *dharmakāya*.[85]

The *dharmakāya*

The notion of the *dharmakāya*, which in early Buddhism meant the teaching of the Buddha in general, was interpreted by the Sarvāstivāda as comprising the eighteen exclusive *dharmas* (*āveṇika*). These are the ten powers, the four kinds of intrepidity, the three foundations of mindfulness, and great compassion; they are the fruits of the immeasurable merit accumulated during three *asaṃkhyeyakalpas*. These qualities are explained in detail in the *Vibhāṣā* as constituting the mental strength of the Buddha.[86] These qualities were attributed to the Buddha at a quite early stage and they are cited in both the Pāli *Mahāsihanādasutta* and the Chinese *Āgamas*.

The concept of the *dharmakāya* was perhaps expounded for the first time in the first of the three Chinese translations of the *Vibhāṣā*, as discussed at the beginning of this chapter. It is stated in the *Vibhāṣā*:

> The *sūtras* delivered by the Buddha state that there are eighty thousand *dharmakāyas*. Question: what quantifies the *dharmakāya*? According to one theory, one *sūtra* is considered a *dharmakāya* and such a *kāya* is counted as the measurement [of a *dharmakāya*]. Thus, the same measurement should apply to all the eighty thousand. According to another theory, the *sūtras* state that mental concentration is a form of measure of a *dharmakāya*. For instance, the *sūtras* speak of the *prahāṇāni*, *ṛddhipādās*, *indriyas*, *balas*, *bodhyaṅgānis* and *mārgas*. Each of these is considered as a form of measurement of a *dharmakāya*. Thus it adds up to eighty thousand. But the counters [of words] say that eight words make a sentence and thirty-two syllables consist of a *śloka*.
>
> Five hundred thousand, again five thousand (*ślokas*).
>
> Five hundred thousand and five thousand (*ślokas*) are the quantity of a *dharmakāya*.[87]

This account suggests that in the earliest stage, probably before the development of Sarvāstivāda, many different theories existed concerning the concept of the *dharmakāya*. In the *Nikāyas* and the *Āgamas*, it is only stated that he who sees the *dharmakāya* sees the Buddha. It is likely that the immediate disciples of the Buddha understood the term *dharmakāya* to mean the actual teachings of the Buddha. However, later followers took it literally as the scripture that contains his teachings and disputed the quantification of the *dharmakāya*. Here the Sarvāstivādins differed, and stated that the eighty thousand *dharmakāyas* mentioned in the *sūtras* are all in the five *skandhas* of *śīla*, *samādhi*, *prajñā*, *vimukti* and *vimukti-jñāna-darśana*, which were thus held to constitute the five divisions of the *dharmakāya*.[88] Sometimes the Sarvāstivādins also explained the *dharmakāya* as consisting of three divisions: *śīla*, *samādhi* and *prajñā*.[89] This perhaps represents the early phase of the Sarvāstivāda concept of the *dharmakāya*, on the basis of which the concept of the eighteen exclusive *dharmas* was ultimately developed.

The question of the eighteen exclusive *dharmas* of the Buddha is a complicated one because there are two lists, one pertaining to the Hīnayāna (mainly the Sarvāstivāda) and the other to the Mahāyāna. The Sarvāstivāda list is a collection of the attributes of the Buddha taken from the early *sūtras*. The ten powers and the four kinds of intrepidity are found in the *Mahāsīhanādasutta* of the *Majjhimanikāya* as well as in the Chinese translations of the *Dīrgha*, *Saṃyukta* and **Ekottarāgamas*.[90] The three foundations of mindfulness are mentioned in the *Saḷāyatanavibhaṅgasutta* of the *Majjhimanikāya* as well as in the corresponding Chinese translation in the **Madhyamāgama*,[91] while compassion is mentioned in numerous places. The Mahāyāna list of the eighteen exclusive *dharmas* is completely different from that above.[92]

Let us first clarify the term 'eighteen exclusive *dharmas*' before proceeding to a detailed discussion of its content. The term is never mentioned in the *Nikāyas* or the *Āgamas*, but is found only in an independent translation of the **Brahmāyuḥsūtra* of the **Madhyamāgama*.[93] A comparison of this independent translation and its counterpart in the **Madhyamāgama* shows that the term was interpolated into the *sūtra* later, given that it was not used in the original version of the *Āgama*. The independent *sūtra* contains two stock passages which are not found in its counterpart: 'the thirty-two major marks and the eighty minor marks of the Buddha' and 'the ten powers, the four kinds of intrepidity and the eighteen exclusive *dharmas*'.

We can see that, first, these stock passages often appear in the post-canonical literature, but never in the early *sūtras*. Second, in addition to the term 'eighteen exclusive *dharmas*', the term 'eighty minor marks' is never used in the *Nikāyas* or the *Āgamas*, but is often found in later works, as we have already seen. Third, the independent translation also refers to a five-coloured light that comes out of the mouth of the Buddha, circles his body three times and then returns into his mouth. Again, this attribute of the Buddha is not mentioned in its counterpart in the **Madhyamāgama*. It is therefore probable that the term 'eighteen exclusive *dharmas*' was interpolated into the independent *sūtra* when it was taken out of the **Madhyamāgama* and independently transmitted. However, the transmitters of the **Madhyamāgama* were faithful to their tradition and kept it relatively uncorrupted even though this text was translated into Chinese a century after the independent *sūtra*. Thus the **Brahmāyuḥsūtra* in the **Madhyamāgama* mentions neither the term 'eighteen exclusive *dharmas*' nor the term 'eighty minor marks'. It is only in the independent translation of it that the term 'eighteen exclusive *dharmas*' occurs.

The term 'eighteen exclusive *dharmas*' is also used in three of the biographical *sūtras* of the Buddha, but scholars are unsure as to which list it refers to although an analysis suggests that these three *sūtras* were either influenced by or belonged to the Mahāyāna. These three biographical *sūtras* are the *Dafangbianfobaoenjing* ('*Sūtra* of the Great Skilful Means [*mahā-upāya*] by Which the Buddha Recompenses the Favour [of his parents]'), the **Mahāyānamahākaruṇāpuṇḍarīkasūtra* and the **Vaipulyamahāvyūhasūtra*.

Judging from the titles, they are all Mahāyāna *sūtras* since the terms used, such as *mahā-upāya* and *vaipulya*, are Mahāyānistic. They further mention names of Mahāyāna bodhisattvas such as Avalokiteśvara and Mañjuśrī.[94] Since they are Mahāyāna *sūtras*, it can be inferred that the eighteen exclusive *dharmas* mentioned are those of the Mahāyāna tradition.

T. Endo is of the opinion that the Theravādins were the first to formulate the eighteen exclusive *dharmas*, which roughly correspond to the Mahāyāna list.[95] The term *aṭṭhādasabuddhadhamma* first appeared between the end of the first and second centuries CE, as it occurs for the first time in the second part of the *Milindapañha* where it is used twice. According to K. Mizuno, the second part of the *Milindapañha* from page 89 to the end was composed in Sri Lanka after the end of the first century CE.[96]

There are two problems concerning the term *aṭṭhādasabuddhadhamma* in the *Milindapañha*. First, it is not clear whether the term refers to the Hīnayāna list or to that of the Mahāyāna. Second, the date of the composition of the second portion of the *Milindapañha* is controversial, and some scholars such as H. Nakamura are of the opinion that it was completed between 250 CE and the time of Buddhaghosa, as T. Endo also indicates.[97] The earliest list of the eighteen *dharmas* of the Theravāda is found only in Buddhaghosa's commentary on the *Dīghanikāya*, but this list never became the standard.[98] It is the list found in Dhammapāla's sub-commentary of the *Dīghanikāya*, a work of the sixth or seventh century CE, that became standard.

We think that the Hīnayāna list of the Sarvāstivādins may have come into being first, on the basis of the following evidence. First, the Sarvāstivāda list of the eighteen exclusive *dharmas* is mentioned in all three versions of the Chinese translation of the *Vibhāṣā*, as discussed above. According to Yinshun, the original version of the *Vibhāṣā* may have been composed in the second century CE, after King Kaniṣka and before the composition of the MPPŚ.[99] This brings the date of the Sarvāstivāda list closer to that of the Theravāda school if we accept Endo's assertion. Second, neither the term 'eighteen exclusive *dharmas*' nor the Mahāyāna list occurs in the early Chinese translations of the **Prajñāpāramitāsūtras* such as the **Aṣṭasāhasrikā* or in two versions of the **Pañcaviṃśatisāhasrikā*: the *Fangguang* and the *Guangzan*. The full Mahāyāna list is mentioned in both Kumārajīva's and Xuanzang's translations of the **Prajñāpāramitāsūtras*.[100] Therefore, the Mahāyāna list probably been introduced into the **Prajñāpāramitāsūtras* later. The Mahāyāna list probably came into being in the third or the fourth century CE as the **Aṣṭasāhasrikā* was translated in the second century CE and Kumārajīva made his translation at the beginning of the fifth century. Third, as discussed above, the Sarvāstivāda list of the eighteen exclusive *dharmas* was not a new creation, but was compiled from material in the early *sūtras*. Thus the list was a development from the Sarvāstivādins analysis of the teachings of the Buddha in the early *sūtras*, while the items in the Mahāyāna list represent a further development. The author of the MPPŚ argues that while the eighteen *dharmas* of the Sarvāstivādins are not exclusive to the Buddha but are shared with *pratyekabuddhas* and *arhats*, the Mahāyāna list of *dharmas* is exclusive to the Buddha.[101] Therefore, it was most probably the Sarvāstivādins who first collected the eighteen items from the early *sūtras* and called them the 'eighteen exclusive *dharmas*'. The term *aṭṭhādasabuddhadhamma* in the *Milindapañha* may refer not to the Mahāyāna list but to the Sarvāstivāda list. The Mahāyānists created another list of eighteen exclusive *dharmas* of the Buddha because they did not agree with the Sarvāstivādins that the eighteen *dharmas* are exclusive to the Buddhas, considering them to be shared with other liberated beings. According to Har Dayal, this occurred in the third century CE.[102]

Let us now examine the four categories of the eighteen exclusive *dharmas*, as discussed in the *Vibhāṣā*.[103]

The ten powers

The essence of the ten powers is defined as wisdom because the mental power of the Buddha is wisdom.[104] They are called powers because they are non-succumbing, non-yielding, indestructible, non-destroying, unchangeable, non-submissive, all-enlightening, enduring, strong, superior and able to overpower others. Therefore, though the *pratyekabuddhas* and the *śrāvakas* also have the eighth and the ninth knowledges, these are not called powers because they do not have the above characteristics. This explanation suggests that probably by the third century CE, the Sarvāstivāda Abhidharmikas had already become extremely meticulous.

The four kinds of intrepidity

The four kinds of intrepidity also have wisdom as their essence because the first intrepidity corresponds to the first power, the second to the tenth power, the third to the second power, and the fourth to the seventh power.[105] They are called intrepidities because they are non-timid, non-terrified, non-collapsible, brave, stable, purified and white in the sense of being pure.

If the ten powers and the four kinds of intrepidity all have wisdom as their essence, what is the difference between them? The Sarvāstivādins explained that each intrepidity has the ten powers and each power also has the four kinds of intrepidity, making forty powers and forty kinds of intrepidity. However, they are different in that qualities such as strength, stability, wisdom and invincibility are powers, while qualities such as bravery, eloquence, fearlessness and their effects are intrepidity.[106]

The three foundations of mindfulness

The three foundations of mindfulness are:

1 When his disciples listen, accept and practise his teaching unanimously and respectfully, the Tathāgata experiences neither joy nor satisfaction, but remains indifferent, in full mindfulness and awareness.
2 When his disciples do not respect, do not hear, do not accept and do not practise his teaching unanimously, the Tathāgata does not experience displeasure or impatience, but remains indifferent, in full mindfulness and awareness.
3 When some of his disciples hear, accept and practise his teaching respectfully, while others do not hear, do not accept and do not practise his teaching, the Buddha does not experience joy or displeasure but remains indifferent, in full mindfulness and awareness.

These three foundations of mindfulness are also included in the first of the ten powers because the Buddha understands the inclinations of beings, has eliminated hatred and attachment, and has achieved the practice of emptiness (*śūnyatā*).[107]

The great compassion

The term 'great compassion' (*mahākaruṇā*) was most probably first introduced by the Sarvāstivādins so that the compassion of the Buddha could be distinguished from ordinary compassion. The **Abhidharmakośabhāṣya* (*Kośa*) of Vasubandhu gives five reasons why the compassion of the Buddha is termed 'great compassion', but both the **Abhidharma(piṭaka)prakaraṇa-śāsanaśāstra* and the **Abhidharmanyāyānusāraśāstra* of Saṅghabhadra list a further four reasons.[108] However, Saṅghabhūti's translation of the *Vibhāṣā*, which is the earliest, gives seven reasons, while Buddhavarma's translation, which is the second, and Xuanzang's translation, which is the latest and longest, give nine similar reasons.[109] Table 2.2 is a comparative table of the reasons given in the above texts.

The comparison in Table 2.2 clearly shows that the reasons given in the two *Vibhāṣā* texts are not presented in an orderly fashion or with sound reasoning. In fact, the seven reasons given in Saṅghabhūti's translation increase to nine in Xuanzang's translation. By contrast, the five reasons given in the *Kośa* are highly condensed and synthesized. It seems that after the creation of the term 'great compassion' of the Buddha, the Sarvāstivādins continued to develop it although the reasons were later condensed into five. This concurs perfectly with the traditional Buddhist view that Vasubandhu wrote the *Kośa* after he had summarized the six commentaries and the *Vibhāṣā* of the Sarvāstivāda school.[110]

Compassion (*karuṇā*) figures in many places in the early *sūtras*, and the Buddha is described as one who is fully accomplished in both wisdom and compassion. However, the Sarvāstivādins distinguished the compassion of the Buddha from ordinary compassion and called it 'great compassion'.

Table 2.2 Comparison of reasons for the doctrine of *mahākaruṇā*

Kośa *of Vasubandhu*	*Two treatises of Saṅghabhadra*	*The* Vibhāṣā *of Saṅghabhūti*	*The* Vibhāṣā *of Xuanzang*
1 Because of its components (*saṃbhāra*): it is produced in fact by a great provision of merit and knowledge.	**1** The same as the left-hand column. Also: It is produced by the great treasure of merit. It is obtained through great endeavour (*prayoga*).	**1** Because of its cultivation: the Buddha makes offerings of his most precious things, unlike a *śrāvaka* who makes one offering to one person or a *pratyekabuddha* who makes several offerings. **3** Because of its great skill in means, it is achieved through practising hundreds and thousands of austerities in three *asaṃkhyeya kalpas*, unlike the *śrāvakas* such as Śāriputra, who achieved *bodhi* by practising earnestly for sixty *kalpas* only, or the *pratyekabuddhas*, who achieved *bodhi* by practising earnestly for a hundred *kalpas*.	**4** Because of its cultivation: it is achieved through the practice of making offerings, the practice of observing precepts, the practice of tolerance, the practice of energy, the practice of meditation, and the practice of wisdom. This is not like the *śrāvakas* and *pratyekabuddhas* who achieved small fruit by practising offering once or by observing precepts for a night or by meditating on a verse of four lines. **5** Because of its earnest endeavour (*prayoga*): it is achieved through practising hundreds and thousands of austerities in three *asaṃkhyeya kalpas*, unlike the *śrāvakas* who achieved *bodhi* by practising earnestly for only sixty *kalpas* and the *pratyekabuddhas* who achieved *bodhi* by practising earnestly for a hundred *kalpas*.*
2 Because of its aspects, of the modality under which it grasps things: it considers things painful because of the threefold suffering.	**2** The same as the left-hand column. Also: It can eliminate the grievous suffering of sentient beings.	**5** Because of its saving beings from the chasm: the Buddha, for example, saves beings from the *pañca gataya*.	**1** Because of its eliminating grievous suffering: it eliminates suffering of the beings in hell, hungry ghosts and animals by taking them out of hell and giving them the happiness of human beings and gods. **2** Because of its eliminating *kleśa*, it takes sentient beings out of the mire of *kleśa* and leads them to the path of the fruit of the saint. **7** Because of its abandoning great happiness and saving people from suffering: it is by great compassion that the Tathāgata abandons the unlimited, superior happiness and saves beings from suffering through wandering in the ten cardinal directions.

Table 2.2 Comparison of reasons for the doctrine of *mahākaruṇā*

Kośa *of Vasubandhu*	*Two treatises of Saṅghabhadra*	*The* Vibhāṣā *of Saṅghabhūti*	*The* Vibhāṣā *of Xuanzang*
3 Because of the object, for it has for its object all beings in the three *dhātus*.	**3** The same as the left-hand column.	**4** Because of its superior benefit: it can bring people to the path of Buddha, *pratyekabuddha*, *śrāvaka* and other worldly benefits, such as wealth and birth in heaven.	**3** Because of its superior benefit: it teaches sentient beings to destroy the three evil deeds and to cultivate the three wholesome deeds so that they may earn various benefits, from obtaining wealth to becoming Mahābrahma and even attaining the final *bodhi*.
4 Because of its evenhandedness: for it is equally concerned with the happiness and benefit of all beings.	**4** The same as the left-hand column.	**7** Because of its excellence: it saves sentient beings by using various skills and means, manifesting in different forms.	**8** Because of its skill in means: it saves sentient beings by using various skills and means, manifesting in different forms. Though the Buddha was in a superior position he helps them all find liberation.
5 Because of its excellence: for no other compassion which has arisen surpasses it.	**5** The same as the left-hand column. Also: It is achieved through the body of a *mahāpurusa*.	**2** Because of its dependence: it arises only in the body of a *mahāpurusa* who has the thirty-two major marks, the eighty minor marks, and the one-fathom rays radiating from his body. His body is golden in colour, and he has a voice like that of the *karaviṅka* bird. **6** Because of being a motivation of great equanimity (*upekṣā*): it benefits sentient beings by motivating the Buddha to help liberate them when he is in a state of great equanimity. In such a state the Buddha is indifferent to everything and nothing can motivate him except great compassion.	**6** Because of its dependence: it arises only in the body of a *mahāpurusa* who has the thirty-two major marks, the eighty minor marks, and the one-fathom rays radiating from the body, the *uṣṇīṣa*, and whose body is golden in colour, unlike the *śrāvakas* and *pratyekabuddhas*. **9** Because of being a motivation of great equanimity (*upekṣā*): it benefits sentient beings by motivating the Buddha to help liberate them when he is in a state of great equanimity. In such a state the Buddha is indifferent to everything and nothing can motivate him except great compassion.

* This explanation seems to be influenced by the Mahāyāna doctrine.

They further explained that the great compassion differs from ordinary compassion in eight ways. Since there are some discrepancies in Leo M. Pruden's English translation of the **Abhidharmakośabhāṣya*, I reproduce here a summary taken directly from the *Vibhāṣā*.[111]

1 With respect to its nature: ordinary compassion is absence of hatred, whereas great compassion is absence of ignorance.
2 With respect to its scope: ordinary compassion takes the form of ordinary suffering, whereas great compassion takes the form of a threefold suffering.
3 With respect to its object: ordinary compassion is concerned with the beings of the *kāmadhātu* only, whereas great compassion is concerned with beings of the three *dhātus*.
4 With respect to its level (*bhūmi*): ordinary compassion is at the level of the ten *dhyānas* – the four *dhyānas*, the four stages above the four *dhyānas*, *antaradhyāna* and the *kāmabhūmi* – whereas great compassion is at the level of the fourth *dhyāna* only.
5 With respect to its support: ordinary compassion arises in *śrāvakas*, *pratyekabuddhas* and Buddhas as well as ordinary people (*pṛthagjana*), whereas great compassion arises only in Buddhas.
6 With respect to its acquisition: ordinary compassion is achieved through detachment from the *kāmadhātu* and the third *dhyāna*, whereas great compassion is achieved through detachment from the *bhavāgra* only.
7 With respect to saving (others): ordinary compassion only arouses sympathy for the act of liberating (others), whereas great compassion not only gives rise to sympathy but also accomplishes the act of liberating.
8 With respect to compassion: ordinary compassion is partial compassion, for it sympathizes only with beings who are suffering, whereas great compassion is turned towards all beings equally.[112]

According to the *Vibhāṣā*, great compassion is found in the fourth *dhyāna* in the *rūpadhātu* and arises depending on the body of a great man (*mahāpuruṣa*). While the great man is still in Jambudvīpa and thus in the *kāmadhātu*, it is not conjoined with *samādhi*. It accounts for all *dharmas* of the past, present and future, the good, the bad, and the neutral, as well as all sentient beings in the three *dhātus*. It does not include, however, the sixteen aspects of the four noble truths. It is neither *śaikṣa* nor *aśaikṣa* and accounts for neither *śaikṣa* nor *aśaikṣa*. Rather, it is of the path of contemplation of the Dharma and of the *saṃvṛtijñāna*. It is obtained either by *prayoga* or when the *kleśas* are eradicated.[113]

The question arises of why the *Vibhāṣā* speaks only of great compassion, and not of great benevolence (*mahāmaitrī*), great joy (*mahāmuditā*) or great equanimity (*mahopekṣā*). The Sarvāstivādins explain that all four should be spoken of as 'great' because: (1) the merit of the Buddha is great; (2) it arises for the benefit and protection of sentient beings; (3) it arises out of his compassion towards sentient beings; (4) it operates with a pure mind, equally and continuously directed towards sentient beings.[114]

These eighteen exclusive *dharmas*, except for the three foundations of mindfulness, were important factors for the Buddha when he preached the Dharma. Through the ten powers, the Buddha established his own position. Through the four kinds of intrepidity, the Buddha destroyed the arguments of the heretics and through great compassion the Buddha's desire to preach was stimulated. Therefore the Buddha accomplished the act of preaching the Dharma by virtue of these fifteen factors. However, the three foundations of mindfulness are not like the powers. They are included in the list of the eighteen exclusive *dharmas* because they are conducive to the Buddha's abiding in equanimity.[115] Here the Sarvāstivādins emphasize the Buddha's quality as a teacher, so conforming with the early Buddhist literature, the *Nikāyas* and the *Āgamas*.

In addition to the eighteen exclusive *dharmas*, the Sarvāstivādins also attributed to the Buddha other qualities such as the seven wonderful *dharmas* and the five holy wisdom *samādhis* which are also described as mental powers.[116] The seven wonderful *dharmas* are that the Buddha: (1) knows the Dharma; (2) knows the meaning (of the Dharma); (3) knows the time (when to preach it); (4) knows the quantity (to preach); (5) knows it for himself (through experience); (6) knows the audience; (7) knows who is born superior and who inferior. These seven wonderful *dharmas* are all functions of the first of the ten powers and belong to conventional knowledge.

The five holy wisdom *samādhis* are:

1. The wisdom that arises from inner attainment knows that the *samādhi* is holy and without defilement.
2. The wisdom that arises from inner attainment knows that the *samādhi* is not attained by the foolish, but is praised by the wise.
3. The wisdom that arises from inner attainment knows that the *samādhi* is enduring happiness.
4. The wisdom that arises from inner attainment knows that the *samādhi* is tranquil, wonderful, the way to calm, and can bring the mind to one-pointedness.
5. The wisdom that arises from inner attainment perceives that *samādhi* is attained through right mindfulness.

The five wisdom *samādhis* are included in the first of the ten powers and all pertain to conventional knowledge.

Other attributes of the Buddha

Other attributes of the Buddha that are discussed in the *Vibhāṣā* cannot be classified as belonging to either the *rūpakāya* or the *dharmakāya*. First, according to the Sarvāstivādins, the smallest unit of time is *kṣaṇa*, the smallest unit of matter (*rūpa*) is an atom (*paramāṇu*) and the smallest unit of naming (*nāma*) is one character.[117] The Buddha was omniscient in the sense that he knew the range of *nāma*[118] as well as the duration of one *kṣaṇa*.[119] In other words, the Buddha knew even the smallest things in the world.

Second, the Buddha did not have any dreams. Since dreams are caused by illusions and the Buddha had eliminated all illusions and habitual force, he was dreamless.[120] Kuiji, the eminent disciple of Xuanzang who translated the *Vibhāṣā*, further commented that undefiled ignorance is the cause of dreams. The Buddha had eliminated all undefiled ignorance,[121] so he had no dreams.[122] However, according to the Sarvāstivādins, the Buddha did sleep because it was necessary for maintaining the health of his physical body. That is why the *sūtras* say the Buddha slept after meals, especially when the day was hot.[123] The Sarvāstivādins distinguished between two kinds of sleep, defiled and undefiled. The sleep of the Buddhas, *pratyekabuddhas* and *arhats* is undefiled because they have eliminated *kleśas*. However, stream attainers to *pratyekabuddhas* and even bodhisattvas have dreams. For instance, Gautama had five dreams before he left the palace, but his dreams were not illusions.[124]

Third, the Buddha could make offerings of wealth and Dharma to all, but nobody can offer Dharma to the Buddha because no one can preach the Dharma to him.[125] *Pratyekabuddhas* could make offerings of both Dharma and wealth to all, but they could not offer Dharma to the Buddha. Śāriputra could make offerings of wealth to all, but could not offer Dharma to the Buddhas or to *pratyekabuddhas*. Maudgalyāyana could make offerings of wealth to all, but could not offer Dharma to Buddhas, *pratyekabuddhas* or Śāriputra. Those who are not intelligent can offer wealth to all, but cannot offer Dharma to the intelligent.

Fourth, the Buddha could utter one sound in one *kṣaṇa* of mind and could utter one word in one *kṣaṇa* of sound because he was swift in verbal response, superior in speech, and had no speech defect.[126] While *pratyekabuddhas* and *śrāvakas* can also make one sound in one *kṣaṇa* of mind, they cannot speak one word in one *kṣaṇa* of sound and they need more *kṣaṇas* to utter a word. However, according to Vasumitra, the Sarvāstivādins held that the Buddha could not expound all doctrines with a single utterance, and not all his speeches were the act of preaching the Dharma, as he also uttered words that did not refer to the truth.[127]

The time needed to become a Buddha

N. Dutt is of the opinion that the Sarvāstivādins cherished Buddhahood as the goal of religious life because it is said in the *Divyāvadāna* that after a discourse, some aspired to *śrāvakabodhi*, some to *pratyekabodhi* and some to *samyaksambodhi*.[128] So it seems that the Mahāsāṃghikas were not alone in holding this position.

In early Buddhism, there was no mention of any definite time period needed for a person to become liberated as everything depended on individual effort. Liberation could even be achieved during this lifetime by following the correct path and striving with zeal. But the necessary period of time was prolonged when the idea of Buddhahood was elevated to an almost unattainable position. This development was due to both faith and reasoning based on the sayings and passages found in the early *sūtras*. As discussed in Chapter 1 above, in early Buddhism the birth of Gautama Buddha on earth was already seen as an extraordinary event marked with supernatural occurrences. Faith together with the bodhisattva practices described in the *Jātaka* provided the foundation for the future developments. Thus, the *Kośa* states that supreme *bodhi* is extremely difficult to attain and can be achieved only by great vows and long-term practice.[129] In the *Vibhāṣā*, the time needed to become a Buddha, from the initial resolution to enlightenment, is said to be three *mahāsaṃkhyeyakalpas* plus another one hundred *kalpas*. During this immeasurable period of time, the bodhisattva practises four *pāramitās* (not six) in order to acquire a great accumulation of knowledge and merit through innumerable heroic deeds.[130]

The *Vibhāṣā* states:

> Upon completion of the first *asaṃkhyeyakalpa*, the bodhisattva is not certain whether he is going to become a Buddha though he has practised various austerities. Upon completion of the second *asaṃkhyeyakalpa*, he is not brave enough to make the announcement 'I will become a Buddha' though he knows that he is certain to become a Buddha. Upon completion of the third *asaṃkhyeyakalpa* while practising for the wonderful marks (*lakṣaṇa*), he is certain to become a Buddha and he makes the lion's roar: 'I will become a Buddha.'[131]

The stipulation of three *asaṃkhyeyakalpas* is probably a creation of the Sarvāstivādins because in three places the *Vibhāṣā* states that all Buddhas practised four or six *pāramitās* for three *asaṃkhyeyakalpas* in order to attain supreme and perfect enlightenment (*Samyaksaṃbodhi*).[132] This position of the Sarvāstivāda is also confirmed by other texts such as the *Kośa*, the **Abhidharma-nyāyānusāra-śāstra* and the **Abhidharma(piṭaka)prakaraṇa-śāsana-śāstra*. For instance the *Kośa* states: 'A bodhisattva has to cultivate the provision of merit and wisdom, six *pāramitās* and numerous austerities for three *asaṃkhyeyakalpas* in order to attain the ultimate enlightenment (*bodhi*).'[133] The other two texts also make the same statement.[134] According to the MPPŚ, the Mahāyānists criticized them, saying:

> 'You said that during the first *asaṃkhyeyakalpa*, [the bodhisattva] did not know whether he would become a Buddha or not. . . . Where did the Buddha say this, in what *sūtra*? Is it in the *Tripiṭaka* of the

> *śrāvakas* or in the Mahāyāna *sūtras*? The disciples of Kātyāyanīpūtra said: 'Although the Buddha did not say it as recorded in the *Tripiṭaka*, yet logically it should be so. The chapter on the bodhisattva in the *Abhidharmavibhāṣā* says so.' Answer: the Mahāyāna *sūtras* state that the bodhisattva knows 'I will become a Buddha' in the first place when he makes a resolution.[135]

In the same treatise, the Mahāyānists criticized the Sarvāstivādins: 'The Buddha said that [he] had accumulated merit in numerous *asaṃkhyeyakalpas* in order to save sentient beings. Why do you say three *asaṃkhyeyakalpas*?'[136] Thus, the Sarvāstivāda clearly held to three *asaṃkhyeyakalpas* as the duration of Bodhisattva practice for Buddhahood but some early Mahāyānists did not agree with this theory.

How long are three *asaṃkhyeyakalpas*? In a long discussion of this in the *Vibhāṣā* nine different opinions are recorded but there is no general agreement. According to both the *Kośa* and the **Abhidharmanyāyānusāraśāstra*, three *asaṃkhyeyakalpas* are in fact infinite.[137]

According to both the *Vibhāṣā* and the *Mahāvastu*, as a bodhisattva the present Śākyamuni Buddha vowed in front of the ancient Śākyamuni Buddha that he also would become a Buddha in exactly the same way as the ancient Śākyamuni Buddha had. He would achieve this when the human life-span was around a hundred years and when people suffered from birth, old age, illness and death in the world of the five defilements (*āyuḥkaṣāya, kalpakaṣāya, kleśakaṣāya, dṛṣṭikaṣāya* and *sattvakaṣāya*).[138] In the course of the first *asaṃkhyeyakalpa*, he met seventy-five thousand Buddhas; the first was the ancient Śākyamuni and the last was Ratnaśikhin. In the second *asaṃkhyeyakalpa*, he met seventy-six thousand Buddhas; Ratnaśikhin was the first and the last was Dīpaṁkara. In the third *asaṃkhyeyakalpa*, he met seventy-seven thousand Buddhas; Dīpaṁkara was the first and Vipaśyin was the last. Then in the extra one hundred *kalpas*, which constituted the final period, the present Śākyamuni worked extremely hard so that he completed the merit required in ninety-one *kalpas* only. During this period, he met six Buddhas; the first was Vipaśyin and the last was Kāśyapa.

The last six Buddhas are mentioned in the *Dīghanikāya* and Dīpaṁkara is also mentioned in the biographical *sūtras* of the Buddha, but the ancient Śākyamuni and Ratnaśikhin Buddhas are not mentioned anywhere in the early *sūtras*. However, the **Abhiniṣkramaṇasūtra* mentions both Dīpaṁkara and the ancient Śākyamuni among many other Buddhas to whom Gautama made offerings. But this *sūtra* mentions fifteen Buddhas before Gautama Buddha. They are Dīpaṁkara, Incomparable in the World, Superior Lotus, Superior Conduct, Superior Virtue, Śākyamuni, Tissa, Pussa (?), Seeing-all-Benefit and then the last six Buddhas. Thus another nine Buddhas are added to the list of the six last Buddhas, though many other Buddhas are mentioned. There is no specific order. The number of Buddhas became more systematized in the *Vibhāṣā*, where the theory of requiring three *mahāsaṃkhyeyakalpas* to become a Buddha is found.

With the gradual extension of the period required to reach Buddhahood, the merit of the Buddha also increased. In early Buddhism, the merit of the Buddha was considered to be manifested as the thirty-two major marks of the great man, which were thought to be the result of the practice of the *pāramitās* in many lives, as described in the *Jātaka* and the *Avadāna*. But according to the *Vibhāṣā*, the Sarvāstivādins asserted that it was only during the extra one hundred *kalpas* that the Buddha practised diligently and acquired the thirty-two major marks, for each of which he completed one hundred merits.[139] The greater merit of the Buddha was the merit of the *dharmakāya*, which consisted of the eighteen exclusive *dharmas* and was the result of practising the *pāramitās* for three *mahāsaṃkhyeyakalpas*. The merit of the *dharmakāya*, according to the Sarvāstivādins, is greater than the merit of the *rūpakāya*, since the latter is impure.

During these three *mahāsaṃkhyeyakalpas*, according to the *Vibhāṣā*, the bodhisattva practises four *pāramitās* instead of six: generosity (*dāna*), discipline (*śīla*), energy (*vīrya*) and wisdom (*prajñā*).[140] The *Vibhāṣā* explains:

> Foreign teachers hold that there are six *pāramitās*, adding patience (*kṣānti*) and meditation (*dhyāna*). But the teachers of Kaśmīra say that the last two are included in the first four. Patience is included in discipline and meditation in intuitive knowledge; they are accomplished upon completion of discipline and wisdom.[141]

Universal virtues common to all Buddhas and differences between them

According to the Sarvāstivādins all Buddhas are equal in three respects:[142]

1 All Buddhas are equal in their cultivation. They have completed the practice of the six *pāramitās* in three infinite *asaṃkhyeyakalpas* and have attained supreme and perfect enlightenment (*Samyaksaṃbodhi*).
2 All Buddhas are equal in the *dharmakāya* in that they have immeasurable merit (*puṇya*) of the eighteen exclusive *dharmas* which are in turn the ten powers (*bala*), the four kinds of intrepidity (*vaiśāradya*), the great compassion (*mahākaruṇā*), and the three foundations of mindfulness (*smṛti-upasthāna*).
3 All Buddhas are equal in their service to beings in that they save hundreds and thousands of *nayutas* of sentient beings and assist them to attain *parinirvāṇa* when they appear in the world.

Apart from these, the *Vibhāṣā* mentions three more aspects in which Buddhas are equal.

4 All Buddhas are equal in intelligence (literally: faculty) in that they abide in its superior grade.
5 All Buddhas are equal in morality in that they have achieved the highest morality.
6 All Buddhas are equal in attainment in that they have attained supreme enlightenment (*Samyaksaṃbodhi*) through the fourth *dhyāna*.

These last three aspects, in fact, can be included in the first of the above three since they are obtained through cultivation. This is why later works such as the *Kośa* do not take the last three aspects into account when they explain the universal virtues of the Buddhas.[143]

The Sarvāstivādins also stated that Buddhas are different: (1) in duration of life; (2) in caste; (3) in *gotra*; (4) in stature; (5) in the duration of their Dharma. Depending on the period during which they appear, their lives are either long or short, they are Kṣatriyas or Brahmins, they belong to the Gautamagotra or Kāśyapagotra, and their bodies are great or small. Whether their Dharma lasts a long or short period of time depends on the conditions of the beings to be converted at the moment of their appearance in that particular world. Since the conditions of the beings to be converted are different, so is the duration of their Dharma.

Taking refuge in the Buddha

The Sarvāstivādins took refuge in the *dharmakāya* of the Buddha and not in the *rūpakāya* because they considered the latter impure, as discussed above. It is stated in the *Vibhāṣā*:

> Some people say that to take refuge in the Buddha is to take refuge in the body of the Tathāgata, which comprises head, neck, stomach, back, hands and feet. It is explained that the body, born of father and mother, is composed of the defiled *dharmas*, and therefore is not a source of refuge. The refuge is the Buddha's fully accomplished qualities (*aśaikṣadharmāḥ*) which comprise *bodhi* and the *dharmakāya*.[144]

The *Kośa* further explains that the Buddha's fully accomplished qualities (*aśaikṣadharmāḥ*) are the knowledge that all the *kleśas* and their related aspects have been destroyed (*kṣaya-jñāna*).[145] But other schools, perhaps precisely the Mahāsāṃghikas, asked:

> If the fully accomplished qualities which comprise *bodhi* constitute the real Buddha, then how do you explain what is said in the *sūtras*? For instance: 'Elders, what is called the Buddha? There is a son from the Śākya clan who left the household with good faith after

> shaving his head and beard, clad in robes, he who is all-knowing (*sarvajña*) is called the Buddha.' Answer: since the Dharma manifestation depends on the physical body, it is not in contradiction with reasoning.[146]

The emphasis of the Sarvāstivāda is on the attainment of Buddhahood, the *dharmakāya*, while the physical body is considered secondary. The *dharmakāya* of all Buddhas is the same. Therefore, according to the Sarvāstivāda, taking refuge in the Buddha is to take refuge in all Buddhas because the term 'Buddha' includes all the Tathāgatas since they are of the same kind.[147] Thus another question arises: since the *dharmakāya* or the Dharma is so important to the Sarvāstivādins, why do they first take refuge in the Buddha and not the Dharma? The Sarvāstivādins explained that the Buddha was the founder. If the founder had not taught, then the Dharma would not have been manifested. Thus the Buddha is seen as the first refuge, just as a patient first seeks a good doctor before asking him for medicine. The patient then seeks a nurse to prepare the medicine. The Buddha is like the doctor, the Dharma like the medicine, and the Saṃgha is the nurse. Such is the order of the three refuges.[148]

The differences between Buddhas, *pratyekabuddhas* and *śrāvakas*

The Sarvāstivādins distinguished Buddhas from *pratyekabuddhas* and *śrāvakas* in seven ways in accordance with the *Vibhāṣā*.

First, with regard to their aspects, there are twenty-one propositions concerning the differences between Buddhas, *pratyekabuddhas* and *śrāvakas*, but these can be summarized as follows.[149] The enlightenment of the Buddhas is thorough and faultless in that they have eliminated all habitual forces, doubt and defiled and undefiled ignorance, and they understand thoroughly the mechanism of dependent origination, but *pratyekabuddhas* and *śrāvakas* do not. The Buddhas have finally achieved both the physical body of a *mahāpuruṣa* and supreme enlightenment, and they have achieved fulfilment of colour, race, eloquence, vows, fruits and analytical inquiry, but *pratyekabuddhas* and *śrāvakas* have not. The Buddhas also possess the eighteen exclusive *dharmas*, a result of the accumulation of merit in three *mahāsaṃkhyeyakalpas*. They know the threefold suffering, they work for the sake of living beings of the three *dhātus*, and regard relatives as well as enemies with total impartiality, while *pratyekabuddhas* and *śrāvakas* do not. The Buddhas are not defiled by the eight worldly *dharmas*, and they can fully liberate beings from difficulties; their merit is incomparable because they have the four kinds of knowledge – knowledge that is unhindered, faultless, unattached and non-retrogressive – while *pratyekabuddhas* and *śrāvakas* again do not.

Second, with regard to the three kinds of retrogression, they consist of (a) that which is acquired; (b) that which has not yet been acquired; and (c) the enjoyment of the merit. Buddhas have only the retrogression of enjoyment because at times Buddhas are known to suspend their enjoyment of the bliss of merit acquired.[150] Buddhas do not have the other two forms of retrogression because they abide in superior faculties and are not retrogressive. *Pratyekabuddhas* have (b) and (c) types of retrogression as they have not attained the superior faculties of the Buddha and sometimes suspend their enjoyment of the bliss of merit. They do not, however, possess the first retrogression because they are also not retrogressive. *Śrāvakas* are divided into two groups: (1) those who are liberated independently of circumstances (*asamaya-vimukta*); (2) those whose liberation is occasional and circumstantial (*samaya-vimukta*). The first type of *śrāvaka* is equal to *pratyekabuddhas*. The second type of *śrāvaka* has all the three kinds of retrogression as indeed they have not attained the non-retrogressive faculties of the three vehicles (*triyāna*) and sometimes they suspend the enjoyment of the bliss of their merit.

Third, with regard to the knowledge that the cankers have been destroyed (*āśravakṣayajñāna*), Buddhas have four kinds of special merit, namely absence of hindrances, knowledge, power and guiding by example, while *pratyekabuddhas* and *aśaikṣa śrāvakas* have only three, as they lack the merit of power.[151] Regarding the knowledge of their own past lives and of other people's past lives, Buddhas have three kinds of special merit: knowledge, power and the absence of hindrances. *Pratyekabuddhas* and *dhyāna śrāvakas* have two merits, knowledge and the absence of hindrances, and *śaikṣa śrāvakas* only have the absence of hindrances.

Fourth, with regard to the *kleśas*, Buddhas have completely eradicated them without any trace or residual effect because the wisdom of Buddhas is sharp and powerful, like the fire at the end of the *kalpa*, burning all things without trace. In the case of *pratyekabuddhas* and *śrāvakas*, although they have eliminated *kleśas* the residual effect is still there because their wisdom is not as sharp as that of Buddhas; this is likened to a worldly fire, burning everything but leaving behind ashes.[152]

Fifth, with regard to knowledge of the minds of all other beings (*paracittajñāna*), Buddhas are able to know the mind of fifteen *kṣaṇas*, *pratyekabuddhas* are able to know three *kṣaṇas*, and *śrāvakas* are able to know two *kṣaṇas* only.[153] It is so because Buddhas are able to exert *paracittajñāna* without any earnest endeavour (*prayoga*) while *pratyekabuddhas* require slight endeavour, and *śrāvakas* need to make an intermediate or strenuous effort.

Sixth, with regard to the four unhindered powers of interpretation (*pratisaṃvid*), Buddhas obtain them when they have attained the knowledge of the cankers being destroyed whereas *pratyekabuddhas* and *śrāvakas* obtain them by earnest endeavour (*prayoga*).[154] The question then arises: if *pratyekabuddhas* also have this power, why do they not preach? The Sarvāstivādins argued that *pratyekabuddhas* not only delight in quietude and cherish solitude but also abhor noise and dislike crowds. Besides, *pratyekabuddhas* focus their minds on *nirvāṇa* when they proceed to preach the Dharma, but once they do so they enter into the peaceful and happy state of *mokṣa* in the second *kṣaṇa* that renders them unable to preach. Buddhas are different because though they delight in happy *mokṣa*, on account of their great compassion (*mahākaruṇā*) and great equanimity (*mahā-upekṣā*) they preach the Dharma.

Seventh, with regard to temperature (*uṣma*), summit (*mūrdhan*) and patience (*kṣānti*), the temperature of Buddhas does not change while that of both *śrāvakas* and *pratyekabuddhas* can change.[155] The same applies to the summit. The patience of *śrāvakas* can change into that of *pratyekabuddhas* but the patience of neither *śrāvakas* nor *pratyekabuddhas* can change into that of Buddhas because patience is not compatible with bad realms. Nor can the patience of *pratyekabuddhas* change into that of *śrāvakas* because patience does not retrogress.

In conclusion, the Sarvāstivādins were rational and developed their concept of the Buddha more on the basis of reason than on faith, because their attitude towards the teachings of the Buddha is that not every word of the Tathāgata is the preaching of the Dharma.[156] Therefore, they were careful in dealing with the *sūtras* and formulated their concept of the Buddha on the basis of the human identity as revealed in early Buddhism, summarizing and synthesizing the teachings concerning the Buddha. They considered the Buddha as a human being and thus *bodhi* made Gautama a Buddha. The Sarvāstivādins explicitly portrayed two aspects of the Buddha: the physical attributes and the spiritual attainments. On the basis of these two aspects they formulated the two-body theory for the first time to explain their concept of the Buddha. The *rūpakāya* is impure though physically perfect while the *dharmakāya* is the embodiment of the Buddha's mental attainments. With regard to the concept of the *rūpakāya*, they formulated the four categories of the Buddha's attributes by adding the eighty minor marks, the golden complexion and the one-fathom halo to the thirty-two major marks. The Sarvāstivāda school was perhaps the first to explain the *dharmakāya* through the eighteen special qualities of the Buddha.

3

THE CONCEPT OF THE BUDDHA IN THE EARLY INDIAN BUDDHIST SCHOOLS

(II) The Mahāsāṃghika and other schools

The Mahāsāṃghikas

The Mahāsāṃghikas' religious philosophy was based more on faith than on reason, and accepted whatever was said by the Buddha or, more precisely, whatever was taught in the *Nikāyas* and the *Āgamas*.[1] As a result, they developed the concept of a transcendental (*lokottara*) Buddha based on the superhuman qualities of the Buddha, as discussed in Chapter 1 above. Two aspects of the Mahāsāṃghikas' concept of the Buddha can be identified: the true Buddha who is omniscient and omnipotent, and the manifested forms through which he liberates sentient beings with skilful means. Śākyamuni was considered but one of these forms. The true Buddha supports the manifested forms that can appear in the worlds of the ten directions. In Mahāyāna Buddhism, the former aspect – the true Buddha – was developed and divided into the concept of the *dharmakāya* and the concept of the *saṃbhogakāya*; the latter aspect – the manifested forms – was developed into the concept of *nirmāṇakāya*. Thus, the Mahāsāṃghikas are the originators of the idea of the *nirmāṇakāya*, and the manifested forms can have many embodiments. Furthermore, they also introduced the theory of numerous Buddhas existing in other worlds.

The origin of Mahāsāṃghika Buddhology

In the case of the Mahāsāṃghikas, unlike the Sarvāstivādins, not much literature survives with which to make a comprehensive study of their concept of the Buddha. There are only three texts available, namely the *Mahāvastu*, the **Lokānuvartanasūtra* and Vasumitra's treatise on the doctrines of early Indian Buddhist schools. Scholars have already confirmed the first two works as belonging to the Mahāsāṃghika or its sub-sect, the Lokottaravāda.[2] As presented in these three works, the concept of the Buddha of the Mahāsāṃghikas is of particular significance. The Buddha is so thoroughly idealized that the historical Buddha is looked upon only as a manifestation; it is the omnipotent and omniscient aspects of the Buddha that are meaningful to them.

In all probability, the transcendental concept of the Buddha of the Mahāsāṃghikas originated from the development of the Buddha's superhuman identity, as discussed in Chapter 1 above. As the Mahāsāṃghikas were faithful followers, they believed in every word of the Buddha and interpreted the passages associated with miracles in the early *sūtras* in an idealistic way. A good example in the *Vibhāṣā* clearly shows how the Mahāsāṃghikas interpreted such passages in the early *sūtras*. In both the **Saṃyuktāgama* and the *Aṅguttaranikāya*, there is a passage that asserts that although the Tathāgata was born in the world and abided in the world, he was not defiled by the worldly *dharmas*.[3] The Mahāsāṃghikas understood and interpreted this passage idealistically, claiming it to mean that the Buddha is pure, without any *āsrava dharmas*, and that this includes his *rūpakāya*, the physical body.[4] The Sarvāstivādins interpreted this passage differently. According to them, the phrase 'the Tathāgata was born in the world and abided in the world' meant that the *rūpakāya* appearing in the world was impure, while 'he was not defiled by the world' referred to the pure *dharmakāya*.[5] Reading this passage in context, we can understand that the Buddha proclaimed this because he had eradicated *āsravas*, the causes for rebirth in this world.[6] Hence, the purity of the Tathāgata carried an ethical not physical, sense. This same passage is repeated three times in the *Vibhāṣā*, and is linked with the Mahāsāṃghika argument, constituting a typical example of the Mahāsāṃghika exegesis of the early *sūtras*.[7] Many pieces of evidence can be found in the early *sūtras* to support the assertion that the Mahāsāṃghikas interpreted the canonical passages in an idealistic way.

The main evidence for the origin of Mahāsāṃghika Buddhology is the *Acchariyābbhūtasutta* of the *Majjhimanikāya* which is also found in the Chinese **Madhyamāgama* with a similar title, but with more descriptions of miracles. The Pāli *sutta* provides a description of twenty miracles that occurred between the Bodhisattva's descent from Tuṣita heaven and the time of his birth on earth, whereas its Chinese counterpart cites twenty-three miracles, only ten of which occurred after the Buddha's birth.[8] The terms used to describe the Buddha in these two versions are also different. The Pāli *sutta* uses the term Bodhisattva, implying that he was not yet enlightened, while the Chinese version uses the term 'World Honoured One' (Bhagavat), probably indicating that his appearance on earth was only a manifestation. The descriptions of the birth of the Buddha are congruent in the two versions although the *sūtra* was transmitted in two different traditions, the Theravāda and the Mahāyāna. This fact in itself suggests the antiquity of such depictions.

The story of the Buddha's birth in the above *sūtra* is as follows. The Buddha descended into his mother's womb from Tuṣita heaven and resided there for exactly ten months without being sullied or smeared by impurities. Immediately after his birth he took seven steps and declared that he was the foremost in the world and that this was his last birth. An immeasurably bright light illuminated the world, reaching the darkest places where the sun and moon cannot penetrate. The ten thousandfold world system shook, quaked and trembled. These last two natural phenomena occurred twice, at the time of the Buddha's descent from Tuṣita heaven and at the time of his birth. The Buddha is described as fully aware and mindful of what was taking place throughout. This story clearly shows that the Buddha was considered a transcendental being.

The first half of the *Nālakasutta* of the *Suttanipāta* is perhaps a forerunner of this story and serves as a basis for the ideas developed in the *Acchariyābbhūtasutta*, for most scholars think that the *Suttanipāta* contains some of the earliest *suttas*.[9] The *Nālakasutta* begins by stating that at the birth of the Buddha, the gods were delighted and danced happily in heaven.[10] Upon perceiving this, the seer Asita inquired about the reason for their happiness, and the gods replied that an incomparable being, the best among all, had been born in the country of the Śākyas in Lumbini garden. He would cause the wheel of the Dhamma to turn for the benefit and happiness of beings. This simple description contains the fundamental ideas found in the *Acchariyābbhūtasutta*: the birth of the Buddha on earth was a wondrous event with the definite purpose of liberating sentient beings. The *Acchariyābbhūtasutta* represents an advanced form of depiction of the Buddha's birth with detailed descriptions of it as a wondrous event. This depiction is further applied to all the other six past Buddhas in the *Mahāpadānasutta* of the *Dīghanikāya*, for all the miracles about Gautama's birth in the *Acchariyābbhūtasutta* are found in this *sutta* in exactly the same format and style. The story of the Buddha's descent into his mother's womb from Tuṣita heaven has become a formula in the *Mahāpadānasutta*. This *sutta* explains that it is in the nature of things (*dhammatā*) that all Buddhas in their last birth descend into the womb of their mother from Tuṣita heaven.[11] All the other miracles accompanying the birth of a Buddha are also said to be in the nature of things.

The *Nālakasutta* makes the important statement that the Buddha was born on earth for the definite purpose of liberating sentient beings. If we trace further the sources of the above statement, it can be found in both the Chinese translation of the **Saṃyuktāgama* and the Pāli *Aṅguttaranikāya*. In one passage, the Buddha preached thus:

> Monks, were not three states found existing in the world, the Tathāgata would not arise in the world, an arahant rightly enlightened; nor would the dhamma-discipline proclaimed by the Tathāgata be shown in the world. What are the three states? Birth, decay and death . . . But since these three states are found, therefore,

> the Tathāgata does arise in the world, an arahant rightly enlightened, and the dhamma-discipline proclaimed by the Tathāgata is shown in the world.[12]

This passage suggests that the advent of the Buddha in the world is not accidental, as is that of ordinary sentient beings driven by *karma*, but has a clear aim, to benefit suffering beings. This is significant because the assertion is put in the mouth of the Buddha himself, whereas in the *Nālakasutta* and the *Acchariyābbhūtasutta*, the statement is said to have been made by the gods and Ānanda respectively. The *Nālakasutta* may have drawn its ideas on the birth of the Buddha from this passage in the *Aṅguttaranikāya* or the **Saṃyuktāgama*.

This analysis of the Buddha's birth suggests that it developed in at least four stages. The passage quoted above from the *Saṃyuktāgama* and the *Aṅguttaranikāya* does not suggest anything mysterious about the rise of the Tathāgata in the world, but it does provide a source of ideas for later development. This is the first stage of the depiction of the Buddha's birth. The *Nālakasutta* represents perhaps the second stage: the birth of the Buddha is already considered a wonderful event. This depiction is further developed in the *Acchariyābbhūtasutta* which contains the entire episode of Gautama's birth, replete with all the miracles. This I would suggest is the third stage. At the fourth stage, in the *Mahāpadānasutta*, the story of the Buddha's birth finally becomes a theory, subsequently applied to all Buddhas. All Buddhist traditions transmitted this theory in their literature, and up to the present time both the Mahāyāna and the Theravāda traditions concur on it. Thus, these developments of the theory concerning the Buddha's birth must have taken place before Buddhism split into different schools. It is thus evident that in early Buddhism, the faithful had already idealized the Buddha and considered the birth of the Buddha on earth not as an ordinary event, but as an atypical event (*adbhuta*). The purpose of his birth is clear, that is to become enlightened 'for the benefit and happiness of all sentient beings'. However, before enlightenment, the aspirant was deemed a Bodhisattva.

From such ideas and theories found in early scriptures the Mahāsāṃghikas asserted that all Buddhas are supramundane (*lokottara*).[13] The *Acchariyābbhūtasutta* provides some vital statements that served as repositories for the idea of the transcendental Buddha of the Mahāsāṃghikas.

First, the Bodhisattva was fully aware and mindful of all events taking place at his birth. Second, the Bodhisattva was not sullied or smeared by impurities when he was born. Third, his mother could see him in her womb, as if she were seeing a gem in her hand. The **Lokānuvartanasūtra* states that the Bodhisattva was not born as a result of the sexual union of father and mother but his body was magically produced, like an illusion.[14] Fourth, the Bodhisattva's mother gave birth while standing. According to Vasumitra, the Mahāsāṃghikas asserted that all bodhisattvas are born from the right side when they come out of their mother's womb. Fifth, the Bodhisattva took seven steps and spoke immediately after his birth. The **Lokānuvartanasūtra* explicitly states that it is in conformity with the ways of the world that the Buddha made such a show when he was born and uttered the words: 'No one in the whole world surpasses me! I shall deliver men of the ten directions!'[15] This suggests that adherents believed that these events could not happen to an ordinary man, but only to a person who was enlightened and made the display for a purpose. It is more than probable that the compilers of both the *Mahāvastu* and the **Lokānuvartanasūtra* were drawing on these ideas when they explained that every act of the Buddha on earth was like a display made for the welfare and happiness of men.[16] The Buddha followed the ways of the world just as much as he followed the transcendental ways. He made a show of standing, walking, sitting and lying down, but he was never tired. He washed his feet and body, though they were not dirty; he cleansed his mouth, though it smelled like a lotus. He ate though he was not hungry, and so forth. These things, the compilers explain, are all due to his being an embodiment of the effects of good actions. Thus, on the foundations laid in early Buddhism, it was the Mahāsāṃghikas who thoroughly idealized the Buddha and asserted that he had become enlightened aeons ago.

In addition to the major evidence above, another six passages can be cited which support this theory of the Mahāsāṃghikas' Buddhology. First, the **Lokānuvartanasūtra* states that 'even if the thunderbolts of the ten directions are combined together to make one sound, it cannot shake one hair of the Buddha because he makes a show of entering into the *samādhi* of no sound.'[17] Similarly, in the *Mahāparinirvāṇasūtra*, the Buddha told the visitor Pukkusa that once, while he was in meditation, rain began to beat down, lightning flashed, and thunderbolts roared; two peasant brothers and four oxen were killed; but he did not hear a sound.[18] There are some striking similarities in the two descriptions: first, the Buddha being in *samādhi*, second, the thunderbolts, and third, the Buddha hearing nothing whatsoever. It seems obvious that the description in the **Lokānuvartanasūtra* is based on the passage in the *Mahāparinirvāṇasūtra*.

Second, the Mahāsāṃghikas asserted that the Buddha's life-span is limitless.[19] In fact, the Buddha's long life-span seems to have been considered by the early compilers of the *Nikāyas* and the *Āgamas*. All versions of the *Mahāparinirvāṇasūtra* state that the Buddha deliberately gave up the remainder of his life at the request of Māra, but if he so wished he could have lived for a *kalpa* or to the end of a *kalpa*.[20] Since a *kalpa* is an extremely long period of time, the Mahāsāṃghikas naturally held that the life-span of the Buddha is limitless.[21] This also supports the assertion that the transcendental conception of the Buddha took root in the minds of Buddhists at a very early date.

Third, according to Vasumitra, the Mahāsāṃghikas asserted that in all that has been expounded by the World Honoured One, there is nothing which is not in conformity with the truth (*ayathārtha*).[22] In the *Aṅguttara*, Bhikkhu Uttara said to Sakka, 'Even so, O King, whatsoever be well spoken, all that is the word of the Exalted One, Arahant, the fully Awakened One, wholly based thereon is both what we and others say.'[23] Thus according to this statement, whatever is well spoken is the words of the Buddha and whatever the Buddha said must have been well spoken. The early Buddhists already thought that all the statements of the Buddha were well spoken. The Mahāsāṃghikas naturally interpreted this passage as meaning that all the words of the Buddha represent the exposition of the Dharma. This was very important to their belief because it is on the basis of such statements in the early *sūtras* that they held every single word of the Buddha to be the truth. The Mahāsāṃghikas' attitude to the words of the Buddha was thus one of the main reasons for their concept of a transcendental Buddha.

Fourth, according to the **Lokānuvartanasūtra*, being like gold, the body of the Buddha could not get dirty, and being like a diamond, it was also supremely pure. His feet were like lotuses to which dust would not cleave, and the Buddha had the mark of a supremely keen sense of taste.[24] This is reminiscent of three of the thirty-two major marks of the Buddha described in the early *sūtras*: (1) the Buddha's body is the colour of gold; (2) his skin is so smooth that no dust cleaves to it; (3) the Buddha's sense of taste is supremely keen. The links between the description in the **Lokānuvartanasūtra* and three of the thirty-two major marks are clear: gold, purity and taste. Thus the various attributes of the Buddha described in the **Lokānuvartanasūtra* may have been developed along the lines of the thirty-two major marks.

Fifth, the **Lokānuvartanasūtra* states that the Buddha knew the *dharmas* of innumerable other Buddhas in other Buddha lands (*Buddhakṣetra*) of the ten directions.[25] According to the *Saṃyutta*, the Buddha knew much more than he taught his disciples; he compared the relationship between what he had actually taught and what he knew to that between the leaves held in his hand and the leaves in the forest.[26] The *Saṃyutta* already suggests that the knowledge of the Buddha is immeasurable. The Mahāsāṃghikas, on this basis, defined the Buddha as omniscient.

Sixth, according to Vasumitra, the Mahāsāṃghikas asserted that the power of the Tathāgata is likewise limitless.[27] This is perhaps a general statement based on the miracles of the Buddha described in the early *sūtras*, for example the miracles by which he converted the three Kāśyapa brothers immediately after his enlightenment, and also the bandit Aṅgulimālya.[28]

All these pieces of evidence suggest that the Mahāsāṃghikas were a group of followers with resolute faith. According to Vasumitra's treatise, the Mahāsāṃghikas asserted that every word spoken by the Buddha is the preaching of the Dharma. This seems to be a clear indication that they took every word in the *Nikāyas* and the *Āgamas* as true sayings of the Buddha himself. This belief led them to develop a transcendental concept of the Buddha on the basis of the superhuman qualities attributed to him in the early *sūtras*.

The pure rūpakāya

Contrary to the Sarvāstivādins, the Mahāsāṃghikas believed the *rūpakāya* of the Buddha was pure. As faithful followers of the Buddha who believed in his every word, they interpreted the relevant passages in the *sūtras* in an idealistic way. The reasons for their belief are found in two texts.

First, it is stated in the *Vibhāṣā*:

> The Vibhajyavādins and the Mahāsāṃghikas regard the *rūpakāya* of the Buddha as pure. Why do they say so? It is because the *sūtras* say: 'The Tathāgata was born in the world and abided in the world, yet was not defiled by the worldly *dharmas*.' They again state that the Buddha had eliminated all the *kleśas* and habitual force (*vāsanā*), and thus the *rūpakāya* was pure.[29]

Second, in his **Abhidharmanyāyānusāraśāstra*, Saṅghabhadra states:

> The Mahāsāṃghikas again said thus: all the *dharmas* in the body of the Tathātaga are pure and thus it is a place for refuge because the *sūtras* say that the body [of the Buddha] is trained or cultivated (*bhāvanā*). The *sūtras* say: 'the body and the mind are trained or cultivated (*bhāvanā*).' If the mind [of the Buddha] is pure after training or cultivation, so is his body.[30]

Three reasons are put forward by the Mahāsāṃghikas for their belief in the pure *rūpakāya* according to these two texts: (1) though the Tathāgata was born and lived in the world, he was not defiled by the world because he was transcendental and his body was only a manifestation; (2) since the Buddha had eliminated all the *kleśas* and habitual force, he was pure both mentally and physically; (3) the Buddha had cultivated both his mind and his body, and so if the mind was pure, logically his physical body would also be pure. The Mahāsāṃghikas thus apparently gave a literal or idealistic interpretation to the two passages in the *sūtras* upon which they established their concept of the *rūpakāya*. This followed from their belief that every word that the Tathāgata preached was the truth, as stated in Vasumitra's treatise.[31] This led them to conclude that the *rūpakāya* of the Buddha should be regarded as pure and transcendental; concomitantly, their emphasis shifted from the historical Buddha to a transcendental one. As this is entirely in contradiction with the Sarvāstivāda concept of the impure *rūpakāya* of the

Buddha, the two schools debated this point. This is discussed in Chapter 5 below.

As described in the three works available, the Mahāsāṃghikas attributed the following qualities to the *rūpakāya* of the Buddha. First, according to Vasumitra, they asserted that the *rūpakāya* of the Buddha is limitless.[32] This perhaps refers to the idea of the *nirmāṇakāya* that can manifest itself in numerous forms, because the Mahāsāṃghikas considered Śākyamuni as one of the bodies of transformation. They had thus already conceived the idea of the *nirmāṇakāya* although they did not use the term. This is borne out by the statement in the **Lokānuvartanasūtra* that the Buddha can appear in numerous forms in countless Buddha lands at the same time.[33]

Second, according to both the **Lokānuvartanasūtra* and the *Mahāvastu*, the body of the Buddha was like a diamond, hence he was not really subject to decay, old age, tiredness, illness, hunger, thirst or human waste, to name but a few. When it was recorded in the early *sūtras* that he was subject to these things, but they were only a display for the sake and good of worldly people in Mahāsāṃghika literature.[34]

Third, the physical strength of the Buddha was so great that he could shake the Buddha lands of the ten directions with one finger, and dry up the water in the sea by simply blowing on it.[35] The text does not say whether the physical strength of the Buddha declined after a certain age. Only the Sarvāstivādins asserted that it declined after he was fifty-five. But as the Mahāsāṃghika concept of the Buddha is transcendental, his strength must be deemed a permanent attribute that would not decline.

The **Lokānuvartanasūtra* also states that the Buddha had a special light that could illuminate the worlds of the ten directions, but he made a show of having a light of seven *chi* so as to be in conformity with the ways of the world.[36] As discussed in Chapter 2 above, the Sarvāstivādins attributed to the Buddha a one-fathom halo radiating from his body. The Mahāsāṃghikas appear to have agreed with the Sarvāstivādins that the Buddha was endowed with special attributes such as light. This, however, was still considered a display.

With regard to the physical body, the Mahāsāṃghikas postulated a Buddha who is over and above sentient beings and who comes into the world with the definite purpose of saving suffering people through manifestation. For them, the Buddha is omniscient and omnipotent, but not as yet omnipresent. These qualities constituted the most important aspect of the Mahāsāṃghikas' concept of the Buddha. On the other hand, Śākyamuni was considered a body of transformation, *nirmāṇakāya*. Although the term was not used by them its connotations and implications are clearly there. Here we see the emergence of the idea of the *nirmāṇakāya* which originated with the Mahāsāṃghikas. Thus the second aspect of their concept of the Buddha is that the Tathāgata makes a display in the world for the sake of sentient beings. However, nowhere in the three texts did the Mahāsāṃghikas use the terms *dharmakāya* and *rūpakāya* as a pair, nor did they formulate a theory of these two bodies, as the Sarvāstivādins did. On the contrary, they envisaged one Buddha body. This difference between the two schools was made clear in the MPPŚ where the concept of the Buddha, though based on the idea of the Mahāsāṃghikas, was actually developed on the basis of the two-body theory of the Sarvāstivāda school.

Aspects of the Buddha

According to the Mahāsāṃghikas, the Buddha is always in the state of *samādhi*. Therefore, (1) he experiences neither sleep nor dreams because sleep is caused by an ignorant or unsettled mind (*viprakṛta*) which is not in the state of *samādhi*, while dreams are caused by phenomena lodged in the mind;[37] (2) the Buddha can preach the Dharma without making any arrangement of words and sentences: his speech just flows of its own accord, and all the words of the Buddha preach the Dharma and contain nothing which is not in conformity with the truth;[38] (3) the Buddha can understand things with his mind in one *kṣaṇa* because the Buddha has trained his mind for numerous *kalpas*.[39]

The Mahāsāṃghikas asserted that many thousand myriad *koṭis* of *asaṃkhyeyakalpas* ago the Buddha accomplished the practice of *prajñāpāramitā*. In other words, the Buddha attained enlightenment not in this life and in this world, but aeons ago. His appearance in this world was out of compassion for suffering people. In order to save them, he made a display of being born as a man and followed the conventions of the world such as *karma*. In the ultimate sense, the Buddha is not affected by anything.[40]

According to the **Lokānuvartanasūtra*, the Buddha is omniscient in the sense that he knows the *dharmas* of all Buddhas of the ten directions as well as of the past, present and future. He understands the essence of the *dharmas* that is emptiness and the nature of the *dharmas* that is formless. He also knows that there is no being in the past, present or future.[41] But in one of the numerous created forms (*nirmāṇakāya*) he preaches numerous *dharmas* to the people in conformity with the ways of the world.

The Buddha is fundamentally empty (*śūnya*), but out of compassion for the world he made a display of wearing clothes, staying in one place, and appearing and disappearing according to the likes and dislikes of the world. In reality, there is no coming and going for the Buddha.[42] This conception of the Buddha marked a new development that had never been discussed in early Buddhism, but was influenced by the **Prajñāpāramitāsūtras*, in which the concept of *śūnyatā* is the central theme. This provides a cluc as to how the Mahāsāṃghikas reached the view that the *rūpakāya* of the Buddha was limitless, for they identify the Buddha with *śūnyatā*. Since *śūnyatā* is limitless in space and ageless in time, so is the *rūpakāya* of the Buddha.

The origin of the idea of contemporaneous Buddhas

The belief in the simultaneous existence of many Buddhas albeit in different Buddha lands (*buddhakṣetra*) was a subject of contention among the early Buddhist schools because it is said in the early *sūtras* that no two Buddhas arise concurrently in one world system.[43] It is most probably the Mahāsāṃghikas who first thought that other Buddhas also exist apart from Śākyamuni in the present era, since they believed that the Buddha could manifest himself in numerous forms and worlds in the ten directions.

Some Japanese scholars have already studied this question in an attempt to establish from which school the ideas about 'contemporaneous Buddhas' originated. Mochizuki Shinko and others assert that this idea is Mahāyānistic, and therefore would have come into being with Mahāyāna Buddhism.[44] But Kyoyu Nishio suggests that the idea of 'contemporaneous Buddhas' originated with the Mahāsāṃghikas.[45] In a study of the question of 'contemporaneous Buddhas' as expounded in both the **Saṃyuktāgama* of the Kāśyapiyas and the **Ekottarāgama* of the Mahāsāṃghikas, he argues that the concept of the Buddha in the **Ekottarāgama* is different from that found in early Buddhism, and that it leaves room for the idea of 'contemporaneous Buddhas' to develop. However, there are many strata of development in the **Ekottarāgama*, which even embraces Mahāyāna ideas, as we have already discussed in Chapter 2 above. This *Āgama* also mentions a Tathāgata named Qiguang (Special Light) who Nishio Kyoyu thinks is apocryphal and was inserted into the text accidentally. Hence, there is every possibility that even in the **Ekottarāgama*, the idea of 'contemporaneous Buddhas' may have been inserted by the Mahāyānists. After a comparative study of the relevant *sūtras* in the Chinese *Āgamas* and the Pāli *Nikāyas*, Fujita Kotatsu maintains that there is no actual mention of 'contemporaneous Buddhas' in the early *sūtras*, only some remote implications.[46] All the above studies were made more than forty years ago, and with the advancement of Buddhist studies, new evidence has been brought to light that supports Kyoyu Nishio's suggestion.

The question of 'contemporaneous Buddhas' is a controversial one which was discussed in at least eight ancient texts, of which the MPPŚ is the earliest. It is stated: 'The Buddha did not say whether there are or are not other Buddhas present in the ten directions, in the *śrāvaka* Dharma.'[47] Here, the author of the MPPŚ uses the term '*śrāvaka* Dharma' in contrast with terms such as 'bodhisattva Dharma' and 'Mahāyāna Dharma', an indication of the early Buddhist teachings contained in the *sūtras* of the *Nikāyas* and the *Āgamas*.[48] So according to this statement, there is no mention of 'contemporaneous Buddhas' in the early *sūtras* or even in the surviving Pāli *Nikāyas*. However, 'contemporaneous Buddhas' are mentioned many times in the extant Chinese translations of the *Āgamas* such as the *Dīrgha*, the *Saṃyukta* and the *Ekottara*.[49] The only explanation for this inconsistency is that these were probably inserted into the *Āgamas* by the transmitters, following the teachings of the schools they belonged to. Scholars have already attempted to ascertain to which schools the *Āgamas* belong, but they are far from reaching a consensus. It is therefore difficult to decide in which school the idea of 'contemporaneous Buddhas' originated.[50]

The author of the MPPŚ argued for the existence of 'contemporaneous Buddhas' in two places.[51] In the summary of his arguments, he gave two main reasons. First, he quoted a verse from the **Dīrghāgama* in which Vaiśravaṇa praised the Buddha, saying: 'Homage to the Buddhas of the past, present and future, and I also take refuge in Buddha Śākyamuni as long as my life endures.'[52] The author argued that there must be many Buddhas at present since Vaiśravaṇa paid homage to the Buddhas of the present era. Second, although the *sūtras* state that there are no two Buddhas in one great *trisāhasra* universe, since there are many great *trisāhasra* universes, there could be many Buddhas at any given time. With regard to the first reason, Lamotte located the verse in the **Āṭānāṭikasūtra*.[53] This *sūtra* is not found in the Chinese translation of the **Dīrghāgama*, however, but an independent translation of it was made by Fatian in 960–1127.[54] This *sūtra* is also found in the Pāli *Dīghanikāya*, entitled the *Āṭānāṭiyasuttanta*, but it does not contain the verse recited by Vaiśravaṇa in praise of the Buddha. Lamotte thinks that the *sūtra* from which the author of the MPPŚ quoted the above verse belonged to the Sarvāstivāda school. He has given two reasons for his assertion.

1 The Sarvāstivāda had 'eighteen great *sūtras*' and according to the **Daśādhyāyavinaya* of this school, one of them is entitled *A zha na jian* (Lamotte: *A tch'a na kien*) meaning '*Sūtra* of Conciliation of the Spirits and Demons'.[55] Lamotte thinks that this refers to the **Āṭānāṭikasūtra*.
2 Four of the 'eighteen great *sūtras*' have been found in Chotscho in Central Asia and published by Waldschmidt. Therefore the *sūtra* from which the author of the MPPŚ quoted the verse must belong to the Sarvāstivāda.

This inference made by Lamotte may not be correct for, according to the MPPŚ, the Sarvāstivādins state: 'There are no [contemporaneous] Buddhas of the ten directions in our Dharma. There are one hundred past Buddhas such as Śākyamuni and Ju chen ruo [Krakucchanda?] and five hundred future Buddhas such as Maitreya.'[56] The well-known Sarvāstivāda texts such as the **Abhidharma-nyāyānusāra-śāstra* and the *Kośa* all confirm this position.[57] The *Kośa* states:

> Sāriputra said, 'I have heard from the World Honoured One with my own ears that there is neither place nor time, neither precedent nor afterwards, two Tathāgatas, fully enlightened, appear in the world. There is only one Tathāgata in one place at a time.'[58]

According to the *Kośa*, the Sarvāstivādins maintained that the Tathāgata could observe only the three great *trisāhasra* universes if he did not make earnest endeavour (*prayoga*). However, infinite universes could be in the sight of his Buddha eyes if he did make earnest endeavour (*prayoga*). The same was true of the other five kinds of direct knowledge (*abhiññā*).[59] Therefore, the Sarvāstivādins asserted that one Tathāgata is sufficient for all universes and there is no need for many contemporary Buddhas to save sentient beings. Thus, the Sarvāstivādins would not have had a *sūtra* containing the contradictory teaching that there are many 'contemporaneous Buddhas' because they maintained that there is only one Buddha, Śākyamuni, in the present era, even though he had already attained *parinirvāṇa*. No contemporaneous Buddhas therefore exist at present. The author of the MPPŚ therefore probably quoted the above verse ('Homage to the Buddhas . . .') from another version of the **Āṭānāṭikasūtra* transmitted by another school. Whoever inserted the verse into the *sūtra* probably did so to support their teaching about contemporaneous Buddhas. This is highly possible because, as discussed above, the Theravāda also has an *Āṭānāṭiyasuttanta* but it does not contain the verse that praises the Buddha. The school that had the version of the **Āṭānāṭikasūtra* containing the above verse was probably the Mahāsāṃghika, because according to their teaching, the Buddha can manifest himself in numerous bodies in numerous worlds at the same time.[60]

Giving the second justification for belief in 'contemporaneous Buddhas', the author of the MPPŚ made an inference on the basis of a passage found in the **Saṃyuktāgama*. He argued that there are conditions and causes for Buddhas to arise in the worlds in the ten directions because in the **Saṃyuktāgama* it is said that there are numerous worlds in the ten directions in which numerous sentient beings are suffering. The Buddha also said that the Tathāgata arises in the world where there is old age, sickness and death.[61] Therefore there must be other contemporaneous Buddhas in the worlds in the ten directions since there are suffering beings in them.[62]

The passage quoted by the author of the MPPŚ is found in both the Chinese translations of the **Saṃyuktāgama*. The first translation was made by Guṇabhadra, and the translator of the second is unknown. Guṇabhadra's translation runs thus:

> Just as the heavy rain that leaves no empty place in the east, in the west, in the south and in the north, in the same way, there are numerous worlds in the east, in the west, in the south and in the north. [Some of them are] in the *kalpa* of formation while [others are] in the *kalpa* of dissolution . . . Thus, the living beings who are subject to birth and death from beginningless time and abide in the *saṃsāra* as dark as a long night, know no origin of suffering.[63]

The second translation reads thus:

> When it rains heavily there is no empty space in the east, in the west, in the south, in the north and in the four corners. Living beings in the numerous worlds in the east live happily, while other numerous worlds with countless beings are in [the *kalpa* of] dissolution, still other numerous worlds are empty with no living beings in them. It is the same with regard to the south, the west, the north, the four corners, above and beneath, [where living beings] are in the cycles of birth and death from beginningless time.[64]

Comparing these two passages, Guṇabhadra's translation mentions the worlds of the *four* cardinal directions while the second translation mentions that of the *ten* directions. So the author of the MPPŚ probably quoted the passage from the Sanskrit version that is closer to the second translation or is actually the original from which it was made. However, there is no consensus among scholars regarding which school the **Saṃyuktāgama* belonged to. Guṇabhadra's translation is generally attributed to the Sarvāstivāda and the second translation to the Mūlasarvāstivāda.[65] So this suggests that the idea of the worlds of the ten directions may have originated from the Mūlasarvāstivāda, a sub-sect of the Sarvāstivāda school. This provides a basis for the idea of the existence of 'contemporaneous Buddhas' of the ten directions.

With the advance of Buddhist studies, we can perhaps be more confident in saying that the idea of 'contemporaneous Buddhas' originated in the Mahāsāṃghika school. This seems to be the case because scholars have come to a general agreement that the **Lokānuvartanasūtra* belongs to the Mahāsāṃghika school, and this *sūtra* mentions the Buddhas of the ten directions in several places. For instance, it states: 'The strength of the Buddha cannot be resisted and he can shake the Buddha lands of the ten directions with one finger.'[66] 'The Buddha knows all the *dharmas* of the countless Buddhas of the ten directions.'[67] 'The Buddha can manifest himself in numerous bodies (*nirmāṇakāya*) and appear in countless Buddha lands, but the body of the Buddha neither increases nor decreases.'[68] 'All Buddhas have one body, the body of the Dharma.'[69] Thus it is evident that the Mahāsāṃghikas already had the notion of the Buddhas in the worlds of the ten directions, and they probably regarded them as manifested bodies of the Buddha.

There are seven other works in which the idea of 'contemporaneous Buddhas' is discussed. They are the **Yogācārabhūmiśāstra*, *Mahāyānasaṃgraha* and its *bhāṣya*, *Kośa*, **Bodhisattvabhūmidharasūtra*, **Abhidharmanyāyānusār-aśāstra* of Saṅghabhadra and **Mahāyānāvatārakaśāstra* of Sthiramati.[70] All seven works argue for the existence of 'contemporaneous Buddhas' for two reasons. First, like the MPPŚ, they hold that there are other contemporaneous

Buddhas in the other great *trisāhasra* universes and that there are numerous worlds in the ten directions. Second, there should be many Buddhas because there are many bodhisattvas who practise for *bodhi*. Although the bodhisattva ideal is primarily emphasized in the Mahāyāna, the concept of 'many bodhisattvas' was already prevalent in Mahāsāṃghika literature. Vasumitra used plural forms in his treatise when he discussed the teaching of the school on the concept of bodhisattva.[71] So this may also suggest that the idea of 'contemporaneous Buddhas' originated with the Mahāsāṃghikas.

The idea of contemporaneous Buddhas in the worlds of the ten directions must predate the rise of Mahāyāna Buddhism because the *Daoxingboruojing*, the earliest Chinese translation of the **Aṣṭasāhasrikāprajñāpāramitāsūtra* (*Aṣṭa*), treats the idea as established. For instance, it is stated:

> Śāriputra, Māra cannot stop him [the bodhisattva] in the mid-way. Why? It is because the present Buddhas in innumerable Buddha lands in the ten directions protect *prajñāpāramitā*. Those who recite, preach, explain it and those who learn, listen to and write it, are also protected by the power of Buddhas.[72]
>
> All the present Tathāgatas, Arhats, Saṃyaksaṃbuddhas in innumerable Buddha lands in the ten directions have attained omniscience by practising the six *pāramitās*.[73]

The *Daoxingboruojing* was translated into Chinese in the second century CE and Conze thinks the basic *Prajñāpāramitā* probably dates back to 100 BCE.[74] Several scholars have suggested that the *Prajñāpāramitā* probably developed among the Mahāsāṃghikas in Southern India, in the Andhra country, on the Kṛṣṇā River.[75] This is because the Mahāsāṃghikas had two famous monasteries near Amarāvati and Dhānyakataka, which gave their names to the schools of the Pūrvaśailas and of the Aparaśailas. These schools each had a copy of the *Prajñāpāramitā* in Prakrit.[76] Moreover, the concept of the Buddha in the *Daoxingboruojing* is based on that of the Mahāsāṃghikas (this is discussed in Chapter 4 below). The Mahāsāṃghikas must, at least, have had a close association with the *Prajñāpāramitā*. All this evidence tends towards the conclusion that the idea of 'contemporaneous Buddhas' in the worlds of the ten directions originated in the Mahāsāṃghika school.

Other early Buddhist schools

The Theravāda

The Theravāda has basically a similar concept of the Buddha to that of the Sarvāstivāda. They are of the opinion that the *rūpakāya* of the Buddha is subject to all the physical frailties of a human being; it is the attainment of *bodhi* that makes a being a Buddha. Buddhas are above benevolence and compassion, but they show benevolence and compassion to living beings.[77] Buddhas possess the knowledge of all aspects of the *dharmas* and complete and detailed knowledge of all things. *Arhats* can, at most, have only partial knowledge.[78] There is no difference between a Buddha and an *arhat* in terms of liberation; Buddhas are only superior to *arhats* in that they are promulgators of the Dharma instead of merely being followers of it.[79] As T. Endo has already comprehensively studied the Theravāda concept of the Buddha, we will not deal with it here in detail.

The Mahīśāsaka

As a Hīnayāna school, the Mahīśāsaka is much more conservative.[80] They maintain not only that the Buddha is part of the Saṃgha, but also that making a separate gift to the Buddha is less meritorious than making one to the Saṃgha as a whole. The Buddha has one and the same path (*mārga*), and one and the same deliverance (*vimukti*) as in the *pratyekabuddhayāna* and *śrāvakayāna*.[81] So the Buddha is barely distinguishable from the *arhats*.

The Dharmaguptaka

The Dharmaguptakas differ from the Mahīśāsakas in that though the Buddha is part of the Saṃgha, making offerings to the Buddha earns greater merit than making them to the Saṃgha. The Buddha has the same emancipation (*vimukti*) as in the *pratyekabuddhayāna* and *śrāvakayāna*, but he is said to have followed a different path (*mārga*).[82]

The Sautrāntika

According to the *Kośa*, the Sautrāntikas are of the opinion that there may be many Buddhas simultaneously.[83] They also believe that ordinary people (*pṛthagjana*) may follow the noble path (*āryamārga*).[84]

The Vibhajyavāda

There is a controversy among scholars as to who really constituted the Vibhajyavāda school.[85] However, scattered evidence found in the *Vibhāṣā* suggests that they were Mahāsāṃghika-Vibhajyavādins because their views on the concept of Buddha were similar to those of the Mahāsāṃghikas. First, both groups believed that the *rūpakāya* of the Buddha is pure and without defilement (*kleśa*) because the *sūtras* say that the Tathāgata was born in the world and abided in the world, but was not defiled by the world.[86] But the Vibhajyavādins go further, stating that a pure mind can also cause birth or continuity such as that of the Buddha, as it is said in the *sūtras* that a bodhisattva in his final birth enters his mother's womb, then abides there and is born with right thought.[87] They assert that the Buddha was pure from the moment he entered his mother's womb. Second, like the Mahāsāṃghikas, they assert that the Buddha is always in *samādhi* because he abides in mindfulness and right view (*samyagdṛṣṭi*); hence the Buddha neither sleeps nor dreams because he has eliminated all hindrances (*nīvaraṇa*).[87]

The Vibhajyavādins also assert that all Buddhas attain one and the same full enlightenment (*saṃyaksaṃbodhi*) which is everlasting, and that they appear in the world at the same time. Although there may be different Buddhas, enlightenment (*bodhi*) is the same. Their argument is based on the *sūtra* that says: 'The Buddha told the *bhikṣus*, "I have attained the old path", so the divine path (*āryamārga*), which is the same to all Buddhas, is *asaṃskṛta*.'[88] Hence, they are also of the opinion that dependent origination (*pratītyasamutpāda*) is *asaṃskṛta* because the *sūtras* say that regardless of whether the Buddha appears in the world or not, the Dharma abides in the world as it is. The Buddha was enlightened by this Dharma and also expounded it to others.[89]

In conclusion, this writer is of the opinion that the teaching on the superhuman aspects of the Buddha developed in early Buddhism is one of the essential causes for the Mahāsāṃghikas' belief in a transcendental Buddha. This belief is founded on their attitude towards the words of the Buddha, which convinced them that all the words of the Tathāgata were the pronouncement of Dharma. As a result, they took everything that was said in the *Nikāyas* and the *Āgamas* as the true words of the Buddha. They arrived at the conclusion that the actual Buddha could not be an ordinary human but must be a transcendental being who is omnipotent and eternal. The historical Buddha was only a body of transformation that appeared in the world for the benefit and happiness of sentient beings. Such manifestations appear not only in this world but in other world systems as well. This is considered great skilful means of the Buddha. It follows therefore that other contemporaneous Buddhas should also exist in the worlds in the ten directions. Hence the Mahāsāṃghikas had already conceived of the idea of *nirmāṇakāya* at a very early stage, although they never used the term. This is shown in their extant literature. Thus, the Mahāsāṃghikas' concept of the Buddha has two distinct aspects: the true Buddha and its manifested forms. These significant developments laid the doctrinal basis for the Mahāyāna concept of the Buddha. In the next chapter, we discuss the concept of the *dharmakāya* in Mahāyāna, which was built upon the concept of the Buddha of the Mahāsāṃghikas.

4

THE ORIGIN AND DEVELOPMENT OF THE *DHARMAKĀYA*

The origin of the *dharmakāya*

The term *dharmakāya* is used in various places in the earliest strata of Buddhist literature, namely the Pāli *Nikāyas* and the Chinese *Āgamas*. The aim of this section is to collect and analyse some of the most significant passages of the *Nikāyas* and their corresponding passages in the Chinese *Āgamas*.[1] There are four relevant passages in which the idea of *dharmakāya* is cited as the teaching of the Buddha.

1

In the first passage under discussion, the idea of treating the Buddha's words as teacher after his death is clearly stated. In the Pāli *Mahāparinibbānasutta*, the Buddha says to Ānanda, 'The Dhamma and Vinaya that have been preached by me will be your teacher after my death.'[2] The fact that the monks took refuge in the Dhamma and Vinaya after the Buddha had passed away is also reflected in the *Gopaka-Moggallānasutta* of the *Majjhimanikāya*.[3] The 'Dhamma and Vinaya' clearly refer to the collection of doctrines and disciplinary rules taught and established by the Buddha. A similar passage is found in all four Chinese versions of the *Mahāparinirvāṇasūtra*, one included in the **Dīrghāgama* and three preserved as independent translations. The basic meaning of the passage is the same as that in the Pāli version although the terminology is different. We now examine the different versions in detail.

First, the relevant passage in the **Dīrghāgama* reads as follows:

> The Buddha said, 'Ānanda, you should not think that after the passing away of the Buddha there is no protection, no support. The Dharma and Vinaya preached by me ever since my enlightenment are your protection and support.'[4]

Second, the passage in the **Buddhaparinirvāṇasūtra* is similar to that above, the only difference being that the Buddha's address was made not to Ānanda alone, but to a group of monks. He said:

> After my *parinirvāṇa*, [you all] should not say that the Buddha is gone and there is no support. The Dharma and Vinaya are [your] support. After my *parinirvāṇa*, [you all] should learn [literally: appreciate] the Dharma and observe the Vinaya generation after generation. You should observe and transmit the two hundred and fifty rules with reverence just as one would revere one's parents.[5]

Third, the passage in the **Parinirvāṇasūtra* is similar to that above in which the Buddha addressed a group of monks:

> You, all disciples, should spur yourselves and not be slackened and lazy, [thinking] that the Buddha is gone and there is no refuge. [You all] should act in accordance with the Dharma, explain the Vinaya rules every fortnight, and recite the *sūtras* on the six observance days so that your minds are set on the Dharma just as in the days when the Buddha was alive.[6]

Fourth, in the **Mahāparinirvāṇasūtra*, translated by Faxian, the passage is very similar to the Pāli version. The Buddha said to Ānanda:

> The *prātimokṣa* rules laid down by me for all *bhikṣus* and the wonderful Dharma I preached in the past will be your great teacher [when I pass away], just as I am now.[7]

Although the first three translations do not state that the Dharma and Vinaya should be considered as 'teacher', similar ideas are implied about the teachings of the Buddha providing protection and support for the monks, who should look upon them with reverence. The idea in the fourth text is exactly the same as that in the Pāli version, which is to take the Dharma and Vinaya as teacher after the Buddha's death. Like the Pāli version, the **Gopaka Maudgalyāyanasūtra* of the Chinese **Madhyamāgama* also reflects the idea of taking refuge in the Dharma after the Buddha's death.[8] Thus the idea of considering the Buddha's preaching as teacher after his death as shown in the early literature in both Pāli and Chinese was common to all the early Buddhist schools. So here the Dharma is the same as the Buddha.

2

In the second passage, the Buddha compares himself to Brahmā. The Pāli passage reads as follows:

> Just as a *brāhmaṇa* would say that he is born of Brahmā, through his mouth, so a *Sakyaputtiyasamaṇa* may say that he is the son of

> the Bhagava, born of his mouth, born of the Dhamma, created by the Dhamma, an heir of the Dhamma (*dhammakāyāda*).[9]

A parallel is clearly being drawn between a *brāhmaṇa* and a *Sakyaputtiyasamaṇa*, and to indicate that *dhammakāya* is equated to *brahmakāya*.[10]

Buddhaghoṣa, commenting on the word *dhammakāya* in the passage in the *Dīghanikāya*, states:

> Why is the Tathāgata said to have a *dhammakāya*? Because the Tathāgata, having thought or devised in his mind the Buddha-word, which is the three *Piṭakas*, aspired to words. Therefore, that body is the Dhamma, because it is made of the Dhamma.[11]

So in the Theravādin understanding, the term *dhammakāya* simply means the teachings of the Buddha.

The same passage is found in the **Dīrghāgama*. It is stated in the text that the Mahābrahmā is another name for the Tathāgata who is the eye of the world, the lord of the world, and the Dharma is the wisdom of the world, the nectar of the world.[12] In the **Saṃyuktāgama*, similar ideas are found in two places. First, the Buddha said to the monks: 'All of you are my sons, born through my mouth, born of the Dharma, the sons of my Dharma.'[13] Second, we find the same passage spoken by Mahākāśyapa who compared himself to the son of the Wheel Turning Monarch (Cakravartin). The passage reads thus: 'Similarly, I am the son of the Buddhadharma, born through the mouth of the Buddha, born of the Dharma, an heir of the Dharma Treasure.'[14]

It is difficult to establish here what Sanskrit word was used for the phrase 'heir of the Dharma', but it is clear that the word Dharma is used in the same sense as in the Pāli *suttas*, to denote the doctrine. That the monks are the sons of the Dharma, born from the mouth of the Buddha, implies that they have gained new lives through the Dharma preached by the Buddha through his mouth. In other words, the Dharma is their mother as well as teacher.

3

The third passage is found in the *Aṅguttaranikāya* where the Buddha said that he is neither a god nor a *gandharva* nor a man, but a Buddha.[15] Some scholars speculate that this is the earliest trace of the Mahāyāna *kāya* concept, but an analysis of the passage shows that the Buddha made the statement because he had destroyed the cankers (*āsravas*) which are the reason why a living being continues to take rebirth in *saṃsāra*.[16] The idea in the corresponding passage in the Chinese **Ekottarāgama* is the same.[17] Thus, this passage does not support any doctrinal implication beyond the concept that the Buddha has completely destroyed the cankers.

4

In the fourth example, a well-known passage of utmost significance in our study, the Buddha declareds that he is the same as the Dharma, and it is only in the Dharma that he is to be seen, not in the physical body. In the Pāli passage, the Buddha makes the following statement to Vakkali: 'Alas, Vakkali! What is there in seeing this vile body of mine? He who sees the Dhamma (*dhammakāyo*), Vakkali, sees me; he who sees me sees the Dhamma (*dhammakāyo*).'[18] However, this statement is not found in the Chinese *Āgamas*, although the story of the sick Vakkali is found in two places, one in the **Saṃyuktāgama* and the other in the **Ekottarāgama*.[19] In this statement, the Buddha is clearly identified with the Dharma. But after careful analysis of the context in which this statement was made, it is clear that the Buddha was stressing the practice of the Dharma and its realization rather than focusing on his physical body. The Buddha said this because the sick Vakkali had made known to him that he had longed to see the Buddha in person for a long time, but due to lack of physical strength he could not do so. There does not appear to be any doctrinal or philosophical implication in the statement of seeing the Buddha in his Dharma. Commenting on this passage, Buddhaghoṣa described the body of the Tathāgata as the supramundane Dhamma in nine divisions.[20] It is clear that Dhamma in this context simply means the teaching of the Buddha, as the 'nine divisions' are the earliest classification of the Buddhadharma. So the Theravāda considered the *Tipiṭaka* as the *dharmakāya*. However, if one considers this statement alongside other similar declarations made by the Buddha elsewhere in the canonical literature, one may find traces from which both the Mahāsāṃghikas and the Mahāyānists could draw certain conclusions concerning the concept of the Buddha.

In many places in both the Pāli *Nikāyas* and the Chinese *Āgamas*, it is stated that the Dharma as dependent origination (*pratītyasamutpāda*) exists eternally whether or not a Buddha arises in the world.[21] And in the **Saṃyuktāgama*, it is further stated that the Buddhas are only the discoverers of this Dharma, dependent origination, but not the inventors.[22] In both the **Madhyamāgama* and the *Majjhimanikāya*, there is another well-known statement that he who sees dependent origination sees the Dharma and he who sees the Dharma sees dependent origination.[23] Thus, when we take all the above statements into consideration, it could be inferred logically that the Buddha is eternal because dependent origination exists eternally and the Buddha is equal to it. The Buddha here is not the flesh and blood historical person but a philosophical concept. That is perhaps why the compilers of the **Prajñāpāramitāsūtras* used the word Tathāgata instead of the word Buddha in their discussions of the relationship between the Tathāgata and *tathatā*, the actual nature of all things.

The authors/compilers of the **Prajñāpāramitāsūtras* probably made their claims for the Buddha's eternity on the basis of the statements discussed above. In the *Daoxingbanruojing*, the earliest **Prajñāpāramitāsūtra* in existence, *tathatā*, the real nature of all phenomena, is described in much the same way as dependent origination is described in the early scriptures. It exists eternally whether a Buddha arises in the world or not. The Tathāgata is identified with *tathatā* in the *Daoxingbanruojing* (to be discussed in detail in the following section). And since *tathatā* is eternal, so is the Tathāgata. Perhaps the ideas expressed in these passages are among the factors that led the followers of the Mahāyāna to speculate that the Dharma corresponds to the *dharmakāya*, which is the real Buddha and which exists eternally. This idea is also reflected in a legendary story concerning the Buddha's trip to Tuṣita heaven to preach the Dharma to his mother.

The *Yizujing*, a biographical *sūtra* on the Buddha, narrates that the *bhikṣuni* Utpalavarṇā was the first to greet the Buddha in person when the latter returned to the earth from Tuṣita heaven.[24] Meanwhile a *bhikṣu* thought that it was better to meditate than to see the Buddha and as a result he obtained the fruit of the first stage (*srotāpanna*) when he meditated on impermanence (*anitya*), suffering (*duḥkha*), emptiness (*śūnyatā*) and the theory of no soul (*anātman*). However, the text neither mentions the name of the *bhikṣu* nor states that he, rather than the *bhikṣuni*, was the first to see the Buddha. Commenting on this story, the MPPŚ states that it was Subhūti (it is probably the author of the MPPŚ who associated Subhūti with this story), not the *bhikṣuni*, who was the first to see the Buddha, because Subhūti meditated on the emptiness (*śūnyatā*) of all *dharmas* and he beheld the *dharmakāya*.[25] This story seems to be an echo of the statement 'seeing the Dharma is seeing the Buddha'. The important point in this story is that the emptiness (*śūnyatā*) of all *dharmas* is considered as the *dharmakāya*. Of course, the MPPŚ is a Mahāyāna text and it naturally contains Mahāyāna ideas.

In addition to the above quotations, the term *dharmakāya* occurs many times in the Chinese *Āgamas*, but corresponding passages are not found in the Pāli *Nikāyas*. First, the term *dharmakāya* is mentioned several times in the introductory chapter of the **Ekottarāgama*, something most probably apocryphal and added by the compilers. The text states: 'Venerable Ānanda thinks that the *dharmakāya* of the Tathāgata will not perish, but will remain for ever in the world, and gods and men will attain enlightenment upon hearing it.'[26] Again:

> Śākyamuni arose in the world with an extremely short life-span, but the *dharmakāya* will remain even though the body in flesh has perished. With the aim of ensuring that the Dharma will not be extinguished [from the world], Ānanda is requested to recite it without hesitation.[27]

A similar passage occurs in chapter forty-eight of the **Ekottarāgama*.[28] In all these places, the doctrinal significance of the term *dharmakāya* is explicit, denoting merely the teaching of the Buddha that will last for ever.

Second, the term *dharmakāya* is mentioned once in a *sūtra* of the **Saṃyuktāgama*, which corresponds to the independent **Aśokasūtra*. The text states:

> The body of the Tathāgata is the *dharmakāya* whose nature is pure . . . The lamp of the Dharma will remain for ever in the world eliminating the darkness of ignorance . . . It is only Ānanda who can remember all [the Buddha's teachings] without forgetting anything when he hears it once only.[29]

This *sūtra* is clearly very late in origin since it mentions King Aśoka. But the implications of the term *dharmakāya* still remain the same, the teachings of the Buddha.

Lastly, the **Ekottarāgama* also mentions three times 'the fivefold *dharmakāya*': discipline (*śīla*), concentration (*samādhi*), wisdom (*prajñā*), liberation (*vimukti*) and the vision of knowledge and liberation (*vimukti-jñāna-darśana*).[30] However, these are not exclusive to the Buddha but are shared by his great disciples such as Kāśyapa and Śāriputra. The fivefold *dharmakāya* schema is late in origin, as it is not mentioned in the Pāli canon. It is strongly arguable that the Chinese **Ekottarāgama* was revised by later compilers as some Mahāyāna elements are found in it, an issue already discussed in Chapter 2 above. The fivefold *dharmakāya* is only found in the post-canonical Pāli texts such as the *Milindapañha* and the *Visuddhimagga*.[31] In his *Visuddhimagga*, Buddhaghoṣa says:

> That Bhagavat, who is possessed of a beautiful *rūpakāya*, adorned with thirty major and eighty minor marks of a great man, and possessed of a *dhammakāya* purified in every way and glorified by *sīla*, *samādhi*, *paññā*, *vimutti* and *vimutti-ñāṇa-dassana*, is full of splendour and virtue, incomparable and fully awakened.[32]

In these passages the term *dharmakāya* simply means the purified body consisting of these five *skandhas* obtained through practice.

The above analysis of the passages found in both the Pāli *Nikāyas* and the Chinese *Āgamas* shows that the term *dharmakāya* was already present in the earliest Buddhist literature. It is evident from these passages that the term *dharmakāya* conveyed the doctrine or the collective teachings of the Buddha, and it possessed no philosophical significance beyond that. The Theravāda retained this concept of the *dhammakāya* at least until the time of Buddhaghoṣa. As discussed above, vague hints of an eternal Buddha may be present in these passages. However, it is only when all the relevant passages and statements are collated that inferences can be drawn and a conclusion reached. It must be remembered that each and every statement the Buddha made was directed at a particular person (such as the sick monk Vakkali) in the context of a particular situation. Therefore, these statements should be read not in isolation but within their own contexts. Hence, it is speculative to draw any conclusion beyond the common understanding that the term *dharmakāya* used in the early Buddhist literature represents the teachings of the Buddha. As discussed in Chapter 2 above, it was the Sarvāstivādins who first related the eighteen purified *dharmas* of the Buddha to the concept of the *dharmakāya*. However, these eighteen *dharmas*, which exist individually in the *Nikāyas* and the *Āgamas*, are the purified mental *dharmas*, the attainment of the Buddha. The Mahāsāṃghikas never used the term *dharmakāya* in any of their literature available to us, but perhaps the true Buddha as discussed in Chapter 3 above can be considered as the *dharmakāya*. However, this elaboration of Buddhology is nothing more than a transcendental, omnipotent and omniscient being. It is only the early Mahāyānists who attributed philosophical and ontological referents to the concept of the *dharmakāya* through the identification of the Tathāgata with *tathatā*, the real nature of all things. Subsequently this *tathatā* became identified with the term *dharmakāya*. Since the *tathatā* is in everything and pervades the universe, thus the *dharmakāya* becomes the cosmic body. In the following section, we concentrate on the Mahāyāna development of the concept of the *dharmakāya* as the contributions made by the early Indian Buddhist schools have already been dealt with.

The Mahāyāna development of the *dharmakāya* concept

The concept of the *dharmakāya* in Mahāyāna literature has greatly advanced from that of the early Buddhist schools. The Mahāyānists developed the concept of the *dharmakāya* through its identification with a number of key terms which they introduced such as *tathatā*, *tathāgatagarbha* and *buddhadhātu*. These new terms and ideas added new dimensions to the notion of *dharmakāya*. Thus the concept of the *dharmakāya* was fundamentally changed and transformed in several different ways in Mahāyāna *sūtra*s and treatises. It acquired both ontological and salvific meanings.

The identification of the Tathāgata with tathatā

The earliest Mahāyāna literature is perhaps the **Aṣṭasāhasrikā Prajñāpāramitā* (*Aṣṭa*), according to the consensus of Buddhist scholars.[33] There exist six versions of the *Aṣṭa*: one in Sanskrit, one in Tibetan and four in Chinese. The four Chinese translations are the *Daoxingbanruojing* translated by Lokakṣema in 178–179 CE, the *Damingdujing* translated by Zhi Qian in

222–229 CE, the *Mohebanruochaojing* translated by Dharmapriya in 382 CE, and the **Prajñāpāramitāsūtra* translated by Kumārajīva, in 408 CE.[34]

In these versions of the *Aṣṭa*, there appears a new term, *tathatā* or suchness, meaning the real nature of all things (*dharmas*), both worldly (*loka*) and transcendental (*lokottara*). The *Aṣṭa* discusses the concept of this new term in numerous places and uses many similes to convey its full meaning. Here we just produce a summary, without giving details. According to the text, this real nature (*tathatā*) is in everything including the Tathāgata and remains one and the same without change at all times. The *tathatā* of the Tathāgata therefore is not different from the *tathatā* of all *dharmas*, and the *tathatā* of all *dharmas* is the same as the *tathatā* of the Tathāgata. The *tathatā* of the Tathāgata is undiscriminated and undifferentiated at all times and in all *dharmas*, because there is only one single true *tathatā* that is unmade, uncreated in all things at all times.

As shown by E. Lamotte in the introduction to his translation of the *Vimalakīrtinirdeśa*, the early Mahāyānists introduced this new concept of *tathatā* on the basis of the early Buddhist teachings.[35] Of the four passages he found in the early scriptures pertaining to the doctrine of the absolute, two are relevant to our study.

First, the nature of things persists, whether or not the Buddha arises in the world. This idea, which is also used to describe *tathatā* in the *Aṣṭa*, is found in many places in both the *Nikāyas* and the *Āgamas*.[36] In early Buddhism, the nature of things is identified with dependent origination upon which the Tathāgata is fully enlightened.[37] The *tathatā* in the *Aṣṭa* is identified with emptiness (*śūnyatā*) by the realization of which a bodhisattva becomes a Tathāgata. Here dependent origination and emptiness refer to the same thing because everything is empty as everything arises dependent on causes and conditions, and apart from causes and conditions, there is no unchanging substance, thus it is empty.

Second, there is a passage in the *Udāna* describing *nibbāna* as: 'unborn (*ajāta*), unbecome (*abhūta*), unmade (*akata*), unformed (*asaṃkhata*)'.[38] A similar description of *tathatā* is also found in the *Aṣṭa*, where *tathatā* is said to be unmade and uncreated, just as discussed above. So the concept of *tathatā* in the *Aṣṭa* has the characteristics of both dependent origination and *nirvāṇa* in early Buddhism. Early Mahāyānists may have thus developed the concept of *tathatā* by combining the ideas of dependent origination and *nirvāṇa*, and finally identifying it with the Tathāgata.

The discussion on *tathatā* in the *Aṣṭa* is as follows. The passage in the oldest extant *Aṣṭa*, the *Daoxingbanruojing*, while problematic, can be elucidated by Kumārajīva's explicit translation of the same text.

> Subhūti, the Tathāgata knows the characteristic of forms (*rūpa*) through perfect wisdom (*prajñāpāramitā*). How does [the Tathāgata] know the characteristic of forms? Because he knows their real

> nature (*tathatā*). Subhūti, the Tathāgata knows the characteristics of sensation, conceptualization, volitional predisposition and consciousness. How does [the Tathāgata] know the characteristic of consciousness? Because he knows their real nature (*tathatā*). Subhūti, the *tathatā* of the five aggregates is what the Tathāgata meant by 'the arising and disappearing'. The *tathatā* of the five aggregates is the *tathatā* of the world; it is the *tathatā* of all things (*sarvadharma*). The *tathatā* of all things is the *tathatā* of the fruits of the stream attainer (*srotāpanna*), the oncereturner (*sakṛdāgāmi*), the non-returner (*anāgāmi*), the worthy one (*arhat*) and the *pratyekabuddha*. The *tathatā* of the *pratyekabuddha* is the *tathatā* of the Tathāgata. All these *tathatās* are actually one without a second, without differentiation, infinite and immeasurable. Thus, Subhūti, the Tathāgata obtains the characteristic of the *tathatā* through perfect wisdom (*prajñāpāramitā*). Subhūti, perfect wisdom thus makes a display of the worlds of all Buddhas and also gives birth to all Buddhas. All Buddhas know the *tathatā* of the world and truly obtain this *tathatā*. Therefore, they are named Tathāgata.[39]

This identification of the Tathāgata with the concept of *tathatā* constituted the foundation of Mahāyāna Buddhology. The early Mahāyānists considered *tathatā* to be the defining principle of Buddhahood. To them, the realization of *tathatā* was enlightenment. The *Aṣṭa* discusses the characteristics of *tathatā* in ten different ways, as follows.[40]

1. The *tathatā* of the Tathāgata has no coming and no going.
2. The *tathatā* of the Tathāgata is the *tathatā* of all *dharmas*, and vice versa.
3. The *tathatā* of the Tathāgata is eternal and has no differentiation.
4. The *tathatā* of the Tathāgata is neither existent nor non-existent.
5. There is no hindrance to the *tathatā* of the Tathāgata or to that of all *dharmas*.
6. The *tathatā* of the Tathāgata and that of all *dharmas* are one and the same, there is nothing that is not *tathatā* because it is unmade.
7. The *tathatā* of the Tathāgata is eternal and undifferentiated, and so is the *tathatā* of all *dharmas*.
8. The *tathatā* of the Tathāgata is neither apart from nor one with all *dharmas*.
9. There is no past, present and future in the *tathatā* of the Tathāgata, or in that of all *dharmas*.
10. There is no difference between the *tathatā* of the Tathāgata and that of the past, that of the present, that of the future, and that of all *dharmas*. A Bodhisattva is named a Buddha when he has attained the highest full enlightenment by means of *tathatā*.

The *Aṣṭa* further states that all *dharmas* are characterized by emptiness (*śūnyatā*), which has no mark, no creator, no destruction, no origin, no birth and no support. These characteristics exist eternally whether a Buddha arises or not. A Tathāgata is so named because he possesses all such characteristics.[41]

The concept of *tathatā* is explained as emptiness (*śūnyatā*), but not in the absolute sense of there being nothing at all. The authors of the *Aṣṭa* were in fact attempting to discard the attitude that everything exists hypothetically. The Mahāyānists were proud of the fact that they taught the emptiness of both the individual (*pudgalanairātmya*) and of phenomena (*dharmanairātmya*), while the Hīnayānists only taught the emptiness of the former and affirmed the real existence of the latter. However, the Mahāyānists took the *tathatā* to be the real nature of all things.

The *Aṣṭa* explains that even the Buddha is empty, comes from nowhere and goes nowhere because all *dharmas* are empty (*śūnya*).

> There is no *prajñāpāramitā*, and no one who practises *prajñāpāramitā*; no one who attains Buddhahood; no all-knowledge (*sarvajñā*), and no one who attains all-knowledge; no Tathāgatahood, and no one who becomes a Tathāgata; no state of being unborn, and no one who attains the state of being unborn; no ten powers, and no one who attains the ten powers; no four kinds of intrepidity, and no one who attains the four kinds of intrepidity. All *dharmas* are pure but no one attains them.[42]

Thus, what is a Buddha? According to the early Mahāyānists, Buddha is emptiness, the true nature of all *dharmas*. Then the question would naturally be asked: how can one become a Buddha if all *dharmas* are empty like a mirage? The text explains in a long passage that one gains full enlightenment neither apart from nor without the *prajñāpāramitā*.[43] This is because the world including the *prajñāpāramitā* is an illusion; it arises dependent on causes and conditions, and therefore one should not become attached to it as real. But, on the other hand, without practising the *prajñāpāramitā*, one will not attain the merits necessary for Buddhahood. So a bodhisattva should practise the *prajñāpāramitā* without even the thought of attaining enlightenment, because the difference between a Buddha and an ordinary sentient being is that the former is without any 'thought' while the latter is full of thoughts and attachments.[44] Therefore, the *Vimalakīrtinirdeśa* speaks of entry into non-duality. A bodhisattva is advised to think: 'I will save countless sentient beings and make them attain *nirvāṇa*, but this Dharma does not lead even one single person to *nirvāṇa*. Why? Because all are in the state of *tathatā*.'[45] However, holding fast to emptiness is also a kind of attachment to be abandoned, for reifying anything existent is attachment. Similarly, thinking that everything does not exist is also attachment. Śāriputra asked: 'What is attachment?' Subhūti replied:

> The thought that form is empty is attachment. The thought that feeling, apperception, volitional formation [literally: birth and death] and consciousness are empty is attachment. The thought that the past *dharmas* are past *dharmas* is attachment. The thought that the present *dharmas* are present *dharmas* is attachment. The thought that the future *dharmas* are future *dharmas* is attachment.[46]

Thus, any activity of the mind is attachment because the mind is originally pure.[47] Non-activity of the mind means that the mind neither observes nor reflects external objects. This is called non-attachment of the mind, which is the mind of the Buddha.[48] Therefore, Tathāgata, *tathatā* and the pure mind are not different, but refer to three aspects of one and the same thing. Observed as the real nature of all *dharmas*, it is called *tathatā*; described as the aspect of mentality, it is the pure mind; and beheld from the angle of bodhisattva practice, it is called Tathāgata. The *tathatā* is emptiness, but not absolute emptiness; it is emptiness unthinkable, indescribable. That is why according to the **Prajñāpāramitāsūtras* the Buddha did not wish to teach immediately after his enlightenment.[49]

The relationship between the Tathāgata and *tathatā* is clearly explained in the *Fangguangbanruojing*, the Chinese translation of the **Pañcaviṃśatisāhasrikā*.[50] The text states:

> All Tathāgatas do not change or move, there is no coming and no going. The Tathāgata is suchness (*tathatā*) which does not arise or disappear. There is no coming and no going because there is no arising, as no-birth is the Tathāgata. Sons of good families, reality does not know the time of coming and the time of going, so reality is the Tathāgata. Empty space does not come and does not go, so emptiness is the Tathāgata. The ultimate truth (*paramārtha*) does not come and does not go, so the ultimate truth is the Tathāgata. The unconditioned (*asaṃskṛta*) does not come and does not go, so the unconditioned is the Tathāgata. Cessation (*nirodha-samāpatti*) does not come and does not go, so cessation is the Tathāgata. Sons of good families, the Tathāgata is not apart from all these *dharmas*, which are the *tathatā* of the Tathāgata.[51]

Here the Tathāgata is identified with the *tathatā*, the pure and real nature of all *dharmas*. So the Tathāgata is one who has not only realized but has also become *tathatā*. In other words, the *tathatā* becomes the essence (*svabhāva*) or, in Makransky's words (in his book *The Buddha Embodied*), 'the defining principle of Buddhahood' in Mahāyāna Buddhism. Therefore, the *Fangguangbanruojing* states: 'The Tathāgata is not to be seen from form-body (*rūpakāya*), because the Tathāgata is *dharmatā* which does not come and does not go. The Tathāgata also does not come and does not go.'[52]

Thus, Tathāgata and *tathatā* are two names of one thing, the empty nature of all *dharmas*.

A passage identical to the above is also found in both the Sanskrit version of the *Aṣṭa* and the small **Prajñāpāramitāsūtra* translated by Kumārajīva. However, in these two *sūtras*, *dharmatā* is replaced by *dharmakāya*.

> All Tathāgatas are not to be seen from the perspective of the form-body (*rūpakāya*), because Tathāgatas are the *dharmakāya*. Sons of good families, the real nature (*tathatā*) of all *dharmas* does not come and does not go, and the same holds for the Tathāgatas.[53]

It is clear that *dharmakāya*, *dharmatā* and *tathatā* are terms with identical meanings.

This is a significant reinterpretation of Buddhahood from that of early Buddhism, and it provided the foundation for the entire Mahāyāna doctrine. The *tathatā*, the real nature of all things, is everywhere and pervades the entire cosmos, so the *dharmakāya* becomes the cosmic body. The *tathatā* is also named the *tathāgatagarbha* because it is the cause of Buddhahood. This *tathāgatagarbha* is called the *buddhadhātu* with regard to sentient beings, for the *tathatā* is covered with all kinds of defilements (*kleśas*), and it is called the *dharmakāya* at the stage of Buddhahood when the defilements are removed and the real nature revealed.

The dharmakāya *as the cosmic body*

In the three earliest Chinese translations of the *Aṣṭa*, the *Daoxingbanruojing*, the *Damingdujing* and the *Mohebanruochaojing*, there is no mention of the term *dharmakāya* although the authors discussed at length the notion of the *tathatā*. It is only in the Sanskrit version and in Kumārajīva's translation of the *Aṣṭa* that the term is used.[54] This has led Lewis Lancaster to think 'that the earliest ideas in Mahāyāna *sūtras* were neither the two-body nor the three-body ones, but rather the notion of one Buddha body'.[55] Y. Kajiyama challenged this view by saying that the older version of the *Aṣṭa* had already made a distinction between the physical body of the Buddha and *tathatā* while not utilizing terms such as *dharmakāya* and *rūpakāya*. He further asserts that the concepts of the *dharmakāya* and the *rūpakāya* were established around 200 CE.[56] Kajiyama is right in that the oldest extant *Aṣṭa*, the *Daoxingbanruojing*, uses two terms 'Buddhakāya' and 'Tathāgata' in the discussion of the concept of the Buddha. The term 'Buddhakāya' is used in the sense of the physical body which is produced by conditions and causes. The *sūtra* uses many metaphors to illustrate that the Buddhakāya is empty and that the Buddha makes a display of such a body only for the sake of sentient beings. In reality, the Buddha has no form, being created and controlled by no one.[57] The term 'Tathāgata', however, denotes one who realizes the *tathatā* of all *dharmas*, the empty nature of both worldly and transcendental things, as discussed above. It is only rarely that the term 'Buddha' is used instead of Tathāgata to denote the state of Buddhahood.

The *Vimalakīrtinirdeśasūtra*, translated first by Zhi Qian, contains the term *dharmakāya*, but its exact connotations are not clear.[58] The text only states: 'The *dharmakāya* of the Tathāgata is not the body made of thought and desire.'[59] Kumārajīva's translation of the *sūtra* rendered the same sentence as: 'The body of all Tathāgatas is the *dharmakāya*, not the body made of thought and desire.'[60] So the true body of the Tathāgata is not the *rūpakāya* but the *dharmakāya*. The meaning of the term *dharmakāya* becomes clear in later translations of the **Prajñāpāramitāsūtras* such as the **Pañcaviṃśatisāhasrikā* (Chinese: *Fangguangbanruojing*), which was translated into Chinese by Mokṣala in 291 CE. The *sūtra* states: 'Whether there is a Buddha or not, the *dharmatā* abides in the *tathatā*, and the *dharmatā* is the *dharmakāya*.'[61] Here the *dharmatā* is the same as *tathatā*, the empty nature of all *dharmas*, because the text says that the *dharmatā* abides in the reality of the Buddha's all-knowing wisdom, which is emptiness.[62] The **Pañcaviṃśatisāhasrikā* translated by Kumārajīva juxtaposes the terms *rūpakāya* and *dharmakāya*. The text explains that Buddhas are to be seen not in the *rūpakāya*, but in the *dharmakāya*.[63]

The concept of the *dharmakāya* became firmly established and expanded once it became identified with the concept of *tathatā*. In later Chinese translations of the Mahāyāna texts the concept of the *dharmakāya* has the characteristics of a cosmic body. This is apparent in Dharmarakṣa's translations such as the *Rulaixingxianjing*, *Dushipinjing*, *Dengmupusasuowensanmeijing*, *Jianbeiyiqiezhidejing* and **Mūkakumārasūtra* which were all translated into Chinese between 266 and 313 CE.[64] The *dharmakāya* in these *sūtras* is described as having the following characteristics. First, there is only one *dharmakāya* in all the Buddhas of the past, present and future, and this one body pervades everywhere in all the Buddha lands of the ten directions. The *Rulaixingxianjing* states: 'The Buddhas of the past, future and present are equal, because the *dharmakāya* is one.'[65] The *Dushipinjing* also affirms: 'It should be known that all Buddhas are but one *dharmakāya*.'[66] 'The *dharmakāya* is one, there is no past, present and future, it is equal in all times.'[67] The *Dushipinjing* further states: 'The *dharmakāya* pervades all the lands of the Buddhas of the ten directions.'[68] The *Rulaixingxianjing* explains that the *dharmakāya* is like empty space that does not have an actual body, so there is nothing it does not hold and there is no place it does not enter, whether with physical form or not.[69]

Second, since the *dharmakāya* has wisdom (*prajñā*) as its body, it cannot be seen. It is only for the sake of sentient beings that it manifests itself in different bodies. The *Rulaixingxianjing* states: 'The *dharmakāya* has wisdom as its body, but ultimately it has no characteristic (*lakṣaṇa*) at all. With one body, the wisdom manifests itself in uncountable bodies and spreads throughout the entire immeasurable cosmos (*dharmadhātu*).'[70] The same *sūtra* further says: 'Seeing nothing is seeing the Tathāgata . . . Why? Because he does not have an actual body, but for the sake of sentient beings, he manifests himself in [different] bodies.'[71] The *Dushipinjing* also states: 'Bodhisattvas understand the wisdom of the Buddha as one, the *dharmakāya*.'[72] The *Jianbeiyiqiezhidejing* confirms this idea by stating that: 'The *dharmakāya*, the body of holy wisdom, has the original vows of all Buddhas.'[73] So the *dharmakāya* is also the support and basis of the manifested bodies in which the Buddha labours for sentient beings.

Third, the *dharmakāya* is pure and eternal. The *Dushipinjing* states: '[The Tathāgata] manifests himself in many impermanent *rūpakāyas*, because gods and people become attached to the *rūpakāya*, but the *dharmakāya* is eternal.'[74] The *Jianbeiyiqiezhidejing* affirms: 'The *dharmakāya* is pure in such a way that the words "go" and "come" do not apply.'[75] The *Dengmupusasuowensanmeijing* says: 'The *dharmakāya* is originally pure.'[76]

The *Dushipinjing* explains that the aim of bodhisattva practice is to attain the *dharmakāya* by merging into the body of the Tathāgata because there is only one *dharmakāya*. 'The body of the bodhisattva enters everywhere and together with all Tathāgatas of the past, present and future, merges into one body . . . Thus the bodhisattva acquires the ultimate *dharmakāya* of immeasurable merits of the Tathāgata.'[77] This is because bodhisattvas and Tathāgatas of the past, present and future practise for one and the same merit by which they will finally merge into one body, the *dharmakāya*.[78] So the eternal and universal *dharmakāya* became the basis of the infinite world as well as the pure nature of all phenomena.

Before the composition of the **Mahāprajñāpāramitāśāstra* at the latest, the *dharmakāya* was taken to mean the cosmic body. In this work, the *dharmakāya* is described as pervading the whole universe. 'The *dharmakāya* pervades the empty space of the ten directions, its dimensions are infinite and limitless, and its form (*rūpa*) is marvellous and dignified with limitless rays of light and voice.'[79] Thus the *dharmakāya* ontologically became the principle of the universe since it is identified with the *tathatā*, the true nature of all *dharmas*.

The development of the dharmakāya *in the* Avataṃsaka

The emphasis of the **Prajñāpāramitāsūtras* is on the *śūnyatā* of everything, including the Tathāgata. As a result, the salvific aspect of the *dharmakāya* became less important. The **Prajñāpāramitāsūtras* state that reading the **Prajñāpāramitāsūtras* is more useful than worshipping the relics of the Buddha, because the *prajñāpāramitā* is the mother of all Buddhas. Hence, the **Prajñāpāramitāsūtras* stress the intellectual aspect of Buddhism and realization through wisdom. One finds, however, that Dharmarakṣa's translation of Mahāyāna texts enhances the salvific aspect by saying that the

Buddha *is* the *dharmakāya*, which is eternal and can deliver suffering sentient beings by its numerous manifestations. This salvific aspect of the Buddha is further developed in the *Avataṃsaka*, which confirms that sentient beings can find liberation just by seeing the *dharmakāya*, encountering its light or hearing its doctrine. The *Avataṃsaka* describes the *dharmakāya* as follows:

> The king of the Dharma peacefully abides in the Dharma Mansion, the light of the *dharmakāya* illuminates all . . . The *dharmakāya* of the Tathāgata is equal to the *dharmadhātu* [cosmos] and manifests itself according to the inclinations of sentient beings for their specific needs. The Tathāgata, the king of the Dharma, liberates sentient beings by taming them according to the law of righteousness.[80]

Thus, the religious aspect of the *dharmakāya* is emphasized through its salvific power.

The first of the three extant Chinese translations of the *Avataṃsaka* was by Buddhabhadra in 418–420 CE, and the second by Śikṣānanda in 695–699 CE. The third consists of only a partial translation, namely the *Gandhavyuha* by Prajñā in 796–798 CE. We focus here mainly on Buddhabhadra's translation because it is the earliest. The other two translations will be mentioned only when appropriate. Śikṣānanda's translation has five more chapters than Buddhabhadra's, though the main body of the *sūtra* is largely the same.[81] Prajñā's translation corresponds primarily to the last chapter in the first two translations, but revised and vastly enlarged.[82]

It is a well-known fact that almost all the Mahāyāna *sūtras* were subject to additions and expansion, and the *Avataṃsaka* is no exception. According to modern scholarship, the *Rulaixingxianjing*, the *Dushipinjing* and the *Jianbeiyiqiezhidejing*, translated by Dharmarakṣa as mentioned above, are the forerunners of the *Avataṃsaka*.[83] They correspond to chapters thirty-two, thirty-three and twenty-two of Buddhabhadra's translation respectively. The *Dengmupusasuowensanmeijing*, also translated by Dharmarakṣa, corresponds to chapter twenty-seven of Śikṣānanda's translation which is not found in Buddhabhadra's translation. On the basis of Dharmarakṣa's translations, the concept of the *dharmakāya* was further developed in the *Avataṃsaka* in the following three ways.

First, the *dharmakāya* is the non-dual reality, the impersonal principle of the universe and ontologically the foundation and support of everything. This notion is developed on the basis of the idea that there is only one *dharmakāya*. The *Avataṃsaka* states:

> There is no dharma in reality. Supreme enlightenment is equal to an illusion and it is named *bodhi* because it does not have the characteristic of bringing together causes and conditions. The present

> Buddha is not a result or product of causes and conditions, the Buddhas of past and future are also the same. All *dharmas* without marks [of bringing together] are the real nature of all Buddhas. If one can thus observe the profound meaning of all *dharmas*, one can see all the Buddhas as well as the true characteristic of *dharmakāya*.[84]

Śiksānanda's translation of the *Avataṃsaka* further states:

> If one knows the real as real, the unreal as unreal, then one is a Buddha. As the Dharma of the Buddha cannot be known, the realization of this is enlightenment. All Buddhas practise in such a way, but no Dharma can be obtained. It should be known that one is many, and many are in fact one [one is reality and many are appearances of that reality]. All *dharmas* do not depend on anything and they arise only when the causes and conditions are brought together. There is no doer and no deed as *dharmas* arise only from actions (*karma*) and thoughts. Then how is it known? It is because there is nothing apart from conditions. All *dharmas* do not exist because a fixed course is not to be attained. All Buddhas abide thus without moving or changing.[85]

Thus every *dharma* is reduced to *dharmakāya* and is equated with the *tathatā*, the real nature of all *dharmas* that does not differentiate, does not think and does not move. Ontologically speaking, the *dharmakāya* is the principle of the universe, and it does not bring together causes and conditions, as it neither arises nor disappears. All phenomena arise due to causes and conditions, and therefore they are not real, but illusions. The only reality is the non-dual *dharmakāya*. All Buddhas, bodhisattvas, worldly and transcendental *dharmas* are in reality the same because they all have the *dharmakāya* as their real nature. But from the phenomenal point of view, they are different. Just as the *Avataṃsaka* says:

> Mañjuśrī, the Dharma is always thus, the King of the Dharma has only one *dharma*, and all liberated people go out of *saṃsāra* along one path. The bodies of all Buddhas are but one *dharmakāya*, one mind and one wisdom, so are the powers and the fearlessness.[86]

The *dharmakāya* abides neither in reality nor in *nirvāṇa*, and manifests itself in any way to purify the world.

Second, the *dharmakāya* possesses skilful means (*upāyakauśalya*) and immeasurable rays of light through which it liberates sentient beings. By the power of skilful means, the Buddha can manifest himself to liberate sentient beings in accordance with their wishes and inclinations. Śikṣānanda's translation of the **Avataṃsaka* states:

> With various kinds of methods the Buddhas can manifest themselves in the worlds in as many ways as the [particles of] water in the ocean according to the wishes of sentient beings. This is the skilful means of the Tathāgata. The *dharmakāya* of the Buddhas is inconceivable and it has no form, no shape and not even the shadow of images, but it can manifest itself in various forms for the many different kinds of sentient beings, allowing them to behold it in accordance with their mentality and wishes.[87]

The text further explains that the *dharmakāya* surpasses all *śrāvakas* and *pratyekabuddhas* in virtues, and it can manifest itself in different life-spans, but its own life-span neither increases nor decreases. It may be reflected in the pure minds of all sentient beings, but the *dharmakāya* itself does not make distinctions as it possesses no thought.[88] The *dharmakāya*, though an impersonal principle lacking movement, change, thought and even action, can manifest itself in different bodies and forms to save sentient beings. This idea is repeatedly expressed throughout the **Avataṃsaka*.

The rays of the *dharmakāya* are immeasurable in that they benefit all sentient beings without discrimination, like the light of the sun. The rays first illuminate bodhisattvas, *pratyekabuddhas*, *śrāvakas*, those who have good roots, and finally all other sentient beings, in that order. Even those who do not have faith in the Buddha can benefit from the light of the *dharmakāya*, just as the blind also benefit from the light of the sun.[89] This light is none other than the light of wisdom of the Buddha. The *sūtra* states:

> Although blind people do not see the sunlight of the wisdom of the Tathāgata, yet they benefit by it.[90]
>
> The Tathāgata possesses the light of wisdom of the *ratnakāya*. Sentient beings will take on the same colour as the Buddha's body if they come into contact with this light. Those who see this light will have the pure dharma eye. Those who encounter this light will eliminate all suffering and attain dignity, wealth, happiness and even ultimate enlightenment.[91]

Thus the Tathāgata is described almost as an omnipotent and almighty godhead, while lacking the power to create the world and sentient beings. This concept of the Buddha served as a precedent for the emergence of the *saṃbhogakāya*.

Third, the *dharmakāya* is the treasure house that contains all the virtues and wisdom of the Buddha. The *Avataṃsaka* states: 'The *dharmakāya* of the Tathāgata is also the same, it is the treasure house of the great wisdom and immeasurable virtues of the great treasure king.'[92] This is because the *dharmakāya*, although it is quiescent, produces all *dharmas*.[93] The attainment of all Buddhas of past, present and future and of the ten directions as well as all the practices of all bodhisattvas are manifested in the body of the Tathāgata, but the *dharmakāya* does not become differentiated.[94] Therefore, the *Avataṃsaka* states:

> The thoughts of the mind, though as numerous as the atoms in a dust heap, are countable; the water in the ocean can be exhausted by drinking; the empty space is measurable and the wind can be caught, but the virtues of the Buddha cannot be measured.[95]

Thus, the development of the concept of the *dharmakāya* in the *Avataṃsaka* prepared the doctrinal foundation for the concept of the Buddha in Mahāyāna Buddhism.

The **dharmakāya** *bodhisattvas*

There are two kinds of bodhisattvas according to the MPPŚ: the *dharmakāya* bodhisattva and the *rūpakāya* bodhisattva.[96] The *dharmakāya* bodhisattvas come either from Tuṣita heaven or other *Buddhakṣetras* to this world to save sentient beings while the *rūpakāya* bodhisattvas come from human beings.[97] The *dharmakāya* bodhisattvas have eliminated all *kleśas* and obtained the six psychic powers; they can manifest themselves in many different bodies and make offerings to all Buddhas of the ten directions.[98] Although the *rūpakāya* bodhisattvas have not eliminated the *kleśas*, some of them have obtained five psychic powers, and others six.[99]

According to the *Avataṃsaka* translated by Prajñā, bodhisattvas acquire the *dharmakāya* when they have completed the practice of the ten *dharmas* in the ten stages (*bhūmi*) of training. In the first stage, the bodhisattva acquires the body of equality because he has realized the real nature of all *dharmas*, the body which is equal and is free from wrong views. In the second stage, the bodhisattva acquires the body of purity because he is free from any transgression of the precepts, thus maintaining constant purity. In the third stage, the bodhisattva acquires the infinite body as he is free from all bad *dharmas* such as desire, hatred, ignorance and jealousy and abides in the supreme *samādhi*. In the fourth stage, the bodhisattva acquires the body of accumulation and cultivation since he always cultivates the *bodhyaṅgas* of all Buddhas. In the fifth stage, the bodhisattva acquires the body of *dharmatā* as he has realized all truths and the nature of all *dharmas*. In the sixth stage, the bodhisattva acquires the body without discursive (*vitarka*) and investigative (*vicāra*) thoughts since he has realized dependent origination (*pratītyasamutpāda*) which, though difficult to explain, is a state free from *vitarka* and *vicāra*. In the seventh stage, the bodhisattva acquires the inconceivable body because he has the skilful means of all Buddhas since he has completed the practice of wisdom. In the eighth stage, the bodhisattva acquires the body of tranquillity since no *kleśa* manifests itself in him and he is free from all worldly matters. In the ninth stage, the bodhisattva acquires the body of emptiness in that the characteristics of this body are limitless and it spreads everywhere. In the tenth stage, the bodhisattva acquires the body of wonderful wisdom as he has gained all-knowledge and a splendid realm. It is at this stage that the bodhisattva acquires the *dharmakāya*. So here the *dharmakāya* bodhisattva is a bodhisattva of the tenth stage.

What then is the difference between the *dharmakāya* of the Buddha and that of the bodhisattva? The *Avataṃsaka* says that there is no difference with regard to the nature of the *dharmakāya*, because the *dharmatā* is equal in both ordinary and extraordinary individuals. But the merits and the powers are different. In the case of the Buddha they are complete and full while in the case of the bodhisattva they are not.[100] However, the power of the *dharmakāya* bodhisattvas is similar to that of the Buddha and they can manifest themselves in numerous *nirmāṇakāyas* to save sentient beings. They may even appear in the form of the Buddha with all the marks of a great man.[101]

The **dharmakāya** *as* **tathāgatagarbha**

As *tathatā*, real nature, exists in all *dharmas*, so it exists in every sentient being. The *tathatā* is identified as the Tathāgata in the **Prajñāpāramitāsūtras* and is again identified with the *dharmakāya* in later *sūtras* such as the *Avataṃsaka*, because the Tathāgata is the *dharmakāya*. Thus, the *dharmakāya* exists in every sentient being, but since it is covered with *kleśas*, it does not become manifest. It is on the basis of such ideas that it is declared in the **Mahāvaipulyatathāgatagarbhasūtra* that all sentient beings have Buddha nature (*tathāgatagarbha*).

> With my Buddha eyes, I (the Buddha) can see that within the *kleśas* such as greed, hatred and ignorance of all sentient beings, there exists Tathāgata wisdom, Tathāgata eyes, and Tathāgata body, sitting cross-legged without moving. Sons of good families, although sentient beings with defiled bodies are in *saṃsāra*, they all have the pure *tathāgatagarbha*, which is endowed with all the virtues and characteristics that I have . . . Thus, sons of good families, upon seeing the *tathāgatagarbha* in all sentient beings, the Buddha preaches this *sūtra* in order to eliminate the *kleśas* and to reveal the *buddhadhātu*. Sons of good families, the Dharma of all Buddhas is thus: whether a Buddha arises or not in the world, the *tathāgatagarbha* in all sentient beings exists eternally and without change, but it is covered with defilements. The Tathāgata arises in the world and preaches the Dharma in order to eradicate defilements and purify supreme wisdom.[102]

The **Mahāvaipulyatathāgatagarbhasūtra* is a very important source for the concept of the *tathāgatagarbha* which it explains through nine similes. The text states clearly that the *tathāgatagarbha* is the same as the *tathatā* and the *dharmakāya*, because they all exist eternally without change whether or not the Buddha arises in the world. It is called the *dharmakāya* at the stage of Buddhahood because pure nature is revealed, and it is called *tathāgatagarbha* or *buddhadhātu* at the stage of sentient beings because the same pure nature is covered with defilements. The **Srīmālādevīsiṃhanādasūtra* states: 'This *dharmakāya* of the Tathāgata in the store of defilement is referred to as *tathāgatagarbha*.'[103] The **Ratnagotravibhāga-śāstra* further explains that the *dharmakāya* of the Tathāgata is in the body of every sentient being. The Tathāgata and the *tathatā* are not different and all sentient beings have the same *tathatā*, which is *buddhadhātu*.[104] The underlying idea is *tathatā*, the real nature of all *dharmas* that links the Tathāgata and sentient beings. The *Buzengbujianjing* states: 'The ultimate truth (*paramārtha*) is the realm of sentient beings, the realm of the sentient beings is the *tathāgatagarbha*, the *tathāgatagarbha* is the *dharmakāya*.'[105] The text continues:

> Śāriputra, this same *dharmakāya*, which is covered with immeasurable *kleśas* and flows in *saṃsāra* [literally: world] from time immemorial and drifts in the ocean of birth and death for as many *kalpas* as the sands in the Ganges River, corresponds to sentient beings. Śāriputra, this same *dharmakāya* that is disgusted by the world, which is full of suffering and birth and death, abandons all desires, performs the ten perfections with eighty-four thousand methods of practice and cultivates *bodhi*, is named bodhisattva.[106]

The text concludes:

> Within the realm of sentient beings there is the *dharmakāya*, and within the realm of the *dharmakāya* there are sentient beings. The realm of sentient beings is the *dharmakāya*, and the *dharmakāya* is the realm of sentient beings. Śāriputra, these two are the same, only the names are different.[107]

So Buddhas and sentient beings are not different in reality, because they have the same *dharmakāya*, but a Buddha is a person who has realized the *dharmakāya* through bodhisattva practices while a sentient being is one who is not aware of possessing this treasure.

The dharmakāya *as* mahāparinirvāṇa

Like the Hīnayāna *Mahāparinibbānasutta*, the Mahāyānists also have their own version of this *sūtra*, which scholars call the Mahāyāna

Mahāparinirvāṇasūtra (MMPS) to distinguish it from the former. One of the main themes of the MMPS is that the Buddha is eternal, a theme very much in contrast with the Hīnayāna idea that the Buddha departed for ever after his final *nirvāṇa*.[108] The Mahāyānists assert the eternity of the Buddha in two ways in the MMPS. They state that the Buddha is the *dharmakāya*, and hence eternal. Next, they reinterpret the liberation of the Buddha as *mahāparinirvāṇa* possessing four attributes: eternity, happiness, self and purity. In other words, according to the Mahāyānists, the fact that the Buddha abides in the *mahāparinirvāṇa* means not that he has departed for ever, but that he perpetually abides in intrinsic quiescence. The Buddha abiding in intrinsic quiescence is none other than the *dharmakāya*. As a result, the Mahāyānists come to identify the *mahāparinirvāṇa* with the *dharmakāya*. There are two ways in which the Mahāyānists declare the eternity of the Buddha.

First, on the basis of the teachings in the early Mahāyāna *sūtras* such as the *Avataṃsaka*, the authors of the MMPS make the assertion that the Tathāgata corresponds to the *dharmakāya*. They draw their ideas from five Mahāyāna *sūtras* to which they refer explicitly: the **Mahāprajñāpāramitā*, the **Saddharmapuṇḍarīka*, the **Śūraṃgamasamādhi*, the **Avataṃsaka* and the **Tathāgatagarbha*.[109] Among the five, the **Avataṃsaka* explicitly states: 'All Buddha bodies are but one *dharmakāya*.'[110] This *dharmakāya* is the real Buddha. It is on this doctrinal foundation that the MMPS declares:

> I [the Buddha] said in a *sūtra* that the Tathāgata has two bodies: the *rūpakāya* and the *dharmakāya*. The *rūpakāya* is the body of transformation manifested by skilful means and this body can be said to have birth, old age, sickness and death . . . The *dharmakāya* has [the attributes of] eternity (*nitya*), happiness (*sukha*), self (*ātman*) and purity (*śubha*) and is perpetually free from birth, old age, sickness, death and all other sufferings . . . It exists eternally without change whether the Buddha arises or not in the world.[111]

In the chapter on the diamond body, the MMPS explicitly states: 'The body of the Tathāgata is not a defiled body sustained by food (*rūpakāya*), but the eternal body, the indestructible body, the diamond body, the *dharmakāya*.'[112] So Buddhahood is nothing other than the *dharmakāya*, and the *rūpakāya* is only considered as a function or skilful means of the *dharmakāya* for work towards the liberation of sentient beings.

Second, the Mahāyānists reinterpret the concept of *nirvāṇa* and distinguish the Buddha's *nirvāṇa* from the *nirvāṇa* attained by *śrāvakas* and *pratyekabuddhas*. To the Mahāyānists, the *mahāparinirvāṇa* possesses the four attributes of eternity (*nitya*), happiness (*sukha*), self (*ātman*) and purity (*śubha*). The MMPS states:

> Happiness can be attained through the elimination of defilements (*saṃyojana*) from the stage of the first *dhyāna* to the stage of neither perception nor non-perception. This happiness can be named *nirvāṇa*, but not *mahāparinirvāṇa*. Why? The *kleśas* may rise again as the habitual force remains. What are the *kleśas* and the habitual force? *Śrāvakas* and *pratyekabuddhas* have them, such as [the thoughts of] 'my body', 'my cloth', 'I go', 'I come', 'I speak' and 'I listen'. They [*śrāvakas* and *pratyekabuddhas*] also think that 'all Tathāgatas attained *nirvāṇa*, the nature of which is without self and happiness, but only eternity and purity.' These are the *kleśas* and the habitual force . . . Thus, the attainment of the people of the two vehicles [*śrāvakas* and *pratyekabuddhas*] is not the *mahāparinirvāṇa*. Why? Because it does not have [the four attributes of] eternity, happiness, self and purity, after which the *mahāparinirvāṇa* is named.[113]

This discussion shows that the Mahāyānists distinguished the liberation of *śrāvakas* and *pratyekabuddhas* from that of the Buddhas. It is only the Buddhas who have attained the *mahāparinirvāṇa*, and in fact the Tathāgatas are always in the state of *mahāparinirvāṇa*, because the *dharmakāya* is intrinsically quiescent. In the chapter on 'The Noble Bodhisattva of the Merit King who Illuminates All', the MMPS further expounds the concept of the *mahāparinirvāṇa* by way of 'great eternity', 'great happiness', 'great self' and 'great purity'. The above chapter explains the latter three attributes while that of 'great eternity' is omitted.[114] The attribute of 'great eternity' may have been omitted during transmission or the authors of the MMPS may have thought that it had already been discussed in many places in the *sūtra*.

The concept of great happiness (*mahāsukha*) is explained as having the following four meanings: (1) the nature of *nirvāṇa* is beyond suffering and happiness, because the happiness of the Buddha is eternal and without change; (2) it is complete quiescence, free from all activities and noises; (3) it is omniscience (*sarvajñā*); (4) the body of the Tathāgata is not the body of *kleśas*, but the indestructible *vajra* body. The *mahāparinirvāṇa* is great happiness possessing these four meanings.

The second concept of 'great self' (*mahā-ātman*) is problematic, granted the Buddhist insistence on non-self. The MMPS expounds the great self as great mastery. The *mahāparinirvāṇa* has the attribute of the great self because the Tathāgata has eight masteries.

1. The Tathāgata can manifest himself in numerous bodies in uncountable worlds in the universe.
2. The Tathāgata can pervade the entire universe with one body as small as a particle of dust while it does not occupy any space since there is no obstruction.

3 The Tathāgata can go anywhere in the universe without any obstacle.
4 The Tathāgata can save countless sentient beings and can manifest himself in numerous other Buddha lands although he always abides in one Buddha field.
5 The Tathāgata has mastery of the six sense organs so that he can use any organ to perceive any of the six sense objects.
6 The Tathāgata penetrates all *dharmas*, but has no thought.
7 The Tathāgata has mastery of speech so that he can expound the meaning of one stanza for many *kalpas*.
8 The Tathāgata is like the empty space that pervades everywhere. The nature of space cannot be seen, and likewise the Tathāgata only makes himself seen through his ability.

This mastery of the Buddha is the great self, which is the *mahāparinirvāṇa*.

Third, the concept of great purity (*mahāśubha*) also has four meanings: (1) *nirvāṇa* is the state where the twenty-five kinds of existence are extinguished;[115] (2) the *karma* of all Buddhas is pure; (3) the body of the Tathāgata is pure owing to the fact that it is eternal; (4) the mind of the Tathāgata is pure since it is free from all *kleśas*. *Mahāparinirvāṇa* is here great purity on account of these four meanings.[116]

The relationship of the four attributes of the *mahāparinirvāṇa* is explained in the *sūtra* in the following words:

> The extinction of the six consciousnesses, which are produced by [the contact of] the internal and external entrances or locations (*ayatana*), is called the eternity. This eternity is again named the self (*ātman*). The eternity and the self are together termed happiness. Then eternity, self and happiness are called purity. Sons of good families, sentient beings are disgusted with suffering and try to eliminate the cause of this suffering. It is called the self when they are liberated from suffering. It is on account of this that I declare eternity, happiness, self and purity.[117]

Thus, among these four attributes of the *mahāparinirvāṇa*, eternity is the core on which the other three are established. Here happiness has not the ordinary sense of enjoyment or excitement, but the sense of abiding peacefully and eternally without any activity. Self is described not in the sense of an eternal soul but in the sense of eternal mastery over oneself so that one can manifest oneself in whatever form one wishes through skilful means with the aim of liberating sentient beings. Purity is described to have the sense that all defilement has been eliminated for ever so that there is no *karma* being accumulated for rebirth in *saṃsāra*. In other words, the Tathāgata's abiding in *mahāparinirvāṇa* means that he abides in eternity. This is one of the three main themes of the MMPS.

The *dharmakāya*, according to the MMPS, also has the same four attributes as the *mahāparinirvāṇa*. It is stated in the *sūtra*:

> The body of the Tathāgata is like diamond and is infinite, it has [the four attributes of] eternity, happiness, purity and self. The mind and the body [of the Tathāgata] are without obstacle because he has the eight kinds of mastery.[118]

> The eternity of the Tathāgata is called self. The *dharmakāya* of the Tathāgata, which has no limit, no obstacle, no birth and no extinction but has the eight kinds of mastery, is also called the self.[119]

'The *dharmakāya* is eternity, happiness, self and purity.'[120] So the *dharmakāya* and the *mahāparinirvāṇa* are identical, because they have the same attributes and qualities. They refer to two aspects of one Buddhahood: the *dharmakāya* is the eternal principle, the fruit of Buddhahood, while the *mahāparinirvāṇa* is the state which is free from all *kleśas*, the aspect of tranquillity of Buddhahood.

Other Mahāyāna texts such as the *Dharmasaṃghītisūtra* and the *Suvarṇaprabhāsottamarāja-sūtra* make the same assertion. The *Dharmasaṃghītisūtra* translated by Bodhiruci in 515 CE discusses two sets of ten ways by which a bodhisattva Mahāsattva knows that Buddhas have attained *mahāparinirvāṇa*. In the first set, two ways are related to the *dharmakāya*. 'Why do Tathāgatas not move and not abide? Being free from these two dharmas the *dharmakāya* does not perish. Since it does not perish and does not rise so Tathāgatas have attained *nirvāṇa*.'[121] 'Tathāgatas are the real *dharmakāya* which is unconditioned. So Tathāgatas attained *nirvāṇa*.'[122] In the second set of ten ways, two are also related to the *dharmakāya*. 'Tathāgatas are free from the conditioned and unconditioned dharmas, only the unconditioned *dharmakāya* is limitless. So Tathāgatas attained *nirvāṇa*.'[123] 'Emptiness is dharma, which is *dharmakāya*, *dharmakāya* is Tathāgata, thus Tathāgatas have attained *nirvāṇa*.'[124]

The *Suvarṇaprabhāsottamarāja-sūtra* translated by Yijing also mentions three sets of ten similar ways by which a bodhisattva Mahāsattva knows that Buddhas have attained *mahāparinirvāṇa*. In each set, it says that the *dharmakāya* is called *nirvāṇa*. In the first set, it states: 'Attaining the true, undifferential and equal *dharmakāya* is called *nirvāṇa*.'[125] In the second set, it states: 'The essence of the Tathāgata *dharmakāya* is true and thus called *nirvāṇa*.'[126] In the third set, it states: 'The empty nature is the true *dharmakāya* and hence called *nirvāṇa*.'[127]

One may thus conclude that the Mahāyānists reinterpreted the concept of *nirvāṇa* so that it became identified with the *dharmakāya*. The **Śrīmālādevīsiṃhanādasūtra* explicitly states: 'Supreme enlightenment (*anuttara-saṃyak-saṃbodhi*) is the realm of *nirvāṇa* and the realm of *nirvāṇa* is the *dharmakāya* of the Tathāgata.'[128] So the Mahāyānists considered that supreme enlightenment, *nirvāṇa*, and *dharmakāya* are the same because they consist of the three dimensions of Buddhahood. In such a context the Buddha's entry into *nirvāṇa* means not that he has gone for ever, but that he is merely abiding eternally in the state of quiescence. This state can be called *mahāparinirvāṇa* as well as *dharmakāya*, as they both have *tathatā* as their essence and are the same in nature.

In the chapter on the life-span of the Buddha, the MMPS explains the concept of *nirvāṇa* in a very special way. It is said that the concept of *nirvāṇa* consists of three dimensions: *dharmakāya*, *vimokṣa* (liberation) and *mahāprajñā* (great wisdom). The relationship of the three is like the word YI ∴ (伊 in Chinese), so that independently none of them can be called *nirvāṇa*. The Tathāgata abides in all three, and for the sake of sentient beings it is called *nirvāṇa*. It is stated in the MMPS:

> What is the secret of the *garbha*? It is like the three dots of the word YI. It cannot be the word YI if the three dots are in a horizontal line and similarly it cannot be the word YI if the three dots are in a vertical line . . . I [the Buddha] am also the same. The *vimokṣa* alone is not *nirvāṇa*; the body of the Tathāgata alone is also not *nirvāṇa*; the *mahāprajñā* alone is also not *nirvāṇa*; that all three *dharmas* are different is also not *nirvāṇa*. I abide peacefully in all three, but for the sake of sentient beings it is called *nirvāṇa*.[129]

Thus, the *mahāparinirvāṇa* has three dimensions: *dharmakāya*, *mahāprajñā* and *vimokṣa*. *Mahāprajñā* is great wisdom, the essence of the Buddhahood; the *dharmakāya* is the fruit of Buddhahood; and *vimokṣa* is liberation resulting from the severance of the *kleśas* through wisdom.

The concept of the *dharmakāya* has finally developed to the stage where the *dharmakāya*, the Tathāgata, *paramārtha* and *nirvāṇa* become one and the same thing because they are in fact different names given to *tathatā*. In his **Buddhagotraśāstra*, Vasubandhu states:

> (1) It is because the Buddha and the Dharma are not separated that the *dharmakāya* is established. (2) It is owing to the fact that the nature [of all *dharmas*] in everything is *tathatā* that the Tathāgata is established. (3) It is by virtue of being free from illusions and confusions that *paramārtha* is established. (4) It is by reason of its intrinsic quiescence that *nirvāṇa* is established. These four meanings and four names are not different from the nature of the Tathāgata.[130]

Vasubandhu further explains that these four names are established for the sake of four kinds of people. It is for the sake of ordinary people that the *tathatā* is called the *dharmakāya*, for they are seen as holding a wrong view of the Buddha body. The *tathatā* is called the Tathāgata because confused beings of the two vehicles, the *śrāvaka* and the *pratyekabuddha*, practised the thought of impermanence while the Tathāgata is eternal. The *tathatā* is called *paramārtha* because some people hold the view that the *tathāgatagarbha* is in existence while others think it is empty, but the *tathatā* is neither in existence nor in non-existence. Lastly, *tathatā* is called *nirvāṇa* for the sake of bodhisattvas at the tenth stage, because only the Buddha attains and becomes the *nirvāṇa*, not bodhisattvas.[131]

The dharmakāya *as non-duality*

Tathatā, the real nature of all *dharmas*, is neither existent nor non-existent, as discussed above. Since the *tathatā* is identified with the *dharmakāya*, the latter is also neither existent nor non-existent. It is stated in the **Avataṃsaka* that the *dharmakāya* is neither reality nor illusion; neither past nor future; neither existence nor non-existence; neither skill in means nor non-skill in means; but it is pure, equal, unconditioned and indestructible.[132] The **Avataṃsaka* further explains why the *dharmakāya* is non-dual. The *dharmakāya* is not past because all kinds of worldly existences are eliminated, it is not future because it does not arise, it is not present because it does not have a physical body. It does not become extinct since it does not have the mark of birth. It is not a reality for it is like an illusion, and it is also not an illusion since it benefits all sentient beings by manifesting itself in the world. It does not go anywhere as it transcends birth and death, and it is not to be destroyed since the *dharmatā* does not change. It has one characteristic for it is free from words of expression, and it has no characteristic as it is empty.[133] Then what is the *dharmakāya* if it does not have any of these qualities? The **Avataṃsaka* uses the following similes to illustrate the *dharmakāya*. 'It is an infinite body, a body with all illusions being eradicated like lightning, a body like a mirage in a dream, a body like an image in a mirror, a body like the pure sun.'[134]

The *dharmakāya* is also the non-duality of unity and differentiation. It is not differentiated, since the *tathatā* is one and the same in everything, and is the support of all Buddhas. It is also not a unity, because many bodhisattvas will become Buddhas through the practice of the six perfections. Thus, it can be summed up in the following sentence: the *dharmakāya* is non-duality of existence and non-existence, of unity and differentiation. However, the *Avataṃsaka* still maintains that the *dharmakāya* is an unconditioned (*asaṃskṛta*) *dharma*.

This issue is taken up and discussed again in the *Laṅkāvatārasūtra* where the *dharmakāya* is identified with the *buddhadhātu*. The bodhisattva Mahāmati asked:

> Is the *dharmakāya* created or uncreated, cause or effect, seer or that to be seen, speaker or that to be spoken of, wisdom or that to be realized by wisdom? With regard to these words, is the *dharmakāya* of the Tathāgata different or not different?[135]

The *Laṅkāvatārasūtra* explains this point in detail in the chapter on the *dharmakāya* and it further develops the concept of non-duality.[136] The Buddha said:

> Mahāmati, the characteristics of the *dharmakāya* of the Tathāgata, the fully Enlightened One, are described as neither created nor uncreated, neither cause nor effect. Why? Because it is wrong either way. Mahāmati, if the Tathāgata is created, then he is impermanent; if impermanent, all created *dharmas* are the Tathāgata, but the Buddha Tathāgata, the fully Enlightened One, is of no such *dharmas*. Mahāmati, if the *dharmakāya* of the Tathāgata is uncreated, then it is no body, so it is wrong to say that there are immeasurable merits generated by all kinds of [bodhisattva] practices and actions. Mahāmati, if it is not created, it is like the horn of a hare or the daughter of a barren woman, because there is no cause for creation and no [physical] body. Mahāmati, if a *dharma* is neither cause nor effect, neither in existence nor in non-existence, then that *dharma* is free from these four kinds of characteristics. Mahāmati, those four kinds of *dharmas* are worldly expressions and sayings. Mahāmati, if a *dharma* is free from these four kinds of *dharmas*, that *dharma* exists but only in name, like the daughter of a barren woman. Mahāmati, the daughter of a barren woman etc. exists only in name and words, just as the discussion of the four kinds of *dharmas*, but the wise would not hold on to it if it falls into the description of the four *dharmas*. Thus, the wise should know [the answers to] all the questions concerning the Tathāgata.[137]

Thus, the *dharmakāya* cannot be described in words such as created or uncreated, cause or effect, because it is non-dual. Here the *dharmakāya* is also non-duality of the conditioned and the unconditioned, because it is neither the created nor the uncreated.

The *Laṅkāvatārasūtra* continues by saying that the *dharmakāya* is neither the same as nor different from the five *skandhas*, *vimukti* and *nirvāṇa*.[138] We have already discussed in the previous section the relationship between the *dharmakāya*, *vimukti* and *nirvāṇa*: they are three aspects of one Buddhahood. The five *skandhas* constitute a sentient being, so the *dharmakāya* is neither the same as nor different from sentient beings. This is clearly based on the idea that all sentient beings have *buddhadhātu*. The text further explains that if a *dharma* exists only in name, then it neither arises nor disappears, like empty space, and it surpasses all words which conceal and cover reality (*prapañca*).[139] That is the characteristic of the *dharmakāya*.[140] Hence, the *dharmakāya* is free from all conceptual constructs (*vikalpa*) and is in fact inconceivable. Therefore, the *sūtra* states that the *dharmakāya* is not absolutely nothing, but a mind-made body (*manomayakāya*) which cannot be understood by *śrāvakas* and *pratyekabuddhas*, or even by the bodhisattvas in the seventh stage.[141] Thus, the non-duality of the *dharmakāya* means that it cannot be conceived by our human minds and expressed in human words because it is beyond logic, reasoning and human imagination.

The **dharmakāya** *as the transformation of support*

In the early Mahāyāna *sūtras*, as discussed above, Buddhahood is the *dharmakāya*, which has two meanings. First, the *dharmakāya* is non-dual ontological reality, the universal suchness that is the essence of Buddhahood, and second, it has the salvific power to liberate sentient beings. It is on this basis that the Yogācārins further developed the concept of the *dharmakāya*, first as the transformation of support and then by the three body theory. Concerning the three bodies, the Yogācāra masters divided the salvific function of the *dharmakāya* into two. One serves to bring bodhisattvas to maturity; this is called *saṃbhogakāya*. The other serves to bring to maturity *śrāvakas* as well as bodhisattvas in their initial stage of liberation; this is called *nirmāṇakāya*. The historical and doctrinal reasons behind the development of the *trikāya* theory are examined in the next chapter where the origin of *saṃbhogakāya* is studied in depth. We will concentrate here on how the *dharmakāya* is expounded by the Yogācāra school.

The **Saṃdhinirmocanasūtra* is perhaps the first Yogācāra text to explain that the *dharmakāya* is the transformation of support, because the **Yogācārabhūmiśāstra* often quotes from it when discussing the concept of the *dharmakāya*. It is stated in the *sūtra*:

> The wonderful *dharmakāya* is obtained through the transformation of support (*āsrayaparāvṛtti*) upon completion of the practice of the ten stages (*bhūmi*) and the *pāramitās* . . . This *dharmakāya* has two inconceivable characteristics: they are (1) freedom from words which cover and conceal the truth (*prapañca*) and (2) freedom from the characteristics of the conditioned (*saṃskṛta*).[142]

The *sūtra* further explains that while *śrāvakas* and *pratyekabuddhas* also have the transformation of support, by which they acquire the body of liberation (*vimuktikāya*), they do not have the *dharmakāya*, because they do not have the immeasurable merits of the Buddha. However, Buddhas, *śrāvakas* and *pratyekabuddhas* are equal as regards liberation (*vimukti*).

It is further stated in the **Saṃdhinirmocanasūtra* that the ultimately pure *dharmakāya* is established when the unattached and unhindered universal wisdom and insight are finally realized through permanent elimination of obstacles caused by the most subtle of *kleśas* and knowledge (*jñeyāvaraṇa*). This is done through the methods of *śamatha* and *vipaśyanā* meditation at the stage of Tathāgatahood.[143] The idea expressed in the *sūtra* is that the *dharmakāya* has pure *tathatā* as its essence and that all the defilements are adventitious. In effect, the transformation of support is the elimination of both *kleśas* and the hindrance of knowledge, and it is through this process that the bodhisattva attains Buddhahood.

In the Yogācāra *śāstra* literature, as Makransky points out, the term *dharmakāya* has two basic meanings: (1) an inclusive sense as the state of Buddhahood in its entirety (including the three bodies); (2) an exclusive sense as the first of the three bodies. The *dharmakāya* in the second definition consists of the *svābhāvakāya*, the essence of Buddhahood.[144] In whichever sense the Yogācāra school perceives it, the *dharmakāya* is the transformation of support.

According to the Yogācāra, the first meaning of the *dharmakāya*, the sense of Buddhahood in its entirety, refers to the three bodies. The author of the *Mahāyānasūtrālaṃkāra* (MSA) sees the three bodies as functions of the purified Dharma realm (*dharmadhātu-viśuddha*). But the author of the *Mahāyānasaṃgraha* (MS) considers that Buddhahood as a whole is the *dharmakāya* which performs three functions pertaining to three different categories of people. The *dharmakāya* or *svābhāvakāya* is exclusively for the Buddhas as only they can realize real nature. The *saṃbhogakāya* is for the great bodhisattvas and the *nirmāṇakāya* is for sentient beings. Since the three bodies are three functional aspects of one Buddhahood, there is no contradiction between them.

The second meaning of the *dharmakāya* is explained in detail in the Yogācāra *śāstras*. The MSA, which is the first text to expound on the three bodies of the Buddha, explains that the *dharmakāya* is the body of essence (*svābhāvakāya*) and its characteristic is that of fundamental transformation. This transformation is the conversion of the eighth consciousness (*ālayavijñāna*) into the mirror wisdom (*ādarśajñāna*) and the seventh consciousness (*manasvijñāna*) into the equality wisdom (*samatājñāna*).[145] The transformation takes place over immeasurable aeons, from the time the bodhisattva attaines the path of direct seeing (*darśana-mārga*), which is the first of the ten stages (*bhūmi*), until he attains Buddhahood. In the ten stages of bodhisattva realization, two kinds of wisdom are achieved: the non-discrimination wisdom (*nirvikalpa-jñāna*) for the maturing of Buddha Dharma and the subsequently acquired wisdom (*pṛṣṭha-labdha-jñāna*) for the maturing of sentient beings. Thus the transformation is completed when all conceptual constructs are eliminated through diamond meditation.[146]

Following the line of thought of the MSA, the MS further explains that the *dharmakāya* is attained through turning away and destroying the store consciousness (*alayavijñāna*), which is transformed into mirror wisdom. The MS expounds the process thus. The permeation (*vāsanā*) of hearing is the seed of the *dharmakāya* and it arises in countering the store consciousness, but it is not comprised within that store consciousness. Since it is an outflow from the transcendent and purest reality realm (*dharmadhātu*), even though a worldly state, it brings about a transcendent mind. All such superior states of mind counter (1) delusory passions, (2) all bad migrations and (3) the decay consequent upon all non-virtuous actions, and enable one to maintain the continuity of life, thus increasing the possibility of an encounter with the Buddhas and bodhisattvas.

Although it is a worldly state, this permeation of hearing is within the *dharmakāya* and is therefore attainable by novice bodhisattvas. As the level of this permeation gradually rises from small to intermediate to high, the maturing consciousness decreases proportionately. The support is hence converted. When that support is entirely converted, the store consciousness will be eliminated altogether, replete with all its seeds.[147]

This exposition of the process of transformation is actually the same as that described in the **Saṃdhinirmocanasūtra*, the elimination of the adventitious defilements (*kleśas*). According to Paramārtha, this is because the seed of the *dharmakāya* flows out from 'the pure reality realm (*dharmadhātu*)', which is nothing but the *tathatā*.[148] This seed brings about the pure mind, which eliminates all the bad *karmas* of the past, present and future, and thus the light of the *dharmakāya* is revealed.

Paul Griffiths and others point out that there is a conceptual problem with regard to the attainment and realization of the *dharmakāya*. If all sentient beings have the *dharmakāya* by the name *buddhadhātu*, then there is no attainment, but rather a realization.[149] That is why Paramārtha's version of the MS makes a distinction between the 'attainment' and 'realization' of the *dharmakāya*. This can perhaps be understood from the explanation given in the **Vijñaptimātratāsiddhiśāstra*: according to the *sūtras* (the **Buddhabhūmisūtra* etc.), the *dharmakāya* is suchness (*tathatā*) while according to the *śāstras* (the *Mahāyānasaṃgraha*), the *svābhāvakāya* is attained by the transformation of the eighth consciousness (*ālayavijñāna*) into the great mirror wisdom (*ādarśajñāna*).[150] Thus, from the point of view of the *sūtras*, the *dharmakāya* can only be realized because it is the suchness of all *dharmas*, while from the point of view of the *śāstras*, it is to be attained because it is a transformation of consciousness into wisdom.

People such as Bandhuprabha in the sixth century were already aware of this problem. He is of the opinion that the *dharmakāya* can only be realized because it is pure suchness (*tathatā*). His arguments in the **Buddhabhūmisūtraśāstra* fall into three steps. He first quoted from three texts – the *Treatise of Praising the Buddha*, the *Mahāyānasūtrālaṃkāra* and the *Vajracchedikā-prajñāpāramitā-sūtra-śāstra-vyākhyā* – to argue that the *dharmakāya* is pure suchness. Then, he argued that transformation of support itself is suchness.

> The *sūtras* and *śāstras* say that ultimate transformation of support (*āśraya*) is the *dharmakāya*. Here the transformation of support (*āśraya*) is none other than the pure *tathatā*, not a counter path [to *kleśas*]. Thus, the *dharmakāya* has only the pure cosmic *tathatā* as its essence (*svābhāva*).[151]

In order to prevent confusion, he further argued in his **Buddhabhūmisūtraśāstra*:

> It is said in the *Mahāyānasaṃgraha* that the *saṃbhogakāya* is attained through the conversion of other consciousness and the *dharmakāya* is attained through the transformation of the *ālayavijñāna*. This is to say that through the elimination of the two kinds of seed of defilement in the eighth consciousness, the pure *dharmakāya* is revealed. It is not the mirror wisdom, because it is the body of enjoyment.[152]

The problem of realization and attainment of the *dharmakāya* is actually the result of looking at one issue from two different angles. The *sūtras* view it from the angle of the essence of Buddhahood, and state that the *dharmakāya*, which is *tathatā*, is intrinsically pure. Hence, there is only realization. But the *śāstras* view it in relation to the practice of bodhisattvas, which is a process of eliminating the adventitious defilements, and therefore it is an attainment. In other words, the transformation of support is the elimination of the seed of defilement. Yogācārins assert that there is only consciousness, and all other things including the defilements are nothing but an illusion. It is stated in the **Ratnagotravibhāgaśāstra* that there are two issues concerning the realization of the *dharmakāya*: the first is to realize that the essence is intrinsically pure, and the second is to realize that all *kleśas* are originally quiescent.[153] Since Yogācāra also affirms that defilements (*kleśas*) are not real but only an illusion, therefore the realization is said towards the essence of the *dharmakāya*, the pure suchness, while the attainment is said towards to the elimination of the adventitious defilements that cover this pure suchness.

As we have seen, the concept of the *dharmakāya* was fully developed and reinterpreted in the Mahāyāna *sūtras* and *śāstras* in two aspects: (1) philosophical and (2) salvific. On the basis of Mahāsāṃghika transcendental Buddhology, the Mahāyānists reinterpreted Buddhahood and identified the Tathāgata with a new concept that they introduced: *tathatā*, the true nature of all *dharmas*. This is a crucial development in that it provides the doctrinal foundation for the Mahāyāna concept of the Buddha. *Tathatā* becomes the underlying principle of Buddhahood, the *dharmakāya*, in later Mahāyāna *sūtras*. Since this underlying principle is the true and eternal Buddha who pervades the entire cosmos, both animate and inanimate, the *dharmakāya* becomes the embodiment of an all-embracing principle that supports the universe. Thus, at the stage of Buddhahood, it is called *dharmakāya* since it is pure and eternal; at the stage of sentient beings, it is called *tathāgatagarbha* or *buddhadhātu* since it is covered with defilement. It is also called the *mahāparinirvāṇa* at the stage of Buddhahood because it is always in quiescence. This is the philosophical development of the concept of the *dharmakāya*. The salvific aspect of the *dharmakāya* also started in the *Prajnaparamitasutras* although its emphasis is on the intellectual aspect of Buddhism. The **Pañcaviṃśatisāhasrikā* explicitly states at the beginning that the Buddha emits beams of light from his whole body before he teaches the *sutra*. Living beings who encounter this light are said to reach liberation. However, in Dharmarakṣa's translation of Mahayana texts the salvific aspect is enhanced by saying that the Buddha is the *dharmakāya*, which is eternal and can deliver suffering sentient beings through its numerous manifestations. This salvific aspect of the Buddha is further developed in the *Avataṃsaka*, which confirms that sentient beings can find liberation just by seeing the *dharmakāya*, encountering its light or hearing its doctrine. The salvific aspect of the *dharmakāya* is later assigned to the *saṃbhogakāya* and the *nirmāṇakāya* to demonstrate the different ways by which its power is used in the deliverance of the great bodhisattvas and sentient beings respectively.

5

THE ORIGIN AND DEVELOPMENT OF THE *SAṂBHOGAKĀYA*

Introduction

The term *saṃbhogakāya*, denoting the body of enjoyment of the Buddha, first appeared in the *Mahāyānasūtrālaṃkāra* (MSA).[1] According to Habito and Makransky, it was in this text that the earliest systematic explanation of the *trikāya* doctrine was formulated.[2] The concept of the *saṃbhogakāya* was most probably introduced to solve the complex problem concerning the physical body (*rūpakāya*) of the Buddha. It was formulated on the basis of the teachings in the early and middle Mahāyāna *sūtras* such as the **Avataṃsaka*. The *rūpakāya* became the central point of contention between the Mahāsāṃghikas and the Sarvāstivādins when the former idealized the Buddha and gradually came to attribute many supernatural qualities to him. Since the Sarvāstivādins did not agree with the Mahāsāṃghikas that the Buddha had these qualities, they debated the purity of the *rūpakāya* of the Buddha for many centuries. These supernatural qualities were further developed in the Mahāyāna *sūtras* when the Mahāyānists attributed to the Buddha immeasurable merit as a result of bodhisattva practice. This in turn caused other problems concerning the *rūpakāya* of the Buddha for the Mahāyānists themselves, such as the contradiction between the short life-span of Śākyamuni and his immeasurable merit. The controversial points of debate from the early Indian Buddhist schools up to the Mahāyāna revolved around the supernatural qualities of the *rūpakāya*, which were not found in the physical body of the historical Buddha and were not described in the *Nikāyas* and the *Āgamas*. Such controversies probably led the author of the MSA to formulate the *trikāya* theory after having summarized the developments concerning the concept of the Buddha in the early and middle Mahāyāna *sūtras* and *śāstras*.

Some Japanese and Western scholars have made studies of the doctrine of the *trikāya*, but few scholars have addressed the origin of the concept of the *saṃbhogakāya*. D. T. Suzuki was perhaps the first scholar to discuss the origin of the concept of the *saṃbhogakāya* in a Western language. He is of the opinion that the *saṃbhogakāya* is vaguely conceived as *niṣyanda-buddha* in the *Laṅkāvatārasūtra*.[3] However, Suzuki states that the concept of the *niṣyanda-buddha* does not include the idea of enjoyment which is implied in the concept of the *saṃbhogakāya*. The notion of the *niṣyanda-buddha* in the *Laṅkāvatārasūtra* refers mainly to its functions and seems to be quite different from the notion of the *saṃbhogakāya* as explained by Asaṅga. There is a vague suggestion in the *sūtra* that the *niṣyanda-buddha* has his abode in Akaniṣṭha heaven where, after arduous training, bodhisattvas attain perfect enlightenment and become Buddhas. It is evident that the *niṣyanda-buddha* 'enjoys' supreme blessedness in this heaven as a result of his long and arduous spiritual training. Thus, Suzuki thinks that the *Laṅkāvatārasūtra* marks the first step in the systematization and formulation of the *trikāya* theory. But he has not traced the development of the concept of the *saṃbhogakāya* any further.

R. Habito, who has conducted a brief survey of the bodies of the Buddha, is of the opinion that the appearance of the *saṃbhogakāya* is the result of a complex development involving the *Jātakas*, the bodhisattva ideal, the concept of the Buddha's merit, the idea of the existence of many other Buddhas, Pure Land Buddhism and other factors.[4] However, he has provided not a detailed study but merely a brief discussion on the background to the rise of the *saṃbhogakāya* theory.

Takeuchi takes a similar approach to that of Habito but places more emphasis on the bodhisattva ideal. He asserts that the concept of the *saṃbhogakāya* is closely connected with the bodhisattva ideal, which in his view evolved concurrently with the concept of the Buddha.[5] The key aspect of the bodhisattva ideal, according to Takeuchi, is the vow that a bodhisattva takes at the beginning of his spiritual training which is binding until the attainment of Buddhahood. In this connection, Amitābha Buddha is considered a *saṃbhogakāya* for he enjoys blessings in the Pure Land as a reward for deeds arising from his vows in front of Lokeśvararāja Tathāgata when he was *bhikṣu* Dharmākara. However, the actual origin and development of the theory of the *saṃbhogakāya* remains unexplained.

The concept of *saṃbhogakāya* probably originated with the concept of merit (*puṇya*) as a reward for the meritorious deeds of bodhisattva practice. It is said in the **Mahāprajñāpāramitāśastra* (MPPŚ) that good as well as great causes result in great rewards, with reference to the superior light and great power that the Buddha possesses.[6] Thus the merit of the Buddha is directly connected with his qualities and attributes. It is evident from different texts that the more merit the Buddha possesses the more numerous the attributes he acquires, including superhuman attributes. Over time, the image of the historical Buddha gradually receded, to the extent that his superhuman character overtook the memory of him as a human being. More and more emphasis was laid on the merit of the Buddha, as it was thought that the appearance of the Buddha in the world was a rare event.[7] As a consequence of this tendency, the merit attributed to the Buddha gradually increased, and this in turn led to an increase in his attributes which pertain not only to physical but also to supernatural qualities. The *Jātaka* marks the first step in the development of the concept of merit and its accumulation by the Buddha during his career as a bodhisattva. Viewed from another angle, it was the bodhisattva career of Siddhārtha Gautama that became expanded with the addition of new dimensions. The *Jātaka* contains 547 stories which portray the Buddha as a bodhisattva practising the *pāramitās* in many lives and in different forms such as king, Brahmin, farmer and even animal such as a monkey, all prior to his Buddhahood. As a result of all his meritorious deeds, the Buddha acquired the reward of the thirty-two major marks and eighty minor characteristics of a great man.

During the period of early Indian Buddhist schools, a bodhisattva was assumed to need to practise for three *mahāsaṃkhyeya kalpas* before he attained enlightenment. During this long period of time, the bodhisattva would acquire a great deal of merit. The Sarvāstivādins stated that in order to gain each of the major marks, the Buddha performed one hundred meritorious acts; and in order to accrue all the merits required for all the thirty-two major marks, the Buddha diligently practised the *pāramitās* for a further ninety-one *mahākalpas*.[8] Thus it is evident that the merit accumulated during the three *mahāsaṃkhyeya kalpas* is immeasurable. However, the Mahāsāṃghika school took a significant step in enhancing the merit of the Buddha. According to the **Lokānuvartanasūtra* of the Mahāsāṃghikas, 'the wisdom, the merits and the power of the Buddha are immeasurable.'[9] As a result of this assumption, the Mahāsāṃghikas attributed many supernatural qualities to the Buddha and made him a transcendent being (*lokottara*), as discussed in Chapter 3 above. This was a major development in the concept of the Buddha during the period of the early Buddhist schools. Following the line of thought of the Mahāsāṃghikas, the Mahāyānists further added to the merit of the Buddha, saying that he accumulated immeasurable merit during three *mahāsaṃkhyeya kalpas* by practising the six *pāramitās* while ascending the ten stages of the bodhisattva career. As stated in the *Avataṃsaka*, it is in this way that the Buddha attained the *dharmakāya*, a state of eternal and blissful quiescence in Buddhahood. As discussed above, the Mahāyānists considered the *dharmakāya* as the Buddha. However, in its function as teacher to the great bodhisattvas who have one more birth to *bodhi*, it is named the *saṃbhogakāya*. And this *saṃbhogakāya* has all the supernatural attributes of the Buddha as a reward for bodhisattva practice. However, it is not easy to follow the process by which the theory of the merit of the Buddha and his attributes was gradually established. Many problems and challenges were posed by the Sthaviras who adhered to the concept of a human Buddha. In the end, however, all such arguments and counter-arguments contributed to the evolution and establishment of the concept of the *saṃbhogakāya*.

The debate between the Sarvāstivāda and Mahāsāṃghika schools on the physical body of the Buddha

During the period of early Indian Buddhist schools, all schools shared a common understanding of the attainments of the Buddha, namely the *dharmakāya*, which consisted of pure *dharmas*. However, in regard to the physical body of the Buddha, opinions were divided as to whether the Buddha was transcendental (*lokottara*); or in other words, whether the Buddha was physically pure or not. This issue became the central point of contention and debate which mainly involved the Mahāsāṃghikas and their sub-schools such as the Lokottaravāda on the one hand, and the Sarvāstivādins representing the Sthaviravāda on the other. The Mahāsāṃghikas asserted that the Buddha is transcendental and that his physical body is pure while the Sarvāstivādins maintained that the Buddha is a human being and, as a result, his physical body is not pure. The *Vibhāṣā*, the encyclopedia of the Sarvāstivāda school, provides us with information on the content of their debates with the Mahāsāṃghikas.

According to the *Vibhāṣā*, the Mahāsāṃghikas held the opinion that the physical body (*rūpakāya*) of the Buddha is pure and without defilement.[10] They gave three reasons to support their assertion. First, the *sūtras* state that the Tathāgata was born in the world, abided in the world, and yet was not defiled by the worldly *dharmas*.[11] Second, the Buddha had for ever eradicated, without exception, all the *kleśas* and habitual forces (*vāsanā*). Third, the Buddha had cultivated both his mind and his body, and if the mind is pure after completion of mental cultivation, then so is the physical body. The Buddha, therefore, is pure and transcendental (*lokottara*). However, the Sarvāstivādins did not agree with them, and asserted the impurity of the physical body of the Buddha. They also found passages in the early *sūtras* to support their view. They argued that on account of ignorance and attachment, both the foolish and the wise obtain their physical bodies with consciousness.[12] The Buddha was included in the category of the wise and his physical body was the result of ignorance and attachment and therefore impure.[13] The Sarvāstivādins further argued that if the physical body of the Buddha was pure and without defilement, then women would not have loved, Aṅgulimālya would not have hated, Uruvilva Kāśyapas would not have shown ignorance about, and the proud Brahman would not have looked down upon the Buddha. Here the argument of the Sarvāstivādins is that a pure body would not give rise to worldly passions such as hatred, love or ignorance; since the physical body of the Buddha had been the source of these emotions, it was not pure. When they were asked to explain the Mahāsāṃghika quotations from the *sūtras*, the Sarvāstivādins gave different interpretations of them.

The Sarvāstivādins interpreted the first quotation of the Mahāsāṃghikas by arguing that the *sūtras* refer to the *dharmakāya*. 'The Tathāgata was born in the world and abided in the world' refers to the *rūpakāya* appearing in the world; 'but was not defiled by the world' refers to the pure *dharmakāya*. On the Mahāsāṃghikas' second point the Sarvāstivādins explained that although the Buddha had eradicated all the *kleśas*, the *rūpakāya* could still cause *kleśas* in others and hence was impure. On the third point, the Sarvāstivādins explained that the phrase 'the body being cultivated' is said in relation to practice against physical defilement (*rūpa kleśa*). When the body is cultivated, the practitioner enters the path and progresses uninterruptedly until liberation.[14] Thus the disagreement between the Sarvāstivādins and the Mahāsāṃghikas about the Buddha's physical body is based essentially on the transcendental qualities of the *rūpakāya* attributed to the Buddha by the Mahāsāṃghikas.

The disagreement on Buddhology between the Mahāsāṃghikas and the Sarvāstivādins is also reflected in their debates on the Buddha as refuge. According to the *Vibhāṣā*, 'some people (or schools) say that to take refuge in the Buddha is to take refuge in the physical body of the Tathāgata, which comprises the head, neck, stomach, back, hands and feet.'[15] Although the text does not provide the name of the school, according to the **Abhidharmanyāyānusāraśāstra* of Saṅghabhadra, it was the Mahāsāṃghikas. Saṅghabhadra stated: 'The Mahāsāṃghikas again said thus: all the *dharmas* in the body of the Tathātaga are pure and are the place for refuge because the *sūtras* say that the body [of the Buddha] is trained or cultivated (*bhāvanā*).'[16] The Sarvāstivādins argued that the physical body of the Tathāgata, born of parents, is not pure, and hence not a place of refuge. Instead, the *dharmakāya* that consists of the Buddha's fully accomplished qualities (*aśaikṣa-dharma*) is the place of refuge. So the basic argument of the two schools still concerns the qualities of the Buddha's physical body.

In his work entitled the *Origin and Doctrines of Early Indian Buddhist Schools*, Vasumitra provides us with more information on the different views of the two schools concerning the transcendental qualities of the Buddha.[17] According to Vasumitra, the Mahāsāṃghikas and their sub-schools such as the Lokottaravāda attributed to the Buddha the following transcendental qualities. The Buddha is always in *samādhi* and always speaks the Dharma with one voice in conformity with the truth. He neither sleeps nor dreams. His life-span, his physical body and his powers are limitless. Contrary to the Mahāsāṃghikas, the Sarvāstivādins maintained that not all the speeches of the Tathāgata proclaim the Dharma, and the Buddha also uttered words that are not in conformity with the truth. Not all the *sūtras* delivered by the Buddha are perfect, for the Buddha himself had said that there were certain imperfect *sūtras*. Nor could the Buddha expound all doctrines with a single utterance.[18] The Sarvāstivādins again stated in the *Vibhāṣā* that the Buddha slept but had no dreams. It is evident from these statements that the two schools had different views on the qualities of the Buddha. The Mahāsāṃghikas believed in a transcendental (*lokottara*) Buddha, both physically and mentally pure and without any worldly defilement. However, the Sarvāstivādins did not agree with them and held a modified view. They distinguished between the attainments of the Buddha, which are the pure *dharmakāya*, and his physical body born of parents, which is subject to old age, illness, death and other worldly conditions.

The Sarvāstivāda concept of the Buddha met with challenges from other schools, primarily the Mahāsāṃghikas. In an attempt to maintain and strengthen their doctrinal position on the concept of the Buddha, the Sarvāstivādins found further support in the *Nikāyas*. This consisted of the eight kinds of wind which are mentioned four times in the *Vibhāṣā* in connection with the body of the Buddha.[19] The eight kinds of wind are (1) gain and (2) loss, (3) praise and (4) ridicule, (5) eulogy and (6) defamation, (7) joy and (8) sorrow. The Sarvāstivādins asserted that sentient beings pursue the eight kinds of wind and the eight kinds of wind pursue sentient beings. The Tathāgata did not pursue the eight kinds of wind, as he was not attached to any of them, although the eight kinds of wind did pursue the Tathāgata. The Tathāgata was not defiled by the worldly *dharmas*. However, the opposing party, most likely the Mahāsāṃghikas, pointed out many problematic incidents in the life of Gautama Buddha, including those of Devadatta and the Buddha's return with an empty bowl, to indicate that the Buddha, in fact, was also affected by the eight kinds of wind.[20] The Sarvāstivādins disputed that the Buddha became neither delighted, attached to, happy or high spirited when he encountered the beneficial winds such as gain, nor was he worried, hateful, angry or low spirited when confronted with the detrimental winds such as defamation. He was not defiled by the world because he did not become attached to any of the eight kinds of wind, but not because his physical body was pure and without defilement.[21] However, the opposing schools were not convinced by their arguments on the problematic incidents in the life of the Buddha, such as his return from the Brahman village with an empty bowl and the slander by Ciñcamānavikā.

Eventually the debate between the Sarvāstivādins and the Mahāsāṃghikas on the Buddha's *rūpakāya* began to focus on these problematic incidents in the life of the Buddha. These incidents were actually the manifestations of what some deemed to be the bad *karma* of the Buddha. This was later classified into a group with ten sub-divisions, with all probability by the Sarvāstivādins.

The Buddha's bad *karma*[22]

The bad *karma* of the Buddha is more than probably an important historical issue concerning the concept of the Buddha because it is found in all the three existing Buddhist traditions: Theravāda, Mahāyāna and

Vajrayana. In the Pāli canon, the Buddha's unskilful deeds are recorded in the *Pubbakammapiloti* of the *Apadāna* and are also referred to in the *Milindapañha*.[23] In the Chinese *Tripiṭaka*, they are found in ten different texts,[24] while in the Tibetan canon there are at least five texts which to some extent address this matter.[25]

The Buddha's bad *karma* refers to ten problematic incidents that happened in the life of the historical Buddha. They fall into three categories: slander from enemies, assaults from enemies and physical illness. It was probably the Sarvāstivādins who associated different stories with each of the ten incidents and explained them as the remaining effect of *karma* performed in the previous lives of the Buddha. The following is a summary of the ten bad *karmas* according to four main texts in which the full stories are given. These include the *Pubbakammapiloti*, the **Pañcaśatasthavirāvadāna*, the **Bhaiṣajyavastu* of the *Mūlasarvāstivāda-Vinaya and the *Xingqixingjing*.[26]

1 It is owing to the remaining effect of the bad *karma* of his slandering an innocent *pratyekabuddha* in a former life that the Buddha suffered the slanderous accusation of Sundarī.
2 It is owing to the remaining effect of the bad *karma* of his jealously slandering a *bhikṣu* with six psychical powers in a previous life that the Buddha suffered the slander of Ciñcamānavikā.
3 It is owing to the remaining effect of the bad *karma* of his wrongly accusing the sage Isigana of being unchaste, when he was a Brahmin teacher with five hundred pupils in a previous life, that the Buddha and his five hundred disciples all suffered slander when Sundarī was murdered.[27]
4 It is owing to the remaining effect of the bad *karma* of the Buddha murdering his brother for wealth in a former birth that Devadatta threw a boulder at him and a splinter wounded his foot.
5 It is owing to the remaining effect of the bad *karma* of his feeling of joyfulness upon seeing fish being killed in a previous life that the Buddha suffered a headache when Vidudabha killed his kinsmen.
6 It is owing to the remaining effect of the bad *karma* of his cursing the disciples of Buddha Vipasyin, saying, 'These bald-headed *śrāmaṇas* should be offered coarse barley', that the Buddha ate horse barley for three months.
7 It is owing to the remaining effect of the bad *karma* of his killing a visiting wrestler in a match, as a wrestler of a king in a former life, that the Buddha suffered backaches.
8 It is owing to the remaining effect of the bad *karma* of his administering a wrong purge to the son of a respectable man as a physician in a former life that the Buddha suffered stomach troubles.
9 It is owing to the remaining effect of the bad *karma* of his reviling Buddha Kāśyapa by saying, 'Bald-headed *śrāmaṇas*, enlightenment is

difficult to obtain', as a Brahman named Jotipāla in a former life, that the Buddha performed six years of severe austerities.

10 It is owing to the remaining effect of the bad *karma* of his knocking over the bowl of a *pratyekabuddha* in a previous life out of hatred that the Buddha returned with an empty bowl from a Brahman village. This is not mentioned in the Theravāda *Pubbakammapiloti*.

The three Chinese texts also mention another bad *karmic* occurrence in addition to the above ten, but this one is late in origin since it is not mentioned in the *Nikāyas* or the *Āgamas*, or indeed in the *Pubbakammapiloti*. It reads thus: in a previous life, the Buddha killed a merchant during a voyage in order to save others. As a result, he suffered in a realm of hell for a substantial amount of time and as a remaining effect of that bad *karma* he suffered from the wooden thorn (*khadira*).

Except for the *Pubbakammapiloti*, which divides the incident with Devadatta into four and makes the number of bad *karma*s twelve, all the other three texts mention ten deeds.[28] The stories associated with the ten incidents in all these texts are almost exactly the same and even the names of the people concerned are quite similar apart from certain negligible details. This suggests that these ten bad *karmas* originally derived from one common tradition. A strong case can be made that these events were collected by the Sarvāstivādins to support their concept of a human Buddha. Textual evidence lends support to this conjecture.

The texts narrating the bad *karma* of the Buddha can be divided into two groups: those accepting them as facts and those rejecting the whole matter. The first group possibly belongs to the Sarvāstivāda school or at least is associated with it, as the theme of these texts conforms with their concept that as a human being the Buddha had bad *karma* in his previous lives. The second group presumably belongs to the Mahāsāṃghikas, or Mahāsāṃghika-Mahāyāna, since these texts conform with their concept of the Buddha: to them the Buddha is transcendental and above our empirical world, and as such is not affected by any bad *karma*.

First, let us discuss the group of texts which accept the bad *karma* of the Buddha. They are five altogether: (1) the *Pubbakammapiloti* of the Pāli *Apadāna*; (2) the *Milindapañha*; (3) the **Pañcaśatasthavirāvadāna*;[29] (4) the *Xingqixingjing*;[30] and (5) the **Bhaiṣajyavastu* of the **Mūlasarvāstivāda Vinaya*.[31] The last survives in both Chinese and Tibetan translations.

The earliest record of the Buddha's bad *karma* is perhaps to be found in two texts: the Chinese translation of the **Pañcaśatasthavirāvadāna* and the *Pubbakammapiloti*. The **Pañcaśatasthavirāvadāna* and the Pāli *Apadāna* in which the *Pubbakammapiloti* is found are similar yet not identical, as pointed out by Lamotte.[32] The *Pubbakammapiloti* records the bad *karma* of the Buddha only, while good *karma* is not mentioned. The one difference is that the bad *karma* of the Buddha is mentioned at the end of the

**Pañcaśatasthavirāvadāna* while the *Pubbakammapiloti* is at the beginning of the Pāli *Apadāna*.

The **Pañcaśatasthavirāvadāna* mentions an invitation extended by the Nāga king to the Buddha and his five hundred elder disciples to have a meal by Lake Anavatapta (Pāli: Anotatta). It was after this meal that each of the Buddha's disciples described his deeds in former existences in verse. In fact, not all of them spoke, as only thirty accounts were recorded. The Buddha's speech was entirely on his unskilful deeds, and there is no mention of any good *karma* at all.[33] The form of the Buddha's speech is straightforward and very brief.

The *Pubbakammapiloti*, following the same pattern, portrays the disclosure made by the Buddha to the community of monks at Lake Anotatta.[34] This text also *only* relates the Buddha's bad *karma* and makes no mention of good *karma* at all. The form of this text, according to Walters, is the same as that of the *Pañcaśatasthavirāvadāna*, straightforward and brief.[35] Heinz Bechert is of the opinion that the Pāli *Apadāna* in which the *Pubbakammapiloti* is found is derived from a recension of the *Anavataptagāthā*, which is part of the *Mūlasarvāstivāda Vinaya* in Tibetan translation.[36] This strongly suggests that the two texts came from one common tradition. Most probably this was the Sthaviravāda to which the Sarvāstivāda belonged; it was from the latter that the sub-sect of the Mūlasarvāstivāda inherited their Vinaya.[37] The Sarvāstivādins were perhaps the first to have collected all the bad *karmas* of the Buddha and compiled them together in order to substantiate their teaching that the Buddha was fundamentally a human being. This was then transmitted to their sub-sect and also influenced other Hīnayāna schools.

The *Pubbakammapiloti* is the only text in the Theravāda tradition that deals solely with the bad *karma* of the Buddha and its unpleasant results. Otherwise the *Apadāna* is devoted exclusively to good *karma*. In fact, much of the Pāli canonical literature, especially the *Jātaka*, devotes itself to the previous good *karma* of the Buddha. Walters, therefore, thinks that the author of the *Pubbakammapiloti* may have drawn his account from a non-Theravāda school of the 'Hīnayāna'.[38] If so, this Hīnayāna school is none other than the Sarvāstivāda. The *Divyāvadāna* of the Sarvāstivāda, according to Walters, provides us with more supporting information on this issue. The text quite often uses the Sanskrit equivalent term *karmaploti*, usually in a stereotypical phrase in which hungry ghosts (*pretas*) inquire of the Buddha the cause of their fate, asking 'What is this strand of *karma*?'[39] Extremely significantly, in one place the *Divyāvadāna* specifically states that 'The previous strands of *karma* have been disclosed at the Great Lake Anavatapta [by the Buddha who was] with the disciples.'[40] So the Sarvāstivādins knew not only the term *karmaploti*, but also the actual context of the discourse made by the Buddha.

Walters also thinks there is a second possibility that the tradition concerning the bad *karma* may have been constructed by the Mahāsāṃghika since the *Mahāvastu-avadāna* narrates a detailed story about the Buddha being slandered by a woman.[41] This is explained as a *karmic* effect of his former unskilful deed of slandering a disciple of Buddha Sarvābhibhu. However, this possibility can be ruled out because the *Mahāvastu* probably originally belonged not to the Lokottaravāda branch but to another Sthaviravāda school. The reason for this assertion is that scholars like N. Dutt are of the opinion that, over the course of time, the *Mahāvastu* was revised by the Lokottaravādins who added introductory chapters.[42] This is highly possible because many texts were revised and enlarged by different schools over the course of time in order to support their teachings. The **Abhiniṣkramaṇasūtra*, as discussed in Chapter 2 above, is a good illustratation of this point. The text is given different titles by different schools according to their own doctrine. At the end of the text it is said that the Mahāsāṃghikas called it the 'Great Matter' (*Mahāvastu*); the Sarvāstivādins called it the 'Great Adornment' (*Mahāvyūha* or *Lalitavistara*); the Kāśyapiyas entitled it the 'Buddha's Former *Nidāna* or *Avadāna*'; the Dharmaguptakas called it 'Śākyamuni's Former Practice' (*Buddhacarita*) and the Mahīśāsakas the 'Root of Vinayapiṭaka' (*Vinayapiṭakamūla*).[43]

The assertion that the collection of the bad *karma* of the Buddha belongs to the Sarvāstivāda is further supported by the **Bhaiṣajyavastu* of the **Mūlasarvāstivāda Vinaya*. The entire story of the Chinese version of the **Pañcaśatasthavirāvadāna* is found in the sixteenth to eighteenth fascicles of the **Bhaiṣajyavastu*, where the content is the same but with some additional information.[44] In this text the number of discourses made by the elders is not thirty but thirty-five. In contrast to the disciples' discourses, which are all in verse, the Buddha's discourse, placed at the end, as it is in the **Pañcaśatasthavirāvadāna*, is entirely in prose and contains detailed stories. Since this text belongs to the Mūlasarvāstivāda, it must have been shared with the Sarvāstivāda. If this supposition is true, the **Pañcaśatasthavirāvadāna* must belong to, or at least be connected with, the Sarvāstivāda.

The *Xingqixingjing*, the latest in the group of texts that accepts the bad *karma* of the Buddha, probably also belongs to the Sarvāstivāda. This *sūtra* has only ten stories devoted to the ten problematic incidents of bad *karma*. The versified introduction of this *sūtra* informs us that it was preached at Lake Anavatapta at the request of Śāriputra who asked the Buddha why he suffered the ten bad *karmas* such as the slander of Sundarī. The ten stories that follow are all independent works, and each story consists of two parts: a prose and a verse section, the latter repeating what is said in the former.[45] The ten stories are quite similar to those found in both the **Pañcaśatasthavirāvadāna* and the **Bhaiṣajyavastu* of the **Mūlasarvāstivāda Vinaya*. It seems that the author of the *Xingqixingjing* compiled his material from these two texts, the verse section from the **Pañcaśatasthavirāvadāna* and the prose section from the **Bhaiṣajyavastu*. These were then combined into a single work. This is particularly true with regard to the verse section.

A comparative study of the verses in both the **Pañcaśatasthavirāvadāna* and the *Xingqixingjing* shows that the author of the latter has simply copied the verses from the former. For our purposes it will be adequate to give two typical examples, the stories of Sundarī and Devadatta, to illustrate how similar the verses are in the two texts (see Table 5.1).

It is clear from Table 5.1 that the verses in the two texts are almost identical except for some minor differences which are largely because they were by two different people at different times. The last four lines of the *Xingqixingjing* version, which are repeated in all the ten stories in the same manner, are probably an addition by the compiler. One possible conclusion to be drawn from this comparison is that the *Xingqixingjing*, which is the latest and most developed account of the Buddha's bad *karma*, also belongs to the Sarvāstivāda. If our conclusion is correct, the theory about the Buddha's bad *karma* most probably belongs to the Sarvāstivādins of a very early period because the *Xingqixingjing* was translated into Chinese by Kang Mengxiang in 207 CE.

Our analysis of the texts which accept the Buddha's bad *karma* strongly suggests that they came from one tradition, which arguably originated in the Sarvāstivāda school. Its followers collected the stories of the bad *karma* not so much for the purpose of supporting their concept of the Buddha, but to refute the concept of the transcendental Buddha of the Mahāsāṃghikas. Initially, the bad *karma* may have been just a rough collection of the problematic incidents in the life of the Buddha. This collection was later added to the last part of the **Pañcaśatasthavirāvadāna*, which was then incorporated in its entirety into the **Bhaiṣajyavastu* of the **Mūlasarvāstivāda Vinaya* with further additions. This **Mūlasarvāstivāda Vinaya* was then translated into both Chinese and Tibetan. The last stage of development of this theory was the *Xingqixingjing*, which was compiled by collecting the verses from the **Pañcaśatasthavirāvadāna* and the prose from the **Bhaiṣajyavastu*. On the other hand, the Theravāda, influenced by the Sarvāstivāda, added it to the *Apadāna* and it is referred to in the *Milindapañha*.

The second group of texts rejects the whole idea of the bad *karma* and considers it a skilful means (*upāyakauśalya*) of the Buddha to save sentient beings. This group apparently belongs to, or at least expounds the doctrine of, the Mahāsāṃghika. The texts include: (1) the **Lokānuvartanasūtra* which survives in both Chinese and Tibetan translations; (2) the *Pusaxingwushiyuanshengjing*, which survives only in Chinese translation; (3) the **Upāyakauśalyasūtra*, which survives in three Chinese and two Tibetan translations; (4) the **Mahāyānadaśadharmakasūtra*, which survives in two Chinese translations; (5) the **Tathāgatapratibimbapratiṣṭhānuśaṃsāsūtra*, which survives in three Chinese and one Tibetan translations; (6) the **Mahāprajñāpāramitāśāstra* attributed to Nāgārjuna; (7) the **Mahāyānāvatārakaśāstra* of Sthiramati.

Table 5.1 The verses on bad *karma*

The *Pañcaśatasthavirāvadāna	*The* Xingqixingjing
Sundarī's slander	
In a former life I was a man named Wenluo, Who slandered an innocent *pratyekabuddha*. People came and tied the wonderful sage, With shackles and chains [the sage] walked slowly like a dying prisoner. On seeing this *śrāmaṇa* who suffered from the chains, I took pity on him and freed him [by offering] myself [to the authority]. Because of this *karma*, [I] suffered in hell for a long time, After being born in the human world I was often slandered by people. A remaining effect of that *karma* was the slander by the heretic Sundarī in my last life.	Formerly, I was named Pure-eye, an actor to cheer others, A *pratyekabuddha* named Delight-in-Emptiness suffered without a cause.[46] [This man] of pure conduct was harassed by people, Abused and chained he was to be banished from the city. On seeing the *pratyekabuddha* being chained and abused, I took pity and caused him to be freed. Because of this *karma*, [I] suffered in hell for a long time, A remaining effect of that *karma* was the slander today. Now this is my last birth in this world, [I] suffered slander from Sundarī. The *karma* is not to be got rid of or be thrown into space, The three *karmas* should be taken care of and never be transgressed. I myself became the Buddha, the hero of the three *dhātus*, And spoke of my past *karma* at Lake Anavatapta.
Devadatta	
[I] fought for wealth with [one of] my three brothers in a former life, Pushed him down to a valley and killed him with a rock. Because of this criminal act [I] fell into the hell of Taishan, Suffered from poison and severe burning and heat. A remaining effect of this *karma* was that Devadatta threw a boulder at me, The boulder fell down and injured the Buddha's toe.	I killed my half-brother for wealth in a former life, Pushed him down from a cliff and threw a rock at him. Because of this *karma* [I] suffered in hell for a long time, In hell [I] was buried in the iron mountain. A remaining effect of this *karma* was that Devadatta threw a boulder at me, A fallen splinter injured [my] foot cutting the big toe. The *karma* is not to be got rid of or be thrown into space, The three *karma* should be taken care of and never be committed with body, mouth or mind. Now I became the Buddha, the hero of the three *dhātus*, And spoke my past *karma* at Lake Anavatapta.

The **Lokānuvartanasūtra* begins with Mañjuśrī asking the Buddha to expound the *upāyakauśalya*.[47] Then the discourse proceeds to describe each of the major events of the Buddha's life, including his day-to-day activities and his preaching, with the intention of reinforcing the idea that the Buddha's appearance in this world is nothing but a deliberate manifestation. In this text it is held that the true nature of the Buddha is beyond the empirical world, supramundane and transcendent (*lokottara*). The text refers to three of the ten incidents of bad *karma*: six years of austerities, illness and the return with an empty bowl. All these events are interpreted not as the remaining effects of bad *karma*, but as skilful means of the Buddha for the benefit of sentient beings.[48] The text states specifically that all *karmas* of the Buddha are nothing but a display.

> Whatever good or bad *karma* the Buddha performed in previous lives would have retribution in later lives. The Buddha showed people that whatever deed one performs would have consequences. It is in conformity with the ways of the world that he makes such a show.[49]

The text further states that the bad *karma* is nothing but a show: 'The Buddha eliminated all evil deeds and had only merits, but he made a display as if enduring a remaining effect of bad *karma*. It is in conformity with the ways of the world that he made such a display.'[50] Here it seems that the text reacts to and also rejects the Sarvāstivāda view that the Buddha genuinely suffered the remaining effect of the bad *karma*.

According to scholars who have made comparative studies of the **Lokānuvartanasūtra* and the relevant part of the *Mahāvastu* of the Lokottaravāda, the **Lokānuvartanasūtra* also belongs to the Lokottaravāda.[51] However, as Bareau claims, ideas of this kind were by no means exclusive to the particular sub-sect of the Mahāsāṃghikas known as the Lokottaravāda (to whom the *Mahāvastu* belongs), but were the common property of the Mahāsāṃghikas in general.[52] As further confirmation of this assertion, the same standpoint on the concept of the Buddha is found in both the **Lokānuvartanasūtra* of the Mahāsāṃghika and Vasumitra's treatise entitled *Origin and Doctrines of Early Indian Buddhist Schools*.[53]

1 According to Vasumitra, the Mahāsāṃghika and its sub-sects such as the Lokottaravāda maintained that 'the divine power of the Tathāgata is limitless'.[54] The *Lokānuvartana* defines the strength or power of the Buddha in four ways and also states that the power of the Buddha is immeasurable.

> The strength of the Buddha cannot be resisted, one finger [of the Buddha] can shake the Buddha lands of the ten directions. But he makes a show of a feeble and exhausted man. It is in conformity with the ways of the world that he makes such a show.[55]

> The physical strength of the Buddha is immeasurable. Although he never has to sit, rise, stand, walk, lie down or go out, he makes a show of a man who sits, rises, stands, walks, lies down and goes out. It is in conformity with the ways of the world that he makes such a show.[56]

> The strength of the Buddha is never exhausted, it is immeasurable and incomparable. But he makes a show of a man who grows decrepit with old age and needs help from people. It is in conformity with the ways of the world that he makes such a show.[57]

> The wisdom, merits and power of the Buddha are immeasurable. The Buddha makes a show of a man of short life-span and lets people know [the works of *karma*]. It is in conformity with the ways of the world that he makes such a show.[58]

2 According to Vasumitra, the Mahāsāṃghikas assert that 'the Buddha is always in *samādhi*'.[59] The **Lokānuvartana* also states that the Buddha is always in *samādhi* in three ways. First,

> The sound of the thunderbolts of the ten directions in combination cannot move even one hair of the Buddha, but he makes a show of having to be in a quiet place in order to enter into *samādhi*. It is in conformity with the ways of the world that he makes such a show.[60]

Second,

> The Buddha is always in *samādhi* even if he ponders on [such things as] essence and appearance, nihilism and externalism. He only makes a show of a man expounding various kinds of *dharma*. It is in conformity with the ways of the world that he makes such a show.[61]

Third,

> All Buddhas are free from worry and are always in *samādhi*, but they make a show of thinking. It is in conformity with the ways of the world that such a show is made.[62]

3 According to Vasumitra, the Mahāsāṃghikas state: 'the length of life-span of the Buddha is limitless'.[63] The **Lokānuvartana* also maintains: 'The body of the Buddha never grows old and feeble but is full of merits. He makes a show of growing old and feeble and it is in conformity with the ways of the world that he makes such a show.'[64]

Thus the **Lokānuvartana* also teaches the Mahāsāṃghikas' doctrinal concept of the Buddha, as expressed in Vasumitra's treatise.

The *Pusaxingwushiyuanshengjing* (*Sūtra* Spoken by the Buddha on (the characteristic marks of) His Appearance as (the result of) Fifty Causes of the Practice of Bodhisattva) is somewhat similar to the **Lokānuvartana*. It starts with the bodhisattva Mañjuśrī requesting the Buddha to expound the causes and conditions of the Tathāgata's being endowed with the thirty-two major and eighty minor marks. Then the text ascribes the two types of attributes to the fifty virtues of the Buddha. For instance,

> The Bodhisattva in his past lives has never destroyed people's houses, but was rather delighted in building houses. For this reason, the Buddha had the strength of Vajras [gods] and was like the mountains of the four directions, and no one could harm the body of the Buddha.[65]

The text describes the body of the Buddha as free from any unpleasant scent or blemish, and states that no bad *karma* reaches the body of the Buddha. Moreover, flies, bees, fleas and other insects are unable to approach the body of the Buddha, which emits an incomparable beam of light. The Buddha does not feel weather extremes and is not hungry, even without food or drink. This *sūtra* expounds the same concept of the Buddha as the Mahāsāṃghikas and rejects the idea of the Buddha's bad *karma*.

The full title of the **Upāyakauśalyasūtra*, according to Paul Harrison, is **Sarva-buddha-mahā-rahasya-upāya-kauśalya-jñānottara-bodhisattva-paripṛcchā-parivarta-nāma-mahāyāna-sūtra*.[66] This *sūtra* clearly belongs to the Mahāyāna because at the end it states that this doctrine of *upāyakauśalya* is not to be taught to inferior individuals of little merit or to *śrāvakas* or *pratyekabuddhas*. This is because such people have not mastered *upāyakauśalya*, and only the Bodhisattva-Mahāsattvas are able to understand this profound teaching.[67] The author refers to the followers of Hīnayāna schools as a whole by the terms *śrāvaka* and *pratyekabuddha* in contrast to Mahāyānist bodhisattvas. The text also mentions the term 'Mahāyāna' three times.[68] Taking all these factors into account, there is little doubt that the text belongs to the Mahāyāna. As Paul Harrison points out, the Mahāyāna was a pan-Buddhist movement or a loose set of movements. The Mahāyānists were members of a *nikāya*, but not all members of a *nikāya* were Mahāyānists.[69] So the author of the **Upāyakauśalyasūtra* was probably a follower of the Mahāsāṃghika and also an adherent of the Mahāyāna.

The *sūtra* has a similar format to that of the **Lokānuvartana*, beginning with the bodhisattva Huishang (Superior Wisdom) requesting the Buddha to expound *upāyakauśalya*.[70] After an account of the Buddha's sixfold explanation, the text describes each of the major events of the Buddha's life from his descent from Tuṣita until his enlightenment. Thereafter the text deals with the Buddha's bad *karma* to demonstrate that all these events were part of deliberate skilful means (*upāyakauśalya*). All ten problematic incidents of the Buddha's bad *karma* in this *sūtra* are described as skilful means employed for the sake of sentient beings. Their purpose was to illustrate that all actions would bring about consequences. In two places the text mentions specifically that the ten problematic events in the life of the Buddha are not the remaining effects of his bad *karma* but only demonstrations.

> The Buddha told Huishang: 'The remaining effects of bad *karma* manifested by the Tathāgata are ten, and they are all *upāyakauśalya* of the World Honoured One. It should be known that it is wrong to say that the Buddha sat at the foot of the *bodhi* tree and attained enlightenment, that the Tathāgata has an iota of blemish or any shortcomings; and it is wrong to say the Tathāgata has not planted the root of goodness or has not completed the [bodhisattva] practice. It is so because [the Tathāgata] has only the white *dharmas* and no blemish at all.' Sons of good families, the Tathāgata has eliminated all unwholesome *dharmas*, how can the World Honoured One suffer any remaining effects of bad *karma*?[71]

This, of course, is an argument put forward by the compiler, namely that the Buddha would not be a Buddha if he had *any* bad *karma*. The Buddha is named Tathāgata because he possesses good deeds and wholesome *karmas* only. Then at the end of the *sūtra*, it states:

> In summary, the remaining effects of the bad *karma* manifested by the Tathāgata are ten, and they should be known as the Buddha's *upāyakauśalya*. The Buddha made a display to demonstrate that there is a consequence to every action. This is for the sake of the common people who have bad thoughts and revere non-*dharma*, it is not because the Buddha had any bad *karma*.[72]

All evidence suggests that the compiler of the **Upāyakauśalyasūtra* knew of the debate between the Sarvāstivāda and the Mahāsāṃghika on the bad *karma* of the Buddha. The compiler must have been a follower of the Mahāsāṃghika and composed this *sūtra* on the basis of the belief of his school. His intention was either to refute the Sarvāstivāda theory of the concept of the Buddha or at least to present its Mahāsāṃghika interpretation.

The **Mahāyānadaśadharmakasūtra*, clearly Mahāyānist, also mentions the ten incidents and explains them as the secret teaching of the Buddha.[73] Thus it states: 'How do Bodhisattva Mahāsattvas understand the Tathāgata's cryptic words? Bodhisattva Mahāsattvas are skilled in understanding exactly the deep and secret meaning hidden in the *sūtra*.'[74] The text goes on to discuss the bad *karmas* individually through questions and answers.

At the end of each discussion, it asserts that it is incorrect to say that the Buddha suffered the consequences of bad *karma*. The Buddha manifested them only for the sake and sympathy of future generations of sentient beings. This *sūtra* considers the bad *karma* as the cryptic words of the Buddha used for the welfare of sentient beings. Thus, the **Mahāyānadaśadharmaka-sūtra* teaches the same doctrine as the Mahāsāṃghikas on the concept of the Buddha.

The **Tathāgatapratibimbapratiṣṭhānusaṃsāsūtra* is a Mahāyāna text that praises the immense merit of making Buddha images.[75] One such merit referred to in the text is being free from retribution for bad *karma*. Then, a question arises in the text on whether the Buddha himself had made any image in the past. The Buddha had after all encountered many unpleasant events in his life such as the Devadatta incident and his illness.[76] The *sūtra* answers this question by saying that the Buddha did make images in the past and he did not suffer from the remaining effect of any bad *karma*. Had this not been the case, the Buddha would not have expounded this *sūtra*. The *sūtra* states that the Tathāgata has an eternal body, the *dharmakāya*, which is free from *any* bad *karma*, and that those incidents were only demonstrations manifested for the sake of sentient beings.

The *Mahāprajñāpāramitāśāstra* (MPPŚ) mentions the bad *karma* when discussing the power and light of the Buddha.[77] The MPPŚ asks: 'If the power of the Buddha is limitless and his merit is immeasurable, how could the Buddha have suffered the retribution of nine bad *karma*?'[78] The text, in fact, lists eleven problematic incidents. As well as the ten mentioned above, it adds that 'the Buddha suffered from fever and Ānanda fanned him from behind.'[79] The MPPŚ answers this question by referring to the two-body theory formulated by the Sarvāstivādins. The *śāstra* explains that the Buddha has two bodies: the *dharmakāya* and the *rūpakāya*. The *dharmakāya* is the true body which pervades the ten quarters of space. Its form is serene, its features are majestic, it is infinitely radiant, and endowed with infinite speech enunciated to save sentient beings of the ten directions. The *rūpakāya* is the manifestation of the *dharmakāya* as it presents the Dharma to living beings such as humans. Therefore, though the Buddha appeared to suffer backache, stomach troubles and other problems, they were nothing but the skilful means (*upāyakauśalya*) of the Buddha. The real body of the Buddha, in fact, is perfect and without any illness because the Buddha had already eliminated *all* bad *karma*. He had also completed the *kuśaladharmas* when he attained enlightenment. It was for the sake of the community of monks that the Buddha made such displays, perhaps in order for the monks to receive proper treatment in the event of illness. In the same text it is again argued that Anuruddha gained the miraculous power of obtaining food by one thought due to the fact that he offered food to a *pratyekabuddha*. The Buddha offered his flesh to sentient beings for many lifetimes; thus he possessed a great deal of merit, and hence did not suffer from hunger. It was only an altruistic display that caused his return with an empty bowl. The author of the text quotes the *Vimalakīrtinirdeśasūtra* where it is said that Vimalakīrti told Ānanda that the Buddha only made a display of suffering illness. However, there is no such passage in the extant *Vimalakīrtinirdeśasūtra* in Chinese translation. The author perhaps quotes from a different version of the *sūtra*.

The *śāstra* refutes explicitly the assertion of the Sarvāstivādins that the Buddha suffered from the remaining effect of past bad *karma*. The author of the *śāstra* also knew of the debate on the bad *karma* and he refuted the Sarvāstivāda position with the Buddhology characteristic of the Mahāsāṃghikas. Here we have evidence of an ancient historical debate on the concept of the Buddha which lasted for several centuries.

The Chinese scholar Yinshun asserts that the author of the MPPŚ solved the problem of the bad *karma* by formulating the two-body theory.[80] But the *śāstra* has not really solved the problem because its author was skewed towards Mahāsāṃghika Buddhology. Even the *trikāya* theory, which in the opinion of the present writer was a result of an attempt to solve this problem, failed to resolve it for even the *trikāya* theory was formulated on the basis of Mahāsāṃghika Buddhology.[81] That the Sarvāstivādins never accepted the *trikāya* theory is proved by a perusal of the extant literature of the Sarvāstivādins. The Theravāda school, for instance, still views the historical Buddha as an excellent human being.

The last text to be examined on this issue is the **Mahāyānāvatārakaśāstra* of Sthiramati. This text mentions some of the problematic incidents in the life of Gautama Buddha.[82] It states that it is wrong to say that the Buddha suffered the remaining effect of bad *karma*, as he had eradicated all unskilful deeds and had immeasurable virtues. Thus, all the texts that reject outright the notion of the Buddha having bad *karma* are closely related to, or at least endorsed the doctrine of, the Mahāsāṃghikas.

This analysis of texts on the Buddha's bad *karma* suggests that the debate on this matter between the Mahāsāṃghikas and the Sarvāstivādins was a serious historical issue which lasted for several centuries. The main argument always revolved round the question of the transcendental qualities and attributes of the Buddha. The Mahāsāṃghikas maintained that the Buddha was transcendental (*lokottara*) and that all bad *karmas* were displays. But the Sarvāstivādins rejected this argument and maintained that the Buddha did actually suffer from the remaining effects of bad *karma* because he was fundamentally a human being. From this debate, we can see how the early schools disputed the Buddha's identity and compiled texts to support their arguments. This suggests that many *sūtras* may have been composed and written by different schools to support their doctrinal teachings. The problem of the Buddha's bad *karma* led on to the question of the Buddha's short life-span. Discussion of this coincided with the ascendancy of the Mahāyāna in the history of Buddhist thought.

The problem of the Buddha's short life-span[83]

The problem of the Buddha's short life-span is reflected in many Mahāyāna *sūtras*. In *sūtras* such as the **Saddharmapuṇḍarīka*, the **Avataṃsaka* and the Mahāyāna *Mahāparinirvāṇasūtra*, a special chapter is devoted to explanation of the issue.

The problem lies in the dichotomy between the Buddha's great merit (*mahāpuṇya*) and his short life-span. The Mahāyāna developed two closely connected concepts, namely the Buddhological variant along with the bodhisattva ideal. The bodhisattva ideal stresses the arduous training that a bodhisattva endures on his way to Buddhahood. It involves the practice of the six *pāramitās* on the ten bodhisattva stages (*bhūmi*) which take three *asaṃkhyeya kalpas* to complete.[84] According to Mahāyāna, a bodhisattva acquires immeasurable merit during this long period of time before the attainment of Buddhahood.[85] As a reward for such great merit, the Buddha enjoys a long and blissful life with marvellous attributes such as limitless light. However, when the Mahāyānists applied this theory to Śākyamuni Buddha, they found that the historical Buddha lived only eighty years on earth during which time he encountered many unpleasant events. This was indeed troubling to the Mahāyāna adepts. But the Buddha's long life-span had already been addressed by the compilers of the early *sūtras* such as the *Mahāparinirvāṇasūtra*. It states that the Buddha could have lived for a *kalpa* or to the end of the *kalpa* if he so wished, but he had deliberately given up his life at the request of Māra.[86] The compilers of the *sūtra* thought that the Buddha could have lived for a *kalpa*. The Mahāsāṃghikas then built on this idea and maintained that the life-span of the Buddha was limitless. However, Vasumitra's treatise does not offer any doctrinal support or explanation for this position. Kuiji, the commentator on Vasumitra's treatise, understood the Buddha of limitless life-span as the *saṃbhogakāya*.[87] Kuiji was an eminent disciple of Xuanzang, the translator of Vasumitra's treatise. Thus, we may safely assume that to at least a significant extent, Kuiji was in agreement with the view of his master.

The problem of the short life-span of Śākyamuni is mentioned in at least seven Mahāyāna texts: the **Saddharmapuṇḍarīka*, the **Śūraṃgamasamādhi*, the **Avataṃsaka*, the **Suvarṇaprabhāsasūtra*, the **Tathāgatapratibimbapratiṣṭhānusaṃsāsūtra*, the **Mahāprajñāpāramitāśāstra*, and the Mahāyāna *Mahāparinirvāṇasūtra*.

The chapter on the life-span of the Tathāgata in the **Saddharmapuṇḍarīkasūtra* states clearly that the Buddha lives for ever, but for the sake of sentient beings he made a display of entering into *parinirvāṇa*.

> Thus, since I have attained Buddhahood, an extremely long period of time has passed. My life-span is an immeasurable number of *asaṃkhyeya kalpas*, and during that time I have remained here

> constantly without ever entering *parinirvāṇa*. Good men, originally I practised the bodhisattva way, and the life-span I acquired then has yet to come to an end, and it will last twice the number of years that have already passed. Now, however, although in fact I do not actually enter *parinirvāṇa*, I announce that I am going to adopt the course of *parinirvāṇa*. This is an expedient means which the Tathāgata uses to teach and convert living beings.[88]

Thus according to the **Saddharmapuṇḍarīkasūtra*, the life-span of the Buddha is in fact immeasurable and it is only as a skilful means for the sake of sentient beings that he announced his *parinirvāṇa*.

In the **Śūraṃgamasamādhisūtra*, the question of Śākyamuni's life-span is posed by the bodhisattva Dṛdhamati.[89] The Buddha told him that his life-span is the same as that of the Buddha Vairocanaraśmipratimaṇḍitavikurvaṇarāja, who lives in a universe named Pratimaṇḍita in the Eastern region thirty-seven Buddha lands away from this Sāha universe. Then Dṛdhamati travelled to that Buddha by supernatural power to enquire about his life-span. That Buddha replied that his life-span was of seven hundred incalculable cosmic periods (*asaṃkhyeyakalpa*) and said: 'My life-span is exactly the same as the life-span of the Buddha Śākyamuni.' At this point, it is stated in the text:

> Then the whole assembly, on learning that the life-span of the Buddha was so inconceivable, experienced great joy and, filled with astonishment, said to the Buddha: Bhagavat, the supernatural power of the Buddhas is astonishing and all their practices are inconceivable. Even though in this universe [the Sāha Lokadhātu], you manifest a very short life-span, in that universe [the Pratimaṇḍita Lokadhātu], your life-span lasts for seven hundred *asaṃkhyeyakalpas*![90]

It is clear that there were followers who were unhappy about the short life-span of Śākyamuni and this *sūtra* thus addresses the problem by attempting to resolve it.

The chapter on the life-span of the Buddha in the **Avataṃsaka* is very short.[91] It is said that one *kalpa* in the Sahā world, the land of Śākyamuni, is a day and night in the world of bliss, the land of Amitābha Buddha. One *kalpa* in the world of bliss is a day and night in the world of Vestment Banner, the land of the Buddha Adamant. This series goes on through billions of worlds. One *kalpa* in the last of these worlds is a day and night in the world of Supreme Lotus, the land of the Buddha Supreme in Goodness, which is filled with great bodhisattvas such as Samantabhadra. Although the text does not specify the length of the life-span of the Buddha in the world of the Supreme Lotus, it nonetheless implies the infinite nature of his life-span.

In the second chapter of the **Suvarṇaprabhāsasūtra*, which also deals with the life-span of the Buddha, it is said that in the past, the bodhisattva Ruciraketu had made offerings to hundreds and thousands of Buddhas and planted the roots of virtue.[92] He reflected on why the life-span of Śākyamuni Tathāgata was only eighty years. He realized that the Buddha taught there were two causes for long life, namely abstaining from killing and making offerings of food. And the Tathāgata practised non-killing in many hundreds of thousands of *asaṃkhyeya kalpas*. He had also completed the ten good *dharmas* and made limitless offerings of food including his own body, bones, marrow, flesh and blood. While the bodhisattva was reflecting thus, the four Buddhas of the four directions appeared and told Ruciraketu that, in fact, the life-span of the Buddha is limitless: 'Just as the water in the sea is immeasurable, the life-span of Śākyamuni Buddha is, like the height of Mount Sumeru, immeasurable.'[93] Here the author attempts to answer the question of Sākyamuni's short life-span by resorting to legend.

The **Tathāgatapratibimbapratiṣṭhānusaṃsāsūtra*, as discussed above in the section 'The Buddha's bad *karma*', is a text praising the merit of making Buddha images, such as having a long life and being free from illness. In the latter half of Devaprajña's translation, it also mentions the problem of the short life-span of the Buddha. It is stated in the text:

> At that time, in the assembly, there was a person, who had not awakened the mind of Mahāyāna, who doubted whether the Tathāgata made Buddha images in the past.[94] If he did, then why was his life-span so short and full of suffering, his land full of impurities?[95]

The *sūtra* answers this question by saying that the Buddha possesses an eternal body, the *dharmakāya*. It is for the sake of sentient beings that he made a display of illness, not to mention attaining *nirvāṇa*. In fact, the Buddha does not have to undergo all these experiences, while he enjoys a blissful infinite life-span abiding in a pure land.

The MPPŚ mentions the short life-span of Śākyamuni in comparison with past Buddhas. It states:

> Ānanda thought that in the past, Buddhas such as Ratnapuṇḍarīka and Dīpaṃkara were all born in the world at a good time. They had immeasurably long life-spans and benefited numerous sentient beings. Śākyamuni Buddha was born into the world at a bad time and had a short life-span. Can he even save all his disciples?[96]

In another place the text also states:

> The life-spans of the Buddhas are different, some are long and some short. The life-span of Buddha Vipaśyin was 84,000 years,

> Krakucchanda's 60,000 years, Kanakamuni's 30,000 years, Kāśyapa's 20,000 years, but the life-span of Śākyamuni was less than 100 years. The life-span of Maitreya will be 84,000 years. The light of Śākyamuni Buddha is only one *zhang* while the light of Maitreya is ten *li*.[97]

Why was the life-span of Śākyamuni so short? The MPPŚ attempts to answer the question by saying that there are two kinds of life-span and light, one manifested and the other concealed. The manifested form is real and limitless, and the concealed form, which is for the sake of sentient beings, is limited and measurable.[98] What the author was trying to express is that the actual life-span of the Buddha – the manifested form – is limitless and immeasurable. But for the sake of sentient beings the Buddha made a show of having lived for eighty years only; this is the concealed form. The *śāstra* gives four reasons why the life-span of Śākyamuni should be limitless.

1. Saving people's lives is the cause of long life. The Buddha saved the lives of an entire village.
2. Practising non-killing is the cause of long life. The Buddha not only practised non-killing, but also showed compassion for all sentient beings.
3. Bodhisattvas obtain long life through the practice of the *prajñāpāramitās* and other virtues. The Buddha has accumulated great virtues by practising them throughout many lives.
4. Among all types of lifetimes, the life of the Buddha is the foremost.

On account of all these merits, the life-span of the Buddha should be limitless, but in order to instruct sentient beings, the Buddha made a display of either long or short life-spans.

The author of the MPPŚ attempted to answer the question of the Buddha's short life-span with logical arguments drawing support from traditional belief. Mahāyānists frequently sought to reconcile paradoxes in this way, as they did when introducing new ideas by compiling a new *sūtra*. The Mahāyāna *Mahāparinirvāṇasūtra* (MMPS) functions primarily to address this problem, as it concentrates to a great extent on the exposition of the idea that the Buddha is eternal. The text reads: 'Mahākāśyapa said, how can the Tathāgata be considered eternal granted the Buddha's statement "It is like the blowing out of the lamp; the flame cannot be found anywhere; so is the Tathāgata when he entered into *nirvāṇa*."'[99] This indicates that Mahākāśyapa, a representative of the conservative Hīnayāna schools, opposed the Mahāyānist idea of the eternity of the Buddha. Therefore, in the chapter on the diamond body, the *sūtra* states that the body of the Tathāgata is eternal because it is an indestructible diamond body, and a *dharmakāya*. It is not a defiled body sustained by food. Then Mahākāśyapa said to the Buddha:

> World Honoured One, I have never seen such bodies as the Buddha described and what I have seen is only the body sustained by food which is to be decomposed into dust. Why? Because the Tathāgata will enter into [final] *nirvāṇa*.[100]

There are two possible reasons for the appearance of Mahākāśyapa and his questions concerning the eternity of the Buddha's body in the MMPS. First, Mahākāśyapa played an important role in the so-called Hīnayāna *Mahāparinirvāṇasūtra*. It was he who lit the fire of the funeral pyre and witnessed the body of the master being burnt. Mahākāśyapa was also the leader of the Saṃgha after the Buddha's death and presided over the first council. The compilers of the MMPS used him as one of the main interlocutors in order to give the new *sūtra* authenticity as it bore the same title as the Hīnayāna version. A second factor, one of the utmost importance to our study, involves Mahākāśyapa's representation of the conservative Hīnayāna schools. This is illustrated by his question, one typical of early Buddhism, concerning the Buddha's entry into *nirvāṇa*. The simile of a lamp being blown out to evoke *nirvāṇa* is even found in the *Saṃyuttanikāya*. Mahākāśyapa's question on the eternity of the Buddha most probably reflects the general attitude of the Hīnayāna schools in contrast to that of the Mahāyāna when the MMPS was composed. The Sarvāstivādins, for instance, held the view that the physical body of the Buddha was subject to human conditions such as birth, old age and death, as discussed in Chapter 2 above. Hīnayānists such as the Sarvāstivādins must have objected to the Mahāyānist declaration that the Buddha is eternal. Consequently, this question became one of the serious issues of debate and contention between the Mahāyāna and the Hīnayāna schools. Perhaps the former school held that there was an urgent need to compose a *sūtra* in order to address the whole matter in an authentic way.

There were already a number of Mahāyāna *sūtras* in existence which devoted a chapter to the problem of the Buddha's life-span. Before the composition of the MMPS, other *sūtras* had put forward arguments for the eternity of the Buddha, as discussed above. But the compilers or authors of the MMPS must have thought this insufficient, and they composed a *sūtra* to address this problem specifically. This view is supported by the three central themes of the MMPS: (1) the Buddha is eternal because the *dharmakāya* exists for ever; (2) the *mahāparinirvāṇa* has four attributes, but eternity is the core; (3) all sentient beings including the *icchantika* (those who do not have good roots) have the *buddhadhātu* (the potential to become Buddhas). The first theme directly addresses the problem while the second functions to bolster the first. The third theme is a further development of the first two.

The second theme, discussed in Chapter 4 above, is a reinterpretation of the concept of *nirvāṇa* found in early Buddhism. According to the MMPS, the *mahāparinirvāṇa* has the four attributes of eternity, happiness, self and purity. Of these, eternity is described as the most important.[101] This may be explained by the belief that the pure self-nature (*svabhāva*) of all *dharmas* is *nirvāṇa* and this pure self-nature is nothing other than *tathatā*. So the concept of the *mahāparinirvāṇa* means eternal quiescence and thus it is the same as the *dharmakāya*, but represents a different aspect of one Buddhahood. The *mahāparinirvāṇa* is the aspect of tranquillity of Buddhahood while the *dharmakāya* is the eternal principle, the fruit of the same Buddhahood. Therefore, to say that the Buddha entered into *nirvāṇa* does not mean that the Buddha was no more, like a fire gone for ever without trace, but that the Tathāgata abides in quiescence.

The third theme is developed from the idea that the *dharmakāya* is eternal and abides in every sentient being. The *sūtra* states: 'The *buddhadhātu* is the Tathāgata, the Tathāgata is the Dharma, which is eternal.'[102] In another place the *sūtra* explains by way of similes that the *buddhadhātu* in all sentient beings is one and eternal. It is said: 'The *buddhadhātu* of all sentient beings, in the same way, is one and eternal and without change, although [sentient beings] take up different bodies in the *saṃsāra*.'[103] From the perspective of sentient beings, the Tathāgata is the *buddhadhātu*, and from the angle of Buddhahood, the Tathāgata is the *dharmakāya*. So the whole MMPS explains the idea that the Buddha is eternal.

This analysis shows that the short life-span of Śākyamuni became a problem when Mahāyānists began to emphasize ever more strongly the merit of the Buddha as a result of immeasurably long bodhisattva practice. It can be seen that although the *sūtras* and the *śāstras* employed various means to resolve the problem, it remained unsolved since the fact that Śākyamuni lived on earth for only eighty years cannot be changed. However, there is not the slightest reference made to the three bodies of the Buddha in these *sūtras* and *śāstras*. It is most probably the case that they were composed before the formulation of the *trikāya* theory.

The concept of the Buddha in the MPPŚ

The concept of the Buddha in the **Mahāprajñāpāramitāśāstra* (MPPŚ) follows fundamentally the two-body theory of the Sarvāstivāda, and its philosophical tenets are based on Mahāsāṃghika Buddhology, as already discussed in chapters 2 and 3 above. The MPPŚ developed the concept of the *dharmakāya* through the expansion of the notion of the Buddha of the Mahāsāṃghikas. It also assimilated the teachings of the Mahāyāna *sūtras* such as the **Prajñāpāramitā* and the **Avataṃsaka*. According to the MPPŚ, the *dharmakāya* pervades the space of the ten directions with majestic form and limitless rays. Its voice is also limitless, always expounding the Dharma in order to save beings. Two terms are used for the second body in the MPPŚ, *nirmāṇakāya* and *rūpakāya*, representing a transitional period in the development of the *trikāya* theory. One finds that the *kāya* theory gradually tends towards the concept of a body of transformation. There are eight places in the MPPŚ where the two-body theory is mentioned. We shall review these in their entirety in order to have a comprehensive discussion on the implications of the two-body theory.

1 The Buddha has two kinds of bodies: the body of *dharmatā* (*dharmatākāya*) and the body born of parents (*rūpakāya*). The *dharmatākāya*, which pervades the space of the ten directions, is infinite, marvellous and wonderful in form (*rūpa*), with limitless rays of light and boundless voice. The audience [which are the *dharmakāya* bodhisattvas] also pervade space and take birth in different places. They manifest themselves in various forms and under different names and save sentient beings constantly through skilful means (*upāyakauśalya*).[104] This *dharmatākāya* can save the beings of the worlds of the ten directions, but the *rūpakāya*, which endures retribution for bad *karma*, preaches the Dharma in a gradual way just as human beings do. Therefore, there is no contradiction [concerning the bad *karma*] since there are two kinds of Buddhas.[105]

2 There are two kinds of Buddha body: the body produced by supernatural power and the body born of parents (*rūpakāya*). The body born of parents is subject to the law of the world of men, thus inferior to that of the gods. It behaves in accordance with the world of men.[106]

3 The *rūpakāya* is characterized by the thirty-two marks and the *dharmakāya* is said to have no mark (*lakṣaṇa*). While the *rūpakāya* is endowed with the thirty-two major and eighty minor marks, the *dharmakāya* is endowed with the virtues of the ten powers, the four kinds of intrepidity, the four kinds of wisdom of unhindered understanding and expression (*catasraḥ pratisaṃvidaḥ*) and the eighteen exclusive *dharmas* and so on.[107]

4 There are two types of Buddha body: the true body and the manifested body (*nirmāṇakāya*). . . . The true body pervades space with rays of light illuminating the ten directions. It always teaches the Dharma with a voice that pervades the ten directions. The living beings of numerous worlds, as many as the sands of the Ganges, listen to its teaching. . . . The *dharmatākāya* presents the Dharma which is comprehensible only to bodhisattvas in their tenth stage, and all people of the three vehicles cannot understand it.[108]

5 The Buddha has two kinds of body, the body born of *dharmatā* (*dharmatākāya*) and the manifested body (*nirmāṇakāya*) in accordance with the world. The retinue of the *nirmāṇakāya* has been

discussed before, while the *dharmatākāya* has the retinue of countless bodhisattvas who have one more birth to *bodhi*. Why? It is said in the '*Sūtra* of the Inconceivable State of Liberation' that 'when the Buddha was about to take birth [in the human world], eighty-four thousand bodhisattvas with one more birth to *bodhi* appeared as the guiding retinue before the Bodhisattva [the Buddha] walked out. It is like the moon being surrounded by clouds.' Again the **Saddharmapuṇḍarīkasūtra* says, 'All the bodhisattvas appearing from the earth are the family retinue, the great retinue, and the bodhisattva retinue.'[109]

6 There are two kinds of Buddha: the *dharmatākāya* Buddha and the manifested Buddha (*nirmāṇakāya*) that accords with the mental conditions of sentient beings. With reference to the *dharmatākāya* Buddha, it is said that upon hearing its name, one will be saved. With regard to the manifested Buddha, it is said that although there were [sentient beings] living together with the Buddha (Śākyamuni), some of them were born in hell on account of their evil *karma*. The *dharmatākāya* Buddha can do anything and fulfil every wish. Why? This is because in the countless *asaṃkhyeya kalpas* the Buddha fully accumulated all the merit (*puṇya*) and attained unhindered knowledge (*prajñā*). Thus he became the divine Lord of sentient beings, only to be seen by the gods and great bodhisattvas.[110]

7 The Buddha has two kinds of body: the *dharmakāya* and the *rūpakāya*. The *dharmakāya* is greater because the benefit it generates is immeasurable.[111]

8 The Buddha has two kinds of body: the *dharmakāya* and the *rūpakāya*. The *dharmakāya* is the true Buddha while the *rūpakāya* exists on account of conventional truth. In relation to the marks (*lakṣaṇa*) of the *dharmakāya*, it is said that the reality of all *dharmas* does not go and does not come. For this same reason, it is said that all Buddhas go and come from nowhere.[112]

In the above eight quotations, the MPPŚ speaks of two bodies of the Buddha: the *dharmakāya* and the *nirmāṇakāya*. Although the terms used may be slightly different in various places, they denote the same things.[113] The text uses two terms, *rūpakāya* and *nirmāṇakāya*, to denote the manifested body with which the Buddha helps sentient beings find liberation. There are three aspects of the *nirmāṇakāya* as described in the text. First, it is the manifested body born of parents, and subject to the law of the human world. Second, the characteristics of the *rūpakāya* are the thirty-two major and eighty minor marks, which are certainly derived from the Sarvāstivāda school. Third, the retinue or dependants of the *rūpakāya* are explained in the MPPŚ with reference to the historical Buddha. 'Śākyamuni, for instance, had Chandaka as servant, Udāyin as playmate, Gautamī, Yaśodharā and other court ladies as family retinue before he renounced the world, and during the six years of austerities, he had five friends as his retinue.'[114] It is clear that the MPPŚ has developed the concept of the *rūpakāya* as a body of transformation following the philosophical idea of the Mahāsāṃghikas while also assimilating the attributes of this concept from both the Sarvāstivādins and the Mahāsāṃghikas.

The concept of the *dharmakāya* in the MPPŚ is explained in a similar way to that of the *rūpakāya*, in terms of its nature, its characteristics and its retinue. First, concerning its nature, the *dharmakāya* is endowed with the following attributes: the ten powers, the four kinds of intrepidity, the four kinds of wisdom of unhindered understanding and expression (*catasraḥ pratisaṃvidaḥ*), and the eighteen exclusive *dharmas*. Here, the eighteen exclusive *dharmas* are Mahāyānistic. The *dharmakāya*, according to the MPPŚ, is endowed with thirty-six mental qualities in total. But the MPPŚ says that the mark of the *dharmakāya* is no mark. The author of the *śāstra* refers to two kinds of truth in his explanation: 'There are two kinds of truth with regard to the Buddhadharma: ultimate truth and conventional truth. In terms of conventional truth, there are thirty-two marks, while in terms of ultimate truth there is no mark.'[115] Then it is asked in the *śāstra*, 'There should be special marks for each of the ten powers and the four kinds of intrepidity etc. How can it be said that the *dharmakāya* has no mark?' The author replies:

> All pure *dharmas* have no mark on account of the sixteen aspects (*ṣoḍaśākārāḥ*) and the three kinds of *samādhi*, but the Buddha taught the Dharma through analysis in order to make sentient beings understand. However, all Buddhadharmas are empty (*śūnya*), possess no mark (*animitta*) and non-contrivance (*apraṇihita*) as their characteristics. They all enter *tathatā*, *dharmatā* and reality.[116]

The author further states,

> With respect to ultimate truth, all Buddhas are empty and they do not come and do not go. If you [Sarvāstivādins] say that the Buddha consists of the five pure aggregates, then it is empty because it is a product of causes and conditions.[117]

Thus, in the MPPŚ the *dharmakāya* is the true nature of all things (*dharmas*), which is empty, has no mark and does not come and does not go. That is the true Buddha. This aspect of the concept of the *dharmakāya* in the MPPŚ has been developed on the basis of that of the **Prajñāpāramitā-sūtras*, the main theme of which is emptiness, as discussed in Chapter 4 above.

Second, concerning its characteristics, the *dharmakāya* is described as pervading the space of the ten directions with a majestic and marvellous form, limitless rays of light and a boundless voice. It always teaches the Dharma in order to liberate living beings, but sentient beings do not perceive the majestic form or hear the marvellous voice because they have much defilement (*kleśas*) accumulated through numerous *kalpas*.[118] It is only the great bodhisattvas who can see the *dharmakāya* and listen to its preaching. The *dharmakāya* of the Buddha is described in the MPPŚ as follows:

> The body of the Buddha is limitless, and so are his rays of light and voice. The merits of moral discipline (*śīla*), concentration (*samādhi*) and wisdom (*prajñā*) of the Buddha are also immeasurable as it is said in the *Guhyakasūtra*.[119]

This means that the Buddha has a marvellous body with the attributes of limitless rays of light and a boundless voice because of gathering great merit by practising the six *pāramitās* for countless *kalpas*.[120] This aspect of the *dharmakāya* is clearly developed on the basis of the philosophical ideas of the true Buddha of the Mahāsāṃghikas through the assimilation of doctrinal teachings in other Mahāyāna *sūtras* such as the *Prajñāpāramitā*.

Third, concerning its retinue, the *dharmakāya* has the retinue of countless great bodhisattvas who have one more birth to *bodhi*. These great bodhisattvas are the audience listening to the preaching of the *dharmakāya*, who can comprehend the Dharma. These bodhisattvas, in turn, save sentient beings with skilful means (*upāyakauśalya*) by taking birth in different lands, under various forms with different names. According to the MPPŚ, there are two kinds of bodhisattvas: the *dharmakāya* bodhisattvas and the ordinary bodhisattvas who are born of *karma*. The *dharmakāya* bodhisattvas can manifest themselves in different forms and take birth in the world of their own will in order to save sentient beings.[121] The ordinary bodhisattvas take birth in the human world on account of *karma* while the *dharmakāya* bodhisattvas come from either other Buddha lands or Tusita heaven. The *dharmakāya* bodhisattvas have the merit of the Buddha, so they are the retinue of the true Buddha.

The above analysis suggests that the MPPŚ developed the concept of the Buddha on the basis of the philosophical ideas in the early Mahāyāna *sūtras* while taking on the two-body theory of the Sarvāstivāda. It is evident that the concept of the *dharmakāya* as depicted in the MPPŚ possesses many qualities and attributes that are characteristic of the *saṃbhogakāya*. These include the marvellous body produced by merit and its retinue of great bodhisattvas who have one more birth to *bodhi*. It was such doctrinal innovations that paved the way for the appearance of the concept of the *saṃbhogakāya*. This marks an important step towards the systematization of thought in the formulation of the *trikāya* theory.

A solution to the complex problem of the physical body of the Buddha

Habito and Makransky point out that the *Mahāyānasūtrālaṃkāra* (MSA) is the first text which gives a systematic explanation of the *trikāya* theory.[122] It is also probably the first text in which the concept of *saṃbhogakāya* as the enjoyment body of the Buddha is found.

The main object of the MSA is to establish Mahāyāna as the teaching of the Buddha.[123] This is because Mahāyāna has been accused of not being the true teaching of the Buddha by other Buddhist schools. There are at least two Mahāyāna *sūtras* which record this historical dispute. The *Daoxingbanruojing*, the earliest extant version of the *Aṣṭa*, states: 'I don't want to listen to [the teachings in the *Daoxingbanruojing*], because all these are not said by the Buddha, but things concerning matters [other than the Dharma].[124] The Sanskrit version of the *Aṣṭa* puts this more clearly: they are 'not the Buddha's words but poetry made by poets'.[125] The **Pratyutpannasamādhisūtra*, which was also translated by Lokakṣema in the second century CE, says,

> Upon hearing this *samādhi*, [they] are not happy and do not believe . . . but [they] speak to each other, 'What is this talk? From where have [the speakers] heard it? This may be created by themselves collectively and therefore this *sūtra* was not taught by the Buddha.'[126]

Similar statements are also found in the *Mahāvaipulya-dhāraṇīratnaprabhāśa-sūtra*, for example 'heretic saying' and 'not spoken by the Buddha',[127] and in the Mahāyāna *Mahāparinirvāṇasūtra*, 'the teachings of *Vaipulyasūtras* are Māra's teachings'.[128] When Mahāyāna appeared in the history of Buddhism, it was criticized as not being the true teaching of the Buddha. The Sarvāstivāda teacher Vasubandhu, before being converted to Mahāyāna, thought that 'Mahāyāna was not the true teaching of Buddha', and he initially did not believe in Mahāyāna teachings.[129] In fact, he initially composed the *Vibhāṣā* in 1,000,000 verses with the intention of condemning Mahāyāna teachings. When the literary composition was finished, Kātyāyaniputra had a stone inscribed with the following proclamation:

> Those who hereafter learn this Dharma must not go out of the country of Kaśmīra. No sentence of the eight books [*Aṣṭagrantha*], no sentence of the *Vibhāṣā* must pass out of the land lest the other schools, or the Mahāyāna, should corrupt the true Dharma.[130]

At the very beginning, the MSA also states:

> Some people doubt whether the Mahāyāna is the true teaching of the Buddha, and that such great merit [of the Buddha] can ever be

> attained. Now, in order to expel their doubts I establish that Mahāyāna really is the teaching of the Buddha.[131]

In the text, the author quotes from nearly thirty *sūtras* and mentioned some of them by their titles, such as the *Prajñāpāramitā* and the *Daśabhūmika*. Some are quoted in general as 'the *sūtra*' or 'the *yathoktaṃ bhagavatā*' without any specific title.[132] The MSA discusses many topics such as *gotra*, *vijñāpti-mātratā*, *dharmadhātu*, *dharmatā*, *tathatā*, *tathāgatagarbha* and *trikāya*. It is obvious that the author of the text analysed and synthesized the existing practices and theories of Mahāyāna developed and established by his predecessors. On that basis, the author took their unelaborated aspects and developed them into more advanced theories. Among all the topics and theories discussed in the MSA, the most distinguishing theory introduced was that of the *trikāya*. It in fact made a tremendous impact on Mahāyāna Buddhism. The author formulated the *trikāya* theory by establishing a new concept, the *saṃbhogakāya*, as an attempt to solve the complex problem concerning the *rūpakāya* of the Buddha. This theory was so successful that it became one of the pillars of Mahāyāna teaching. In order to clarify this point, we have to examine the author and the background to the composition of the MSA to establish the position of Mahāyāna and its relationship with the Hīnayāna schools.

There is a controversy among scholars over the authorship of the MSA. The original Sanskrit text does not give the name of the author, but merely states at the end: 'mahāyānasūtrālamkare-suvyavadāta-samaya-mahābodhisattva-bhāsite'.[133] However, the Chinese translation mentions that both the text and its commentary (*bhāṣya*) were composed by bodhisattva Asaṅga, while the Tibetan tradition attributes the text to bodhisattva Maitreya and its commentary to Vasubandhu.[134] Although there is no consensus regarding the authorship of the MSA all the arguments are centred on three persons: Maitreya, Asaṅga and Vasubandhu.[135] Maitreya is a controversial figure connected with the legendary future Buddha and hence most scholars express a sceptical attitude to his historical identity.[136] However, Asaṅga and Vasubandhu, who were great Mahāyāna teachers, are real historical personages whose dates are relatively settled.[137] Therefore, they seem to be the more possible candidates for authorship of the MSA.

There are two early sources in Chinese concerning the lives of Asaṅga and Vasubandhu: the *Life of Vasubandhu* translated by Paramārtha (499–569 CE) and Xuanzang's *Datangxiyuji* ('The Record of the Western Regions'). These two sources basically agree that Asaṅga and Vasubandhu were brothers born into a Brahmin family in Puruṣa-pura in North India.[138] They both became Buddhist monks of the Sarvāstivāda school, were later converted to Mahāyāna Buddhism, and wrote many treatises on it. Some of these are available today in both Chinese and Tibetan translations. We can see two pictures from this brief account of the lives of Asaṅga and Vasubandhu.

First, Asaṅga and Vasubandhu lived in an age when the Sarvāstivāda was very influential but gradually declining and giving way to the new and attractive movement of Mahāyāna, which was gaining ground progressively in terms of both followers and doctrinal elaboration. Many new Mahāyāna *sūtras* came into existence and many treatises were written, through which the Mahāyānists reinterpreted many of the concepts in early Buddhism and also introduced many new concepts establishing a revisionist path to Buddhahood.[139] Thus the Mahāyāna attracted many people, including eminent personages such as Asaṅga and Vasubandhu. Such a climate in Northwest India during the third to fourth centuries is also evidenced by another eminent Sarvāstivādin scholar, the controversial Nāgārjuna, who later became a Mahāyānist and composed the **Mahāprajñāpāramitāśāstra*, as discussed by Lamotte.[140] However attractive the Mahāyāna teachings might have appeared to be, they were not accepted by all the Buddhist schools, especially the Sthaviras who rejected and vehemently criticized the new teaching as not that of the Buddha. This situation is clearly recorded in both the MSA and the *Mahāyānasaṁgraha* in which the authors list many reasons defending Mahāyāna not only as the teaching of the Buddha but also as the superior teaching.[141]

We think that the doctrinal conflict between Mahāyāna and Hīnayāna was much more serious than is generally believed because even today the Theravādins do not accept the Mahāyāna teachings on Buddhology or the bodhisattva ideal. The Mahāyāna *Mahāparinirvāṇasūtra* is good evidence for this conflict because, as discussed above, this *sūtra* was most probably compiled to defend the Mahāyāna tenet that the Buddha is eternal. The date of the compilation of the *sūtra* was possibly between the third and fifth centuries, according to Shih Hengching.[142] The *sūtra* quotes from five other Mahāyāna *sūtras*: the **Mahāprajñāpāramitā*, the **Saddharmapuṇḍarīka*, the **Sūrāṃgamasamādhi*, the **Tathāgatagarbha* and the **Avataṃsaka*. The latest of these is the **Tathāgatagarbha*, which was translated into Chinese for the first time by Faju in 290–306 CE, while the first copy of the MMPS was obtained by Faxian in India around 405 CE.[143] So the MMPS was probably compiled before the end of the fourth century, approximately the time when both Asaṅga and Vasubandhu were active in India. In the prevailing conditions, the author of the MSA, as a great Mahāyāna teacher, would have felt a heavy responsibility and duty to compose a work that reinforced the new teaching.

Second, both Asaṅga and Vasubandhu learned and mastered the teachings of both Sarvāstivāda and Mahāyāna. In fact they must have been very familiar with the teachings of all schools, as demonstrated by their extant works. The author of the MSA possessed expertise in the Buddhology of all schools, summarized the existing doctrines on Buddhology including those of the Hīnayāna schools, in particular the Sarvāstivāda, and formulated the theory of the *trikāya*.[144] Therefore, he must have been aware of all the problems concerning the physical body of the Buddha, the debate between the Sarvāstivādins and the Mahāsāṃghikas, and the conflict between the short life-span of Śākyamuni and his great merit as described in Mahāyāna *sūtras*.

It appears certain that the author of the MSA composed the work after summarizing the teachings in the early Mahāyāna *sūtras* in order to establish that Mahāyāna was an authentic teaching of the Buddha. One of the most important issues discussed by the author is the concept of the Buddha, which has become a subject of contention among the different schools over a period of several centuries. The Hīnayāna schools represented by the Sarvāstivāda did not accept the transcendental concept of the Buddha of the Mahāsāṃghikas, the concept that was to form the basis on which the Mahāyānists established their own concept of the Buddha. As a result, the Hīnayāna schools also rejected the Mahāyāna concept of the Buddha. Contemporary Theravādins do not subscribe to the *trikāya* theory. However, the *trikāya* theory and the bodhisattva ideal are two of the main doctrinal developments of Mahāyāna Buddhism. Of the two concepts, that of the Buddha is more important because the main aim of the Mahāyānists is to attain Buddhahood rather than arhatship. To the Mahāyānists, bodhisattva practice is merely a means to this end. The epistemological status of the Buddha was a central topic of all Buddhist schools, for it was naturally important for them to establish their specific concept of the Buddha, the founder of their various doctrines. Therefore, in order to establish Mahāyāna as the teaching of the Buddha, the author of the MSA first had to establish a theory on the Buddha's status. This was vital for the formulation of the remaining teachings of Mahāyāna such as the bodhisattva ideal. It was also important to explain the origins of the Mahāyāna *sūtras* which were not found in the *Āgamas* or the *Nikāyas*, but from which the author expounded the Mahāyāna teaching.

Under such circumstances, the author of the MSA formulated the *trikāya* theory by establishing a new concept, that of the *saṃbhogakāya*. This was advanced to resolve the paradox concerning the Buddha's *rūpakāya*. The *saṃbhogakāya* was established on the basis of the teachings on the concept of the Buddha in the early and middle Mahāyāna *sūtras* such as the **Prajñāpāramitā* and the **Avataṃsaka*, as we have discussed in the previous chapters. The author of the MSA explains the concept of the *saṃbhogakāya* as the body of enjoyment, which is eternal, enjoying the *dharmas* in the great assembly of bodhisattvas.[145] In his *Mahāyānasaṃgrahabhāṣya* Vasubandhu elucidates this point further, stating that the sole purpose of the *saṃbhogakāya* is to bring bodhisattvas to maturity.[146] All the transcendental qualities of the Buddha developed by the Mahāsāṃghikas along with the early Mahāyāna *sūtras*, while not found in the physical body of the historical Buddha or in the *Nikāyas* and the *Āgamas*, are attributed to this new concept, the *saṃbhogakāya*. This includes the second and third aspects of the concept of the *dharmakāya* in the MPPŚ: the marvellous and wonderful body produced by merit and the great bodhisattva retinue. The *saṃbhogakāya* represents the aspect of the Buddha's merit as manifested in boundless light and limitless life-span. It includes many other attributes via the enjoyment of *dharmas* in the assembly of great bodhisattvas. The historical Buddha is considered only a body of transformation (*nirmāṇakāya*) through which he made a show of being born in North India, attaining enlightenment and then entering into *parinirvāṇa*. Whatever bad *karma* or troubles he encountered are considered as skilful means to save sentient beings. In the ultimate sense, Buddhas never suffer. This aspect of the Buddha is designated the *nirmāṇakāya*, which can manifest itself in any form anywhere in order to help sentient beings attain *nirvāṇa*. The *dharmakāya* is the essence of Buddhahood, the realization of the true nature of all *dharmas*, as well as the principle of the universe, and it is therefore the support of the other two *kāyas*. The theory of *trikāya* is so fundamental to Mahāyāna teachings that it is found in many Mahāyāna *sūtras* and *śāstras*, and exerts tremendous influence on Buddhism in India, China and other Buddhist countries.

The development of the *saṃbhogakāya*

The term *saṃbhogakāya* is translated into Chinese in two ways: the body of enjoyment and the reward body. This indicates two aspects of the concept.[147] First, the *saṃbhogakāya* is translated as the body of enjoyment, sharing Dharma with bodhisattvas, when viewed from the standpoint of this function. Second, the *saṃbhogakāya* is translated as the reward body of the Buddha, on account of his long arduous training as a bodhisattva, with regard to the great merit of the Buddha. These two aspects are closely connected to each other and cannot be separated. However, in the later Chinese translations, ever more emphasis was placed on the second aspect of the concept of merit, so that the term *saṃbhogakāya* was more often rendered as the reward body. Makransky has studied the term *saṃbhogakāya* and, after comparing the meaning of the Sanskrit word with the Tibetan translation, suggested that it should be translated as 'embodiment [of Buddhahood] in communal enjoyment of dharma' or 'embodiment for communal enjoyment of dharma'.[148] Here it is clear that Makransky stressed only the first meaning of the term. But according to the MSA, the predominant feature of the *saṃbhogakāya* is the achievement of benefit for oneself, while the predominant feature of the *nirmāṇakāya* is the achievement of benefit for others.[149] In this sense, the *saṃbhogakāya* is the body of enjoyment of the achievement which is the reward of bodhisattva training. However, Makransky neglects the second aspect of the term *saṃbhogakāya*, the reward of great merit. Makransky says that the prefix *saṃ* signifies 'together with' or 'mutual'. According to Monier Williams, *saṃ* is used as a preposition or prefix to verbs and verbal derivatives to express the meaning of 'completeness', 'thoroughness', 'intensity' and 'union'.[150] For instance, in *saṃbuddha*, the prefix *saṃ* means 'completely', 'thoroughly'. Thus, *saṃbuddha* means 'the completely enlightened one'. Hence, *saṃbhoga* means 'complete or thorough enjoyment'.[151] Therefore, when the two aspects of the term are considence, *saṃbhogakāya* can perhaps be translated as 'the body of complete enjoyment of the reward'.

It is on account of these two aspects of the concept that the *saṃbhogakāya* was developed dualistically in later works. The *svasaṃbhogakāya* was developed from the reward aspect of the *saṃbhogakāya*, while the *parasaṃbhogakāya* is developed from the aspect of the enjoyment of Dharma. Thus, the *svasaṃbhogakāya* is the body of enjoyment for the benefit of oneself and the *parasaṃbhogakāya* is the body of enjoyment for the benefit of others. In his **Buddhabhūmisūtraśāstra*, Bandhuprabha states: 'There are two kinds of *saṃbhogakāya*: the *svasaṃbhogakāya* that is accomplished by practising [the *pāramitās*] during the three *asaṃkhyeya kalpas*, and the *parasaṃbhogakāya* for the enjoyment of the Dharma with bodhisattvas.'[152] The **Vijñaptimātratāsiddhiśāstra* further explains:

> The *svasaṃbhogakāya* is the ultimately and completely pure form-body which is eternal and universal. It is the infinite real merit (*kuśaladharma*) achieved through the accumulation of both wisdom and merit during the three *asaṃkhyeya kalpas* of practising [the *pāramitās*] by all the Tathāgatas. It is to continuously enjoy the pleasure of the Dharma for oneself into the infinite future without interruption. The *parasaṃbhogakāya* is the wonderful body of pure merit manifested by the Tathāgatas through the *samatājñāna* [wisdom of sameness]. It abides in a Pure Land, manifests great miracles, turns the wheel of righteous Dharma and eliminates the net of doubts for all bodhisattvas in the ten stages so they may enjoy the pleasure of the Mahāyāna Dharma.[153]

It is evident from these two major works that the merit of the *saṃbhogakāya* as the result of bodhisattva practice is ever more strongly emphasized. The logical outcome is the concept of the *saṃbhogakāya* elaborated in these two aspects, as discussed at the beginning of this section. The **Vijñaptimātratāsiddhiśāstra* explains that the *svasaṃbhogakāya* is infinite and endowed with endless marks and attributes which are the products of immeasurable merit. Although merit and wisdom do not belong to matter (*rūpa*) and the form of the *svasaṃbhogakāya* cannot be measured, it is omnipresent on account of the *dharmakāya*, its realization and support. By the practice of gradually transforming pure consciousness into a Pure Land from the time of enlightenment to the infinite future, the *svasaṃbhogakāya* abides in the Pure Land. It represents the maturing of causes and conditions relevant to the particular Pure Land. The *parasaṃbhogakāya* is also infinite and abides in its own Pure Land. This Pure Land is the maturing of the causes and conditions created through altruistic practice. As a result, the wisdom of equality and great compassion are manifested in different Pure Lands, the size and quality of which change in accordance with one's level on the ten *bhūmis*.

As we have seen, the need to find a solution to the complex problem concerning the physical body of the Buddha is one of the principal driving forces behind the emergence of the *saṃbhogakāya*. The doctrinal foundation of the *saṃbhogakāya* was already present in the early and middle Mahāyāna *sūtras* such as the **Prajñāpāramitā* and the **Avataṃsaka* collections. Contention over the problem first began between the Mahāsāṃghikas and the Sarvāstivādins when the former thoroughly deified the Buddha and attributed numerous supernatural qualities to him. In the course of time, the Buddha was termed *lokottara*. Transcendental qualities such as the infinite and blissful life of the Buddha were further developed in the Mahāyāna *sūtras* as a result of the Mahāyāna's emphasis on the merit of the Buddha accumulated by bodhisattva practice. However, the fact that the historical Buddha lived for *only* eighty years on earth and was confronted with many difficulties proved problematic for the Mahāyānists. The MPPŚ attempted to solve the problem by utilizing the two-body theory of the Sarvāstivāda while doctrinally relying on the teachings of the **Prajñāpāramitāsūtras*. It is stated that the real Buddha is the *dharmakāya* possessing a majestic form with a great retinue of bodhisattvas, and expounding the Dharma perpetually. The *nirmāṇakāya* is a mere manifestation for the sake of sentient beings. It is in such a doctrinal and historical environment that the *trikāya* theory appeared in the MSA, formulated through the establishment and addition of the concept of *saṃbhogakāya*.

6

THE ORIGIN AND DEVELOPMENT OF THE *NIRMĀṆAKĀYA*

The origin of the *nirmāṇakāya*

The idea of the *nirmāṇakāya* most likely has its origin in the idea of the mind-made body (*manomayakāya*) found in early Buddhism. Both are magically created through supernatural power (Skt: *ṛddhi*, Pāli: *iddhi*).[1] The mind-made body is mentioned at least three times in the *Nikāyas*, and it always precedes the description of the six supernatural powers (*abhiññā*), except in the *Poṭṭhapādasutta*. In both the *Sāmaññaphalasutta* of the *Dīghanikāya* and the *Mahāsakuludāyisutta* of the *Majjhimanikāya*, it is stated that a meditator concentrating with a pure mind will be able to create from his coarse physical body another refined body. This created body is made of mind (*manomaya*), its form having all his original body's limbs, and complete with all faculties.[2] The process of mentally creating another body from one's own is compared to the act of drawing out a reed from its sheath, a sword from its scabbard, or a snake from its slough. The *Visuddhimagga* explains that if a meditator wishes to create a mind-made body, he should emerge from the basic fourth *jhāna* (Skt: *dhyāna*), advert to his own body and resolve that the body is hollow.[3] This ability to double oneself is named 'the knowledge of the mind-made body (*manomaya iddhi ñāṇa*)' in the *suttas*. So it is a creation by the supernatural power of *iddhi* attained through the practices of *jhāna*. This is also mentioned in the Chinese **Dīrghāgama*, but in a different *sūtra* which corresponds to the *Ambatthasutta* of the *Dīghanikāya*.[4] The description of supernatural power and even the similes used are exactly the same as in the Pāli version.

The *Poṭṭhapādasutta* of the *Dīghanikāya* also mentions the mind-made body as one of the three modes of existence, namely: the material (*oḷārika*), the immaterial (*manomaya*) and the formless (*arūpo atta-paṭilābho*).[5] The mind-made body belongs to the second mode. It possesses a form with all greater and lesser limbs complete and all organs perfect. Buddhaghosa explains that this second mode of existence corresponds to the realm of form (*rūpabhava*), which in turn is equated to the sixteen worlds of the

Brahman gods, and is attained by the practice of the four ecstasies (*jhāna*).[6] However, it seems that this mind-made body is produced not by the power of *iddhi* but by virtue of conduct.

The power of *iddhi* is also the first of the six kinds of direct knowledge (*abhiññā*): called the *iddhividhañāṇa*, it is the knowledge of the modes of supernatural power.[7] Under the power of *iddhi*, eight kinds of magic power are mentioned and the first one is 'having been one, he becomes many; having been many he becomes one'.[8] In the *Visuddhimagga*, Buddhaghosa explains that to exercise this kind of psychic power, the meditator should enter the fourth *jhāna* as a basis for direct knowledge and emerge from it. Then he must resolve on the number of forms he wishes to create. He again attains the fourth *jhāna*, emerges and resolves. Thus, he can create as many as 'a hundred, or a thousand forms' akin to himself which perform the same actions as the original form.[9] This magical power of self-multiplication as the first of the six supernatural powers (*abhijñā*) is also mentioned in both the Chinese **Dīrghāgama* and the **Ekottarāgama*.[10]

According to the *Sāmaññaphalasutta*, the attainment of the first direct knowledge is higher than the attainment of 'the knowledge of the mind-made body (*manomaya iddhi ñāṇa*)'.[11] This is why the *suttas* always mention the mind-made body first, as the compilers describe spiritual attainments in ascending order. The *iddhi* power of the mind-made body can create only one body at a time while the *iddhi* power of the *iddhividhañāṇa* can create as many bodies as one wishes. Of course, the *suttas* only mention 'many' and not 'a hundred, or a thousand' as does the post-canonical work of the *Visuddhimagga*.

The *Paṭisambhidāmagga* describes another supernatural power of *iddhi* which is called the power of transformation (*vikubhaṇa iddhi*). The text reads as follows:

> He abandons his normal appearance and shows the appearance of a boy or the appearance of a *nāga*, the appearance of a *supanna* [winged demon], the appearance of an *aśura*, the appearance of the ruler [Indra] of the gods, the appearance of some deities, the appearance of a Brahmā, the appearance of the sea, the appearance of a rock, the appearance of a lion, the appearance of a tiger, the appearance of a leopard; he manifests as an elephant, he manifests as a horse, he manifests as a chariot, he manifests as a foot soldier, or he manifests as a manifold military array.[12]

This is obviously a further development on the basis of the *iddhi* power discussed above, since through the power of transformation (*vikubhaṇa iddhi*) the meditator not only creates many human forms but also transforms himself into whatever form he wishes, for example a god or a lion. This kind of supernatural power of self-transformation is not explicitly mentioned in the *suttas*, but it is implied in certain quotations. The *Mahāparinibbāṇasutta*, for instance, states that the Buddha used this power to transform himself into the appearance of whatever audiences he was addressing, such as Brahmins, householders, various categories of *devas*.[13] This idea is much closer to the idea of *nirmāṇakāya*. However, this *iddhi* is not exclusive to the Buddha alone, but is available to all his disciples as well as the *śrāmaṇas* of other Indian traditions with some attainment of *jhāna*. Devadatta, for instance, is described in the **Ekottarāgama* as having changed himself into the form of a small boy through the power of *ṛddhi* and then changed back to his original form again in the presence of Prince Ajātaśatru.[14]

It should be noted that in the *Yogācārabhūmiśāstra*, the *nirmāṇakāya* is also described in the first of six supernatural powers (*abhijñā*). The text states that the Buddhas and bodhisattvas are able to manifest themselves in different bodies (*nirmāṇakāya*), different voices and different objects for the sake of sentient beings.[15] In the **Buddhagotraśāstra*, Vasubandhu also states that the *nirmāṇakāya* is manifested through *dhyāna*.[16] There is an important similarity between the *nirmāṇakāya* and the magically created body, whether it be a mind-made body or a creation of the first of the six *abhijñās*. They are all produced by the supernatural power of *ṛddhi* obtained through *dhyāna*. In fact, the concept of the *nirmāṇakāya* includes all the variations of the created bodies found in early Buddhism: self-multiplication and self-transformation. Through self-multiplication, the Buddha can create infinite *nirmāṇakāyas* in the form of a Buddha and through self-transformation he can transform himself into whatever shape he wishes to take, such as *nirmāṇakāyas* in animal forms.

The supernatural power of *ṛddhi*, which plays a key role in creating magical bodies, is still mundane. In early Buddhism the *rūpakāya* of the Buddha was never conceived as a product of the power of *ṛddhi*. Even the modern Theravādins and the Sarvāstivādins of yore never thought that Śākyamuni was magically arisen. It is perhaps the Mahāsāṃghikas who, taking the idea of the mind-made body, first conceived the idea that the historical Buddha, as a *rūpakāya*, was a magical creation for the sake of sentient beings, while the true Buddha was eternal and omniscient.

The **Lokānuvartanasūtra* states that every act of the Buddha is a display for the sake of sentient beings. In reality the Buddha is unaffected by any worldly conditions such as illness and other forms of suffering. It mentions specifically that the Buddha can manifest himself in numerous bodies and appear in countless Buddha lands, but the body of the Buddha neither increases nor decreases.[17] Therefore, with Mahāsāṃghikas, terms like *rūpakāya* and *nirmāṇakāya* have a congruent reference. However, the term *nirmāṇakāya* does not occur in the literature of the Mahāsāṃghika.

The development of the *nirmāṇakāya*

The formulation of the nirmāṇakāya

From the very beginning, the Mahāyānists accepted the Buddhology of the Mahāsāṃghikas in its entirety, as shown in Chapter 4 above. However, early Mahāyāna *sūtras* such as the **Prajñāpāramitā* rarely use terms such as *rūpakāya* or *nirmāṇakāya*. The *Aṣṭa*, for instance, narrates that bodhisattva Sadāprarudita saw a magically produced Buddha with a wonderful body endowed with the thirty-two marks when he was cultivating the *prajñāpāramitā*. That Buddha instructed him to go to the east to learn the *prajñāpāramitā*; once there he met the bodhisattva Dharmodgata.[18] Here the idea of *nirmāṇakāya* is expressed but the term is not used. In the Chinese translation of the **Pañcaviṃśatisāhasrikā Prajñāpāramitā*, there is a discussion between the Buddha and Subhūti concerning the created Tathāgata.[19] Subhūti asked the Buddha what the difference was between the real Tathāgata and the created one. The Buddha taught Subhūti that there was no difference as they both performed the same function. Subhūti next asked whether the created Tathāgata functioned independently. The Buddha replied in confirmation and to illustrate this point, the Buddha told Subhūti that there was a Buddha named Suśānta in the past. Suśānta magically created another Buddha who lived for a *kalpa* instructing people in bodhisattva practice after he entered *parinirvāṇa*. People did not know that it was only a magically created Buddha. Subhūti asked whether making offerings to the real Tathāgata earned different merit from offerings to the created one. The Buddha replied that there was no difference as all merits lead to the cessation of suffering.

The important point in this dialogue is that the magically manifested Buddha performs acts for the sake of sentient beings in exactly the same way as the actual Buddha. In later Mahāyāna *sūtras* these acts for the sake of sentient beings are called the *karma* of the Buddha performed through the *nirmāṇakāya*. Thus the concept of the *nirmāṇakāya* was formulated in terms of a created Buddha, and not a created body. It was not until the third century with Dharmarakṣa's translation of the *Rulaixingxianjing* ('*Sūtra* on the Appearance of the Tathāgata'), which corresponds to chapter thirty-two (on the appearance of the Ratnarājā Tathāgata) of the **Avataṃsaka*, that the term *nirmāṇakāya* with full connotations appeared.[20]

The text states:

> Tathāgata, representing ultimate reality, is the great king of Dharma by his supreme wisdom, and always enjoys the pleasure of the Dharma through manifestations. The nature [of the Tathāgata] is quiescence spread all over the cosmos (*dharmadhātu*). The cloud of

> the *dharmakāya* pervades everywhere and manifests itself [in different bodies] in accordance with the inclination of sentient beings. Sometimes, he manifests the body of supreme enlightenment for sentient beings and pours down the rain of Dharma. He also manifests the *nirmāṇakāya* and showers the Dharma rain. He may also manifest the constructed body (*samāropa*?) and bring down the Dharma rain. Or he manifests the *rūpakāya* and rains various grades of the Dharma rain. Or he manifests the body of merit and rains the Dharma rain. Or he manifests the wisdom body and rains, or manifests a body in accordance with the situation [of the beings to be saved].[21]

This passage is important in that it describes the *buddhakāya* as having two aspects. First, it includes the *dharmakāya* as the real Buddha pervading the cosmos. Second, it includes the various kinds of bodies manifested in accordance with the inclination of sentient beings. Concerning the manifested bodies, the text lists several types, the *nirmāṇakāya* being one of them. It should be noted that the *Rulaixingxianjing* is perhaps one of the earliest texts in which the term *nirmāṇakāya* is found because the terms used for the manifested bodies are not merged into one fixed concept. But among them, the term *nirmāṇakāya* is the most appropriate because it encompasses all the variations and differences of the manifested bodies. The idea of the manifested bodies developed gradually and matured finally in the **Avataṃsaka* where the ten Buddha bodies were formulated. This will be discussed in the next chapter.

In the **Avataṃsaka*, the term *nirmāṇakāya* became widely used and its ramifications were made clear. For instance, the *sūtra* states:

> When Buddhas appear in different worlds, they establish sentient beings in the reality of truth through the Door of Wisdom by manifesting inconceivable Tathāgata *nirmāṇakāyas* and illuminating infinite Buddha lands and Dharma realms.[22]

> The Tathāgata has a mark of the great man named the Wheel Cloud of Pure Dharma Illumination. . . . Immeasurable *nirmāṇakāyas* of the Tathāgata are born from it.[23]

The Buddha, according to the **Avataṃsaka*, can manifest an ocean of *nirmāṇakāyas* even from one pore of his bodily hairs, which fill up the whole universe.[24] Each of these inconceivable *nirmāṇakāya* manifestations is endowed with the infinite light of wisdom as well as all the major marks, just like the great bodhisattva Samantabhadra.[25] The *nirmāṇakāyas* always expound Dharma according to the inclination of sentient beings.[26] Sometimes they teach sentient beings various types of bodhisattva practice through example and even manifest great *nirvāṇa* for the sake of suffering beings.[27]

In another section, the **Avataṃsaka* states that the Buddha can create as many bodies as atoms of infinite Buddha lands from each pore of his bodily hairs at every thought moment. These *nirmāṇakāyas* of the Tathāgata turn the wheel of Dharma like a wheel of fire.[28] They eliminate all the doubts of sentient beings by taming them and adorning them with Mahāyāna wisdom. They illuminate all *dharmas*, open up all the treasure of Dharma, preach bodhisattva practices, and make complete the sun of wisdom of the Mahāyāna.

In the chapter on 'The Entry into the Universe' of the **Avataṃsaka*, the *sūtra* states that Śākyamuni was Vairocana Buddha who descended from Tuṣita heaven and took abode in the womb of Mahāmāyā.[29] The **Brahmajālasūtra*, which is the Vinaya text of bodhisattvas, states that Śākyamuni was originally named Vairocana, abiding in a lotus platform with a thousand petals. He manifests a thousand Śākyamunis, one in each of the petal worlds in which there are a hundred million Sumerus, a hundred million suns and moons, a hundred million Jambudvīpas and a hundred million Śākyamunis sitting under the *bodhi* tree preaching the bodhisattva doctrine.[30] In this *sūtra*, Śākyamuni is considered the *nirmāṇakāya* of Vairocana. As previously discussed, the Mahāsāṃghikas already believed that Śākyamuni was not the real Buddha but a manifestation through skilful means for the sake of sentient beings. It is only in the **Brahmajālasūtra* that Śākyamuni is named the *nirmāṇakāya*. The **Mahāprajñāpāramitāśāstra* expresses this point in explicit terms. It states,

> When a bodhisattva attains complete enlightenment, he can manifest a short or long life-span in accordance with the life-span of beings to be saved in various lands. Śākyamuni, for instance, lived only around a hundred years in this Sahā world, while in the World of Adornment he lived for seven hundred *asaṃkhyeya kalpas*.[31]

Śākyamuni is thus considered the *nirmāṇakāya* of Vairocana while Vairocana is considered the *saṃbhogakāya* of Śākyamuni. Quoting from a *sūtra* entitled 'The Chapter on the Thirty-Third Heaven',[32] the *sūtra* states that in the east there are numerous Buddhas in different worlds, some are adorned with gold and full of *arhats*, some adorned with silver and full of *pratyekabuddhas*, while some are adorned with the seven precious objects and full of irreversible bodhisattvas. All these Buddhas are different manifestations of Śākyamuni.[33]

The relationship between the *dharmakāya* and the *nirmāṇakāya* is compared in the **Avataṃsaka* to the moon and its reflections in different waters.[34] The moon is only one, but its reflections are numerous. First, although the *dharmakāya* is the same in all Buddhas, the *nirmāṇakāya* can be numerous and manifest in various forms in different Buddha lands. Second, the *dharmakāya* is always in quiescence without birth and death, rise and fall, but the *nirmāṇakāya* displays various acts such as birth, enlightenment and *parinirvāṇa* for the sake of sentient beings. Third, the *dharmakāya* does not differentiate and is the same to all, but the *nirmāṇakāyas* are manifested in accordance with the inclination of sentient beings. The *nirmāṇakāya* can have long or short life-spans, possess different light, and appear in different forms. For instance, Amitābha has an infinite life-span and possesses limitless light while Śākyamuni lived only eighty years on earth.[35] The *nirmāṇakāya* is thus a channel through which the *dharmakāya*, the real Buddha in Mahāyāna Buddhism, performs the Buddha activities (*karma*) by skilful means.

The **Saṃdhinirmocanasūtra*, along the line of thought of the **Avataṃsaka*, further explains that the *nirmāṇakāya* is the reflection of the light of wisdom of the *dharmakāya* which is attained through the practice of the perfections (*pāramitā*) and skilful means. But *śrāvakas* and *pratyekabuddhas*, who have only the body of *vimokṣa*, do not have such attributes.[36] Here, it is in the **Saṃdhinirmocanasūtra* that the distinction is made between the Buddhas and the *śrāvakas* and the *pratyekabuddhas* concerning the *nirmāṇakāya*. It is only the Buddhas who possess *nirmāṇakāyas*, in contrast with the *śrāvakas* and *pratyekabuddhas* because they do not have such great merit.

The development of the nirmāṇakāya

After its formation, the concept of the *nirmāṇakāya* was further developed mainly by the Yogācāra school. The **Saṃdhinirmocanasūtra*, which is a major text of this school, explains that the major characteristic of the *nirmāṇakāya* is its function in the preservation of the Dharma in the world through skilful means.[37] Through *nirmāṇakāyas*, all Tathāgatas perform Buddha deeds of preaching the Dharma to liberate sentient beings in conformity with the ways of the world. The *nirmāṇakāya* is manifested in the world in the following ways: entering the womb, being born in the family of a king or a family with great merit, indulging in desire, leaving home, practising asceticism, and attaining perfect enlightenment after abandoning asceticism. It is obvious that the *sūtra* takes the life of Śākyamuni, the historical Buddha, as an example to illustrate the skilful means of the *nirmāṇakāya*.

The **Yogācārabhūmiśāstra* explains the manifestations of the *nirmāṇakāya* in detail and states that the Buddhas and bodhisattvas perform activities for sentient beings in three ways through magically produced bodies, objects and voices.[38] First, the Buddhas and bodhisattvas can manifest various forms of *nirmāṇakāyas* in infinite worlds of the ten directions to benefit countless sentient beings. Some *nirmāṇakāyas* preserve the Dharma by teaching it, while others disappear after the completion of the activities of bringing beings to spiritual maturity. Second, Buddhas and bodhisattvas can produce various objects miraculously, such as food, cloth, vehicles and even jade for sentient beings to enjoy. Third, Buddhas and bodhisattvas can manifest voices miraculously either through *nirmāṇakāyas*, through the air, or through any inanimate object. These voices always teach sentient beings the Dharma that not only augments pure faith in the ignorant, but also makes indolent people remorseful and inspires them to practise diligently.

One may feel that there is not much difference between the *dharmakāya* and the *nirmāṇakāya* since the latter is only a reflection of the former. Hence there is no need for the existence of a *nirmāṇakāya*. It is probably to refute this kind of thought that Asaṅga lists eight reasons for the existence of the *nirmāṇakāya* in his *Mahāyānasaṃgraha*. If there is no *nirmāṇakāya*:

1 it is not possible for those bodhisattvas who have long since obtained irreversible concentration to be born in Tuṣita heaven or among men;
2 it is not possible that those bodhisattvas who have long since remembered their previous births should not have complete understanding of writing, calculation, mathematics, illustrations, crafts, scholarship and the enjoyment of and indulgence of sensual desire;
3 it is not possible that those who have long since understood the difference between good and bad presentations of doctrines should take heretics as their masters;
4 it is not possible that those who have understood the excellent doctrine concerning the path of the three vehicles should practise asceticism;
5 it is not possible that, upon leaving behind a hundred million Jambudvīpas, a bodhisattva should realize complete awakening and set in motion the wheel of doctrine at only a single location;
6 If, without manifesting the skilful method of complete awakening, a bodhisattva were to perform the activities of a Buddha in the other Jambudvīpas by means of bodies of transformation, then he might also attain complete awakening in Tuṣita heaven;
7 Why can one not admit that a Buddha appears in all Jambudvīpas at the same time? No sacred text or argument invalidates this assertion;
8 The doctrine of a multiplicity of bodies of transformation does not contradict the sacred text, which says that two Tathāgatas do not arise in the same world since the term 'world' in the text indicates the four continents of a single Jambudvīpa and not a trichiliocosm.[39]

The first five reasons provide a summary of the career of the historical Buddha, while the last three reasons reflect a debate on two issues. These – as has been pointed out by Paul Griffiths and others – are the question of the multiplicity of Buddhas and of the reconciliation of it with the tradition that there is only one Buddha in one world system at a given time. This, in fact, reflects the debate on Mahāyāna Buddhology between the Mahāyānists and the Sarvāstivādins, as discussed in Chapter 4 above. The Hīnayānists refused to accept the idea that Śākyamuni was only a *nirmāṇakāya* while the

Buddha is transcendental. This debate is also reflected in another discussion concerning the *nirmāṇakāya*.

In his *Mahāyānasaṃgraha* Asaṅga lists six reasons why Buddhas do not remain permanently in their *nirmāṇakāyas*:

1 on completion of their activities in delivering sentient beings who need to be brought to maturity;
2 to prevent a lack of desire for cessation caused by desire for the Buddha's eternal body;
3 to prevent disrespect towards the Buddha caused by lack of understanding of the teaching of the profound doctrine;
4 to arouse longing for the Buddha, lest those who see him continually take him for granted;
5 to induce sentient beings to develop personal effort as they no longer have the teacher among them;
6 to induce those under training to reach maturity quickly by not abandoning their own efforts.[40]

These reasons actually form a continuous argument to support the statement that the *nirmāṇakāya* is different from the *dharmakāya*. The *Mahāyānasaṃgraha* explains that it is not possible that Buddhas enter *parinirvāṇa* without working for sentient beings after enlightenment because it contradicts their original vows and practices. In their initial stage as bodhisattvas Buddhas made vows to benefit sentient beings. Therefore the *nirmāṇakāya* is a necessary means for Buddhas to perform the activities they pledged and to appear repeatedly in the world for the benefit of sentient beings.[41] According to the *Mahāyānasaṃgraha*, the *nirmāṇakāya* performs eight acts in the world in order to benefit sentient beings. They include descending from Tuṣita heaven, being born, indulging in desire, leaving home, practising various forms of asceticism, attaining great enlightenment, turning the wheel of Dharma, and entering *parinirvāṇa*.[42]

In his **Buddhagotraśāstra*, Vasubandhu states that the *nirmāṇakāya* has great compassion (*mahākaruṇā*) as its essence, ecstasy (*dhyāna*) as the basis for manifestation, and five kinds of capability through wisdom (*prajñā*). The five kinds of capability are the following: (1) making sentient beings feel aversion to *saṃsāra*; (2) facilitating their entry into the noble path; (3) making them abandon their attachment; (4) making them believe in the great Dharma; and (5) making predictions (*vyākaraṇa*) on their great enlightenment (*bodhi*).[43] This text says that Buddhas manifest fourteen acts in the defiled world through the *nirmāṇakāya*. These are their different births (*jātaka*), ascending to and descending from Tuṣita heaven, entering the womb, taking birth, learning skills, being a playful boy, leaving home, practising asceticism, coming to the *bodhi* tree, defeating Māra, attaining enlightenment, turning the wheel of Dharma, entering *parinirvāṇa*.

These are the activities of the *nirmāṇakāya* through which sentient beings are helped to become mature. It is clear that these fourteen activities are a further expansion of the eight acts in the *Mahāyānasaṃgraha*. They are modelled on the life of Śākyamuni who is considered a *nirmāṇakāya* by the Mahāyānists.

In the same work, Vasubandhu also states that the *nirmāṇakāya* has three aspects.

1 It is like the reflections of the moon in different waters.
2 It is produced by the power (of *dhyāna*) through the original vows.
3 It has a beginning as well as an end, for the *nirmāṇakāya* is manifested in accordance with specific conditions.[44]

After the formulation of the *trikāya* theory, the concept of the *nirmāṇakāya* was further developed by assimilating the ideas of Buddha lands and the bodhisattva ideal. The *nirmāṇakāya* is described as living in either a pure or an impure land, for the maturing of ordinary people, *śrāvakas*, *pratyekabuddhas*, as well as bodhisattvas who have not yet entered into the *bhūmis*. The **Buddhabhūmisūtraśāstra* states that the *nirmāṇakāya* has the characteristic of magical manifestation and it has the mastery of transformation through which all altruistic acts are accomplished. Produced by pure *karma*, the *nirmāṇakāya* lives in either pure or impure lands, manifests in various forms and teaches various *dharmas*. It brings ordinary bodhisattvas, *śrāvakas*, *pratyekabuddhas* and sentient beings to maturity. It allows them to enter the *bhūmis* and leave the three realms (*dhātu*) as well as the suffering states (*durgati*).[45]

The **Vijñaptimātratāsiddhiśāstra* also states:

> The *nirmāṇakāya* means that the Tathāgatas, through the Wisdom of Fulfilment of Deeds (*kṛtyānuṣṭhāna-jñāna*), manifests infinite bodies of transformation in accordance with the types [of sentient beings]. It lives in either pure or impure land, preaches the Dharma and displays supernatural powers for bodhisattvas who have not entered the *bhūmis*, *śrāvakas* and *pratyekabuddhas* as well as sentient beings in accordance with their inclinations. It benefits them with various things.[46]

Two kinds of *nirmāṇakāya* are distinguished in the above descriptions: (1) the *nirmāṇakāya* in the form of a Buddha with the thirty-two major and eighty minor marks for saving *pṛthagjanas* (human beings), *śrāvakas* and *pratyekabuddhas* as well as bodhisattvas who have not entered the *bhūmis*; (2) the *nirmāṇakāya* in the form of an ordinary human being, an animal, or even a ghost for liberating different forms of sentient beings. The best example of the first type of *nirmāṇakāya* is Śākyamuni Buddha and it is in reference to this type that the eight or fourteen acts are mentioned. The examples for the second type are found in the *Jātaka* stories where the Buddha appears in appropriate forms to save various beings. The ancient Chinese masters called these two kinds of *nirmāṇakāya* the assumed body (*Yingsheng* in Chinese), and the magically produced body (*Huasheng* in Chinese) respectively.[47] The magically produced body, according to the **Suvarnaprabhāsottamasūtra*, entails that the Tathāgata manifests various bodies in accordance with the mentality, activity and the realms of sentient beings in appropriate places, times and doctrines.[48] The term 'assumed body' occasionally means the body of enjoyment for the great bodhisattvas (*parasaṃbhogakāya*). Therefore, the assumed body can be either a *nirmāṇakāya* or a *saṃbhogakāya* according to the audience to which the Buddha appears. The Buddha appears in the form of the *saṃbhogakāya* before an assembly of bodhisattvas who have already entered into the *bhūmis* and in the form of a *nirmāṇakāya* before other audiences.

In summary, the *nirmāṇakāya* probably originated from the idea of the mind-made body (*manomayakāya*) found in early Buddhism. This idea was first taken up by the Mahāsāṃghikas when they argued that Śākyamuni was a manifestation come to liberate sentient beings and that the Buddha is not bound by worldly conditions. The Mahāyānists, accepting the Buddhology of the Mahāsāṃghikas in its entirety, further developed this idea and formulated the concept of the *nirmāṇakāya*. They argued that the *dharmakāya* is the Buddha. Śākyamuni was only a *nirmāṇakāya* manifested in the world out of compassion for sentient beings. Thus, the concept of the *nirmāṇakāya* has the following aspects. It has the *dharmakāya* as its support, great compassion as its essence and transformation as its activity. It manifests itself in either a pure or impure land through the power of concentration (*dhyāna*) for the sake of bringing maturity to sentient beings, *śrāvakas*, *pratyekabuddhas* and bodhisattvas who have not entered the *bhūmis*. It is manifested in different forms in accordance with the inclinations of the audience to be addressed and its context. It performs eight or fourteen acts in accordance with the state of the world if the *nirmāṇakāya* is in the form of a Buddha.

7

THE ATTRIBUTES OF THE BUDDHA AND OTHER BUDDHAS IN EARLY AND MIDDLE MAHĀYĀNA *SŪTRAS*[1]

In the previous chapters, we discussed the origins and development of the three bodies of the Buddha. This chapter focuses on two aspects of the concept of the Buddha: first, the attributes and qualities of the Buddha that have not yet been discussed; second, the other Buddhas in the early and middle Mahāyāna *sūtras*. These two aspects also contributed to the formulation of the *trikāya* theory.

The light of the Buddha

The idea that the Buddha had bodily light emerged very early. According to both the Pāli and the Chinese versions of the *Mahāparinirvāṇasūtra*, the Buddha's body radiated light during the night of his final passing away.[2] According to this *sūtra*, there were two occasions on which the Buddha's body radiated light: the night when he attained full enlightenment and the night before his final *nirvāṇa*, as there was no remaining element of clinging.[3] However, followers of the Buddha thought that he must have emitted bodily light on many other occasions in a similar way. According to the **Mahāprajñāpāramitāśāstra* (MPPŚ), the Buddha's body emitted light on various occasions. These include his descent from Tuṣita heaven, his birth, his attaining enlightenment, the first turning of the wheel of Dharma, the defeat of the heretics, his *parinirvāṇa*, and also many occasions when the Buddha delivered important *sūtras* such as the **Prajñāpāramitā* and the **Saddharmapuṇḍarīka*.[4] To this bodily light was added another light, the light of the Buddha's wisdom. It is said in the MPPŚ that there are two kinds of light of the Buddha: the physical light (*rūpa-prabhā*) and the light of wisdom (*prajñā-prabhā*).[5] For the purpose of saving sentient beings, the Buddha emits the physical light from his body, and for the purpose of differentiation and analysis of the general and individual characteristics of all *dharmas*, he sheds the light of wisdom.[6] The physical light can again be divided into two categories. The first is the light actually emitted from the physical body of the Buddha, such as the one-fathom halo that radiates from his body constantly and without interruption. The second is the light that appears through the supernatural power of the Buddha on certain occasions, such as the preaching of important *sūtras*.[7] It should therefore be called the light of the supernatural power. Thus, the light of the Buddha can be further classified into three types: (1) the physical light; (2) the light of the supernatural power; and (3) the light of wisdom.[8]

The physical light

The physical light of the Buddha is formed by a one-fathom halo. As discussed in Chapter 2 above, there is no mention of this attribute in the *Nikāyas* or the *Āgamas*, in which the Buddha is only described as having skin the colour of gold as one of the thirty-two marks. It was in the period of the early Indian Buddhist schools that the attribute of the one-fathom rays became one of the qualities of the Buddha. There was a debate as to whether it belonged among the thirty-two marks of a great man. As a result, some of the biographical *sūtras* of the Buddha such as the *Atītapratyutpanna-hetuphala* included it in the list of the thirty-two marks while many others did not. Nevertheless, the one-fathom halo was included in the thirty-two marks in all the relevant Mahāyāna *sūtras* and it became a standard expression.

As discussed in Chapter 2 above, it is perhaps the Sarvāstivādins who first conceived of the Buddha as having a one-fathom halo radiating from the four sides of his body. This idea most probably originated from the mark of the golden-coloured skin of the Buddha described in early Buddhism. According to the *Vibhāṣā*, the light emanating from a one-fathom halo constantly radiates from the Buddha's body day and night.[9] Thus, it is deemed 'normal' or 'constant light'. The MPPŚ further explains that this normal bodily light is different in every Buddha. For instance, Maitreya Buddha has the normal light of ten *li* (five kilometres) emanating from his body.[10] Amitābha Buddha, on the other hand, has infinite bodily light, and according to the **Amitāyurbuddhadhyānasūtra*, it is for this reason that he is so named.[11] Śākyamuni, had immeasurable bodily light, but he displayed it in one-fathom rays in accordance with the disposition of people in the Sahā world, as stated in the *Vibhāṣā*.[12] The **Prajñāpāramitāsūtras* incorporated the attribute of the Buddha's bodily light into the bodhisattva ideal and made it one of the ten accomplishments to be fulfilled by bodhisattvas in the ninth stage.[13] Thus, it has become a standard expression in Mahāyāna Buddhism that the Buddha possessed physical 'light measuring one fathom radiating from all sides of his body'. In most images of the Buddha this is depicted by a circle around his head.

The light of supernatural power

The light of supernatural power of the Buddha can be divided into two kinds: (1) the light emitted from bodily marks such as his white hair; (2) the light emitted from all over his body. First, the mark of the white hair is a special attribute of the Buddha and the Mahāyānists pay special attention to it. It is said that the white hair always emits immense beams of light whenever the Buddha is about to deliver an important *sūtra*. The chapter on meditation on the physical marks in the **Buddhadhyānasamādhisāgarasūtra* states that the Tathāgata has uncountable marks of greatness, and in each mark there are eighty-four thousand minor marks, all of them emitting beams of light. None of them, however, can compare with the merit of the mark of white hair (*ūrṇā-kośa*).[14] The *sūtra* states that through the mark of white hair the Buddha emitted immense beams of light at different stages in his life, both as a prince and as a Buddha. In particular, when the Buddha battled with Māra, the white hair emitted beams of light in the ten directions as bright as billions of suns. Māra and his retinues saw billions of wondrously produced Śākyamunis, and each had a white hair as long as five *zhangs* (about sixteen metres) on his forehead. In the white hair of every Buddha there are immeasurable beams of light and in each beam of light there are numerous manifested Buddhas that also have white hair.[15] It was this magical light of the white hair that subdued Marā, the evil one.

In his **Daśabhūmikasūtraśāstra* Vasubandhu states that the light of the white hair has eight kinds of *karma* and two kinds of bodies.[16] They are:

1. the *karma* of enlightenment, where bodhisattvas feel the aid bestowed by the Buddha when the light illuminates their bodies;[17]
2. the *karma* of cause as the *asaṃkhyeya* beams of light have immeasurable rays of light as retinue;
3. the *karma* of expansion and diminution, which illuminates the *asaṃkhyeya* worlds when expanding and is reduced to normal light when diminishing;
4. the *karma* of cessation, which brings various kinds of anguish to cessation in all suffering realms;
5. the *karma* of subjugation, which outshines the light of Māra's palaces and deprives him of his power to terrify and disturb sentient beings who are going to be liberated;
6. the *karma* of veneration, which can manifest the inconceivable power of the Buddha;
7. the *karma* of manifestation, which illuminates the worlds of the ten directions and bestows the Tathāgata's power upon the teachers (of the Dharma) as well as bodhisattvas;
8. the *karma* of invitation, which can produce voices and speak verses.

For instance, on the web platform of the great light cloud, a voice speaks verses inviting the Buddha to ascend to his seat. The two bodies of the light of the white hair are: the body that can travel like a comet to all the Buddha lands, and the body that abides in empty space like the sun. The *sūtra* says that the light constructs a web platform of great light in the air, and the body abides there illuminating all worlds at all times. Living beings in different worlds can see each other and listen to the teaching of the Buddha as in one assembly.

In the **Avataṃsaka* there are descriptions of the light emanating from the marks of the Buddha. These are found in two chapters dedicated to the marks of the Buddha, one on the major and the other on the minor marks.[18] These marks do not correspond to the traditional thirty-two major and eighty minor marks, and they are called the Ocean of Marks of the Tathāgata. The *sūtra* cites ninety-seven major marks and each mark, which is decorated with various jewels, emits immeasurable beams of light illuminating all the worlds of the ten directions. The **Avataṃsaka* version translated by Śikṣānanda says at the end of chapter thirty-four that 'Vairocana Buddha has as many such marks of greatness as atoms in ten Flower Treasury oceans of worlds, each limb adorned with sublime marks of myriad jewels.'[19] Here Vairocana Buddha is none other than Śākyamuni, because it is said in the following chapter that Vairocana Buddha descended from Tuṣita heaven and was born in the human world, in the house of King Śuddhodana.[20] Thus, Śākyamuni Buddha was endowed with countless marks of greatness from which emanated immeasurable beams of light.

The chapter on 'The Merit of Light of the Buddha's Minor Marks' in the **Avataṃsaka* states that the Buddha has a minor mark named 'king of ocean' from which a light called 'pure effulgence' emits beams together with seven million *asaṃkhyeya* beams as retinue.[21] The *sūtra* then describes how the wheel mark on the sole of the Buddha's feet has a light named 'king of universal light'. From this, together with the minor mark of 'the king of ocean', emanate forty kinds of light. Among them a light called 'pure virtue' illuminates as many worlds as the atoms in six billion Buddha lands, causing all sentient beings to develop and mature according to their various actions and inclinations.

Another kind is the light of the Buddha's supernatural power which is only emitted when he delivers a special *sūtra* or on a special occasion. The **Saddharmapuṇḍarīka*, one of the earliest Mahāyāna *sūtras*, describes how the Buddha emitted immense rays of light from the white hair between his eyebrows before he preached the *sūtra*.[22] The light illuminated the eighteen thousand Buddha lands in the eastern direction. The light penetrated everywhere, reaching downward as far as the Avīci hell and upward to Akaniṣṭha heaven. People from the Sahā world could see the Buddhas. The sentient beings and the bodhisattvas in those lands could also hear the expounding of the *sūtra*.[23]

The **Prajñāpāramitāsūtras* describe five kinds of light miraculously emanating from the whole body of the Buddha before he taught the *sūtra*, and living beings who encounter this light are thought to reach liberation. This light, according to the *sūtra*, is a result of the concentration called King of Concentration (*samādhirājasamādhi*), which contains all *samādhis*. First, the Buddha emitted immense rays of light from the wheel marks on his feet. Second, the Buddha emitted immeasurable rays of light from all over his body from feet to head. Third, the Buddha emitted immeasurable rays of light from all the pores of his body. Fourth, the Buddha emitted natural or ordinary rays of light, which extended for a fathom from all four sides of his body. Fifth, he emitted immeasurable rays of light from his tongue when he stretched it out. On each of the rays from his tongue was a treasury of lotuses with a thousand petals emitting golden light, and on each lotus a sitting Buddha preached the six *pāramitās*. All these five kinds of rays release immeasurable light. These rays illuminate all Buddha lands of the great *trisāhasra* universe in the ten directions. Living beings who encountered such rays of light would attain supreme and perfect enlightenment (*anuttara-saṃyak-saṃbodhi*). Thus, Śākyamuni Buddha showed the eternal body to all beings in the great *trisāhasra* universe by magical power.[24]

The MPPŚ describes what is probably the most spectacular mythical power of the Buddha. It is said that Ānanda once feared that Śākyamuni might pass away without completing his task (Buddha work) of saving sentient beings. In order to allay his fear, Śākyamuni entered into the *samādhi* known as 'the Sun Rising' and from all the pores of his body emitted immense beams of light illuminating as many worlds as the grains of sand in the Ganges River in the ten directions. In each beam, there appeared a seven-jewelled lotus with a thousand petals in which was a sitting Buddha. All these Buddhas appeared in as many worlds as the grains of sand in the Ganges River to save sentient beings.[25] Thus, the light here symbolizes the salvific power of the Buddha. The *Avataṃsaka* states that all Buddhas have the embellishment of supreme and immeasurable beams of light, and each beam has numerous webs of light as retinue, which illuminate the Buddha lands of the ten directions and eliminate the darkness in all the worlds.[26]

According to the **Daśabhūmikasūtraśāstra*, the light of the Buddha has three kinds of *karma*: to benefit those who encounter it, to awaken faith, and to subjugate pride.[27] However, Fazang explains that the light has four kinds of meaning: (1) to make manifest the wonderful and majestic Buddha body and Dharma; (2) to awaken faith; (3) to help the suffering; (4) to convene assemblies from afar.[28]

This analysis suggests that the Mahāyānists greatly developed the attribute of light and considered it the salvific power of the Buddha through which sentient beings are liberated. Early Buddhism advocated that one could attain liberation only through one's own energetic strife and so the Buddha was regarded as only a teacher or guide. But in Mahāyāna Buddhism, liberation could be attained only through the power of the Buddha as manifested in the light he emits. The Buddhist attitude towards liberation thus underwent a major change from being the result of reliance on oneself to being the result of reliance on Buddhas and bodhisattvas such as Amitābha and Avalokiteśvara. The salvific power of the Buddha was believed to be strengthened and expanded through the light of supernatural power.

The light of wisdom

The light of wisdom corresponds to the light of *dharmakāya* because the *dharmakāya* has wisdom as its essence, as discussed in Chapter 4 above. It is stated in the MPPŚ: 'The infinite *dharmatākāya* pervades the space of the ten directions, its form is majestic and wonderful, its light and voice are immeasurable.'[29] Again, 'This infinite *dharmatākāya* or Buddhakāya has limitless light and its voice expounding the Dharma pervades the Buddha lands of the ten directions.'[30] The **Saṃdhinirmocanasūtra* concurs by saying that the *dharmakāya* is attained through the accumulation of merit by the practice of skilful means (*upāyakauśalya*) and wisdom (*prajñā*). From the *dharmakāya*, the light of great wisdom emanates and various *nirmāṇakāyas* are manifested.[31] According to the *Avataṃsaka*, all Buddhas have supreme adornments of light from which emanate countless beams of light, each of which is accompanied by webs of light as retinue. These beams of light illuminate all Buddha lands of the ten directions, destroy the darkness in all worlds and reveal innumerable Buddhas who perform Buddha activities.[32] This is because all Buddhas have one and the same *dharmakāya*, and from the wheel of the great wisdom emanate various kinds of light of wisdom.[33] Although the *dharmakāya* always emits light and preaches the Dharma, sentient beings who have defilements do not see it or hear it, just as the blind are not able to see the sun. Only those who have pure minds are able to see the *dharmakāya*.[34] The Yogācārins further explain that the light of wisdom means the light of 'the non-discrimination wisdom' and 'the subsequently obtained wisdom', which are inherent in the *dharmakāya*.[35]

The light of the *dharmakāya* can be interpreted in two ways. First, the *dharmakāya* emits immense light because it is intrinsically pure and endowed with immeasurable merit. Second, the light of the *dharmakāya* is the light of the Dharma of the Buddha, which destroys the darkness of ignorance and the defilements of sentient beings. Let us discuss the first aspect. As seen in Chapter 4 above, the *dharmakāya* is identified with suchness (*tathatā*), which is pure from beginningless time. The *Shimoheyelun* ('Elucidation of Mahāyāna') attributed to Nāgārjuna explains that from time immemorial, suchness (*tathatā*) is by nature endowed with every excellent quality such as the light of great wisdom illuminating the entire Dharma realm.[36] Suchness (*tathatā*) is called the *tathāgatagarbha* when latent and the *dharmakāya* when manifest. The **Sarvadharmaratnottara(-artha)-saṅgīti-śāstra* attributed to bodhisattva Shanji (Kuśalaśānti?) also states that the *tathatā* has no mark and is free from cognitive objects, its self-nature is pure, and it possesses great light.[37] The **Avataṃsaka* further states that all Buddhas have *dharmakāya*, which is pure and eternal, illuminating all equally.[38] Thus the *dharmakāya* emits light because its nature is pure.

The light of the Dharma of the Buddha is discussed in many *sūtras*. The *Daśabhūmikasūtra* states:

> One body of the Tathāgata (*dharmakāya*) brings down the rain [of Dharma] in the realm of Dharmatā, it preaches the [Dharma] womb of all times which contains the supreme teaching of Dharma. This is the light of Dharma.[39]

The **Avataṃsaka* states:

> The pure and wonderful *dharmakāya* of the bodhisattvas is produced from the true Dharma of all Buddhas. The bright and pure Dharma light benefits all sentient beings through the preaching of infinite Dharma that destroys their sufferings and worries.[40]

Then in chapter eight, the **Avataṃsaka* says that bodhisattvas preach the four noble truths through various means and thus they emit inconceivable beams of light through which they save sentient beings.[41] According to the text there are forty-four kinds of light and sentient beings are enlightened by encountering them. These beams of light are given various names and each is aimed at a particular group of sentient beings. For instance, the light of non-greediness enlightens those who are greedy, the light of coolness enlightens those who violate the discipline, the light of tranquillity enlightens those whose minds are confused, and the light of wisdom adornment enlightens those who are ignorant. This, in Mahāyāna Buddhism, is called the Dharma Door, which means the method of practice. There are countless Dharma Doors because there are numerous kinds of sentient beings. Therefore, the Buddha has immeasurable beams of light of Dharma corresponding to the inclinations of sentient beings.

The light of Dharma is a subject of discussion in both the **Yogācārabhūmiśāstra* and the *Mahāyānasaṃgraha* (MS). The **Yogācārabhūmiśāstra* describes three kinds of light: the light countering darkness, the light of Dharma and bodily light.[42] The light countering darkness is categorized into three: (1) the light of the moon and stars in the night; (2) the light of the sun in the daytime; (3) the light of bright objects such as fire and jewels. They counter three kinds of darkness: the darkness of the night; the darkness caused by clouds; and the darkness of houses and caves. Bodily light is the light radiating naturally from the bodies of sentient beings. The light of Dharma is the observation of phenomena through feeling, thought and contact, or by the practice of reciting the names of Buddhas. It counters three kinds of darkness, ignorance, doubt and sluggishness (*styāna*), because it can reveal the nature of all *dharmas*. In other words, the light of Dharma is the knowledge obtained through observation as well as energetic practice.

The MS states that a bodhisattva attains, as one of the five results of practice, right and comprehensive knowledge of the light of the great Dharma, which is infinite and indiscriminate.[43] The Chinese master Chengguan (738–839), after having carefully examined both the MS and its commentaries, stated that the light of Dharma has four meanings.[44] First, according to Vasubandhu's commentary, the light of Dharma is the wisdom of Dharma as well as the infinite *dharmas* to be realized by wisdom. Vasubandhu explains that the light of Dharma is comprehensive knowledge of the infinite and undifferentiated *dharmas* of the ten directions, such as skilful study and recitation of the written texts.[45] Second, according to Asvabhāva's commentary on the MS, the light of Dharma is wisdom, as he explains that it has the function of illumination.[46] Third, according to Paramārtha's translation of Vasubandhu's commentary on the MS, the light of Dharma has two kinds of wisdom: experiential wisdom and undefiled, non-discriminating wisdom.[47] Fourth, according to the *Kośa*, the light of Dharma is the light opposing ignorance. These four meanings of the light of Dharma still focus on wisdom that is attained through both learning and practice.

The retinue of the Buddha

There are two kinds of retinue of the Buddha according to the MPPŚ. They are: (1) the family or internal retinue such as Yaśodharā and Ānanda, who formed the retinue of Śākyamuni Buddha; (2) the retinue of great bodhisattvas who have one more birth to *bodhi*, such as Maitreya and Mañjuśrī. The first retinue belongs to the *rūpakāya* and the second belongs to the *dharmatākāya*.[48] The MPPŚ discusses only the two Buddha bodies, but if we apply these two kinds of retinue to the three-body theory, the worldly retinue would belong to the *nirmāṇakāya* and the great bodhisattva retinue would belong to the *saṃbhogakāya*. This is because the *saṃbhogakāya* only enjoys the Dharma with great bodhisattvas, not with others, according to the *Mahāyānasūtrālaṃkāra*.[49] In other words, the *saṃbhogakāya* would only have the great bodhisattvas as retinue, while the *dharmakāya* in the three-body theory is the support and base of the other two bodies.

The idea of the bodhisattva retinue emerged very early. For instance, the **Pañcaviṃśatisāhasrikā* lists twelve accomplishments (*samanvāgama*) to be attained by a bodhisattva in the ninth stage (*bhūmi*), one of which is the accomplishment of the bodhisattva retinue.[50] The twelve accomplishments are obviously modelled on the life of Śākyamuni, an issue that has already been discussed by Hisao Inagaki.[51] In other words, Śākyamuni before his enlightenment was considered by the compilers to be a bodhisattva of the ninth stage because a bodhisattva of the tenth *bhūmi* is already a Buddha according to the **Prajñāpāramitāsūtras*.[52] The **Saddharmapuṇḍarīkasūtra* also states that bodhisattvas that emerged from the earth are all great retinues of the Buddha.[53] The **Prajñāpāramitāsūtra* defines 'bodhisattva retinue' by stating that the Buddha has only bodhisattvas as his retinue.[54] It is also said in the MPPŚ that there are Buddhas who have only bodhisattvas as their retinue, Buddhas who have only *śrāvakas* as their retinue and Buddhas who have both bodhisattvas and *śrāvakas* as their retinue.[55] It is clear that the Buddhas who have only bodhisattvas as their retinue are not the *rūpakāya* or the *nirmāṇakāya* but the *saṃbhogakāya* according to the *trikāya* theory.

The **Daśabhūmikasūtra* explains in detail that a bodhisattva can manifest different numbers of bodhisattva retinues in each of the ten stages (*bhūmi*). These vary from a hundred in the first stage to as many as the atoms in the *asaṃkhyeya* great *trisāhasra* universe in the ninth stage.[56] In the *Avataṃsaka*, such bodhisattva retinues are mentioned frequently. Examples include the chapters on Vairocana Buddha and 'The Awakening Light of the Tathāgata' which mention immeasurably great bodhisattva retinues that visited the Buddha from the ten directions. In chapter nine, it is said that the Buddha travelled to the top of Mount Sumeru. In the following chapter, many bodhisattvas came and praised the Buddha in verse. The text states, 'The pure bodhisattva assembly, the great retinue of all Buddhas, who come from the ten directions, sit cross-legged.'[57] By the time the *Avataṃsaka* appeared as a collected and accumulated *sūtra* compilation, the theory that Buddhas possessed numerous great bodhisattvas as their retinue was already accepted.

This is demonstrated in chapter five of the *Avataṃsaka*, on the awakening light of the Buddha. The text describes how the Buddha, from beneath the wheel mark of his feet, emitted a hundred billion light beams, illuminating the entire great *trisāhasra* universe.[58] The Buddha was seen sitting on a lotus lion throne surrounded by as many bodhisattva retinues as the atoms in the ten Buddha lands. By magic power, from each of the ten directions, one great bodhisattva visited the Buddha with as many bodhisattvas as atoms in the ten Buddha lands. The light beams passed through this universe and illuminated ten Buddha lands in the eastern direction, where people perceived the Buddha in the same majestic form. The same happened for the other nine directions. Similarly, the light beams of the Buddha passed another eight times while extending to a hundred thousand billion Buddha lands in each of the ten directions. And just as the first time in each extension, from each of the ten directions one great bodhisattva was seen visiting the Buddha with as many bodhisattvas as atoms in the ten Buddha lands. In this description there is no mention of *śrāvakas* or *pratyekabuddhas*, thus it is a huge assembly of the great bodhisattvas. This Buddha is none other than the *saṃbhogakāya* as defined by the *Mahāyānasūtrālaṃkara*.

These Buddhas, together with their great bodhisattva retinues, are not seen by sentient beings. What are these Buddhas? The ancient Chinese masters such as Fazang (643–712) found it very difficult to categorize the main interlocutory Buddha of the *Avataṃsaka* into any one of the three bodies. Some argued that it was the *nirmāṇakāya* as the Buddha attained enlightenment under the *bodhi* tree. Others maintained that it was the *saṃbhogakāya*, as Vairocana was a form of Śākyamuni abiding in the Pure Land of the lotus womb (*padma-garbha-loka-dhātu*).[59] These Chinese masters had the three Buddha bodies in their minds when they examined this *sūtra*. However, the *sūtra* came into existence before the *trikāya* theory was formulated. As a result, the compilers of the *Avataṃsaka* lacked the notion of the three Buddha bodies. They described the glorious and luminous Buddhas with reference to other early Mahāyāna *sūtras*. Therefore, the only conclusion we can draw is that the attributes of the bodhisattva retinue of the *saṃbhogakāya* were already current in the **Avataṃsaka*.

In fact, the **Avataṃsaka* is the only text that develops the salvific aspect of the Buddha, in the sense that all the qualities and attributes of the *saṃbhogakāya*, the mythological or almighty Buddha, are described, but without the technical term. The *Avataṃsaka* is presented as a teaching aimed at the assembly of great bodhisattvas. The Chinese master Fazang, who established the Huayan school based on the **Avataṃsaka*, even believed that the Buddha had taught the *Avataṃsaka* to the great bodhisattvas in the second week after his enlightenment.[60]

The twenty-one qualities of the Buddha

The *Dushipinjing* is probably the first text to list the qualities of the Buddha in twenty-one sentences. As discussed in Chapter 4 above, the *Dushipinjing*, which was translated by Dharmarakṣa in the third century, corresponds to the chapter on 'Detachment from the World' in the **Avataṃsaka*.[61] In fact, these twenty-one sentences are found in the two translations of the **Avataṃsaka* by Buddhabhadra and Śikṣānanda.[62] They also appear at the beginning of the **Buddhabhūmisūtra*.[63] However, according to Chengguan, the commentator of the **Avataṃsaka*, it was Asaṅga who called them the twenty-one qualities of the Buddha and discussed them in his *Mahāyānasaṃgraha*.[64] Thereafter the phrase was used by the commentators of the *Mahāyānasaṃgraha*, Vasubandhu and Asvabhāva, as well as Bandhuprabha, the commentator of the **Buddhabhūmisūtra*.[65]

The twenty-one qualities were considered by Asaṅga to consist of the purest wisdom of the Buddha.

1 The first sentence, which says that 'the Bhagavat has attained the supreme and pure enlightenment', is a key sentence, and the other twenty qualities are explanations of this pure enlightenment. Bandhuprabha explains

that the Buddha is rightly and fully enlightened on all conditioned and unconditioned *dharmas*. In other words, the Buddha knows all things, both worldly and transcendental.

2 The Buddha arises in a non-dual course, which is explained by Asaṅga as the quality of arising without any obstacle whatsoever to knowing. Asvabhāva further explains that this is the wisdom of non-obstruction which knows all things in their categories and differences without obstacles and doubt. However, Bandhuprabha is of the opinion that the Buddha abides neither in *saṃsāra* nor in *nirvāṇa*, which are considered obstacles. Sentient beings abide in *saṃsāra* and therefore they have defilement (*kleśas*), while *śrāvakas* and *pratyekabuddhas* abide in *nirvāṇa* and do not perform actions to benefit others.

3 The Buddha enters into the state of no characteristics. Asaṅga explains that this is the quality of enabling entrance into pure suchness without the duality of the conditioned and the unconditioned. Asvabhāva says that the Buddha not only enters suchness himself but also causes others to enter it.

4 The Buddha abides in the abode of Buddhas. Asaṅga explains that the quality of the Buddha's abode is such that the Tathāgata's activity is effortless and uninterrupted. Bandhuprabha says that the Buddha abides in compassion and observes the world day and night to save sentient beings.

5 The Buddha attains the state of nature that is equal in all Buddhas. Asaṅga explains that this is the quality of the absence of differentiation in support, intention and activity in the *dharmakāya*. Chengguan further explains that the support is suchness, or pure wisdom, while the intention is the mind of sharing happiness. The activity means that all Buddhas benefit others through the *saṃbhogakāya* and the *nirmāṇakāya*.[66]

6 The Buddha has arrived at the state of non-obstruction. Asaṅga explains that this is the quality of opposing all obstacles to practice. The commentators explain that the Buddha has attained the wisdom of liberation by eliminating both *kleśas* and the obstacles to knowledge.

7 The Buddha has attained irrefutable Dharma. Asaṅga explains that this is the quality of suppressing all heretical doctrines.

8 The Buddha performs deeds without obstacles. Asaṅga explains that this is the quality of arising in the world without being defiled by the worldly states. Bandhuprabha, on the contrary, explains that this is the quality of suppressing Māras, for obstacles such as form (*rūpa*) cannot disturb the Buddha.

9 The Dharma established by the Buddha is inconceivable. Asaṅga explains that this is the quality of true doctrine validly established.

10 The Buddhas are equal in all three times. Paramārtha's translation of the *Mahāyānasaṃgraha* explains this as the quality of responding to

the questions of others through the four skilful answers. Xuanzang's translation explains it as the quality of prophecy (*vyākaraṇa*).[67] Bandhuprabha also explains that this is the quality of prophesying the past as well as the future without any obstacle.[68]

11 The Buddha can manifest different bodies in all the worlds. Asaṅga explains that this is the quality of manifesting the *saṃbhogakāya* and the *nirmāṇakāya* in all worldly realms.

12 The Buddha has unhindered wisdom in all things. Asaṅga explains that this is the quality of resolving the doubts of others.

13 All practices of the Buddha are for great enlightenment. Asaṅga explains that this is the quality of introducing others to various practices that will lead to great enlightenment.

14 The Buddha's wisdom is found in all things. Asaṅga explains that this is the quality of understanding things that arise in the future.

15 The Buddha makes various manifestations without any differentiation. Asaṅga explains that this is the quality of manifestation in accordance with the aspirations of sentient beings. But Bandhuprabha asserts that it is the quality that pertains to the pure body that will not give rise to defilement.

16 The Buddha has the wisdom of non-discrimination that all bodhisattvas seek. This is the quality of taming sentient beings and being the support of countless bodhisattvas.

17 The Buddha has attained the perfection of non-dual abode. Asaṅga explains that this is the quality of the fullness of perfection of the *dharmakāya*. Bandhuprabha explains that the abode itself is the *dharmakāya* because suchness is non-dual.

18 The Buddha has attained the wonderful liberation of wisdom which is infinite. Asaṅga explains that this is the quality of making manifest various pure Buddha lands in accordance with the aspirations of sentient beings. Bandhuprabha explains it as the merit of the *saṃbhogakāya* which is different in every Buddha. But Chengguan explains that the Pure Lands manifested by the Buddha are of two kinds: the Pure Land of the *nirmāṇakāya* and the Pure Land of the *saṃbhogakāya*.

19 The Buddha has attained the Buddha stage (*bhūmi*) of impartiality without extremes. Asaṅga explains that this is the quality of infinity and undifferentiation of the three Buddha bodies in all worlds. Bandhuprabha says that this is the quality of suchness, because it is free from all characteristics and is therefore impartial to all Buddhas.

20 The Buddha attains the ultimacy of the reality realm (*dharmadhātu*). Asaṅga explains that this is the quality of engendering benefit and happiness for all sentient beings to the limit of the birth-death cycle. Bandhuprabha says that this is the quality of the Buddha's attainment which exhausts the entire cosmos and which is the fruit of the practice of the Dharma.

21 The attainment of the Buddha extends to the limit of empty space and the infinite future. Asaṅga explains that this is the quality of inexhaustibility. Bandhuprabha explains on the contrary that the Buddha performs beneficial deeds both for himself and for others without exhaustion.[69]

These twenty-one qualities are a summary of the attributes of the Buddha that were developed in the early and middle Mahāyāna *sūtras* before the **Avataṃsaka* was finalized. Bandhuprabha claims that these are the twenty-one supreme and special qualities of the Buddha which are achieved through the attainment of pure *bodhi*, Buddhahood.[70] In his commentary on the *Avataṃsaka*, Fazang further explains that these are the twenty-one qualities of the *saṃbhogakāya*, the fruit of the Buddha.[71] This would appear to be accurate, as the **Avataṃsaka* goes on to describe the bodhisattvas who have one more birth before *bodhi* and who have come from the ten directions of the world to attend the assembly. Thus it would follow that the Buddha mentioned in the chapter on 'Detachment from the World' in the *Avataṃsaka* pertains to the *saṃbhogakāya* aspect.

The ten Buddhas and ten Buddha bodies

The **Avataṃsaka* is perhaps the first text to mention the ten Buddhas in the chapter on 'Detachment from the World' and the ten Buddha bodies in the chapter on 'The Ten Stages' (*bhūmi*).[72] These have become subjects of discussion in almost all the commentaries on the *sūtra* written by Chinese masters. As discussed in Chapter 4 above, the **Avataṃsaka* was first translated into Chinese by Buddhabhadra in 398–421 CE. The chapter on 'Detachment from the World' as an independent *sūtra* entitled the *Dushipinjing* (the *sūtra* on 'The Crossing Over of the World') was translated even earlier by Dharmarakṣa in 265–316 CE. The *Dushipinjing* already mentions that bodhisattvas have ten ways of seeing Buddhas, but it does not cite the names of the ten Buddhas given in the chapter on 'Detachment from the World' in the **Avataṃsaka*.[73] Asaṅga, the author of the *Mahāyānasaṃgraha*, must have known the **Avataṃsaka*, the ten Buddhas and the ten Buddha bodies mentioned therein, and these probably served as a basis for him to formulate the three-body theory.

The ten Buddhas

The first of the ten Buddhas mentioned in the **Avataṃsaka* is the Buddha of Attainment of Full Enlightenment (*Samyak-saṃbuddha*), or the Buddha of Non-attachment, peacefully abiding in the world after the attainment of Buddhahood.[74] Fazang explains that the Buddha of Non-attachment is so named because the Buddha is attached neither to *nirvāṇa* nor to the world.[75] Non-attachment means that the Buddha manifests himself in the world through attaining enlightenment and passing away into *nirvāṇa*. This is the general statement while the other nine are further explanations.[76]

The second is the Buddha of the Vow (*Praṇidhāna Buddha*). Fazang explains that as the Buddha has no more obstacles and the great vow has been accomplished, the vow is essentially the same as the Buddha. It also means that all merits are accrued under the vow of the Buddha so that the Buddha can fulfil all the wishes of sentient beings. Hence the name the Buddha of the Vow.

The third is the Buddha of the Reward of Action (*Karmavipāka Buddha*) who can inspire profound faith in others. Fazang explains that all meritorious *dharmas* correspond to the effects of *karma* of sentient beings. This certainty of reward inspires faith in others.

The fourth is the Buddha of Preservation of the True Teaching (*Nirmāṇakāya-Buddha*) in accordance with the world. Fazang explains that all merits support understanding and practice. Chengguan explains that it is the relics (*śarīra*) of the Buddha as well as his perfect voice, which travels through the past, the present and the future, that preserve the true teaching of the Buddha in accordance with the dispositions of sentient beings.[77]

The fifth is the Buddha of Nirvāṇa (*Nirvāṇa Buddha*) who for ever abides over on the other shore. Fazang explains that a manifestation of the Buddha in the world serves to demonstrate the act of passing into *nirvāṇa*.

The sixth is the Buddha of the Cosmos (*Dharmadhātu Buddha*) who pervades everywhere. Chengguan explains that the *dharmakāya* pervades the entire cosmos (*dharmadhātu*) which itself is the body of the Buddha.

The seventh is the Buddha of Mind (*Manas Buddha*) who abides peacefully. Both Fazang and Chengguan explain that the mind is the Buddha. Chengguan adds that it is in a perfect state of peace that is pure consciousness.

The eighth is the Buddha of Concentration (*Samādhi Buddha*), who is infinite and without attachment. Fazang explains that the Buddha is always in *samādhi* and is attached to nothing.

The ninth is the Buddha of Fundamental Nature (*Tathatā Buddha*), who does not change. Fazang explains that the true nature of all *dharmas* is thus absolute, and it is by the realization of this nature that one becomes enlightened.

The tenth is the Buddha of Wish Fulfilment or the Buddha Adapting to Capacities who serves all. Fazang explains that the Buddha can manifest himself in accordance with the various capacities of sentient beings to fulfil their wishes effortlessly. All those to be liberated are under the power of the Buddha.

Fazang further explains that the ten Buddhas can also be classified into five pairs. The first two are a pair since the first Buddha is effectual and the second is causal, for one becomes a Buddha by a great vow. The third and the fourth are a pair in that the third is the direct reward and the fourth is the dependent reward. The fifth and the sixth are a pair in that the fifth is the eternal *nirvāṇa* and the sixth is the infinite *dharmadhātu*. The seventh and eighth are a pair in that the seventh is the manifestation of the mind and the eighth is concentration without attachment. The ninth and the tenth are a pair in that the ninth is true nature which does not change, and the tenth is the function that spreads all over the cosmos. These ten Buddhas are in fact the merits of one Buddha, because the text states that all the Buddha bodies are included in the *dharmakāya*, which has one mind and one wisdom.[78]

The ten Buddha bodies

The **Avataṃsaka* also mentions two categories of ten Buddha bodies, which a bodhisattva in the eighth stage (*bhūmi*) comprehends. The first ten bodies are: (1) the body of sentient beings; (2) the body of lands; (3) the body of the reward of action; (4) the body of *śrāvakas*; (5) the body of *pratyekabuddhas*; (6) the body of bodhisattvas; (7) the body of Tathāgatas; (8) the body of wisdom; (9) the *dharmakāya*; (10) the body of empty space. The body of lands is the physical world. The first, the third and the sixth pertain to the world of sentient beings. The rest pertain to the world of the enlightened.

The body of a Tathāgata itself contains ten bodies: (1) the body of enlightenment, the manifestation of a Buddha body attaining enlightenment; (2) the body of the vow, aspiring to be born in Tuṣita heaven; (3) the body of transformation; (4) the body of preservation of the true teaching, this being the relics of the Buddha; (5) the body adorned with excellent physical characteristics due to great merit; (6) the body of power with all the rays of light to subdue sentient beings; (7) the body manifested at will according to occasion; (8) the body of merit and virtue; (9) the body of wisdom; (10) the *dharmakāya*, the quintessential Buddha body.[79]

Zhiyan (602–668), the second patriarch of the Huayan school, called the first group the ten Buddhas of the realm of understanding. Bodhisattvas, with their pure and true wisdom of awakening, perceive that the Dharma realm is the Buddha with ten aspects (bodies). He similarly called the second group the ten Buddhas of the realm of practice, because bodhisattvas achieve the fruit of the Buddha when they complete their practice.[80] A bodhisattva, according to the **Avataṃsaka*, attains ten kinds of Buddha qualities by practising the ten perfections (*pāramitā*).[81] Chengguan says that these qualities are the ten Buddha bodies.[82]

1 A bodhisattva obtains the wonderful marks of the Buddha through the practice of generosity (*dāna*). This is the Buddha body endowed with excellent physical marks.
2 A bodhisattva obtains the pure Buddha body through the practice of discipline (*śīla*). This is the mind body.
3 A bodhisattva obtains the inconceivable body of the Buddha through the practice of patience (*kṣānti*). This is the body of enlightenment.

4 A bodhisattva obtains the invincible body of the Tathāgata through the practice of energetic striving (*vīrya*). This is the body of preservation of the true teaching.
5 A bodhisattva obtains the pure and incomparable body of the Buddha through the practice of meditation (*dhyāna*). This is the body of merit and virtues.
6 A bodhisattva obtains the pure body of Dharma of the Tathāgata through the practice of *prajñā*. This is the *dharmakāya*.
7 A bodhisattva obtains the pure physical body of the World Honoured One through the practice of skilful means (*upāya*). This is the body of transformation.
8 A bodhisattva lives for a *kalpa* for the benefit of sentient beings through the practice of vows (*praṇidhāna*). This is the body of the vow.
9 A bodhisattva obtains the pure body that travels to all Buddha lands through the practice of power (*bala*). This is the body of power.
10 A bodhisattva obtains the pure body which makes sentient beings happy through the practice of knowledge (*jñāna*). This is the body of wisdom.

The ten Buddha bodies, according to Chengguan, are the same as the ten Buddhas and they are the ten virtues of one Buddha body, the *dharmakāya* which pervades the entire cosmos.[83] Therefore, the ten Buddha bodies are perfectly interfused without any obstacle. In his commentary on the **Avataṃsaka*, Chengguan further explains that the Buddha body is both principle and practice, one and many, support and substance, preacher and Dharma, beings and non-beings, cause and effect, profound and infinite, three bodies and ten bodies, because it has the same cloud as the *dharmakāya*.[84]

Kuiji, the eminent disciple of Xuanzang, explains that the *nirmāṇakāya* is composed of the first five of the ten Buddhas: the Buddha of enlightenment, the Buddha of the vow, the Buddha of reward of action, the Buddha of preservation of the true teaching, and the Buddha of *nirvāṇa*.[85] The *dharmakāya* is composed of the *dharmadhātu* Buddha and *tathatā* Buddha, while the *saṃbhogakāya* is composed of the Buddha of mind, the *samādhi* Buddha and the Buddha of wish fulfilment. However, Chengguan holds a different opinion. He asserts that the *nirmāṇakāya* is composed of the body of enlightenment, the body of the vow, the body of transformation and the body of preservation of the true teaching.[86] The body of mind and the body of power can be the enjoyment body for others (*parasaṃbhogakāya*) as well as the *nirmāṇakāya*. The body of merit and virtue, the body of wisdom and the body endowed with excellent qualities can be either of the two kinds of *saṃbhogakāya* or the *nirmāṇakāya*. The body of *dharmatā* is the *dharmakāya*. The ten Buddhas and the ten Buddha bodies are extremely complicated in comparison with the three bodies, which describe the concept of the Buddha in a simple and clear manner. However, it is evident that the ten Buddha bodies provided the doctrinal foundation for the formulation of the *trikāya* theory.

A model for the *trikāya* theory

In his *Studies in the Laṅkāvatāra Sūtra*, D. T. Suzuki states that the *Laṅkāvatāra* marks a step towards the systematization of the concept of the Buddha, as it mentions three Buddhas. This, he claims, is much like the three bodies of the *trikāya* theory.[87] The *Laṅkāvatāra* mentions the Dharma-buddha, Dharmatā-buddha, Mūlatathāgata and the Tathatājñāna-buddha as comparable to the *dharmakāya*. Equivalent to the *saṃbhogakāya*, we find the Niṣyanda-Buddha and the Dharmatā-niṣyanda-buddha. Comparable to the *nirmāṇakāya* is the Nirmāṇa Buddha. In the Chinese translations of the *Laṅkāvatāra*, the wisdom Buddha is added to the three mentioned above, and thus the number of Buddhas becomes four. The Niṣyanda-Buddha is very different from the concept of the *saṃbhogakāya* because, as Suzuki states, it does not carry the meaning of enjoyment. The remaining two Buddhas are similar to the *dharmakāya* and the *nirmāṇakāya*. However, Suzuki emphasizes the fact that the *Laṅkāvatāra* distinguishes Buddha personalities in terms of Buddha, not in terms of body (*kāya*) which has more of a synthesizing value.[88]

The **Anuttarāśrayasūtra* translated by Paramārtha represents perhaps the last stage in the development of the concept of the Buddha before the formulation of the *trikāya* theory. The **Anuttarāśrayasūtra* mentions three bodies of the Buddha without giving their names.

It is stated in the *sūtra*: 'Ānanda, what are the practices and abodes of the *bodhi*? Three bodies are manifested by three reasons. First the reason of profound meaning, second the reason of the magnificent and great cause, and third the reason of immeasurable merit.'[89] The *sūtra* explains that the first body has five characteristics and five kinds of merit. The five characteristics are those of being: (1) unconditioned (*asaṃskṛta*); (2) inseparable; (3) non-dual; (4) free from all obstacles; (5) pure by nature. The five kinds of merit are those of being: (1) immeasurable; (2) uncountable; (3) inconceivable; (4) exclusive (to the Buddhas); (5) ultimately pure. The *sūtra* further states that the five kinds of merit are exclusive in the two senses of being, first, not knowable to sentient beings, *śrāvakas* and *pratyekabuddhas* for they are beyond their knowledge, second, not generally attainable for it is the Buddha alone who can attain them. Five kinds of *dharmas* are exclusive to *bodhi*: profound suchness (*tathatā*), immovable mastery, purity belonging to the undefiled realm, wisdom without obstacles, and complete benefit to sentient beings. This description suggests that the first body is none other than the *dharmakāya*.

The second body, which possesses great wisdom (*mahāprajñā*) and great compassion (*mahākaruṇā*) as its essence, flows out from pure *dharmakāya* and manifests all the infinite merit of the Tathāgata. It has five kinds of merit consisting of: (1) non-discrimination; (2) spontaneity (acting without pondering); (3) benefiting sentient beings in accordance with their mentality;

(4) inseparability from the *dharmakāya*; (5) never abandoning sentient beings. It should be noticed that *niṣyanda* signifies either to 'flow out' or 'flow down'. So the Niṣyanda-Buddha in the *Laṅkāvatāra* has some connection with the second body. However, this second body does not have the meaning of enjoyment as does that of the *saṃbhogakāya*.

The third body, which has the form element (*rūpa*) as its essence, flows out from wisdom (*prajñā*) and great compassion. It has four kinds of merit: (1) the thirty-two major marks; (2) the eighty minor marks; (3) majesty and virtue;[90] (4) power. It has the faculties, capacities, nature and actions of sentient beings. It manifests various kinds of birth in the impure Buddha lands, such as Tuṣita, descent from Tuṣita, taking birth in the mother's womb, being born, being a boy, learning the eighteen sciences, playing in the garden, going forth and practising austerities, coming to the abode of attaining enlightenment, turning the wheel of Dharma at Vārāṇasī, and entering into *parinirvāṇa* at Kuśinagara. This is unmistakably the *nirmāṇakāya*.

The **Anuttarāśrayasūtra* describes the three bodies, in the third chapter on *bodhi*, as the function of Buddhahood. *Mahāyānasūtrālaṃkāra* also discusses the three bodies, in the chapter on *bodhi*, as the function of Buddhahood.[91] This does not seem to be coincidental. It is possible that the author of the MSA constructed the *trikāya* theory by modelling the three bodies of the **Anuttarāśrayasūtra* through a synthesis of philosophical teachings on the concept of the Buddha as presented in early Mahāyāna *sūtras*. There are two reasons for this assertion.

First, the **Anuttarāśrayasūtra* was composed earlier than the MSA according to Nakamura, who ascribes this *sūtra* to the first of the three periods of scriptures explaining the concept of *tathāgatagarbha*.[92] The MSA, along with the **Buddhagotraśāstra* and the *Mahāyānasaṃgraha*, is ascribed to the second period. This dating of the **Anuttarāśrayasūtra* is also confirmed by Vasubandhu's two works: the **Buddhagotraśāstra* and the **Mahāyānasaṃgrahabhāṣya*, both of which were translated into Chinese by Paramārtha. In these two works, Vasubandhu quoted from the **Anuttarāśrayasūtra* five times, four times in the former and once in the latter, to support his thesis.[93] So the **Anuttarāśrayasūtra* must have been in existence when Vasubandhu wrote these two treatises. Hakuju Ui holds the opinion that the **Anuttarāśrayasūtra* was composed around 350 or before 400 CE, and D. Tokiwa is of a similar opinion, namely that this *sūtra* came into existence in the age of Asaṅga and Vasubandhu.[94] However, Takasaki maintains that the **Anuttarāśrayasūtra* was composed after Vasubandhu's works, some time in the late fifth or the early sixth century, but he has not given any strong evidence to support his assertion,[95] which seems to have no basis.

Second, the **Anuttarāśrayasūtra* discusses *bodhi* under ten topics: (1) essence (*svabhāva*); (2) cause (*hetu*); (3) obstacle (*paripanthā*); (4) result (*phala*); (5) activity (*karma*); (6) endowment or quality (*yoga*); (7) function (*vṛtti*); (8) eternity (*nitya*); (9) exclusiveness (*āveṇika*); (10) inconceivability (*acintya*).[96] The MSA discusses *bodhi* under six topics: (1) essence (*svabhāva*); (2) cause (*hetu*); (3) result (*phala*); (4) activity (*karma*); (5) endowment or quality (*yoga*); (6) functional modes (*vṛtti*).[97] The six topics of the Yogācāra school are probably a further development on the basis of the ten in the **Anuttarāśrayasūtra*, which are less systematic.

The **Anuttarāśrayasūtra* explains the essence of *bodhi* as the conversion of support through righteous and proper practice of the ten perfections (*pāramitā*) and the ten stages (*bhūmi*), which are inconceivable to *śrāvakas* and *pratyekabuddhas*. The Dharma to be converted is the *tathāgatagarbha* which has suchness (*tathatā*) as the result and which is the pure Dharma realm. There are four requirements for *bodhi*: (1) willingness to practise Mahāyāna; (2) practice of the perfection of wisdom (*prajñāpāramitā*); (3) practice of breaking the gate of the *samādhi* of empty space; (4) practice of the Tathāgata's great compassion. These show some overlap. However, the *Mahāyānasaṃgraha* explains the essence and requirements of the *dharmakāya* clearly, stating that the former is the suchness and the latter is the practice of the ten stages (*bhūmi*).[98]

The **Buddhabhūmisūtra* also mentions three bodies in a verse at the end, but without giving any explanation. It states: 'the Buddhas said that the purified realm of Dharma (*dharmadhātuviśuddha*) has a [three-fold] differentiation of function: essence, enjoyment of dharma, and transformation.'[99] The commentator of the **Buddhabhūmisūtra* explains these as the three bodies.[100] Thus, the three bodies in the **Anuttarāśrayasūtra*, the three Buddhas in the *Laṅkāvatāra* and the three functions of the purified Dharma realm in the **Buddhabhūmisūtra* may have served as a model for the formulation of the *trikāya* theory in the MSA.

Other Buddhas and their lands

Belief in the simultaneous existence of many Buddhas in different lands came into being very early, and was probably developed by the Mahāsāṃghika school, as discussed in Chapter 3 above.[101] The early Mahāyānists followed this line of thought and significantly developed the idea. As a result, numerous Buddhas came into existence, each one having their own particular world of responsibility. Many scholars have discussed the origins of Buddha lands or fields (*Buddhakṣetra*), and put forward various opinions. In a recent article, Jan Nattier says that it was a 'logical' necessity of the bodhisattva ideal.[102] As many bodhisattvas opt for Buddhahood and only one can become a Buddha in a given world at one time, others must either wait for their turn like Maitreya or go to other worlds to realize Buddhahood.[103] As a result of this necessity, other Buddha fields were conceived. Jan Nattier is right in saying that a new way of understanding the emergence of 'Pure Land' ideas should be sought within Indian Buddhism and the idea that these paradise-like realms are a concession for the underachieving laity no longer holds much conviction. Much less is the evidence for the incorporation of foreign (e.g. Iranian) or non-Buddhist (e.g. Hindu) ideas into the process of its conception. Nattier's assertion is supported by the following seven ancient works: the **Yogācārabhūmiśāstra*, *Mahāyānasaṃgraha* and its *bhāṣya*, *Kośa*, **Bodhisattvabhūmidharasūtra*, **Abhidharmanyāyānusāraśāstra* of Saṅghabhadra and **Mahāyānāvatārakaśāstra* of Sthiramati.[104] They all argue that there should be many Buddhas because there are many bodhisattvas who practise for *bodhi* at the same time. Since there are many Buddhas there also should be many Buddha lands for them to practise in.

The origin of Pure Lands is a complex problem that involves various aspects of Buddhist thought. In addition to the causes discussed by scholars, the following may have contributed to the emergence of Pure Lands. It was most likely a creation for the majority of lay and monastic Buddhists who were less inclined towards a *nirvāṇa* interpreted as an inactive and indefinable state likened to the blowing out of a lamp. The Tathāgata was said to be found nowhere after the attainment of *parinirvāṇa* in early Buddhism. *Nirvāṇa* was perhaps being identified too closely with nihilism. Thus as a natural consequence, life in a trouble-free land such as Sukhāvatī became an appealing trend in Buddhist thought. A glimpse of the promises (vows) made by both Akṣobhya and Amitābha will suffice to support this. In the *Sukhāvatīvyūhasūtra*, Amitābha made the following vows concerning the inhabitants of his land:

> [21] When I become a Buddha, may all the bodhisattvas and arhats in my realm have life-spans of innumerable *kalpas*.
>
> [23] All have light on the crowns of their heads.[105]
>
> [15] May all bodhisattvas in my realm have bodies the colour of burnished purple gold, with the thirty-two major and eighty minor marks, and may they all be like Buddhas.

Amitābha also made vows concerning his land:

> [1] May there be in my realm no species that flit and wriggle, no animals and *pretas*.
>
> [3] 'May my realm be spontaneously composed of the seven precious substances, be of great extent, vast and boundless, and extremely pleasant. May dwellings for living, clothing, food and drink all arise spontaneously, like those of the king of the sixth heaven.

These are just examples, and similar promises are found in many of the vows of Amitābha. People who are born in these Pure Lands are assured of the upward way in their spiritual path, because they all attain the non-retrogressive state (*avaivartika*). In Mahāyāna *sūtras*, the following four Buddhas along with their Pure Lands are prominent and influential: Akṣobhya and Abhirati, Amitābha and Sukhāvatī, Maitreya and Tuṣita, and Vairocana and the Pure Land of the Lotus World.

Akṣobhya and Abhirati

Akṣobhya is perhaps the first of the contemporaneous Buddhas to be mentioned by name in the early Mahāyāna *sūtras*. Apart from the **Akṣobhyavyūha*, the *Daoxingbanruojing*, one of the earliest versions of the *Aṣṭa* in existence, states that a female devotee will be reborn in the Pure Land of Akṣobhya after many *kalpas* if she has no fear after listening to the **Prajñāpāramitāsūtra*.[106] Belief in Akṣobhya and his Pure Land was already established when the *Daoxingbanruojing* came into existence. Amitābha is not mentioned in this *sūtra* although Lokakṣema is the translator of the **Akṣobhyavyūha*, the *Daoxingbanruojing*, and the *Sukhāvatīvyūha*.[107] Jan Nattier, who has studied the *Akṣobhyavyūha* and compared it with the *Sukhāvatīvyūha*, also supports the assertion that Akṣobhya is the first contemporaneous Buddha to be named in these *sūtras*. She states that the ideas in the *Sukhāvatīvyūha* represent a further development of those found in the **Akṣobhyavyūha*.[108]

Not much study has been carried out on how and why Akṣobhya came into existence. There is an interesting discussion on the origin of Akṣobhya in Yinshun's work, the *Chuqidacheng Fojian Zhi Qiyuan Yu Zhankai*.[109] He is of the opinion that Akṣobhya was modelled on one of the great disciples of Śākyamuni Buddha, Aṅgulimāla, who was a notorious bandit before he entered the Order. He points out that there are some similarities between Akṣobhya and Aṅgulimāla. First, according to the *Akṣobhyavyūha*, Akṣobhya, while a bodhisattva, made vows that women in his Buddha land would safely give birth to new babies and be free from all womanly difficulties and defilements. As a result, women in his land are endowed with great virtues.[110] Similarly, according to the *Aṅgulimālasutta* of the *Majjhimanikāya*, Aṅgulimāla had been advised by the Buddha to say the following words to a woman who was about to give birth to a baby: 'Sister, since I was born, I do not recall that I have ever intentionally deprived a living being of life. By this truth, may you be well and may your infant be well!'[111] Second, Akṣobhya made a vow before a Buddha known as 'Great Eyes' when he learned to practise the bodhisattva way. He pledged not to bring forth anger, malice or ire towards any living being until his attainment of Buddhahood. As a result, he was named Akṣobhya, the Unperturbed.[112] Aṅgulimāla was also renamed Ahiṁsā after he became a monk. They were both renamed on a similar basis although the Sanskrit words 'Ahiṁsā' and 'Akṣobhya' are different.

In the **Akṣobhyavyūha*, Akṣobhya is described as emitting intense light that outshines even the sun and the moon, but the *sūtra* never mentions his life-span.[113] His life is clearly modelled on Śākyamuni, for he is described as having descended from Tuṣita heaven, become a Buddha and finally attained *nirvāṇa*. The inhabitants of Abhirati are mainly *arhats*, as the *sūtra* states that this is a land where arhatship is easy to attain because there is no Māra.[114] Bodhisattvas are also mentioned as members of this society, but the bodhisattva path is intended only for those who take up religious practice zealously, granted the demands of practice. The *Akṣobhyavyūha* represents perhaps a transitional stage between arhatship and Buddhahood which is the final aim of Mahāyāna Buddhist practice.

Amitābha and Sukhāvatī

Amitābha is perhaps the most widely known Buddha of the other contemporaneous Buddhas. Many studies conducted by Japanese as well as Western scholars have expressed various opinions concerning his origins. The theories proposed by these scholars can be classified into three categories: first, those proposing non-Indian origin, mainly the sun worship of Zoroastrianism; second, those proposing origin within non-Buddhist Indian mythology; and third, those proposing origin within Buddhist thought itself.[115] All these theories have been formulated on the basis of two factors: the limitless life-span and the infinite light of Amitābha; but the first and second theories cannot explain both aspects. We now examine the third in greater detail. First, concerning the limitless life-span, in the period of the early Buddhist schools there was already a tendency to eternalize the Buddha. The Mahāsāṃghikas stated that the life-span of Buddhas is limitless, as we have seen in Chapter 3 above. On the basis of Mahāsāṃghika thought, the Mahāyānists further developed and eternalized the Buddha. Amitābha is perhaps the first Buddha in the history of Mahāyāna who is conceived as possessing an infinite life-span. Second, the physical light of the Buddha was also described as early as the *Mahāparinirvāṇasūtra*, as shown at the beginning of this chapter. These ideas developed during the period of the early Buddhist schools, which ascribed to the Buddha a bodily light, one of the marks of a great man. In the **Prajñāpāramitāsūtras*, the Buddha is already described as emitting infinite physical light. Akṣobhya is also described as having infinite light. Hence the image of Amitābha as having infinite light and a limitless life-span has its doctrinal basis in a number of *sutras*. There was no need for the Mahāyānists to borrow foreign ideas to establish the concept of Amitābha since its two keys elements, the limitless life-span and the infinite light, were already present in Buddhist thought.

In ancient China, there was a debate over whether Amitābha was a *nirmāṇakāya* or a *saṃbhogakāya*. Huiyuan (334–416), Zhiyi (538–597) and Jizang (549–623) were of the opinion that Amitābha was a *nirmāṇakāya* whereas Shandao (613–681) held the opinion that he was a *saṃbhogakāya*, an opinion which became very influential in Chinese Buddhist thought.

However, evidence seems to be in favour of Amitābha being a *nirmāṇakāya*, as will be discussed in the last section of this chapter.

The inhabitants of Sukhāvatī are a mixture of bodhisattvas and *arhats*, but bodhisattvas are always mentioned before *arhats*. Bodhisattvas are considered to be in the three superior grades of the nine classes found in the **Amitāyurbuddhadhyānasūtra*.[116] The bodhisattva path is taken for granted and Buddhahood is the sole aim of the members of this Pure Land. Amitābha and Sukhāvatī are a further development of Pure Land thought, going beyond Akṣobhya and Abhirati.

Maitreya and Tuṣita

Maitreya was already a well-known figure in early Buddhism as a future Buddha, but his Pure Land came into existence after those of Akṣobhya and Amitābha. In the **Ekottarāgama*, there is a *sūtra* which says that Śākyamuni entrusted his teachings to the four great disciples and asked them not to enter *nirvāṇa* until Maitreya's advent in the world.[117] The text further explains that Maitreya will have three assemblies and 9.6 billion beings will attain arhatship in the first assembly, 9.4 billion in the second and 9.2 billion in the third. It seems that arhatship was easily obtained in the time of Maitreya because individuals of that time possessed high moral character. It is perhaps this idea of awaiting Maitreya's appearance in the world that gave rise to the idea of being born in his Pure Land of Tuṣita. There are two reasons for being reborn in Tuṣita and waiting there rather than in this Sahā world. First, if one remains in this world, one may not be a human at the time when Maitreya appears. One may thus lack the chance to attend the great assemblies of Maitreya and listen to his teaching. Second, if one is reborn in Tuṣita, one is ensured attendance at the assemblies of Maitreya when he descends to this world. One will reach Buddhahood after attaining the irreversible stage through listening to Maitreya's preaching in the Pure Land. The *Maitreya-vyākarana* states that one will be reborn in Tuṣita heaven if one practises strenuously and recites the name of Maitreya. One will overcome the bad *karma* accumulated in nine billion *kalpas* and attain the irreversible stage through listening to Maitreya's preaching. One descends from Tuṣita to listen to Maitreya, to meet all the Buddhas of the present (*bhadra-kalpa*) and the next age (*nakṣatra kalpa*), and then to receive predictions given by all these Buddhas.[118]

Vairocana and the Pure Land of the Lotus World

The earliest mention of Vairocana Buddha is perhaps in the second chapter of the **Avataṃsaka* translated by Buddhabhadra in 317–402.[119] In this *sūtra*, Vairocana is described as having attained enlightenment immeasurable *kalpas* ago and abiding in the world born from the lotus (*padma-garbha-loka-dhātu*) which was purified by him in as many *kalpas* as there are atoms in the *asaṃkhyeya* worlds while he was a bodhisattva.[120] The infinite beams of light of Vairocana illuminate the worlds of the ten directions and great bodhisattvas as numerous as the atoms of one billion Buddha worlds, each accompanied by as many bodhisattva retinues as the atoms of one Buddha world. They all attend Vairocana's assembly and listen to his teaching. Each of these bodhisattvas emits as many beams of light as the atoms of ten Buddha worlds from each pore of his body and from each beam there appear as many bodhisattvas as the atoms of ten Buddha worlds. All these bodhisattvas are capable of teaching by employing various Dharma Doors (methods of practice) to liberate numerous sentient beings from suffering within one thought moment. As many sentient beings as the atoms of Mount Sumeru become established in virtue and wisdom. Thus they are not ordinary bodhisattvas, but bodhisattvas of higher attainment. The Pure Land of Vairocana is then described in the *sūtra*, but there is no mention of *arhats*. The Pure Land of Akṣobhya may thus be distinguished to from that of Vairocana. In the Pure Land of Akṣobhya, arhatship is the main goal while the bodhisattva path is recommended only for a few. In Amitābha's land the bodhisattva path enjoys a wider following than the *arhat* path. The Pure Land of Vairocana is of the highest level, for only bodhisattvas are found there. For this reason, Fazang and other ancient Chinese masters considered Vairocana to be the *saṃbhogakāya*.

Vairocana Buddha in the **Avataṃsaka* may be considered the *saṃbhogakāya* of Śākyamuni and the Lotus World his Pure Land. In the chapter on the light of the minor marks of the Buddha in the **Avataṃsaka*, it is stated that when Vairocana passed away in Tuṣita heaven and took abode in the womb of Mahāmāyā in the family of Śuddhodana, many bodhisattvas also came to Jambudvīpa.[121] In the chapter on the entry into the *dharmadhātu* of the **Avataṃsaka*, Mahāmāyā says to Sudhana:

> I have already accomplished the Dharma Door of Great Vow and Wisdom, by which I became the mother of Vairocana Tathāgata. From my right side I gave birth to Prince Siddhartha in the palace of Śuddhodana in Kapilavastu in Jambudvīpa.[122]

It is explicit that the authors of the **Avataṃsaka* considered that Śākyamuni and Vairocana were the same Buddha in different bodies. The **Brahmajālasūtra*, the Vinaya text of bodhisattvas reputed to be translated by Kumārajīva, gives us a clear picture of the relationship between Śākyamuni and Vairocana. This *sūtra* states that Śākyamuni was originally named Vairocana, who lives in the world of a lotus platform with a thousand petals. He manifests a thousand Śākyamunis, one in each petal world with a hundred million Sumerus, a hundred million suns and moons, a hundred million Jambudvīpas and a hundred million Śākyamunis each sitting under a *bodhi* tree expounding the bodhisattva doctrine.[123] In this *sūtra*, Śākyamuni is clearly considered to be a *nirmāṇakāya* of Vairocana.

The classification of Buddha lands

The term *Buddhakṣetra* (Buddha land) has two meanings. First it is the land in which the Buddha performs the Buddha activities to liberate sentient beings. Second it is the Pure Land in which only Buddhas live. One of the **Prajñāpāramitāsūtras* states: 'The three kinds of sages and the ten categories of holy ones live in the fruit of their actions, it is only the Buddha who abides in the Pure Land.'[124] Here the three kinds of sages means the *śrāvakas*, *pratyekabuddhas* and *bodhisattvas* before the attainment of the ten stages (*bhūmi*), while the ten categories of holy ones means the bodhisattvas of the ten stages. The first type of *Buddhakṣetra* can be either pure or impure. Only the liberated live in pure lands, such as the Sukhāvatī and Tuṣita. By contrast, in this Sahā world the liberated and sentient beings live together. The first type of *Buddhakṣetra* originated first, along with the idea of other Buddhas. It is modelled on Śākyamuni Buddha and his land. The development of the concept of Pure Land can be roughly divided into three stages.

First, belief in the existence of *Buddhakṣetras* is already found in the second century CE. Both the **Akṣobhyavyūha* and the *Sukhāvatīvyūha* translated by Lokakṣema have descriptions of Pure Lands. These Pure Lands are modelled on the ordinary world, for descriptions of the physical world in these two *sūtras* are very similar to our Sahā world. Like Śākyamuni, the Buddhas in these lands will attain *nirvāṇa* after they have disseminated their teachings. The only difference between these Pure Lands and our Sahā world is that the former are pure and full of liberated ones such as bodhisattvas and *arhats* while the latter is impure. This represents the first and primary development of the concept of *Buddhakṣetra*.

The second stage is the development of the Pure Land in which only the Buddhas live by sharing the enjoyment of Dharma together with great bodhisattvas. The *Rulaixingxianjing* states that the land of the Buddha is immeasurable. The bodhisattvas are as many as the atoms in a hundred thousand Buddha lands. They all attend the assembly by the virtue of the Buddha's power.[125] The **Avataṃsaka*, as discussed above, states that Vairocana Buddha abides in the Pure Land of the Lotus World with countless bodhisattvas who come from the ten directions to listen to his teaching.[126] It is said in the *Shizhuduanjiejing* ('*Sūtra* on the Cutting of the Tie of Passions in the Ten Dwellings') that north of our Sahā world, as many Buddha lands as the sand particles in 1.3 billion Ganges Rivers away, there lies a world called Immovable. The Buddha teaching there is named Illuminating Mind. In this land, even the names of *śrāvakas* and *pratyekabuddhas* are unknown, and there are only the trainees of the Mahāyāna who have attained the bodhisattva stages (*bhūmi*).[127] In these descriptions, the physical appearance of these Pure Lands is completely different from our Sahā world, as they are built on lotuses. Both the **Avataṃsaka* and the **Brahmajālasūtra* state that Vairocana lives in a great Lotus World. The **Brahmajālasūtra* even says that the lotus has a thousand petals (as described above). The Buddhas in these Pure Lands live eternally because there is no mention of their *parinirvāṇa*. The inhabitants of these Pure Lands are only bodhisattvas.

The third stage is the development of the *dharmatā* land in which only the *dharmakāya* Buddha abides, with no bodhisattvas. This type of Buddha land is precisely in accord with the second meaning of the term *Buddhakṣetra*. The **Vijñaptimātratāsiddhiśāstra* translated by Xuanzang states that the *dharmakāya* has the *dharmatā* as its abode. Although the body and the land are one and the same, on account of its characteristics it is called a body, and on account of its nature it is called a land.[128] Kuiji further explains that the land of *dharmatā* is *tathatā*, the true nature of all things. It is called a body on account of the meaning of enlightenment, and a land on account of the nature of *dharmatā*.[129] Thus the *dharmakāya* and its land are one and the same, as both possess *tathatā*, the true nature of all things, as their substance.

Buddhakṣetras are closely related to the issue of Buddha bodies. Hence, the Buddha lands are classified mainly in accordance with the *trikāya* theory. Lamotte has made a good survey of this, albeit limited to Indian works, *sūtras* and *śāstras* translated into Chinese.[130] Ancient Chinese scholars analysed the theory of *Buddhakṣetra* and classified them into various categories. They have been systematized into two, three or four types in accordance with the Buddha bodies under consideration.

The two types of *Buddhakṣetra* are the real and the created. According to Kuiji, the real Pure Land is the land of *dharmatā*, in which only the *dharmakāya* Buddha abides. All other *Buddhakṣetra* belong to the created type, which is either pure or impure and in which the *rūpakāya* Buddha abides.[131] The three types of *Buddhakṣetras* are classified according to the three Buddha bodies, the land of the *dharmakāya*, the land of the *saṃbhogakāya* and the land of the *nirmāṇakāya*. The most influential classification is the four types of Buddha land. There are two Chinese Buddhist schools that propose different classifications of these Buddha lands.

First, the Tiantai school classifies Buddha lands into the following four: (1) the land in which both sentient beings and the liberated abide; (2) the land in which liberated ones with minor defilement such as *arhats*, *pratyekabuddhas* and bodhisattvas before entering the *bhūmis* abide; (3) the land in which only great bodhisattvas abide; (4) the land of eternal serenity and illumination in which only Buddhas abide. This classification is simple and also includes all the variations and differences of the Buddha lands described in the *sūtras*. However, this is a classification utilizing the Buddhas as loci, and not the inhabitants of the Pure Land themselves.

Second is the Faxiang school or Cittamātratā that classifies *Buddhakṣetras* into four in accordance with the four Buddha bodies.

First is the Pure Land of true nature in which only the *dharmakāya* Buddha abides. Kuiji explains that the land of the *svabhāvakāya* is *tathatā*, the true nature of all *dharmas*. Therefore, the *dharmakāya* and its *kṣetra* are one and the same. It is called a *kāya* on account of its characteristics of enlightenment and a *kṣetra* on account of its true nature (*dharmatā*). The Buddha *kāya* and *kṣetra* are neither form, nor mind, nor associated mental activities, but are established by reason of true nature.[132] Therefore, it cannot be described in terms of size. On account of its characteristics, it is infinite like all-pervading empty space. All Buddhas attain this same *dharmatā* land which is one and without any sustenance and which is entered through the gate of signlessness (*animitta*) because one realizes the suchness (*tathatā*) of all *dharmas* by the observation of *animitta*. According to the Yogācāra, the *dharmatā* land is the *dharmatā* mind, non-discriminating transcendental wisdom (*nirvikalpakajñāna*).[133]

Second is the Pure Land of *svasaṃbhogakāya* in which only the Buddhas abide. Sthiramati states,

> There is a Pure Land where there is no suffering and which is not produced by the force of *karma* and *kleśa* . . . but produced by great vow, supportive cause and pure skilful (*kuśala*) deeds. This land is inconceivable and known only to the Buddhas, not known even by those who have attained pure *samādhi*, let alone those liberated ones who still possess *vitarka* and *vicāra* thoughts.[134]

Kuiji asserts that this is the Pure Land of the *svasaṃbhogakāya*, which is pure consciousness (the *āryavijñāna*) associated with mirror wisdom (*ādarśajñāna*). Mirror wisdom transforms itself into a pure *Buddhakṣetra* adorned with various jewels. It consists of the maturing of pure causes that a bodhisattva cultivates while in training. The transformation commences the moment the bodhisattva becomes a Buddha and lasts eternally. The land of the *svasaṃbhogakāya* pervades the entire cosmos without limit and each Buddha produces a different, limitless *svasaṃbhogakāya* land without obstruction by magical power. This land is sustained by the enjoyment of *dharmas* and is entered through the gate of wishlessness (*apraṇihita*) as Buddhas have no desire in the three realms (*dhātu*).

The above two kinds of Buddha lands are exclusively for Buddhas without retinue. The only difference between the two is that the Pure Land of the *dharmakāya* is one and the same to all Buddhas while the Pure Land of the *svasaṃbhogakāya* is specific to each Buddha.

Third is the Pure Land of *parasaṃbhogakāya*, where the Buddha abides by sharing the enjoyment of Dharma with the great bodhisattvas. Different *sūtras* present this Pure Land differently but give it a common factor, the lotus by which it is established. According to the *Brahmajālasūtra*, Vairocana Buddha sits on a great lotus with a thousand petals and each petal is a world in which there is a Śākyamuni, the *nirmāṇakāya*.[135] Similarly in the **Daśabhūmikasūtraśāstra* Vasubandhu states that when a bodhisattva enters the *samādhi* of *sarvajñā-jñāna*, a great treasure lotus appears on which the bodhisattva sits. This bodhisattva is surrounded by many other bodhisattvas sitting on lotuses.[136] But according to the **Yogācārabhūmiśāstra*, there is a Pure Land which is beyond the Śuddhāvāsa heaven where bodhisattvas in the tenth stage are born.[137] According to Asvabhāva, the western Sukhāvatī is the Pure Land where the great bodhisattvas live.[138] Kuiji explains that just as an ordinary kingdom consists of the people as inhabitants in the physical world, the land of the *parasaṃbhogakāya* consists of great bodhisattvas as inhabitants with gold and silver as surroundings. This Pure Land manifests as large or small, superior or inferior, according to the temperament of the great bodhisattvas of the tenth *bhūmi*.[139] The great bodhisattvas enter this Pure Land through the gate of great emptiness (*śūnyatā*) and are sustained by the enjoyment of the dharma.

Fourth is the land of the *nirmāṇakāya*, which is either pure or impure. The Pure Lands in which liberated ones such as *arhats* and bodhisattvas abide include Sukhāvatī of Amitābha and Abhirati of Akṣobhya. The impure lands in which both the liberated ones and sentient beings live include the Sahā world. This is similar to the first category of the Tiantai school. The Buddha in this land is the body of transformation arisen out of compassion for suffering beings.

Amitābha and Akṣobhya as *nirmāṇakāyas*[140]

Japanese scholars such as Takeuchi, following Chinese masters such as Daochuo (562–645), assert that Amitābha is a *saṃbhogakāya*.[141] Daochuo was perhaps the first person to make such an assertion explicitly in writing.[142] In his *Anleji* Daochuo states, 'Amitābha in the present is a *saṃbhogakāya* and the paradise land adorned with jewels is a Reward Land.'[143] However, in the same text some questions were raised: 'The *saṃbhogakāya* is eternal. Why does the '*Sūtra* on Avalokiteśvara's Prediction' state that after the *parinirvāṇa* of Amitābha, Avalokiteśvara bodhisattva would become a Buddha?' Daochuo replies:

> This is the *saṃbhogakāya* that manifests birth and death, it is not that it really attains *nirvāṇa*. The *sūtra* also states that after the *parinirvāṇa* of Amitābha, those sentient beings who have good roots in deep faith are still able to see the Buddha. This is a testimony.[144]

However, Daochuo's argument is weak, as David Chappell has pointed out. Nevertheless, it has exercised a tremendous influence on Chinese Pure Land Buddhism.[145]

Before Daochuo, Amitābha was regarded as a *nirmāṇakāya* according to his *Anleji*. 'According to ancient tradition, Amitābha is considered as a *nirmāṇakāya* by all and his Buddha land is also a land for a *nirmāṇakāya*.'[146] This is confirmed by David Chappell's analysis of Amitābha in the writings of Sengzhao (375–414), Jingying Huiyuan (523–592) and Zhiyi (538–597).[147] So Amitābha, like Śākyamuni, should be considered a *nirmāṇakāya* and not a *saṃbhogakāya*.

Before going into detailed discussion, we must first clarify the definition of the three *kāyas*. According to the concept of *trikāya* as explained in the *Mahāyānasūtrālaṃkāra*, all three *kāyas* are equal and eternal. 'On account of their base (*āśraya*), mind (*āśaya*) and *karma*, the three *kāyas* are equal. With regard to their essence (*svabhāva*), non-interruption and continuity, the three *kāyas* are eternal.' The commentary on the *Mahāyānasūtrālaṃkāra* explains:

> By the three kinds of *kāyas*, all Buddhas are completely equal. On account of their base, all Buddhas are equal with regard to *svabhāvakāya* because the *dharmadhātu* is the same. On account of their mind, all Buddhas are equal with regard to the *saṃbhogakāya* because the Buddha mind is the same. On account of their *karma*, all Buddhas are equal with regard to the *nirmāṇakāya* because the Buddha's deeds are the same. Again, all Buddhas are eternal with regard to the *svabhāvakāya* because the *svabhāva* is eternal and without defilement. All Buddhas are eternal with regard to the *saṃbhogakāya* because they teach the Dharma without interruption. All Buddhas are eternal with regard to the *nirmāṇakāya* because though it disappears from here it reappears there.[148]

The three *kāyas* manifested by Buddhas as defined above are both equal and eternal, but the *nirmāṇakāya* disappears from one place and reappears in another place in order to liberate sentient beings. Such disappearance and reappearance are the *parinirvāṇa* and the birth of a *nirmāṇakāya*, which are the activities of a Buddha. According to the *Mahāyānasaṃgraha*, the *nirmāṇakāya* performs eight acts in the world in order to benefit sentient beings. They include descending from Tuṣita heaven, being born, indulging in desire, leaving home, practising various forms of asceticism, attaining great enlightenment, turning the wheel of Dharma, and entering *parinirvāṇa*.[149] However, there is no such thing concerning the concept of the *saṃbhogakāya*. In accordance with this definition Amitābha should be considered a *nirmāṇakāya* on the following three grounds.

First, according to the *Sukhāvatīvyūha*, when Amitābha was a *bhikṣu* named Dharmākara, he made twenty-four or forty-eight vows to become a Buddha before Lokeśvararāja Tathāgata.[150] He also vowed to have his Buddha land so pure that it would be free from all evils such as those found in our Sahā world. Accordingly, Dharmākara attained enlightenment and became Amitābha Buddha in his Pure Land, Sukhāvatī. Śākyamuni, in the same way, also became a Buddha in this Sahā world after he made vows to liberate suffering sentient beings in front of the ancient Buddha Śākyamuni in the first *asaṃkhyeya kalpa.*[151] It is also said in the MPPŚ that Śākyamuni vowed to liberate those in the defiled world through the Dharma. He did not appear in the world to enjoy happiness and wealth.[152] If Śākyamuni is regarded as a *nirmāṇakāya*, then in the same way Amitābha should also be regarded as a *nirmāṇakāya* because they both became Buddhas in their respective Buddha lands in accordance with their vows for the sake of specific living beings.

How does one explain that Amitābha enjoys a limitless life-span and immeasurable light in his Sukhāvatī due to his past merit? The answer to this question is that Amitābha's qualities of a limitless life-span and immeasurable light are adaptations to accord with and liberate particular living beings in Sukhāvatī who also enjoy long life-spans. The situation is similar to that of Śākyamuni, who made a display of having lived for only eighty years in order to accommodate the expectations of sentient beings in our Sāha world. In fact, he could have enjoyed an immeasurable life-span, as explained in the **Saddharmapuṇḍarīkasūtra*. The **Avataṃsaka* states, 'There are Buddhas appearing in [different] worlds making a display of *rūpakāyas* which pervade the cosmos (*dharmadhātu*), some have short life-spans while others live for limitless *kalpas*.'[153] The author of the MPPŚ also explains this point clearly: 'Thus the life-spans of all Buddhas are, in fact, immeasurable, but they make displays of either short or long life-spans [in accordance with the beings of that particular world] in order to liberate them.'[154]

The *Vimalakīrtinirdeśasūtra* makes the same point, 'All Buddhas and Tathāgatas are equal in merit, but they make displays of having different Buddha lands in order to teach and liberate sentient beings.'[155]

The *Vimalakīrtinirdeśasūtra* states,

> Ānanda, all Buddhas are the same so far as the perfections of the Buddha qualities are concerned. These include: their forms, colours, radiance, bodies, marks, nobility, morality, concentration, wisdom, liberation, gnosis, vision of liberation, strengths, fearlessness, special Buddha qualities, great love, great compassion, helpful intentions, attitudes, practices, paths, the length of lives, teaching of the Dharma, development and liberation of living beings, and purification of Buddha lands. Therefore, they are all called *Samyaksaṃbuddhas*, Tathāgatas, and Buddhas.'[156]

Second, in all three Chinese translations of the *Sukhāvatīvyūhasūtra* (T12, no. 361, no. 362 and no. 364), it is said that once Amitābha attains *parinirvāṇa*, the Bodhisattva Avalokiteśvara will become a Buddha, the lord of Sukhāvatī, who in turn will teach there.

> After the *parinirvāṇa* of Amitābha, Bodhisattva Alougen [Avalokiteśvara][157] will attain Buddhahood and will be the lord teaching the Dharma. He will liberate individuals of the world as well as gods of the eight directions, above and below, by facilitating the *nirvāṇa* of all beings. His merits will be the same as Amitābha.[158]

There is no *parinirvāṇa* with regard to the *saṃbhogakāya* as it is eternal. The *nirmāṇakāya*, though eternal, makes a display of birth, enlightenment and *parinirvāṇa*, as Śākyamuni Buddha did. It follows that Amitābha cannot be regarded as a *saṃbhogakāya*, for he also attains *parinirvāṇa*.

Third, according to the MSA, the *saṃbhogakāya* enjoys the Dharma to its fullest realization by sharing it *only* with the assembly of great bodhisattvas.[159] The commentary on the MSA explains it thus:

> All Buddhas have three bodies, the first is the *svabhāvakāya* and its characteristic is transformation. The second is the *saṃbhogakāya* which shares the food of Dharma with the great assembly. The third is the *nirmāṇakāya* which works for the benefit of beings through its manifestations. It should be noted that the *svabhāvakāya* is the support of both the *saṃbhogakāya* and the *nirmāṇakāya*.[160]

In the *Mahāyānasaṃgrahabhāṣya*, Vasubandhu explains this point further by saying that the *saṃbhogakāya* serves only to bring bodhisattvas to maturity.

> [The statement] '*Dharmakāya* is the support for various *saṃbhogakāyas*' means that the *saṃbhogakāyas* are supported by the *dharmakāya*. Why must they be thus supported? It is because they bring all bodhisattvas to maturity. Without [the help of] such *saṃbhogakāyas*, bodhisattvas who have entered the first stage (*bhūmi*) would not come to maturity. [The statement] 'it is the support for the various *nirmāṇakāyas*' illustrates that these *nirmāṇakāyas* are supported by the *dharmakāya*. Why must they be thus supported? It is because they generally bring all *śrāvakas* to maturity. Without the help of these *nirmāṇakāyas*, *śrāvakas* of little faith and meagre understanding would not come to maturity. The term 'generally' should be understood to imply the inclusion of bodhisattvas who are in the stages of [initial] understanding and practice.[161]

From these explanations, it is clear that the *saṃbhogakāya* shares the pure Dharma with great bodhisattvas, bringing only bodhisattvas to maturity. The *nirmāṇakāyas* bring to maturity the *śrāvakas* as well as bodhisattvas in their initial stage. Amitābha, however, teaches various kinds of beings aside from bodhisattvas and *arhats*. The larger *Sukhāvatīvyūhasūtra* explains:

> When Amitābha delivers a *sūtra* to bodhisattvas and *arhats* who assemble in the teaching hall, immeasurable bodhisattvas, *arhats*, gods, people and other beings fly to where Amitābha is, sit down and listen to the *sūtra* after paying their respects [to Amitābha]. . . . After Amitābha has proclaimed the *sūtra* to bodhisattvas and *arhats*, among the gods and people, those who have not attained the path attain it, those who have not attained *śrotāpanna* attain it . . . *sakṛdāgāmin* . . . *anāgamin* . . . *arhat*, and those who have not attained the irreversible (*avaivarta*) stage of the bodhisattva career attain it.'[162]

Since Amitābha teaches various kinds of beings in his Sukhāvatī in addition to great bodhisattvas, Amitābha cannot be regarded as a *saṃbhogakāya*. More intuitively he is to be regarded as a *nirmāṇakāya* as he attained Buddhahood for the sake of particular beings possessing a long life-span and special powers. As quoted above, Vasubandhu explains that it is the *nirmāṇakāya* which brings to maturity the *śrāvakas* as well as the bodhisattvas. In the same way, Akṣobhya does the same work in his Buddha land Abhirati. He is a *nirmāṇakāya* manifested for the sake of particular beings, with specific reference to womankind. Śākyamuni, Amitābha and Akṣobhya attained enlightenment in their respective Buddha lands of Sahā, Sukhāvatī and Abhirati in accordance with their vows. Belonging to the same category, they assumed different *nirmāṇakāyas* in order to teach and liberate particular beings in their respective Buddha lands. Śākyamuni lived for only eighty years because the life-span of people in the Sahā world is around a hundred years while Amitābha had a long life because the beings in the Sukhāvatī generally have long lives. In the end the three Buddhas attain *parinirvāṇa* in their Buddha lands after they have completed their Buddha activities. Since Śākyamuni is considered a *nirmāṇakāya*, Amitābha and Akṣobhya must also be regarded in the same way.

CONCLUSION

The five basic stages in the development of the concept of the Buddha

As we have seen, the development of the concept of the Buddha is a complex issue. It involves many key aspects of Buddhist thought such as the goal of Buddhist practice – Buddhahood, the bodhisattva ideal and the notion of *nirvāṇa*. These developments can be described as a process of evolution from the Buddha envisaged as a human teacher in early Buddhism to a philosophical and abstract concept in the Mahāyāna. Even in the time of the early Indian Buddhist schools, attempts were made to understand or interpret what or who the Buddha was. The interpretations of these early schools were closely connected with the historical Buddha since the life of Śākyamuni had a strong influence upon them. It is the early Mahāyānists who thoroughly interpreted the notion of the Buddha in an ontological way. The *dharmakāya* was rendered as an impersonal principle supporting all phenomena in which the historical Buddha played an insignificant role. It was on this basis that the *trikāya* theory was formulated through the analysis and synthesis of the doctrinal developments in the early and middle Mahāyāna *sūtras*. Five basic stages can be identified in the development of the concept of the Buddha.

The first stage is the Buddha as a human teacher and guide in early Buddhism albeit with many supernatural qualities attributed to him, for example the thirty-two marks of a great man. In the earliest Buddhist literature, namely the *Nikāyas* and the *Āgamas*, two identities of the Buddha are clearly distinguishable: the human teacher and the superhuman being. As discussed in Chapter 1 above, the superhuman aspect of the Buddha falls into two categories: the miracles performed by Gautama Buddha and the miracles that occurred as a result of natural phenomena. The latter category does not affect the personality of the Buddha. The first, as analysed, is included in the six modes of higher knowledge that are attainable by a human. Although the story of the Buddha in the early *sūtras* is deeply embedded in legends and mythology, the human identity is vividly apparent in his illness and old age as well as in the troubles of his life within and outside the community of monks.

In the second stage of the early Indian Buddhist schools there emerged two different interpretations of the notion of the Buddha on the basis of the two identities of the Buddha present in early Buddhism. The Sarvāstivādins established the two-body theory: the *dharmakāya* and the *rūpakāya* based on the teachings of the *Āgamas*. They insisted that the *dharmakāya* corresponded to the real Buddha to be taken refuge in. It was thus not the impure *rūpakāya* that was to form the object of refuge, although they essentially advocated the human version of the Buddha. The Sarvāstivādins believed that what made Gautama a Buddha was his attainment of *bodhi*, which was comprised of purely mental qualities. According to the **Mahāvibhāṣā* these purely mental qualities consisted of the eighteen *dharmas* exclusive to the Buddha, which are known collectively as *dharmakāya*, as shown in Chapter 2 above. This interpretation of the concept of the Buddha is rational and analytical since there is nothing innovative about it. It represents only a synthetic summary of what is taught in early Buddhism. On the other hand, the Mahāsāṃghikas interpreted the Buddha as a transcendental being on the basis of the Buddha's superhuman qualities also revealed in the *Āgamas*. After all, it is well known that they took whatever was said by the Buddha as an enunciation of Dharma. This interpretation added two new dimensions to the notion of the Buddha. First, the real Buddha was perceived as exalted above mankind, omniscient and almighty. Second, the appearance of the Buddha on earth, including his daily activities, is considered a display for the sake of liberating sentient beings. The Buddha was not therefore subject to the laws of the human world.

The third stage is the ontological interpretation of the concept of the Buddha by the early Mahāyānists on the basis of Mahāsāṃghika Buddhology. The early Mahāyānists reinterpreted the notion of the Buddha as having the nature of the *tathatā*, which they introduced. According to them, *tathatā*, which is the true nature of all things both transcendental and worldly, is the *dharmakāya*, for both possess the same characteristics: (1) they are intrinsically pure and eternal; (2) they are one and the same in all Buddhas of the past, present and future. Since *tathatā* inheres in all objects and pervades the entire universe, the *dharmakāya* becomes a cosmic body as well as the principle supporting all phenomena. This is why the *dharmakāya* is regarded as the Buddha. This understanding of the notion of the Buddha is very different from that of the early Indian Buddhist schools. The Mahāyānists concentrated exclusively on the abstract notion of the Buddha, not on the historical Buddha. This provides the foundation for the Mahāyānist doctrine of the concept of the Buddha.

The fourth stage is the identification of the *dharmakāya* with many new concepts such as *tathāgatagarbha* and *mahāparinirvāṇa*, which were introduced by the Mahāyānists along with the composition of the Mahāyāna *sūtras* and *śāstras*. These new concepts added new dimensions to the notion of the Buddha, expanding its connotations. According to the

**Mahāvaipulyatathāgatagarbhasūtra*, all sentient beings possess Buddha nature (*tathāgatagarbha*), although it is covered with defilements. When the defilements are eliminated, pure *dharmakāya* is revealed. The *tathāgatagarbha* is called *buddhadhātu* at the level of sentient beings, and *dharmakāya* at the level of Buddhahood. Buddhas are not different from sentient beings in an ultimate sense since all possess the same *tathatā*, but from the perspective of conventional truth they are different, as Buddhas do not have *kleśas*. According to the Mahāyāna *Mahāparinirvāṇasūtra*, however, the *mahāparinirvāṇa* of the Buddha is different from the liberation of the *śrāvakas* and *pratyekabuddhas* in that it has four attributes: eternity, happiness, self and purity. The attribute of eternity is the crux of the concept of *mahāparinirvāṇa* since the other three attributes are established on its basis, as discussed in Chapter 4 above. Therefore, the Buddha's abiding in *mahāparinirvāṇa* does not imply that he is gone for ever, but means he eternally lives in intrinsic quiescence. Thus, in his **Buddhagotraśāstra*, Vasubandhu asserts that terms such as Tathāgata, *dharmakāya*, *paramārtha* and *nirvāṇa* are all congruent since they ontologically have *tathatā* as their essence. They are given different names because each of them denotes a specific aspect of Buddhahood. Thus, the notion of the Buddha in the Mahāyāna is entirely different from that of early Buddhism. Ontologically it is the ultimate reality and salvifically it is the transcendent being who establishes sentient beings in enlightenment.

The fifth stage is the formulation of the *trikāya* theory, the climax in the progressive development of the concept of the Buddha. The *trikāya* theory is a result of the complex development of Mahāyāna thought. From early to middle Mahāyāna *sūtras* we can see that the concept of the Buddha developed considerably and acquired many transcendental qualities and attributes such as magical light and salvific power. These qualities were expanded and strengthened as Mahāyānist theories developed. The **Avataṃsaka* compilation represents perhaps the last stage before the formulation of the *trikāya* theory by providing the doctrinal foundation for it. On the other hand, the debates on the transcendental qualities of the Buddha in early Indian Buddhist schools identified the problem of the short life-span of Buddha Śākyamuni in Mahāyāna *sūtras*. It was an important issue to which many Mahāyāna *sūtras* devoted a special chapter, as shown in Chapter 5 above. This served as significant impetus for the further development of the concept of the Buddha. One of the reasons Yogācāra masters such as Asaṅga and Vasubandhu established the *trikāya* theory rooted in the doctrines of the Mahāyāna *sūtras* was thus to solve the complex problem concerning the ontological status of the Buddha.

APPENDIX

Chronology of Chinese translations of Mahāyāna *sūtras* and *śāstras*

In this chronology, the major translators and their representative translations have been chosen in order to illustrate that they roughly reflect the development of Buddhist thought in India. The date of the first translation is used in cases where more than one translation of the same text is extant. This is because the first translation reflects the date of appearance of the particular text.

Lokakṣema (178–189)

**Ajātaśatrurāja-sūtra* (佛說阿闍世王經), T15, no. 626.
**Akṣobhyatathāgatasyavyūha-sūtra* (阿閦佛國經), T11, no. 313.
Daoxingbanruojing (a version of the *Aṣṭa* 道行般若經), T8, no. 224.
**Lokānuvartana-sūtra* (佛說內藏百寶經), T17, no. 807.
**Pratyutpanna-buddhasammuhkāvasthitā-samādhi-sūtra* (般舟三昧經), T13, no. 418.

Others (194–199)

**Caryānidāna-sūtra* (修行本起經), T3, no. 184, tr. Mahābala, together with Kang Menxiang, 197.
**Madhyametyukta-sūtra* (中本起經), T4, no. 196, tr. Dharmaphala together with Kang Menxiang, 207.
Xingqixingjing (佛說興起行經 *Nidānacaryā-sūtra*?), T4, no. 197, tr. Kang Menxiang, 194–199.

Zhi Qian (222–280)

Damingdujing (a version of the *Aṣṭa* 大明度經), T8, no. 225.
**Jñānamudrāsamādhi-sūtra* (佛說慧印三昧經), T15, no. 632.
**Kumāra-kuśalaphala-nidāna-sūtra* (太子瑞應本起經), T3, no. 185.
**Pūrṇamukhāvadāna-śātaka* (撰集百緣經), T4, no. 200.

Sukhāvatīvyūha-sūtra (佛說阿彌陀三耶三佛薩樓佛檀過度人道經), T12, no. 362.
**Vimalakīrtinirdeśa-sūtra* (佛說維摩詰經), T14, no. 474.
Yizu-jing (佛說義足經 '*Sūtra* on the Sufficiency of Truth'), T4, no. 198.

Mokṣala (291)

**Pañcaviṃśatisāhasrikā Prajñāpāramitā-sūtra* (放光般若經), T8, no. 221.

Dharmarakṣa (266–313)

**Buddhasaṅgīti-sūtra* (諸佛要集經), T17, no. 810.
Dengmupusasuowensanmei-jing (等目菩薩所問三昧經 '*Sūtra* on a *Samādhi* Asked by the Bodhisattva Samacakṣus'), T10, no. 288.
Dushipin-jing (度世品經 '*Sūtra* of the Chapter on Going Across the World'), T10, no. 292.
Jianbeiyiqiezhide-jing (漸備一切智德經 '*Sūtra* on Making Gradually Complete All the Wisdom and Virtue'), T10, no. 285.
**Maitreya-paripṛcchā-sūtra* (彌勒菩薩所問本願經), T12, no. 349.
**Mañjuśrībuddhakṣetraguṇavyūha-sūtra* (文殊師利佛土嚴淨經), T11, no. 318.
**Mūkakumāra-sūtra* (佛說無言童子經), T13, no. 401.
**Pañcaśatasthavirāvadāna-sūtra* (佛五百弟子自說本起經), T4, no. 199.
**Pañcaviṃśatisāhasrikā Prajñāpāramitā-sūtra* (光讚經), T8, no. 222.
Pusaxingwushiyuansheng-jing (菩薩行五十緣身經) [*Sūtra* spoken by the Buddha on (the characteristic marks on) his person as (the result of) fifty causes of the practice of *bodhisattva*], T17, no. 812.
Rulaixingxian-jing (如來興顯經 '*Sūtra* Spoken by the Buddha on the Manifestation of the Tathāgata'), T10, no. 291.
**Samantaprabhāsa-sūtra* (普曜經), T3, no. 186.
**Saddharmapuṇḍarīka-sūtra* (正法華經), T9, no. 263.
**Sucintidevaputra-sūtra* (須真天子經), T15, no. 588.
**Tathāgatamahākāruṇikanirdeṣa-sūtra* (大哀經), T13, no. 398.
**Upāyakauśālyasūtra* (慧上菩薩問大善權經), T12, no. 345.

Sanghabhūti (381–385)

Vibhāṣāśāstra (鞞婆沙論), T28, no. 1547, tr. Saṅghabhūti, Dharmanandin, Buddharakṣa, 383.

Kumārajīva (402–413)

**Brahmajāla-sūtra* (梵網經), T24, no. 1484.
**Daśabhāṇavāravinaya* (十誦律), T23, no. 1435.
**Daśabhūmika-sūtra* (十住經), T10, no. 286.

**Daśabhūmikavibhāṣā-śāstra* (十住毘婆沙論), T26, no. 1521, attrib. Nāgārjuna.
**Dhyānaniṣṭhitasamādhi-sūtra* (坐禪三昧經), T15, no. 614, by Saṅgharakṣa.
**Kāruṇikārājā-prajñāpāramitā-sūtra* (仁王般若波羅蜜經), T8, no. 245.
**Mahālaṅkāra-sūtra-śāstra* (大莊嚴經論), T4, no. 201, attrib. Aśvaghoṣa.
**Mahāprajñāpāramitā-śāstra* (大智度論), T25, no. 1509, attrib. Nāgārjuna.
**Maitreya-vyākaraṇa-sūtra* (佛說彌勒下生成佛經) T14, no. 454.
**Pañcaviṃśatisāhasrikā Prajñāpāramitā-sūtra* (摩訶般若波羅蜜經), T8, no. 223.
**Prajñāpāramitāsūtra* (a version of the *Aṣṭa* 小品般若波羅蜜經), T8, no. 227.
**Saddharmapuṇḍarīka-sūtra* (妙法蓮華經), T9, no. 262.
**Satyasiddhi-śāstra* (成實論), T32, no. 1646, by Harivarman.
**Śūraṃgamasamādhi-sūtra* (佛說首楞嚴三昧經), T15, no. 642.
**Vimalakīrtinirdeśa-sūtra* (維摩詰所說經), T14, no. 475.

Buddhabhadra (410–421)

**Buddhadhyānasamādhisāgara-sūtra* (佛說觀佛三昧海經), T15, no. 643.
**Buddhāvataṃsaka-mahāvaipulya-sūtra* (大方廣佛華嚴經), T9, no. 278.
**Mahāvaipulya-tathāgatagarbha-sūtra* (大方等如來藏經), T16, no. 666.

Dharmakṣena (414–426)

**Bodhisattvabhūmidhara-sūtra* (菩薩地持經), T30, no. 1581.
Buddhacarita (佛所行讚), T4, no. 192, by Aśvaghosa.
**Karuṇāpuṇḍarīka-sūtra* (悲華經), T3, no. 157.
Mahāparinirvāṇa-sūtra (大般涅槃經), T12, no. 374 (Mahāyāna version).
**Suvarṇaprabhāsa-sūtra* (金光明經), T16, no. 663.

Guṇabhadra (435–468)

Laṅkāvatāra-sūtra (楞伽阿跋多羅寶經), T16, no. 670.
**Prakaraṇapāda-śāstra* (眾事分阿毘曇論), T26, no. 1541, attrib. Vasumitra.
**Saṃyuktāgama* (雜阿含經) T2, no. 99.
**Śrīmālādevīsiṃhanāda-sūtra* (勝鬘師子吼一乘大方便方廣經), T12, no. 353.

Others (437–520)

**Abhidharmavibhāṣāśāstra* (阿毘達磨毘婆娑論), T28, no. 1546, tr. Buddhavarman and Daotai, 437–439.
**Mahāyānadaśadharmaka-sūtra* (佛說大乘十法經) T11, no. 314, tr. Saṅghapāla, 506–520.

**Ratnagotravibhāga-Mahāyānottaratantra-śāstra* and *Vyākhyā* (究竟一乘寶性論), T31, no. 1611, author unknown, tr. Ratnamati, 508.

Bodhiruci (508–535)

Buzengbujian-jing (佛說不增不減經 '*Sūtra* on Neither Increasing Nor Decreasing'), T16, no. 668.
**Daśabhūmikasūtra-śāstra* (十住經論), T26, no. 1522, by Vasubandhu.
Laṅkāvatāra-sūtra (入楞伽經), T16, no. 671.
**Mahāsatyanirgranthaputra-vyākaraṇa-sūtra* (大薩遮尼乾子所說經), T9, no. 272.
**Sandhinirmocana-sūtra* (深密解脱經), T16, no. 675.

Buddhaśanti (525–539)

**Mahāyānadaśadharmaka-sūtra* (大寶積經・大乘十法會), T11, no. 310.9.
Mahāyānasaṃgraha of Asaṅga (攝大乘論), T31, no. 1592.

Paramārtha (546–569)

**Abhidharma-kośavyākhyā-śāstra* (阿毘達磨俱舍釋論), T29, no. 1559, by Vasubandhu.
**Anuttarāśraya-sūtra* (佛說無上依經), T16, no. 669.
**Buddhagotra-śāstra* (佛性論), T31, no. 1610, by Vasubandhu.
Mahāyānasaṃgraha (攝大乘論), T31, no. 1593, by Asaṅga.
**Mahāyānasaṃgrahabhāśya* (攝大乘論釋), T31, no. 1595, by Vasubandhu.
**Samayabhedavyūhacakra* (部執異論), T49, no. 2033, by Vasumitra.

Xuanzang (645–664)

**Abhidharma-dharmaskandhapāda-śāstra* (阿毘達磨法蘊足論), T26, no. 1537, attrib. Śāriputra (Sanskrit version), Mahāmaudgalyāyana (Chinese version).
**Abhidharma-jñānaprasthāna-śāstra* (阿毘達磨發智論), T26, no. 1544, attrib. Kātyāyanīputra.
**Abhidharma-kośa-śāstra* (阿毘達磨俱舍論), T29, no. 1558, by Vasubandhu.
**Abhidharma-nyāyānusāra-śāstra* (阿毘達磨順正理論), T29, no. 1562, by Saṅghabhadra.
**Abhidharma(piṭaka)prakaraṇaśāsana-śāstra* (阿毘達磨藏顯宗論), T29, no. 1563, by Saṅghabhadra.
**Abhidharma-prakaraṇapāda-śāstra* (阿毘達磨品類足論), T26, no. 1542, attrib. Vasumitra.
**Abhidharma-vijñānakāyapāda-śāstra* (阿毘達磨識身足論), T26, no. 1539, attrib. Devaśarman.

Buddhabhūmi-sūtra (佛說佛地經), T16, no. 680.
Buddhabhūmisūtra-śāstra (佛說佛地經論), T26, no. 1530, by Bandhuprabha.
Mahāyānābhidharmasaṃyuktasaṅgīti-śāstra (大乘阿毗達磨雜集論), T31, no. 1606, by Sthiramati.
Mahāyānasaṃgrahabhāśya (攝大乘論釋), T31, no. 1597, by Vasubandhu.
Mahāyānasaṃgrahabhāśya (攝大乘論釋), T31, no. 1598, by Asvabhāva.
Mahāyānasaṃgraha (攝大乘論本), T31, no. 1594, by Asaṅga.
Mahāvibhāṣāśāstra (大毘婆沙論), T27, no. 1545.
Mahāprajñāpāramitā-sūtra (大般若波羅蜜多經), T5, T6, T7, no. 220.
Pañcavastukavibhāṣā-śāstra (五事毘婆沙論), T28, no. 1555, attrib. Dharmatrātā.
Samayabhedavyūhacakra (異部宗輪論), T49 (2031), by Vasumitra.
Sandhinirmocana-sūtra (解深密經), T16, no. 676.
Vijñāptimātratāsiddhi-śāstra (成唯識論), T31, no. 1585, by Dharmapāla and nine others.
Yogācārabhūmi-śāstra (瑜伽師地論), T30, no. 1579, attrib. Maitreya.

Yijing (695–713)

Bhaiṣajyavastu of the *Mūlasarvāstivāda-vinaya* (根本說一切有部藥事), T24, no. 1448.
Maitreya-vyākaraṇa-sūtra (佛說彌勒下生成佛經), T14, no. 455.
Mūlasarvāstivādavinaya (根本說一切有部毘拉耶), T23, no. 1442.
Saṃghabhedavastu of the *Mūlasarvāstivāda-vinaya* (根本說一切有部破僧事), T24, no. 1450.
Suvarṇaprabhāsottamarāja-sūtra (金光明最勝王經), T16, no. 665.

NOTES

INTRODUCTION

1 Louis de La Vallée Poussin (1906) 'Studies in Buddhist Dogma: The Three Bodies of the Buddha (Trikāya)', *Journal of the Royal Asiatic Society of Great Britain and Ireland*, pp. 943–77; C. Akanuma (1922) 'The Triple Body of the Buddha', *Eastern Buddhist*, vol. 2, pp. 1–29.
2 G. Nagao (1973) 'On the Theory of Buddha-body (Buddhakāya)', *Eastern Buddhist*, vol. 6, no. 1, pp. 25–53.
3 N. Dutt (1978) *Mahāyāna Buddhism*, Delhi: Motilal Banarsidass.
4 S. Takeuchi (1983) 'Buddhakan no hensen', in Akira Hirakawa, ed., *Daijō Bukkyō*, vol. I, Tokyo: Shunjusha, pp. 166–70.
5 John Makransky (1997) *Buddhahood Embodied: Sources of Controversy in India and Tibet*, New York: State University of New York Press.
6 Nāgārjuna is traditionally considered the founder of Mahāyāna Buddhism. Thus, Mahāyāna arose in the second century CE according to tradition.
7 E. Conze (1960a) *The Prajñāpāramitā Literature*, s-Gravenhage: Mouton, p. 9. Masao Shizutani, basing himself chiefly on epigraphical records and the dates of the Chinese translations of Mahāyāna *sūtras*, made a proposal that proto-Mahāyāna was in its inception during 100 to 1 BCE.
8 Japanese scholars such as Masao Shizutani have also used the dates of Chinese translations in their studies of the development of Mahāyāna *sūtras*. Cited from H. Nakamura (1996) *Indian Buddhism: A Survey With Bibliographical Notes*, Delhi: Motilal Banarsidass, p. 152.
9 See K. Ch'en (1972) *Buddhism in China: A Historical Survey*, Princeton, NJ: Princeton University Press, p. 60.
10 T55, 73c.
11 T24, 822a, 232b–c; T22, 955a, 174b; T23, 274a; Pāli Vinaya, II. 139.
12 For a general discussion of the date of the Buddhist canon, see Max Muller's Introduction to his translation of the *Dhammapada: The Sacred Books of the East*, Oxford: Clarendon Press, vol. X, part I.

1 THE CONCEPT OF THE BUDDHA IN EARLY BUDDHISM

1 An earlier version of this chapter was originally published in the *World Hongming Philosophical Quarterly*, vol. 2002, June, under the same title (Internet URL:

www.whpq.org or www.whpq.net). The term 'early Buddhism' indicates the teachings of the Buddha as revealed in the Pāli *Nikāyas* and the Chinese *Āgamas* which are considered by scholars to be the earliest form of Buddhist literature.

2 According to the *Acchariyābbhūtasutta* of the *Majjhimanikāya*, soon after the Buddha was born he said: 'I am the highest in the world; I am the best in the world; I am the foremost in the world. This is my last birth; now there is no renewal of being for me' (M iii, 123). This clearly shows the superhuman aspect of the Buddha.

3 These scholars include E. C. M. Senart (1875) *Essai sur la légende du Bouddha: son caractère et ses origines*, Paris: Imprimerie nationale, and also Hendrich Kern, A. Barth, R. Otto and Ananda Coomaraswamy.

4 B. G. Gokhale (1994) *New Light on Early Buddhism*, London: Sangam Books, pp. 107–8.

5 The *Sekhasutta* of the *Majjhimanikāya* (M i, 354) records that once when the Buddha suffered from back pain he asked Ānanda to speak on higher training. Similarly, Moggallāna (S iv, 183–4; T2, 316b), Sāriputta (D iii, 200; T1, 49c; A v, 122, 125) and Anuruddha (T1, 551c–552b) were asked to preach on his behalf under similar circumstances. Stomach troubles of the Buddha are mentioned in many places in the canon such as *Vinaya*, ii, 210; *Theragāthā*, 185; S i, 174–5. They are also found in the *Dhammapada* commentary, iv, 232 and the *Theragāthā* commentary, I, 311.

6 The Pāli version, D ii, 127–8, the four Chinese translations: T1, 18b, 164c, 180a, 197b.

7 The *Mahjjimanikāya* commentary, i, 465, and the *Dīghanikāya* commentary, iii, 974.

8 The *Saṃyuttanikāya* commentary, i, 200.

9 *Vinaya*, i, 279.

10 Miln. 135.

11 The *Udāna*, 165–7.

12 According to the *Saṃyuttanikāya*, the Buddha sometimes walked for a large part of the night and then washed his feet before going to bed (S i, 106).

13 S v, 217.

14 D ii, 100. The English translation is adapted from T. W. Rhys Davids (tr.) (1995), *The Dialogues of the Buddha*, Oxford: PTS, vol. II, p. 107. These words of the Buddha are also found in three of the Chinese translations of the *Mahāparinirvāṇasūtra*: T1, 15b, 164c, 180a.

15 T1, 472a. This *sūtra* must be of a late date since it contains praises of Ānanda as an attendant of the Buddha for twenty-five years. Ānanda's role is corroborated by a similar account in the Southern Tradition found in the commentary on the *Dhammapada*.

16 The *Dīghanikāya* commentary, ii, 573. For an explanation of the term *gāvuta* see An Yang-Gyu (1998) 'Buddhology in the *Mahāparinibbāna Suttanta* and Its Commentary, with an Annotated Translation of Buddhaghosa's Commentary', unpublished Ph.D. thesis, University of Oxford, p. 257, footnote 2.

17 Vinaya, ii, 257–71; S i, 262.

18 According to the *Samantapāsādikā* (iii, 613f.), they were all from Sāvatthi and were originally acquaintances. Finding a living hard to obtain, they entered the Order under the two chief disciples. They decided among themselves that it was unwise for them all to live in the same place, and they therefore divided themselves into three groups. Each group had five hundred monks attached to it. Of the three groups, the followers of Paṇḍuka and Lohitaka were the most virtuous.

Unlike the others, they did not transgress Vinaya rules. Cited from G. P. Malalasekera, ed. (1937) *Dictionary of Pāli Proper Names*, vol. I, London: John Murray, p. 926.

19 The Pāli Vinaya, i, 84f., 104, 106, 111, 113, 114, 138, 160, 170, 185, 189, 192, 194, 203f., 216, 285, 306, 316; ii, 73, 105ff., 145ff., 213ff., 241, 262, etc. The Chinese *Tripiṭaka*: T1, 191, 217, 360; T3, 149; the *Dhammapada* commentary, iii, 48f., 330, 382. Cited from Malalasekera, *Dictionary*, p. 926.

20 T2, 279c. *Cullavagga*, iv, 4. 4–11. The nun Mettiyā was persuaded by a group of monks to accuse Dabba Mallaputta of having an affair with her. After an investigation, the charge was found to be false.

21 Vinaya, ii, 262, 266, 269, 271, 276. Cited from Malalasekera, *Dictionary*, p. 926.

22 M iii, 153.

23 S ii, 208; T2, 300c–301a.

24 S ii, 223–4. The translation is adapted from Mrs Rhys Davids (tr.) (1990) *The Book of Kindred Sayings*, vol. II, Oxford: PTS, pp. 151–2.

25 *Mahāvagga*, i, 31.

26 S ii, 13.

27 S ii, 50. There is another case of a monk returning to lay life in S iv, 102.

28 *Cullavagga*, i, 32–4. The story of Ariṭṭha is also found in M i, 130.

29 His defection is given in the *Pāṭikasutta* of the *Dīghanikāya* and his return to lay life is given in the *Mahāsīhanādasutta* of the *Majjhimanikāya* (M i, 68). The *Sunakkhattasutta* (M no. 105) was apparently expounded to him by the Buddha before he joined the Order.

30 M i, 170–1; T1, 777b. During the time of the Buddha, people judged whether a person was or was not an *arhat* by their serenity of countenance which is an expression of inner peace. For instance, Sāriputta took Assaji to be an enlightened person due to his appearance (Vinaya, i, 40).

31 A ii, 36–7; T2, 28a–b.

32 A. Naughton (1991) 'Buddhist Omniscience', *Eastern Buddhist*, vol. 24, no. 1, p. 32.

33 The discussions held between Gautama Buddha and the wanderer Udāyin are found in the *Mahāsakuludāyisutta* and the *Cūlasakuludāyisutta*, numbers 77 and 79 of the *Majjhimanikāya*. There are several Udāyins mentioned in the *Nikāyas*. According to Mrs Rhys Davids (*Psalms of Brethren*, Oxford: PTS, 1909, p. 288, footnote 2) there are three Udāyins who are the disciples of the Buddha: Kāludāyin, Udāyin the great, and a Brahmin Udāyin. The person in our discussion is a wanderer Sakuludāyin.

34 M i, 108; T1, 603b; T2, 743a.

35 Cited from Ñāṇamoli, Bhikkhu (tr.) (1995) *The Middle Length Discourse of the Buddha*, Boston: Wisdom Publication, endnote 226.

36 S i, 112; T2, 772a–b.

37 The *Dhammapada* commentary, iii, 257.

38 Vinaya, i, 39–44.

39 M i, 6.

40 M i, 258.

41 M i, 132.

42 This is referred to in Ñāṇamoli, *The Middle Length Discourse*, endnote 249.

43 Vinaya, ii, 188, 'Sāriputtamoggallānānam pi kho ahaṃ Devadatta bhikkhusaṃghaṃ na nissajjeyyaṃ, kim pana tuyhaṃ chavassakhelāpakassā'ti'. It is also mentioned in the **Dharmaguptakavinaya* (T22, 592b), 我尚不以僧付舍利弗目連，況汝癡人涕唾之身豈可付囑, the **Daśabhāṇavāravinaya*, (T23, 258b),

舍利弗目連有大智慧神通，佛尚不以眾僧付之，況汝噉唾癡人死人，而當付囑, the **Mūlasarvāstivādadavinaya* (T23, 701c), 汝之癡人，如舍利子大目連，我尚不以苾芻 僧伽而見付囑，況汝癡人，食人洟唾，而相付囑, the **Mūlasarvāstivādavinaya Saṃghabhedavastu* (T24, 169b), 如我舍利弗大目揵連，弟子中聰明智慧，梵行神通證羅漢果，我今尚自不以苾芻僧伽而見付囑，豈可況汝無智癡人食唾者乎. This incident is also referred to in the *Abhayarājakumārasutta* (M i, 393). The meaning of the quotation is basically the same in the Vinaya of all these schools and traditions although the wording is slightly different. This suggests that it is probably historical in nature.

44 A iii, 401. The translation is taken from E. M. Hare (tr.) (1995) *The Book of the Gradual Sayings*, vol. III, Oxford: PTS, p. 287.

45 T2, 567a–c.

46 According to the *Sāmagāmasutta* (M ii, 243–4), in his last few years the Buddha observed that Jain monks split after the death of their Master because of different views and understandings on the teachings of their Master.

47 T27, 601c–602a.

48 D ii, 96. The translation is taken from Rhys Davids, *The Dialogues*, vol. II, p. 103.

49 D ii, 102. The translation is taken from Rhys Davids, *The Dialogues*, vol. II, p. 110. It is also mentioned in the *Saṃyuttanikāya*, v, 258.

50 The praise of the Licchavis is mentioned in all the four Chinese versions: T1, 13c, 164a, 179b, 194b, but the praise of the city of Vesālī is only found in two: T1, 165a, 180b.

51 The *Apadāna*, i, 299–301.

52 The *Apadāna*, i, 299–301, verses 7–9; *Jātaka*, iv, 187f.; the *Dhammapada* commentary, iii, 178f.; the *Itivuttaka* commentary, 69.

53 The *Udāna*, iv, 8; the *Udāna* commentary, 256ff.; the *Dhammapada* commentary, iii, 474f.; the *Saṃyutta* commentary, ii, 528f.; the *Jātaka*, ii, 415f.; and the *Apadāna*, i, 299–301, verses 4–6. According to the commentary of the *Majjhimanikāya*, this incident is also referred to in the *Bāhitikasutta* of the *Majjhimanikāya*, where King Pasenadi is said to have asked Ānanda about it.

54 The thirty-two marks of a great man are mentioned in many early *sūtras*: the Pāli *suttas* such as the *Mahāpadānasutta*, D ii, 17–19; the *Lakkhaṇasutta*, D iii, 143–4; the *Brahmāyusutta*, M ii, 136–7; the Chinese translations such as the **Dīrghāgama*, T1, 5a–b; the **Madhyamāgama*, T1, 686; 883c–884a; the **Saṃghabhedavastu* of the **Mūlasarvāstivādavinaya*, T24, 108c–109a and the *Mahāvastu*, i, 226; ii, 29.

They are also referred to in many biographies of the Buddha in Chinese translations: the **Lalitavistara*, T3, 496a–b; the *Fangguangdazhuangyejing*, T3, 557a; the **Kumārakuśalaphalanidānasūtra*, T3, 474a; the **Atītapratyutpannahetuphalasūtra*, T3, 627a–b; the **Abhiniṣkramanasūtra*, T3, 692c–693a; the **Samadattamahārājasūtra*, T3, 940b–c.

55 For instance, H. Nakamura (1987) *Gotama Buddha*, Los Angeles and Tokyo: Buddhist Books International, p. 513.

56 Rhys Davids, *The Dialogues*, vol. iii, pp. 134–5. T. Endo (1997) *Buddha in Theravāda Buddhism: A Study of the Concept of Buddha in the Pāli Commentaries*, Colombo: The Buddhist Culture Center, pp. 139–40. The passages concerning the *mahāpurisa* are found in the *Saṃyuttanikāya*, v, 158, the *Suttanipāta*, verses 1040–2, and the *Dhammapada*, verse 352.

57 A ii, 35.

58 The *Dhammapada*, verse 352.

59 H. Nakamura is of the opinion that it is the Buddhists who first formulated the list of thirty-two marks. Cited from Endo, *Buddha in Theravāda Buddhism*, p. 139.
60 M ii, 133–4.
61 The *Suttanipāta*, 106.
62 D ii, 211; M ii, 140. This is also referred to at M ii, 166f.
63 T49, 15b.
64 D ii, 133–4. This is also mentioned in all the four Chinese translations: T1, 19c, 168b–c, 184a, 198b–c.
65 Some prominent features of the thirty-two marks of the Buddha make him immediately recognizable. The Buddha, for instance, had such long arms that the palms of his hands could touch and rub against his knees when he was not stooping. He had wheels with a thousand spokes and ribs and complete hubs on the soles of his feet. See the *Lakkhaṇasutta* of the *Dīghanikāya*, iii, 142–4.
66 M iii, 238–47. *Sutta* no. 140.
67 W. Rahula (1985) *What the Buddha Taught*, London: Gordon Fraser, p. 7, footnote 2.
68 M iii, 155.
69 T2, 629b.
70 W. Pachow (1986) 'A Hermeneutical Approach to the Supernatural Phenomena in Buddhist History', *Chinese Culture*, vol. XXVII, no. 1, p. 31.
71 The *adbhuta-dharma* includes three kinds of miracles or wonderful things: the miracles associated with the Buddha, the miracles of the Dharma and the miracles of the *ārya* Saṃgha. But, according to the *Vibhāṣā* (T27, 660b), the term *adbhuta-dharma* originally meant the miracles of the Buddha.

> What is *adbhuta-dharma*? It is the accounts in the scriptures of the miracles associated with the Triple Gem (*triratna*). But other teachers say that it is the accounts of disciples in praise of the Buddha's marvellous deeds or miracles such as Śāriputra who praises the Buddha for his great merit and Ānanda who praises the wonderful things about the Buddha.

Here what 'other teachers say' solely concerns the miracles of the Buddha. The Chinese translation of the *Lalitavistara* states: 'The *adbhuta-dharma* is such as Ānanda who praises the Buddha for his wonderful things' (T4, 643c). But, according to the MPPŚ, 'The Buddha manifested various kinds of wonderful things and sentient beings were amazed and thought it was marvellous (*adbhuta*). This is *adbhuta-dharma*' (T25, 308a). So *adbhuta-dharma* originally only included the miracles of the Buddha.
72 A ii, 130–5.
73 M iii, 118–24. The Sanskrit counterpart of this *sutta* is found in the Chinese **Madhyamāgama* (T1, 469c–471c), but it is slightly longer than the Pāli one which narrates the miracles from the appearance of the Bodhisattva in Tuṣita heaven to his birth on earth. The Chinese version includes another ten miracles different from the ones mentioned in the Pāli version.
74 The *Bhūmicālasutta* of the *Aṅguttaranikāya* iv, 307. The same *sūtra* is also found in T1, 477b–478b. An earthquake is also mentioned in the Chinese **Ekottarāgama*, T2, 753c–754a.
75 S v, 288–90.
76 Gokhale, *New Light on Early Buddhism*, p. 98.

77 The *Iddhipāda-Saṃyutta* states that both *samaṇas* and Brahmins could gain the first five modes of higher knowledge (S v, 275ff.). It is only the Buddhist recluses who could achieve the sixth, the knowledge of *āsravas* being destroyed.

78 The *Dīghanikāya*, *sutta* no. 2, the **Dīrghāgama*, *sūtra* no. 27.

79 M i, 247–9.

80 The stereotype text of *iddhi* found in all the four *sutta* collections (e.g. D i, 78) is as follows:

> Now, O Bhikkhus, the monk enjoys the various magical powers (*iddhi-vidhā*), such as being one he becomes manifold, and having become manifold he again becomes one. He appears and disappears. Without being obstructed he passes through walls and mountains, just as if through the air. In the earth he dives and rises up again, just as if in the water. He walks on water without sinking, just as if on the earth. Cross-legged he floats through the air, just like a winged bird. With his hand he touches the sun and moon, these so mighty ones, so powerful ones. Even up in the Brahma-world he has mastery over his body.

81 Vinaya, *Mahāvagga*, i, 15–34; I. B. Horner (tr.) (1992–1993) *The Book of Discipline*, Oxford: PTS, vol. iv, pp. 24–46.

82 D ii, 89.

83 D ii, 103.

84 D ii, 129.

85 M i, 330.

86 M ii, 99.

87 M ii, 135.

88 D iii, 112–13.

89 The monastic rules concerning the prohibition on performing miracles are found in the *Vinaya*, ii, 112–13. See also the *Cullavagga*, v, 8; Horner, *The Book of Discipline*, vol. v, p. 151.

90 Gokhale, *New Light on Early Buddhism*, p. 107.

91 The list of the ten powers is given in M i, 69–72; A v, 33–6; the **Dīrghāgama*, T2, 41b–c; the **Saṃyuktāgama*, T2, 186c–187a; the **Ekottarāgama*, T2, 776b–c, 859a. The list of the four kinds of intrepidity is given in M i, 71–2. But both the ten powers and the four kinds of intrepidity are mentioned in numerous places in the *Nikāyas* and the *Āgamas*.

2 THE CONCEPT OF THE BUDDHA IN THE EARLY INDIAN BUDDHIST SCHOOLS (I)

1 The term 'early Indian Buddhist schools' refers to the eighteen or twenty schools mentioned in Vasumitra's treatise **Samayabhedavyūhacakra*.

2 'Early *sūtras*' refers to the *sūtras* in the *Nikāyas* and the *Āgamas*, which are common to both the Theravāda and the Mahāyāna and are considered by scholars to be the earliest Buddhist literature.

3 Yinshun (1994) *Chuqi Dacheng Fojian Zhi Qiyuan Yu Zhankai*, Taipei: Zhengwen Publication, p. 167. This scholar believes that the author of the MPPŚ is Nāgārjuna. He puts forward eight points in support of his assertion.

NOTES

1 As the text was translated by a committee, even if additions were made they were not necessarily the work of Kumārajīva. Further, phrases in the text such as 'in Chinese we say' were inserted by the translators for the convenience of the Chinese audience, and were not 'fabrications' by Kumārajīva.
2 The tradition that claims the existence of a version of the text in one thousand fascicles is unfounded. Evidence suggests that the original text contained 136 fascicles.
3 Kumārajīva may have learned the Mahāyāna tradition of Kashmir and the work of the scribe Shengyu on the project contains errors.
4 The MPPŚ selects from a number of divergent views, affirming the interpretations of various schools, and is not necessarily biased in favour of the Sarvāstivāda.
5 The Sarvāstivādins did not have a *Kṣudrakapiṭaka* and made little use of stanzas and legends, whereas the MPPŚ makes extensive use of these materials as a legitimate vehicle for Buddhist doctrine. The *Jātaka* and *Avadāna* materials are taken from throughout India, and are not limited to Northern India. In fact, the author is intimately connected with Southern India.
6 Nāgārjuna lived to be old and may have quoted from the works of his disciple Aryadeva. Further, Nāgārjuna's early and later works may differ stylistically. Hence, stylistic differences alone are insufficient evidence to support the claim that the MPPŚ and the **Madhyamakaśāstra* are the works of different authors.
7 The fact that the MPPŚ is not mentioned in late Indian and Tibetan *Madhyamaka* works may have resulted from a temporary discontinuity in knowledge about Nāgārjuna in the history of Buddhism.
8 The MPPŚ and the **Daśabhūmikavibhāṣā* are consistent: they are not the works of two different authors.

This abstract is cited from Yinshun (1990) 'The Authorship and the Translation of the MPPŚ', *Dongfang Zongjiao Yanjiu*, vol. ii, pp. 9–70.

4 According to Yinshun himself, the *Vibhāṣā* was composed after King Kaniṣka and before the composition of the MPPŚ, in the second century CE, because in the treatise itself, it is said that 'in the past, the King Kaniṣka' (Yinshun (1968) *Shuoyiqieyoubu De Lunshu Yu Lunshi Zi Yanju*, Taipei: Zhengwen Publication, 209–14). For a brief survey of the *Vibhāṣā* compendia, see C. Willemen, B. Dessein and C. Cox (1998) *Sarvāstivāda Buddhist Scholasticism*, Leiden, New York and Cologue: Brill, pp. 229–39.

5 T55, 73c. Yinshun is of the opinion that the real author of the *Mahāvibhāṣāśāstra* is neither Kātyāyanipūtra nor the five hundred great *arhats*; he thinks it was first compiled by Pilouni (Vilani?), was then revised and enlarged by Sitapāni and was again revised and supplemented by Daxi (Dasa?). Thus, it became three versions: the small, the medium and the large. The compilers collected their material from various sources and consulted and also commented on the opinions of the different *abhidharmika* teachers. Therefore, it is not wrong to say that the authors of the treatise are the five hundred great *arhats*.

6 Yinshun, *Shuoyiqieyoubu*, p. 228.

7 T27, 871c–872a, 229a, 391c–392a. This quotation of the Mahāsāṃghikas is found in the **Saṃyuktāgama*, T2, 28b and the *Aṅguttaranikāya*, ii, 37.

8 T28, 463b.
9 T28, 176b.
10 T27, 229a, 392a, 871c.
11 Yinshun, *Shuoyiqieyoubu*, p. 212.
12 T25, 92a, 104b, 273a, 341c, 343a, 579c, 756c.
13 T25, 86c, 91c, 92a, 154c, 155a, 255b, 273a.
14 Lamotte has traced many quotations of the *Vibhāṣā* in the MPPŚ. See the Chinese translation of his article: E. Lamotte (1990) 'Dazhidulun De Zhuozhe Jiqi Fanyi', *Diguan*, vol. 62, p. 125.
15 T25, 92a.
16 T25, 273a.
17 T25, 341b–c.
18 Lamotte, 'Dazhidulun', pp. 125–6.
19 F. E. Reynolds (1977) 'The Several Bodies of the Buddha: Reflections on the Neglected Aspects of Theravāda Tradition', *History of Religions*, vol. 16, no. I, p. 380.
20 N. Dutt (1930) *Aspects of Mahāyāna Buddhism and Its Relation to Hīnayāna*, London: Luzac & Co, pp. 138–40.
21 This stock passage is found in many places in the three versions of the *Vibhāṣā*, T27, 159c, 361b, 428c, 590b, 698a, 730a, 891c; the **Abhidharmavibhāṣāśāstra*, T28, 267b–c, 271c, 322a, 590b; and the **Vibhāṣāśāstra*, 440b, 496b, 517c.
22 T27, 392b.
23 This quotation is found in the **Saṃyuktāgama* (T2, 83c–84a), but the expression is slightly different. The Chinese is as follows: 爾時，世尊告諸比丘：愚癡無聞凡夫，無明覆，愛緣繫，得此識身。內有此識身，外有名色，此二因緣生觸。此六觸入所觸，愚癡無聞凡夫苦、樂受覺，因起種種。云何為六？眼觸入處，耳、鼻、舌、身、意觸入處。若黠慧者，無明覆，愛緣繫，得此識身。如是內有識身，外有名色，此二緣生六觸入處。六觸所觸故，智者生苦、樂受覺，因起種種。何等為六？眼觸入處，耳、鼻、舌、身、意觸入處。愚夫、黠慧，彼於我所修諸梵者，有何差別？

A similar phrase is found in the Pali *Saṃyuttanikāya* (ii, 23–5):

> The wise man (compare) with the fool. For the fool (wise man), brethren, cloaked by ignorance and tied to craving, this body is wrought (worked) on this fool (wise): there is just this body and names-and-shapes without (outside): thus this pair. Because of the pair (there is) contact, just six spheres of sense. Touched by these, or one of them, the fool (wise) experiences pleasure and pain.

The translation is taken from C. A. F. Rhys Davids and F. L. Woodward (tr.) (1997) *The Book of Kindred Sayings*, Oxford: PTS, vol. II, p. 19.
24 T27, 392a, 871c.
25 T27, 863b. 第四，正知入母胎，住出亦爾， 第四入母胎為菩薩。
26 T27, 863c–964a.
27 T27, 872a.
28 T27, 872a.
29 T27, 899c.
30 The *Milindapañha*, vol. I, 75, the **Nāgasena Bhikṣu Sūtra*, T32, 700c, 716a.
31 At the end of page 89 of the *Milindapañha*, the text states: 'Concluded are the questions and answers to Milinda's questions.' The same statement

is given in the Chinese translations of the **Nāgasena Bhikṣu Sūtra*. So it is clear that the part from page 1 to 89 of the *Milindapañha* is the original. The Theravādins added the latter part, according to scholars such as Kogen Mitsuno.

32 The date of the composition of the *Milindapañha* itself is a problematic issue. See I. B. Horner's introduction to her translation, *Milinda's Questions*, vols I and II, London: Luzac & Company, 1963. For a detailed argument brought forward by scholars, see Guang Xing (1994) '*Nāgasena Bhikṣu Sūtra*: An Annotated Translation and Study', unpublished M.Phil. thesis, University of Kelaniya.

33 The Chinese *Avadānas* in which only the thirty-two major and eighty minor marks are mentioned are shown in the table that follows.

The thirty-two major and eighty minor marks

中本起經 T4, 159c, 301b, 334a	三十二相八十種好
大方便佛報恩經 T3, 152b	三十二相八十種隨形之好
過去現在因果經 T3, 645b	三十二相八十種好
大莊嚴論經 T4, 335a, 301b	三十二相八十種好
佛本行集經 T3, 871a, 697b,	三十二相八十種好
697a, 695c, 695a, 693c	以三十二大人之相，莊嚴其身，具足八十種好

34 The **Madhyametyuktasūtra* (T4, no. 196) was translated by Dharmaphala together with Kang Meng-xiang in 207. The *Dafangbianfobaoenjing* (T3, no. 156) was translated under the Eastern Han dynasty 25–220 CE., but the name of the translator is lost. The **Atītapratyutpannahetuphalasūtra* (T3, no. 189) was translated by Guṇabhadra in about 420–479.

35 The Chinese *Avadānas* in which the first two and the fourth categories of the Buddha attributes are mentioned are given in the table below.

Thirty-two major and eighty minor marks and the light

撰集百緣經 T4, 237a, 256c, 256a	三十二相八十種好	光明暉曜如百千日
法句譬喻經 T04, 587c	三十二相八十種好	光明洞達照耀天地
悲華經 T3, 182b, 198b, 203a,	三十二相八十種好	常光一尋174c
188a, 186b, 222a	百福德成就一相174c	
大乘本生心地觀經 T3, 329c	三十二相八十種好	大光明照十方界
眾許摩訶帝經 T3, 971a, 969a	三十二相八十種好	光明莊嚴

The dates of translation of these *sūtras* are as follows: the **Pūrṇamukhāvadānaśataka*, 223–253; the **Dharmapadāvadānasūtra*, 290–306; the **Karuṇāpuṇḍarīkasūtra*, 397–439; the **Mūlajātahṛdayabhūmidhyānasūtra*, 785–810; and the **Samadattamahārājasūtra*, 982–1001.

36 T3, 532b. Apart from the **Samantaprabhāsasūtra*, translated by Dharmarakṣa in 308, there is another version of the *Lalitavistara* in Chinese translation, the **Vaipulyamahāvyūhasūtra*, translated by Divākara in 683.

37 The Chinese *Avadānas* in which all the four categories of the Buddha's attributes are mentioned are shown in the table below.

Four categories of the attributes of the Buddha

出曜經 T4, 675c, 659b, 621a	三十二相八十種好	紫磨金色	圓光七尺
菩薩本行經 T3, 109a	三十二相八十種好	身紫金色	
菩薩本行經 111b	三十有二八十種好		光明晃煜
大乘悲分陀利經 T3, 239c, 248b, 234c, 268a, 248a	三十二大人之相八十種好		
大乘悲分陀利經 242a	三十二相八十種好百福莊嚴皆悉具足	若瞿盧樹紫磨金色	身有圓光
賢愚經 T4, 371b, 443b	三十二相八十種好	身紫金色	光曜人目
賢愚經 433a	三十二相八十種好		光照天地
賢愚經 431a	三十二相八十種好		
賢愚經 418c	三十二相八十種好	身黃金色	
佛説興起行經 T4, 173a	三十二相八十種好	身色如金山	面如月滿光如日明
方廣大莊嚴經 T3, 616c	三十二相八十種好		
方廣大莊嚴經 612c	三十二相八十種好	巨身丈六紫磨金色	
方廣大莊嚴經 601c	三十二相八十種好		身光赫然如日初出
方廣大莊嚴經 584a	三十二相八十種好		圓光一尋
修行本起經 T3, 464b	三十二相八十種好	身如金剛殊妙難量	
修行本起經 461a	三十二相八十種好		光明普照三千世界
佛説鹿母經 T3, 457c	三十二相八十種好	軀體金色	威光無量
師子月佛本生經 T3, 444a	三十二相八十種好	身紫金色方身丈六	皆放光明如紫金山
菩薩本生鬘論 T3, 343a	三十二相八十種好	佛身相作黃金色	無量光明
菩薩本生鬘論 342c	三十二相八十種好	作黃金色	無量光明
生經 T3, 100c	三十二相八十種好		威神光光不可稱限
生經 87b	三十二相八十種好	體長丈六	光明超日

38 The *Apadāna*, I, 156.

39 T32, 704a.

40 N. Dutt (1978b) *Buddhist Sects in India*, Delhi: Motilal Banarsidass, p. 135.

41 T. W. Rhys Davids (tr.) (1890) *The Questions of King Milinda*, Oxford: Clarendon Press, Part I, Introduction, p. XI; M. Winternitz (1988) *History of Indian Literature*, vol. II, Delhi: Motilal Banarsidass, p. 142, n. i. Pelliot, Demiéville and J. Rahder are also of the same opinion.

42 For instance, Alasanda in Pāli, A-li-san in Chinese, which is identified as Alexandra Island, is an island town in West India. Yavana in Pāli, Daqing in Chinese, is a Bactrian country in West India. Again Kashmir, Ji-bin in Chinese, is in Northwest India; Sāgala, or Se-jian in Chinese, is identified as Sialkot in West India. Most of the rivers in the Chinese version – Heng, Xin-ta, Si-ta, Pa-cha and Shipi-i-r, which are identified by Dr Kogen Mizuno ('On the Recensions of Milindapañha', *Summary of the Research Studies of University of Komazawa*, vol. 17, 1959) as Gaṅgā, Sindhu, Śītā, Vakṣu and Sarasvatī, are in Northwest India except for the Gaṅgā. All these names of places suggest Northwest India as the place of compilation for the original.

43 T27, 888a–889a.
44 T27, 887c–888a.
45 T27, 889c–890b.
46 T. Endo (1997) *Buddha in Theravāda Buddhism: A Study of the Concept of Buddha in the Pāli Commentaries*, Colombo: The Buddhist Culture Center, pp. 156–63.
47 *Buddhavaṃsa-aṭṭhakathā*, p. 32. The translation is taken from Endo, *Buddha*, p. 159.
48 T27, 890b.
49 T27, 886c.
50 T27, 889b.
51 T27, 889a.
52 The *Mahāparinirvāṇasūtra*, T1, 12b, the **Aśokasūtra*, T2, 166c. The *Buddhavaṃsa* refers to the term *anubyañjana* (xxi, v, 27) while the *Apadāna* talks of eighty minor marks (i, 156). However, Endo is of the opinion that the Theravāda Pāli tradition borrowed the notion from the Sanskrit tradition. See Endo, *Buddha*, p. 47.
53 The three other translations are: the **Buddhaparinirvāṇasūtra*, T1 (5), translated by Śrāmaṇa Bai Fazhu during the Western Jin Dynasty of 265–317 CE; the **Parinirvāṇasūtra*, T1 (6), translator lost, but listed under Eastern Jin Dynasty (317–420 CE) and the **Mahāparinirvāṇasūtra*, T1 (7), translated by Faxian in 399–414 CE.
54 T2, 599a, 615c, 623b, 664a, 664b, 678b, 686a, 686b, 754b, 758a, 769b, 788b, 799c.
55 T2, 615c, 664a, 788b.
56 Yinshun (1991) *Yuanshi Fojian Shengdian Zhi Jicheng*, Taipei: Zhengwen Publication, pp. 764–74.
57 T2, 550a.
58 T2, 640a.
59 The *Apadāna*, i, 156. The *Buddhavaṃsa*, XXI, v, 27, only mentions 'minor marks' (*anubyañjana*), but does not specify the number eighty. The *Milindapañha*, 75, mentions the term 'eighty minor marks' (*asīti-anubyañjana*), together with the thirty-two major marks and a one-fathom halo.
60 The **Abhiniṣkramaṇasūtra*, T3, 696a–697a, and the **Vaipulyamahāvyūhasūtra*, T3, 557b–c.
61 T3, 532b.
62 H. Nakamura (1996) *Indian Buddhism: A Survey with Bibliographical Notes*, Delhi: Motilal Banarsidass, p. 132.
63 T3, 932a. 摩訶僧祇師，名為大事；薩婆多師，名此經為大莊嚴；迦葉維師，名為佛生因緣；曇無德師，名為釋迦牟尼佛本行；尼沙塞師，名為毘尼藏根本。
64 T3, 655a.
65 T3, 682a.
66 The *Milindapañhaṭīkā*, 17–18, the *Jinālaṅkāraṭīkā*, 198. Cited from Endo, *Buddha*, p. 144.
67 Endo, *Buddha*, pp. 144–5.
68 T25, 255c. The MPPŚ mentions 'such as the eighty minor marks you believe are not found in the *Tripiṭaka*' when the author discusses the eighteen exclusive *dharmas* with the Sarvāstivādins.
69 T25, 255c. The MPPŚ states that 'You do not believe in the Mahāyāna, so you cannot quote from it [the Mahāyāna *sūtras*] as evidence. You should quote from the *śrāvaka* teaching as support' when the author discusses the eighteen exclusive *dharmas* with the Sarvāstivādins.

70 The *Buddhavaṃsa*, i, v, 45; the *Vimānavatthu*, 213.
71 *Encyclopedia of Buddhism*, Sri Lanka: Government of Sri Lanka, 1958, vol. 2, fascicle 3, p. 380.
72 The Chinese phrase is '左光'. Here the Chinese word '左' which literally means 'left' standing for 'superior' or 'better'.
73 T27, 506a.
74 The **Atītapratyutpannahetuphalasūtra*, translated by Guṇabhadra in 420–468 CE., T3, 627b. The **Samadattamahārājasūtra*, T3, 940b20, tr. Faxian in 982–1001.
75 T24, 109a; T6, 967c; T8, 395c; T25, 90c.
76 T27, 506a–b. The author of the MPPŚ (T25, 311c) also explains that Śākyamuni possesses a one-fathom halo while Maitreya has the bodily halo of ten *li*, equal to five thousand metres.
77 The *Buddhavaṃsa*, i, v, 15; vii, v, 24; xiii, v, 2, etc. The commentaries: *Dīghanikāya* commentary, iii, 918, 972; *Majjhimanikāya* commentary, ii, 167; *Saṃyuttanikāya* commentary, iii, 48; *Aṅguttaranikāya* commentary, i, 10; *Buddhavaṃsa* commentary, 41, 87. It explains that these rays are usually said to consist of six colours: blue, yellow, red, white, crimson and a combination of the five colours. The *Sāratthappakāsinī* gives the length of then rays as eighty hands.
78 The *Saṃyuttanikāya* commentary, iii, 47.
79 T8, 1b, 147b–c, 217b.
80 T27, 207b.
81 T27, 620c–621a. The *sūtra* states that the Buddha helped sentient beings to attain perfection when he saw they had some defect. He also restored the dilapidated monasteries and stupas and renovated statues of Buddhas and bodhisattvas. Due to such good *karma*, the Buddha had a glorious body without any defect.
82 T27, 154b–156b.
83 T2, 857c–859a. It was translated by Dharmarakṣa in the Western Jin dynasty, 265–316 CE.
84 According to the *Vibhāṣā* (T27, 657b), there are two theories regarding the Buddha's deliberately giving up his life: a one-third theory and a one-fifth theory. According to the one-third theory, the Buddha had the life-span of 120 years, but he gave up forty years of his life. According to the one-fifth theory, the Buddha had the life-span of one hundred years, but he gave up twenty years of his life.
85 T27, 601c–602b. The *Vibhāṣā* mentions two other similar explanations. First, harming the body of the Buddha is only harming the master whereas splitting the Saṃgha is the destruction of what the master respects, the Dharma. Second, harming the Buddha is counted only as the sin of *prayoga* while splitting the Saṃgha means planning for a long time, one to four months. The Buddha is not distressed mentally by being harmed physically, but splitting the Saṃgha would result in the suffering of many beings.
86 The full description of the eighteen exclusive *dharmas* of the Hīnayāna can be found in the *Vibhāṣā* (T27, 156c–160c), the **Abhidharmakośabhāṣya* (T29, 140a–141b), the **Nyāyānusaraśāstra* (T29, 746a–750a) and the **Abhidharma(piṭaka)prakaraṇa-śāsanaśāstra* (T29, 955c–958a). But the description given in the *Vibhāṣā* is much the most comprehensive and great compassion is explained again in 428a–430c. The three foundations of mindfulness are also explained again in 942b–943a.
87 T28, 459a–b.
88 T28, 459b.

89 T28, 472c. 或曰：此中說三分法身，戒身定身慧身，彼不害一切眾生者是戒身；我不為他，他不為我者是定身；諸所習法，皆是盡法者是慧身，如三身三戒三思惟亦爾。

90 The list of the ten powers can be found in M i, 69–72; A v, 33–6; the **Dīrghāgama*, T2, 41b–c; the **Saṃyuktāgama*, T2, 186c–187a; the **Ekottarāgama*, T2, 776b–c; 859a. The list of the four kinds of intrepidity can be found in M i, 71–2. But both the powers and the intrepidity are mentioned in numerous places in the *Nikāyas* and the *Āgamas*.

91 The *Saḷāyatanavibhaṅgasutta*, M iii, 221–2. There is a *sūtra* in Chinese translation having the same title and contents as the Pāli one, T1, 693c–694a.

92 The eighteen exclusive *dharmas* of the Mahāyāna are as follows.

1 The Tathāgata has no bodily defects.
2 He has no speech defects.
3 He has no faintness of memory.
4 He has no notion of diversity.
5 He has no thoughts which are not composed.
6 His equanimity is not affected by any non-knowledge.
7 He has no loss of zest.
8 He has no loss of energy.
9 He has no loss of memory.
10 He has no loss of wisdom.
11 He has no loss of deliverance.
12 He has no loss of knowledge and vision of deliverance.
13 All bodily actions of the Tathāgata are preceded and accompanied by knowledge.
14 All vocal actions of the Tathāgata are preceded and accompanied by knowledge.
15 All mental actions of the Tathāgata are preceded and accompanied by knowledge.
16 With regard to the past he has knowledge and vision that are free of attachment and obstacles.
17 With regard to the future he has knowledge and vision that are free of attachment and obstacles.
18 With regard to the present he has knowledge and vision that are free of attachment or obstacles.

This can be found in the *Prajñāpāramitāsūtras*, T6, 967a–b; T8, 255c–256a; T8, 395b; the MPPŚ, T25, 247b.

93 T1, 885a–b. This independent **Brahmāyuḥsūtra* was translated by Zi Qian in the Wu dynasty, 222–280 CE. But the **Madhyamāgama*, in which the counterpart of the **Brahmāyuḥsūtra* is found, was translated by Gautama Saṅghadeva in 397–398 CE. A comparison of the independent **Brahmāyuḥsūtra* and its counterpart shows that there are many interpolations in Zi Qian's translation regarding the attributes of the Buddha, such as the term 'eighteen exclusive *dharmas*', the term 'eighty minor marks' and the five-colour light from the mouth of the Buddha. However, there is no mention of these terms in Saṅghadeva's translation at all. This suggests that the transmitters of the **Madhyamāgama* were very faithful to their tradition. Though the **Madhyamāgama* was translated more than a hundred years later than the independent **Brahmāyuḥsūtra*, it still keeps its pure tradition. This makes

the study of Buddhist literature, especially the Chinese translations, more difficult.

94 The term 'eighteen exclusive *dharmas*' is mentioned twice in the *Dafangbianfobaoenjing* (T3, 136c, 161a), once in the **Mahāyānamahākaruṇāpuṇḍarīkasūtra* (T3, 288b) and once in the **Vaipulyamahāvyūhasūtra* (T3, 611b).

95 Endo, *Buddha*, pp. 130–1.

96 The date of the composition of the *Milindapañha* itself is problematic. The two Chinese translations entitled **Nāgasena Bhikṣu Sūtra* (T32, nos 1670a and b) correspond only to the pages 1–89 of the PTS edition of the *Milindapañha* edited by Trenckner. The second portion from pages 90 to the end of the text was composed in Sri Lanka. The term *aṭṭhādasabuddhadhamma* is used twice on pages 105 and 285. See Endo, *Buddha*, p. 115. For detailed arguments, see Guang Xing, '*Nāgasena Bhikṣu Sūtra*'.

97 Endo, *Buddha*, p. 115.

98 Cited from ibid., p. 119. *Dīghanikāya* commentary, iii, 994.

99 Yinshun, *Shuoyiqieyoubu*, p. 212.

100 T8, 395b, T6, 967a–b.

101 T25, 255c.

102 H. Dayal (1932) *The Bodhisattva Doctrine in Buddhist Sanskrit Literature*, London: Routledge & Kegan Paul, p. 23.

103 T27, 156c–157c.

104 The ten powers are as follows.

1 The Tathāgata truly knows the possible as the possible and the impossible as the impossible.
2 The Tathāgata truly knows the function of *karma* in the past, present and future with regard to place, cause, object and maturation.
3 The Tathāgata truly knows the impurity, purification, categories and purity of meditations, liberations, concentrations and attainments.
4 The Tathāgata truly knows the world endowed with diversifications and multiple dispositions.
5 The Tathāgata truly knows the different aspirations of other living beings and individuals.
6 The Tathāgata truly knows the degree of the moral faculties of other living beings and individuals.
7 The Tathāgata truly knows the path that leads to different destinies.
8 The Tathāgata recollects his previous existences over a period of many worlds that evolve and dissolve.
9 The Tathāgata sees with his divine and pure eye the appearance and passing away of living beings.
10 The Tathāgata truly knows that the cankers have been destroyed in him.

105 The four kinds of intrepidity are that the Buddha has: (1) intrepidity in asserting that he has attained perfect enlightenment; (2) intrepidity in asserting that he has destroyed all defilements; (3) intrepidity in explaining to people those elements which hinder the realization of the Dharma; (4) intrepidity in expounding the method of liberation.

106 T27, 159a–b.

107 T27, 942b–943a.

108 The *Kośa*, T29, 0141a; another translation of the *Kośa-bhāṣya*, T29, 292a; the **Abhidharma(piṭaka)prakaraṇaśāsanaśāstra*, T29, 957b; and the **Abhidharmanyāyānusāraśāstra*, T29, 749b.

109 Saṅghabhūti's translation of the *Vibhāṣā*, T28, 496b–c; Xuanzang's translation of the *Vibhāṣā*, T27, 159b–160a. The reasons given in Buddhavarma's translation are very much the same as those in Xuanzang's translation.
110 Yinshun, *Shuoyiqieyoubu*, pp. 650–4.
111 Leo M. Pruden translated the **Abhidharmakośabhāṣya* into English from the French translation of Xuanzang's Chinese translation of the original Sanskrit version. Pruden's translation is at third remove from the original, so there may be some changes.
112 T27, 160b.
113 T27, 159b–160b.
114 T27, 428a.
115 T27, 160c.
116 T27, 160c–161a.
117 T27, 701a–b. 有為法有三分齊，謂時色名，時之極少謂一剎那，色之極少為一極微，名之極少為依一字。 Here, name (*nāma*) means concepts or non-physical phenomena as contrasted with the *dharmas* contained in the category of form (*rūpa*). It refers to those existences categorized under feeling, apperception, volition and consciousness.
118 T27, 74a.
119 T27, 201c.
120 T27, 194a.
121 There are two kinds of ignorance: the defiled and the undefiled. The defiled ignorance includes all the *kleśas* and it has *avidyā* as its essence. The undefiled ignorance has inferior wisdom as its essence. The Buddha has eliminated both, but the *pratyekabuddhas* and the *śrāvakas* have eliminated only the defiled ignorance.
122 Z. Yao (1996) *Yibu zonglun lun*, Taiwan: Foguang Publication, p. 163. Kuiji helped Xuanzang in all his translation works, such as the *Vibhāṣā*. Therefore he was particularly well versed in the teachings of the Sarvāstivāda. So his commentary on Vasumitra's treatise on the doctrine of Buddhist schools is based on the knowledge which he acquired and learned from Xuanzang. His comments on different schools are therefore always in agreement with the *Vibhāṣā*. According to Kuiji, some schools assert that the Buddha also had dreams but we do not know which schools he based this claim upon.
123 The *sūtras* frequently state that the Buddha slept when he was tired, but there is no mention of his dreams. For instance, the *Sekhasutta* mentions that the Buddha went to sleep when he got back pains after a day's preaching (M i, 354). Again, the **Saṃyuttanikāya* iv mentions that the Buddha slept on a similar occasion (S iv, 183–4).
124 According to the *Vibhāṣā*, Vasumitra says that there are five causes for dreams. (1) They are caused by others, such as gods, ghosts, medicine, relatives' thought, etc. (2) They are caused by previous sight or hearing of something or one's learning and practice of something. (3) They are omens for either good or bad. (4) They are caused by thought, doubt and desire. (5) They are caused by illness. The text also gives seven causes for dreams in the Vedas. They are caused by previous sight, hearing, experience, desire, thought, illness or as an omen. T27, 193c–194a.
125 T27, 153b.
126 T27, 72b.
127 J. Masuda (1922) *Origin and Doctrines of Early Indian Buddhist Schools*, *Asia Major*, vol. II, fascicle I, Leipzig: Verlag Asia Major, p. 52.
128 Dutt, *Aspects of Mahāyāna Buddhism*, p. 26. Divyā, 226, 271.
129 T29, 63c. 無上菩提甚難可得，非多願行無容得成。

130 Leo M. Pruden's translation of the **Abhidarmakośabhāṣya* (1990), 3, 480. According to the *Vibhāṣā* T27, 892b, the foreign teachers say that there are six *pāramitās*, but the Kashmir teachers say that patience (*kṣānti*) is included in discipline and meditation in wisdom.
131 T27, 886c.
132 T27, 85a–b, 131b, 624a–b.
133 T29, 63c. 菩薩要經三劫無數，修大福德智慧資糧，六波羅蜜多百千苦行，方證無上正等菩提。
134 *Abhidharma-nyāyānusāra-śāstra*, T29, 523c and *Abhidharma(piṭaka)prakaraṇa-śāsana-śāstra*, T29, 957c.
135 T25, 92a.
136 T25, 92b.
137 The *Kośa*, T29, 63b–c, the **Abhidharmanyāyānusāraśāstra*, T29, 523c.
138 T27, 890a–893a. The *Mahāvastu*, i, 1. In the Pāli sources (*Cariyāpitaka*, i, 1.1 etc.), the career of the Bodhisattva is four *asaṃkheyyas* in length plus a hundred thousand *kappas*.
139 T27, 887c–891b.
140 T27, 892a.
141 T27, 892b.
142 This is discussed in three places in the *Vibhāṣā*: T27, 85a–b, 131b, 624a–b; also in T28, 104a. However, a full discussion is found in the following three works: the *Kośa-bhāṣya*, T29, 141b–c; the **Abhidharma(piṭaka)prakaraṇaśāsanaśāstra*, T29, 957c–958a; and the **Abhidharmanyāyānusāraśāstra*, T29, 749c–750a.
143 Elsewhere in the *Vibhāṣā* (T27, 479c), it states that Buddhas are similar in five ways. (1) Regarding *dhyāna*, all Buddhas attained *bodhi* through the fourth *dhyāna*. (2) Regarding *prayoga*, all Buddhas completed the practice of six *pāramitās* in three *mahāsaṃkhyeya kalpas*. (3) Regarding the object, all Buddhas attained *bodhi* through observation of the four noble truths. (4) Regarding the aspect, all Buddhas practised the path according to the sixteen characteristics. (5) Regarding work, all Buddhas eliminated *kleśa* by the power of the way of purity (*anāśravamārga*) and liberated numerous sentient beings to *parinirvāṇa*.
144 T27, 177a.
145 T29, 76b. 何等名為佛無學法？謂盡智等及彼隨行，非色等身，前後等故。
146 T27, 177b.
147 T27, 177c.
148 T27, 178c.
149 T27, 735b–c.
150 T27, 315b–c.
151 T27, 530c.
152 T27, 77a–c.
153 T27, 515b–c.
154 T27, 904a–905a. The four unhindered powers of interpretation are dharma or the letter of the law, *artha* or its meaning, *nirukti* or the form of expression and *pratibhāna* or in eloquence.
155 T27, 33b.
156 Masuda, *Origin and Doctrines*, p. 52. At the beginning of Vasumitra's work, there are five verses, of which the last one reads as follows: 'when the teachings of the Buddha are closely examined, the fundamentals are the *āryan* truths. Like [one] who gathers gold from [heaps of] sand, [out of untruths] one should pick up the truths.' (See Masuda, *Origin and Doctrines*, p. 13.) This reflects the attitude of the Sarvāstivāda concerning the teachings of the Buddha.

NOTES

3 THE CONCEPT OF THE BUDDHA IN THE EARLY INDIAN BUDDHIST SCHOOLS (II)

1 The Mahāsāṃghikas asserted that all the words of the Buddha preach the Dharma and contain nothing which is not in conformity with the truth. Vasumitra's **Samayabhedavyūhacakra* translated by Xuanzang, T49, 15b.
2 P. Harrison (1982) 'Sanskrit Fragments of a Lokottaravādin Tradition', in A. L. Hercus, ed., *Indological and Buddhist Studies: Volume in Honour of Professor J. W. de Jong on his Sixtieth Birthday*, Canberra: Faculty of Asian Studies, p. 213.
3 T2, 28b12; A ii, 37; S iii, 140.
4 T27, 229a, 391c–392a, 871c.
5 T27, 229a, 391c–392a, 871c.
6 T2, 28b12.
7 N. Dutt also thinks it likely that the Mahāsāṃghika concept of the Buddha is based on the utterances found in the *Nikāyas*, such as 'I am the all-conqueror, I am omniscient, I am untouched by all worldly objects. I am perfect in this world; I am a teacher incomparable; I am the only enlightened, tranquilized and have extinguished everything' in the *Majjhimanikāya*. See N. Dutt (1978b) *Buddhist Sects in India*, Delhi: Motilal Banarsidass, p. 71. The quotation is from M i, 171.
8 M iii, 118–24; T1, 469c–471c.
9 Scholars like V. Fausböll think that the *Suttanipāta* belongs to the oldest strata of Buddhist literature. He considers that most of the *Mahāvagga* and nearly all the *Aṭṭhakavagga* are very old. He bases this conclusion on the language and the contents. See V. Fausböll (1881) *The Suttanipāta: A Collections of Discourses*, vol. X, part II, *The Sacred Books of the East*, Oxford: Clarendon Press, p. xi. Thus the *Nālakasutta* perhaps belongs to a later stage of development.
10 The *Suttanipāta*, verses 679–98.
11 D ii, 12–15.
12 A v, 144. The English translation is taken with a few changes from F. L. Woodward (tr.) (1995) *The Book of the Gradual Sayings*, Oxford: PTS, vol. 5, p. 99. Similar passages are found in T2, 95c, 199c. The Chinese translation gives the three states as old age, illness and death, in contrast with the Pāli version: birth, decay and death.
13 J. Masuda (1922) *Origin and Doctrines of Early Indian Buddhist Schools*: *Asia Major*, Leipzig: Verlag Asia Major, vol. II, fascicle I, p. 18.
14 T17, 751c.
15 T17, 751c.
16 The *Mahāvastu*, i, 167–70; the **Lokānuvartanasūtra*, T17, 751c–752a.
17 T17, 752b, lines 24–6.
18 D ii, 130–3. This incident is also found in the four Chinese translations of the *Mahāparinirvāṇasūtra*: T1, 19a–b, 168a–b, 183c–184a, 198a–b.
19 Masuda, *Origin and Doctrines*, p. 20.
20 T1, 15c, 165a, 180b; T24, 387c; *Divyāvadāna*, 201; D ii, 103; S v, 259; A iv, 309; the *Udāna*, vi, 62. According to the *Vibhāṣā* (T27, 657b) there are two accounts of the Buddha's giving up the remainder of his life. The first is that the Buddha gave up one-third of his life because the life-span of the Buddha is 120 years. The second is that the Buddha gave up one-fifth of his life because the life-span of the Buddha is a hundred years. This of course is a rational explanation of the Sarvāstivādins.
21 A *kalpa* is the longest period of time in Indian cosmology. It is an age, the life cycle of a world or a universe, an unimaginably long period of time. According to Monier Williams, a *kalpa* is a fabulous period of time. It is a day of Brahma or

one thousand Yugas, a period of 4,320 million years of mortals, measuring the duration of the world. A month of Brahma is supposed to contain thirty such *kalpas*. According to the *Mahābhārata*, twelve months of Brahma constitute his year, and one hundred such years his lifetime; fifty years of Brahma are thought to have elapsed, and we are now in the *svetavārāha-kalpa* of the fifty-first; at the end of a *kalpa* the world is annihilated. Buddhists are not in agreement on the length of a *kalpa*, except for it being an immeasurably long period of time. M. Williams (1986) *A Sanskrit–English Dictionary*, Tokyo: Meicho Fukyu Kai, reprint, p. 262c.

22 Masuda, *Origin and Doctrines*, p. 19.

23 A iv, 163–4. The translation is taken from Woodward, *The Book of the Gradual Sayings*, vol. 4, p. 112.

24 T17, 752a–b.

25 T17, 752b.

26 S v, 437.

27 Masuda, *Origin and Doctrines*, p. 19.

28 M ii, 99.

29 T27, 671c.

30 T29, 557b.

31 Masuda, *Origin and Doctrines*, p. 19.

32 Ibid., pp. 19–20.

33 T17, 753b. Masuda thinks that 'the *rūpakāya* of the Tathāgata' means the *saṃbhogakāya*, not the *nirmāṇakāya*. He probably thinks in terms of infinite size, not infinite number. But at this stage the idea of the *saṃbhogakāya* had not yet been conceived, while the idea of the *nirmāṇakāya* already existed, as Śākyamuni was considered a *nirmāṇakāya*.

34 T17, 752a.

35 T17, 752a–c.

36 T17, 751c. *Chi* (尺) is a Chinese measurement, three *chi* are similar to one metre and ten *chi* are equal to one *zhang* (丈).

37 Z. Yao (1996) *Yibu zonglun lun*, Taiwan: Foguang Publication, p. 163, Kuiji's commentary.

38 Masuda, *Origin and Doctrines*, p. 20.

39 Yao, *Yibu*, p. 164.

40 T17, 751c, 752b.

41 T17, 752b–753a.

42 T17, 752b.

43 This statement is found in many places: (1) the early *sūtras*: D ii, 225, iii, 114; M iii, 65; A i, 27; **Dīrghāgama*, T1, 31a; 79a; **Madhyamāgama*, T1, 724a; (2) later works: *Milindapañha*, 236; *Mahāvastu*, iii, 199; *Kośa*, iii, 198–201 (Chinese translation: T29, 64c–65a); Chinese translation of the *Mahāyānasaṃgraha*, T31, 132b, 151c.

44 Cited from K. Nishio (1938) 'A Study of Many Buddhas in the Present Period', *Bukkyō Kenkyū*, vol. 2, no. 4, p. 142.

45 Ibid., pp. 149–55.

46 F. Kotatsu (1958) 'An Aspect of the Buddhas, Found in the Early Buddhist Scriptures, with Reference to the Present-Other Worlds Buddhas', *Indogaku Bukkyōgaku Kenkyū*, vol. VI, no. 2, March, p. 70.

47 T25, 126b, 以是故佛於聲聞法中，不言有十方佛，亦不言無。

48 T25, 235c. 復次，為聲聞説法中無大慈悲心，大乘法中一句雖少，有大慈悲；聲聞法中皆自為身，大乘法中廣為眾生；聲聞法中無欲廣知諸法心，但欲疾離老病死，大乘法中欲了了知一切法；聲聞法功德有限量，大乘法中欲盡諸功德，無有遺餘，如是等大小乘差別。(T25, 619c) 復次聲聞法易解易知故言具足，菩薩法佛法難解難知故言當學。復次聲聞法總相，但知苦知苦因知苦盡知盡苦道...... 菩薩摩訶薩如大醫。 Sometimes the author of the MPPŚ also uses the term *śrāvaka Dharma Tripiṭaka* such as 何經中有是語？若聲聞法三藏中說，若摩訶衍中說？(T25, 92a).

49 **Dīrghāgama*: T1, 76c, 163b, 255b; **Saṃyuktāgama*: T2, 131a, 322a, 410a; **Ekottarāgama*: T2, 708c–710a, 773a.

50 See the latest study on this issue, C. Willemen, B. Dessein and C. Cox (1998) *Sarvāstivāda Buddhist Scholasticism*, Leiden, New York and Cologuc: Brill, pp. 7–9.

51 T25, 93a–c, 126a–c.

52 T25, 93b. This verse is quoted again at T25, 126a. My translation is directly rendered from the Chinese original.

53 E. Lamotte (1992) 'Shi Chupinzhong Pusa', *Diguan*, vol. 69, pp. 92–4, footnote 93.

54 T21, no. 1245. 《毘沙門天王經》，法天譯。

55 T23, 174b.《十誦律》:'阿吒那劍(晉言鬼神成經)'。

56 T25, 93b.

57 This passage is found in many Sarvāstivāda texts such as the *Abhidharma-kośa-śāstra*, T29, 64c–65a; the *Kośa*, T29, 222c; the *Abhidharma-nyāyānusāra-śāstra*, T29, 524c; and the *Abhidharma(piṭaka)prakaraṇaśāsana-śāstra*, T29, 857c.

58 T29, 64c.

59 T29, 64c. 謂若世尊，不起加行，唯能觀此三千大千，若時世尊發起加行，無邊世界皆佛眼境，天耳通等例此應知。

60 T17, 753b.

61 This saying of the Buddha is found in the *Aṅguttaranikāya*, v, 144: 'Tayo bhikkhave dhammā loke na saṃvijjeyyuṃ, na Tathāgato loke uppajjeyya arahaṃ sammāsambuddho . . . Katame tayo? Jāti ca jarā ca maraṇañ ca.' It is also found in two places in the Chinese **Saṃyuktāgama*: T2, 95c, 199c.

62 T25, 125c–126a.

63 T2, 243.

64 T2, 488b.

65 For further information on the schools of the *Āgamas* see C. Willemen *et al.*, *Sarvāstivāda*, pp. 7–8.

66 T17, 752a. 佛力不可當，持一指動十方佛刹。

67 T17, 752b. 佛悉曉了，十方不可計諸佛所有經法。

68 T17, 753b. 佛化分身在無央數，不可復計佛刹悉遍至，佛身亦不增亦不減。

69 T17, 753a. 諸佛合一身，以經法為身。

70 The **Yogācārabhūmiśāstra*, T30, 499b–500b; the **Bodhisattvabhūmidharasūtra*, T30, 902a–b; the *Kośa*, T29, 64c–65a; the *Mahāyānasaṃgraha*, T31, 112a, 151b; the **Mahāyānasaṃgrahaśāstrabhāṣya*, T31, 266a–c, 319b, 378a–b, 447b–448c; the **Abhidharmanyāyānusāraśāstra*, T29, 423b; and the **Mahāyānāvatārakaśāstra*, T32, 43c.

71 Masuda, *Origin and Doctrines*, p. 21. All bodhisattvas are born from the right side when they come out of their mother's womb.

72 T8, 446a.

73 T8, 462a.

74 E. Conze (1960) *The Prajñāpāramitā Literature*, s-Gravenhage: Mouton, p. 9.

75 For references see E. Lamotte (1954) 'Sur la formation du Mahāyāna', *Asiatica*, p. 386, n. 49. Cited from Conze, *Prajñāpāramitā Literature*, p. 9.

76 Cited from ibid.

77 Dutt, *Buddhist Sects*, p. 215.

78 *Kathāvatthu*, 62: 'Thānāthānādini hi sāvakā padesena jānanti. Tathāgatā nippadesena iti. Tāni uddesato sādhāraṇāni; neddesato asādhāraṇāni . . . niddesato sabbākaravisayataṃ samdhāya paṭikkhipati.' Cf. *Mahāvastu*, i, 158.
79 See S iii, 66; also Dutt, *Buddhist Sects*, p. 103.
80 The term 'Hīnayāna' used in this book indicates all schools apart from Mahāyāna. Vajrayāna is also considered Mahāyāna.
81 Masuda, *Origin and Doctrines*, p. 62.
82 Ibid., 64.
83 Cited from Dutt, *Buddhist Sects*, p. 176.
84 Masuda translates this proposition as 'the average man (*pṛthagjana*) also possesses the potentiality of becoming a Buddha' (*Origin and Doctrines*, p. 68). But this may mislead the reader into thinking that the Sautrāntika already had the idea that all sentient beings have the potential to become Buddhas, as the Mahāyānists believe.
85 On the Vibhajyavādins, see Dutt, *Buddhist Sects*, pp. 208–10.
86 T27, 871c.
87 T27, 308c–309a. 謂或有執，不染污心亦令有相續，如分別論者。問：彼何故作此執？答：彼依契經故作此執，謂契經說，菩薩正知入母胎，正知住母胎，正知出母胎。 既有正知入母胎者，正知即在，不染污心故，不染污心亦令有相續。
87 T27, 410b–c. There are five hindrances: (1) sensuous lust; (2) ill will; (3) physical and mental torpor and languor; (4) restlessness and worry; (5) doubt.
88 T27, 479c. 如分別論者，彼作是說：唯一無上正等菩提，常住不滅，隨彼彼佛出現世間，能證者雖異，而所證無別。如一龍象，妙飾莊嚴，雖有多人次第乘御，而彼龍象前後是一。問：彼何故作此執？答彼依契經。如契經說：佛告苾芻，我證舊道， 故知聖道定是無為。
89 T27, 116c. 或復有執，緣起是無為，如分別論者。問：彼因何故作如是執？答：彼因經故，謂契經說： 如來出世若不出世，法住法性，佛自等覺，為他開示，乃至廣說，故知緣起是無為法。

4 THE ORIGIN AND DEVELOPMENT OF THE *DHARMAKĀYA*

1 N. Dutt has already collected and analysed the passages in the Pāli *Nikāyas* on the concept of the Buddha in his *Mahāyāna Buddhism*, Delhi: Motilal Banarsidass, pp. 138–40.
2 D ii, 154.
3 M, no. 108.
4 T1, 26a.
5 T1, 172b.
6 T1, 188a.
7 T1, 204b–c.
8 T1, 654b.
9 S ii, 221; M iii, 29; D iii, 84. Similar passages are also found in M i, 12f, ii, 84, iii, 195, 224.
10 N. Dutt is also of the same opinion that in this passage the word Dhamma has no metaphysical meaning at all.
11 *Sumaṅgalavilāsinī*, iii, 865. *Dīghanikāya* commentary, iii, 865: 'Kasmā Tathāgato Dhammakāyo ti vutto? Tathāgato hi tetipiṭakaṃ Buddhavacanaṃ hadayena cintetyā vācāya abhinīhari. Ten' assa kāyo Dhammamayattā Dhammo va.'
12 T1, 37b.
13 T2, 457b.

14 T2, 303c.
15 A ii, 38.
16 Cited from Dutt, *Mahāyāna Buddhism*, p. 140.
17 T2, 717c–718a.
18 S iii, 120: 'Alam Vakkali kiṃ te pūtikāyena diṭṭhena. Yo kho Vakkali dhammaṃ passati so maṃ passati. Yo maṃ passati so dhammaṃ passati.' The translation is taken from C. A. F. Rhys Davids (tr.) (1995) *The Book of Kindred Sayings*, Oxford: PTS, vol. III, p. 103, with a few changes.
19 The **Saṃyuktāgama*, T2, 346b; The **Ekottarāgama*, T2, 642c.
20 The *Sāratthapakāsinī*, ii, 314: '*Yo kho, Vakkali, dhamman* ti, idha Bhagavā 'dhammakāyo kho dasseti. Nava-vidho hi lokuttara-dhammo Tathāgatassa kāyo nāma. Idāni therassa tiparivaṭṭa-dhamma-desanam ārabhanto *tam kim maññasī* tiādim āha.'
21 It is found in various places in the early scripture: *Saṃyutta*, ii, 25; **Saṃyukta*, T2, 84b, 85b–c; *Aṅguttara*, I, 286. This idea is also found in a number of secondary sources such as *Visuddhimagga*, 518; **Pañcaviṃsati*, 198; **Aṣṭasāhasrikā*, 274; *Laṅkāvatāra*, 143; **Daśabhūmika*, 65.
22 The statement that neither the Buddha nor any other person is the inventor of the law of dependent origination is found only in the Chinese **Saṃyuktāgama* (T2, 85b–c), *sūtra* number 299, but not in the Pāli canon, according to C. Akanuma (1956) *The Comparative Catalogue of Chinese Āgamas and Pāli Nikāyas*, Tokyo: Hajinkaku-Shobo, p. 45, number 17. It is said that Śākyamuni attained enlightenment through the realization of this very Law and he then preached it to all sentient beings.
23 T1, 467a, 象跡喻經, M I, 191. Even the title of the *sūtra* in which this passage is found in both the **Madhyamāgama* and the *Majjhimanikāya* is the same: the *Mahāhatthipadopama*.
24 T4, 185c. This *sūtra* contains sixteen stories and the story of the *bhikṣuni* Utpalavarṇā is the fourteenth.
25 T25, 137a.
26 T2, 550a.
27 T2, 549c.
28 T2, 787b.
29 T2, 168b.
30 T2, 711c, 712b, 772c.
31 The *Milindapañha* mentions the five factors of *dharmakāya* on page 98. However, the first part of the Pāli text from page 1 to 89 is earlier than the part from page 90 to the end, as it corresponds quite well to the Chinese translation of the **Nāgasena Bhikṣu Sūtra*, which is the counterpart of the Pāli text. And on page 89, there is a concluding sentence as follows: 'Here ends the answering of the problems of the questions of Milinda.'
32 Vsm. 234.
33 L. Lancaster (1975) 'The Oldest Mahāyāna Sūtra: Its Significance for the Study of Buddhist Development', *The Eastern Buddhist* (new series), vol. 8, no. 1, p. 30.
34 Ibid., pp. 31–3. We will not refer to the Tibetan translation in our research since it is of a much later date.
35 E. Lamotte (1976) *The Teachings of Vimalakīrti*, London: PTS, pp. lx–lxi.
36 'Uppādā vā tathāgatānaṃ anuppāda vā tathāgatānaṃ ṭhinā va sā dhātu dhammaṭṭhitatā dhammaniyāmatā idappaccayatā.' S ii, 25; 若佛出世，若未出世，此法常住. **Saṃyuktāgama*, T2, 84b; A I, 286.
37 S ii, 25.
38 *Udāna*, 80.

39 T8, 558b. The following table is a comparison of a passage on the *tathatā* found in two translations of the *Aṣṭa*: the *Daoxingbanruojing* and Kumārajīva's translation.

Comparison of the *Aṣṭa*: the *Daoxingbanruojing* and Kumārajīva's translation

The Daoxingbanruojing *(T8, 450a)*	*Kumārajīva's translation (T8, 558b)*
怛薩阿竭知色之本無，如知色本無，痛癢思想生死識亦爾。何謂知識？知識之本無。何所是本無，是欲有所得者，是亦本無。怛薩阿竭亦本無，因慧如住。何謂所本無，世間亦是本無，何所是本無者，一切諸法亦本無，如諸法本無，須陀洹道亦本無，斯陀含道亦本無，阿那含道亦本無，阿羅漢道、辟支佛道亦本無，怛薩阿竭亦復本無。一本無無有異，無所不入，悉知一切。是者須菩提，般若波羅蜜即是本無，怛薩阿竭因般若波羅蜜，自致成阿耨多羅三耶三佛，照明持世間，是為示現。怛薩阿竭因般若波羅蜜，悉知世間本無無有異。如是須菩提，怛薩阿竭悉知本無，爾故號字為佛。	復次須菩提，如來因般若波羅蜜知色相，雲何知色相？知如如。須菩提，如來知受想行識相，雲何知識相？知如如。須菩提，五陰如即是如來所說出沒，如五陰如即是世間如，五陰如即是一切法如，一切法如即是須陀洹果如，斯陀含果、阿那含果、阿羅漢果、辟支佛道如，辟支佛道如即是如來如。是諸如皆是一如，無二無別無盡無量，如是須菩提，如來因般若波羅蜜，得是如相。如是須菩提，般若波羅蜜，示諸佛世間，能生諸佛，諸佛知世間如，如實得是如故，名為如來。

As the table shows, they are almost identical. However, this passage is not found in the Sanskrit version of the *Aṣṭa*. It is likely that Lokakṣema's translation represents the earliest version, the Sanskrit version being the latest and Kumārajīva's translation falling in between.

40 *Daoxingbanruojing*, T8, 453b, Kumārajīva's translation of the *Aṣṭa*, T8, 562b–c.

41 *Daoxingbanruojing*, T8, 450a–b, Kumārajīva's translation of the *Aṣṭa*, T8, 558c.

42 T8, 468a.

43 T8, 466a–b.

44 T8, 439a.

45 T8, 427c.

46 T8, 442b–c.

47 T8, 442c. 心者本清淨，可有所作。

48 T8, 427b.

49 T8, 335a.

50 The *Fangguangbanruojing* (T8, no. 221) was translated by Mokṣala in 291 CE.

51 T8, 145a.

52 T8, 145b.

53 T8, 584b. This is a passage from Kumārajīva's translation of the *Aṣṭa*. See also E. Conze (1960) *The Prajñāpāramitā Literature*, s-Gravenhage: Mouton, p. 216.

54 Kumārajīva translated two versions of the **Prajñāpāramitāsūtra*: the small version (no. 227) is a translation of the *Aṣṭa* and the large version (no. 223) is a translation of the **Pañcaviṃśatisāhasrikā*. There are two pieces of textual evidence to support the assertion that the small version is similar to the extant Sanskrit version of the *Aṣṭa*. First, in the chapter on suchness (Chinese: T8, 561a–563c; E. Conze (tr.) (1970) *Aṣṭasāhasrikā Prajñāpāramitā-sūtra*, Calcutta: The Asian Society, pp. 113–20), both versions mention that Subhūti was born after the Tathāgata since the suchness in the Tathāgata and Subhūti is the same, not different. Second, near the end of this chapter, both versions also mention

Pūrṇa (Chinese: Pūrṇamaitrāyaṇīputra), who suggests that Śāripūtra should ask Subhūti whether there is a bodhisattva vehicle. However, in the three early translations, there is no mention of Pūrṇa and Subhūti being born after the Tathāgata.

55 Lancaster, 'The Oldest Mahāyāna Sūtra', p. 36.

56 Y. Kajiyama (1989) *Banruo Sixiang*, Chinese translation by Xu Yangzu, Taipei: Faer Publication, pp. 65–6.

57 T8, 476b–477b.

58 This *sūtra* was translated into Chinese between 222 and 229 CE. See Lamotte, *The Teachings*, p. xci.

59 T14, 523c. In this discussion, we use the chronology of the Chinese translations because the date of the composition of the *Prajñāpāramitāsūtras* is impossible to determine as yet.

60 T14, 542a.

61 T8, 67c.

62 T8, 15b. The *Fangguangbanruojing*: the *dharmatā* abides in the reality of the Buddha, the *sarvajñā*, which is neither in existence nor to be seen, because it is empty internally and externally and is empty in both existence and non-existence.

63 T8, 584b.

64 Dharmarakṣa was active in China from 266 to 313 CE, and belonged to the early translators.

65 T10, 592c. 去來今佛，一切悉等，為一法身。

66 T10, 639c. 解知諸佛皆一法身。

67 T10, 659b. 解法身一，無去來今，平等三世。

68 T10, 627a. 然其法身，皆遍十方，諸佛世界。

69 T10, 598b. 如虛空界，無所不苞，無所不入，或至一切有色無色，有形無形，有處無處，亦無所至，亦無有來，則無有身，以無身故，無所不周，佛身如是。

70 T10, 592c. 法身慧體，究竟無相。... 慧以一身，示於無量所行之體，周於無限法界之裏。

71 T10, 598b. 無所見者，為見如來 ... 所以者何，用無身故，如來身者，欲以開化眾生之故，因現身耳。

72 T10, 640a. 菩薩解了佛慧，為一法身。

73 T10, 458b. 以致法身至聖慧體，具足諸佛本所志願。

74 T10, 653b. 諸天人民，著於色身，故現色身，如是無常，法身常存。

75 T10, 479a. 法身清淨，壞來至義。

76 T10, 577c. 又如法身，本之清淨。

77 T10, 637a. 其菩薩身，普無不入，(與)諸去來今如來至真，同合一身，是為十身。菩薩住此，逮成如來不可盡業無極法身。

78 T10, 582a. 彼菩薩，與過去當來今現在諸佛，而行一德本，彼菩薩(與諸如來)合為一身，以法身無踰者。

79 T25, 121c. 是法性身，滿十方虛空，無量無邊，色像端正，相好莊嚴，無量光明無量音聲。

80 T9, 399c.

81 Chapters two, three, four, five and twenty-seven are new additions in Śikṣānanda's translation because they are not found in Buddhabhadra's translation.

82 Prajñā's translation is in forty fascicles, but the first thirty-nine are an expansion on the basis of the last chapter of the first two translations, 'The Entry into the Cosmos (*dharmadhātu*)', and the last fascicle corresponds to chapter thirty-one of Buddhabhadra's translation and chapter thirty-six of Śikṣānanda's translation, 'The Practice of Universal Good'.

83 Yinshun (1994) *Chuqi Dacheng Fojian Zhi Qiyuan Yu Zhankai*, Taipei: Zhengwen Publication, pp. 1000–6.
84 T9, 444a.
85 T10, 83b.
86 T9, 429b.
87 T10, 37c.
88 T9, 617a.
89 T9, 616a–c.
90 T9, 616c.
91 T9, 617b.
92 T9, 617b. 如來法身亦復如是，為大寶王功德積聚大智慧藏。
93 T9, 599b.
94 T9, 399b.
95 T10, 444c.
96 T25, 342a.
97 T25, 336c. 一從他方佛國來生，二從兜率天上來，三從人道中來。T25, 337b 彼二處來者是法身菩薩，變身無量以度眾生，故來生是間，人道中者皆是肉身。
98 T25, 342a, 146c.
99 T25, 342a.
100 T10, 808a–b.
101 T9, 455a.
102 T16, 457c. The translator of this *sūtra* is Buddhabhadra who also translated the sixty-fascicle *Avataṃsaka*. He was active in China in 398–412 CE and a contemporary of Kumārajīva. They helped each other in their translation works. There is another translation of the **Tathāgatagarbhasūtra* done by Amoghavajra in the eighth century.
103 T12, 221c. 如是如來法身不離煩惱藏名如來藏。
104 T31, 828b. There are three meanings to the Tathāgata's saying that all sentient beings have the *tathāgatagarbha*. First, the *dharmakāya* of the Tathāgata is in each and every sentient being, so the *gāthā* says that the *dharmakāya* pervades everywhere. Second, there is no difference between the Tathāgata and the *tathatā*, so the *gāthā* says that the *tathatā* is no difference. Third, all sentient beings truly have the *tathatā*, the *buddhadhātu*, so the *gāthā* says that there is truly the *buddhadhātu*.
105 T16, 467a. 第一義諦者即是眾生界，眾生界者即是如來藏，如來藏者即是法身。
106 T16, 467a.
107 T16, 467b.
108 The MMPS has three themes: (1) the Buddha is eternal because the *dharmakāya* exists for ever; (2) the *mahāparinirvāṇa* has four virtues; (3) all sentient beings including *icchantika* (those who do not have the good roots) have the potential to become Buddhas (*tathāgatagarbha*).
109 See K. Kawamura (1972) 'Sūtras Quoted in the *Mahāparinirvāṇasūtra*', *Indogaku Bukkyōgaku Kenkyū*, vol. XX, no. 2, pp. 54–9.
110 T9, 429b. 一切諸佛身，唯是一法身。
111 T12, 567a.
112 T12, 382c. 如來身者，是常住身，是不壞身，是金剛身，非穢食身，是則法身。
113 T12, 502b.
114 T12, 502c–503a.
115 The twenty-five kinds of existence refer to the twenty-five sub-realms of the three realms, where sentient beings transmigrate from one to the other. In the desire realm (*kāmadhātu*) there are fourteen existences, in the form realm

(*rūpyadhātu*) there are seven existences, and in the formless realm (*arūpyadhātu*), four existences. The twenty-five are grouped into the Four Evil Destinies, the Four Continents, the Six Heavens of Desire, the Four Meditation Heavens, the Heaven of the Five Pure Abodes, and the Four Spheres of the Formless Realm. Cited from C. Muller, ed. (2001) *Digital Dictionary of Buddhism*, available online, http://www.acmuller.net/ddb/.

116 T12, 502c–503b.

117 T12, 596a.

118 T12, 545c.

119 T12, 556c.

120 T12, 567a. 法身即是，常樂我淨。

121 T17, 611a. 云何如來不行不住？離彼二法，法身不滅，不滅不生，是故如來名得涅槃。

122 T17, 611b. 如來即實法身，身即無為，是故如來名得涅槃。

123 T17, 611c. 如來遠離有為無為法故，唯有無為法身，不可限量，是故如來名得涅槃。

124 T17, 611c. 空者即是法，法者即是法身，法身者即是如來，是故如來名得涅槃。

125 T16, 407a. 證得真實無差別相平等法身故，名為涅槃。

126 T16, 407a. 如來法身，體是真實，名為涅槃。

127 T16, 407a. 空性即是真法身故，名為涅槃。

128 T12, 220c. 阿耨多羅三藐三菩提者，即是涅槃界，涅槃界者即是如來法身。 In the teachings of the Yogācāra school, *nirvāṇa* is divided into four types. The first is the *nirvāṇa* of the originally pure self-nature. It is the principal and suchness of all *dharmas*. All sentient beings have it equally but it is neither the same as nor different from all *dharmas*. It is free from all characteristics and differentiation. This type of *nirvāṇa* is the *dharmakāya*. The second is the *nirvāṇa* with remainder (*sopadhiśeṣa nirvāṇa*) that the hindrances due to defilement are extinguished. The third is the *nirvāṇa* without remainder (*nirupadhiśeṣa nirvāṇa*) that the hindrances due to defilement in the mind are cut off, and the body is also extinguished. The fourth is the non-abiding *nirvāṇa* (*apratiṣṭhita nirvāṇa*) that both the hindrances due to defilement and the hindrances of knowing are cut off, and a deep wisdom is attained wherein *saṃsāra* and *nirvāṇa* are not distinguished. Not abiding in *nirvāṇa* nor disliking *saṃsāra*, one teaches sentient beings yet does not become attached to the world. See also the *Vijñāptimātratāsiddhi-śāstra*, T31, 55b and Muller, *Digital Dictionary*.

129 T12, 376c.

130 T31, 821a.

131 T31, 812a–b.

132 T9, 599b.

133 T9, 723a. T10, 372b.

134 T9, 599b. 無窮盡身，滅眾虛妄如電光身，如幻夢身，如鏡像身，如淨日身。

135 T16, 550a.

136 This chapter is only found in the version of the *Laṅkāvatārasūtra* translated by Bodhiruci in 513 CE. According to D. T. Suzuki, the *Laṅkāvatārasūtra* is 'a collection of notes unsystematically strung together' (Suzuki (1930) *Studies in the Laṅkāvatāra Sūtra*, London: George Routledge, p. 17). Thus five versions of the Sanskrit original were already in existence when Śikṣānanda translated this *sūtra* for the fourth time (ibid., p. 9). So the *Laṅkāvatārasūtra*, like other Mahāyāna *sūtras*, was subject to additions and revisions. However, it was finalized before the formulation of the *trikāya* theory because this theory is not mentioned in

any version of the *Laṅkāvatārasūtra*. Suzuki thinks that the *Laṅkāvatārasūtra* represents the last stage before the *trikāya* theory was formed.

137 T16, 550a

138 T16, 550b.

139 According to Nāgārjuna, *prapañca* means words, which conceal and cover reality, are nothing but subjective counterfeits, and lead further into ignorance and affliction. But, according to the **Yogācārabhūmiśāstra* (T30, 815a), 'The words which can bring meaningless speculations and discriminations are called *prapañca*. Why? Because they do not increase an iota of wholesome *dharma*, but conversely they increase bad *dharma* when one utters them. This is named *prapañca*.'

140 T16, 550c.

141 T16, 551a.

142 T16, 685a. There are two complete Chinese translations of the **Saṃdhinirmocanasūtra*, one by Bodhiruci, the other by Xuanzang. These two translations are almost identical.

143 T16, 678c, 702a.

144 John J. Makransky (1997) *Buddhahood Embodied: Sources of Controversy in India and Tibet*, New York: State University of New York Press, p. 61.

145 T31, 606b–607b.

146 T31, 625c–626b.

147 See Xuanzang's translation of the MS, T31, 136c; Paramārtha's translation of the MS, T31, 117a–b.

148 T31, 174a.

149 P. Griffiths, H. Noriaki, J. P. Keenan and P. L. Swanson (1989) *The Realm of Awakening: A Translation and Study of the Tenth Chapter of Asaṅga's Mahāyānasaṃgraha*, New York: Oxford University Press, p. 93.

150 T31, 58a. The **Vijñaptimātratāsiddhiśāstra* does not mention the title of the *sūtra* and the *śāstra*. However, they are supplied in its commentary written by Xuanzang's great disciple Kuiji who assisted him in his translation. See also Louis de La Vallée Poussin's translation: *Vijñāptimātratāsiddhi: la Siddhi de Hiuan-Tsang*, vol. II, Paris: Librairie Orientaliste Paul Guenther, 1929, p. 706.

151 T26, 326a.

152 T26, 326a.

153 T31, 824c.

5 THE ORIGIN AND DEVELOPMENT OF THE *SAṂBHOGAKĀYA*

1 Both Chinese translations of the *Avataṃsaka*, one by Buddhabhadra in 317–420 CE and the other by Śīkṣānanda in 695–699 CE, include the term 'the reward body of *karma*' among the ten kinds of body (T9, 565b, 565c, 661c; T10, 200a, 200b, 201b, 201c). These ten kinds of body include the body of sentient beings, the body of land, the reward body of *karma*, the *śrāvaka* body, the *pratyekabuddha* body, the bodhisattva body, the Tathāgata body, the wisdom body, the body of doctrine, and the body of space. The 'reward body of *karma*' does not mean the enjoyment body of the Buddha.

2 R. Habito (1978) 'The Development of the Buddha-body Theory', *Shūkyō Kenkyū*, vol. L2-2, no. 237, p. 11; J. Makransky (1997) *Buddhahood Embodied: Sources of Controversy in India and Tibet*, New York: State University of New York Press, p. 54.

3 D. T. Suzuki (1930) *Studies in the Lankavatara Sutra*, London: George Routledge, pp. 308–8.
4 Habito, 'The Development', pp. 10–11.
5 S. Takeuchi (1983) 'Buddhakan no hensen', in Akira Hirakawa, ed., *Daijō Bukkyō*, Tokyo: Shunjusha, vol. I, pp. 166–70.
6 T25, 121b–c.
7 The *Parinirvāṇasūtra*, T1, 182b–c; the *Mahāparinirvāṇasūtra* translated by Faxian, T1, 203b; the *Aṅgulimālyasūtra*, T2, 539c; the *Ekottarāgama*, T2, 578a; the *Sūtra on Ānanda's Fellow Student*, T2, 874c. D II, 149. The **Dīrghāgama*, T1, 31a, 79a.
8 T27, 890c.
9 T17, 753b lines 28–9.
10 T27, 871c–872b, 391c–392b.
11 This quotation of the Mahāsāṃghikas is found in the **Saṃyuktāgama*, T2, 28b12 and the *Aṅguttaranikāya*, ii, 37. But in two other places of the *Mahāvibhāṣā* (T27, 229a, 391c–392a) it is said that this view was held by the Mahāsāṃghikas with no mention of the Vibhajyavādins.
12 This quotation of the Sarvāstivāda is found in the **Madhyamāgama*, T1, 645b and the *Aṅguttaranikāya*, iv, 43.
13 T27, 871c–872b.
14 T29, 557b.
15 T27, 177a–b. 謂或有謂，歸依佛者，歸依如來頭項腹背，及手足等所合成身。
16 T29, 557b. 然大眾部復作是言，如來身中，所有諸法，皆是無漏，盡是所歸。
17 Translated from the Chinese text into English by J. Masuda (1922) *Origin and Doctrines of Early Indian Buddhist Schools*, *Asia Major*, Leipzig: Verlag Asia Major, vol. II, fascicle I, pp. 18–21.
18 Ibid., p. 52.
19 T27, 229a–b, 391c–392c, 735c, 871c–872a.
20 The opposing party states the following.

 1 The Buddha received three hundred thousand robes in one day from householder Ujaluo. This is gain.
 2 The Buddha returned with an empty bowl from a Brahmin village. This is no gain.
 3 The name of the Buddha reached Akaniṣṭha heaven when he attained enlightenment. This is the honour of fame.
 4 The Buddha was subjected to slander by the women Sundarī and Ciñcamānavikā. His tarnished reputation was thereafter known throughout the sixteen great kingdoms. This is disgrace.
 5 The Brahmins had pure faith in him because the facial complexion of the Buddha did not change (in debate). This is praise.
 6 The Brahmin Bhāradvāja cursed the Buddha with five hundred verses. This is defamation.
 7 The Buddha enjoyed incomparable mental and physical happiness which is not experienced by sentient beings. This is happiness.
 8 The Buddha also suffered from headaches, back pain, a *khadira* thorn and a splinter in his foot. This is suffering. T27, 871c–872b.

21 T27, 871c–872a.
22 An abstract of this section with the title 'The Bad Karma of the Buddha' has been published in *Buddhist Studies Review*, vol. 19, no. 1, 2002, pp. 19–29.
23 In the Theravāda tradition there is another source relevant to this issue, a Sāmmatīya list of sixteen incidents transmitted by Daśabalaśrīmitra in his

Saṃskṛtāsaṃskṛta-viniścaya. It is probably a Dhammarucika list in a Sinhalese work of the fourteenth century or earlier called *Detis Karmaya*, which allegedly describes thirty-two such incidents. The manuscript of this work is preserved in the British Library. See K. D. Somadasa (1989) *Catalogue of the Hugh Nevill Collection of Sinhalese Manuscripts in the British Library*, Henley-on-Thames: Pali Text Society, vol. 2, pp. 122–3. Since this is a very late work it does not fall into the scope of our discussion of the debate on the physical body of the Buddha in the period of the early Buddhist schools.

24 The ten texts are (1) the **Pañcaśatasthavirāvadāna*, T4, 190a–202a; (2) the *Xingqixingjng*, T4, 163c–174b; (3) the **Bhaiṣajyavastu* of the **Mūlasarvāstivāda Vinaya*, T24, 94a–97a; (4) the **Lokānuvartanasūtra*, T17, 773a–774c; (5) the *Pusaxingwushiyuansheng Jing*, T17, 773a–774c; (6) the **Upāyakauśalyasūtra*, T11, 594c–607c; T12, 156a–165c, 166a–178b; (7) the **Mahāyānadaśadharmakasūtra*, T11, 154c–157a, 767b–769a; (8) the **Tathāgatapratibimbapratiṣṭhānusaṃsāsūtra*, T16, 788a–788c, 788c–790a, 790a–796b; (9) the **Mahāprajñāpāramitāśāstra*, T25, 121c; (10) the **Mahāyānāvatārakaśāstra*, T32, 37b–c.

25 The five Tibetan texts are: (1) the **Upāyakauśalyasūtra* translated by Gos Chos grub (Chinese Wu Facheng) based on Dharmarakṣa's rendition (Taisho no. 345); (2) the **Upāyakauśalyasūtra* translated by Dānaśīla, Karmavarman and Ye shes sde from Sanskrit; (3) the **Bhaiṣajyavastu* of the **Mūlasarvāstivāda Vinaya*; (4) the **Lokānuvartanasūtra*; and (5) the **Tathāgatapratibimbapratiṣṭhānusaṃsāsūtra*.

26 The Tibetan translation of the **Anavataptagāthā* will not be dealt with here as the present writer does not specialize in Tibetan sources. I will refer to it only through the works of other scholars. According to Paul Harrison (1995b), 'Some Reflections on the Personality of the Buddha', *The Otani Gakuko*, vol. 18, no. 1, pp. 48–69, the Tibetan text refers to these several times as *las kyi rgyud bcu po*, i.e. Skt: *daśa-karma-ploti/pluti*.

27 For this *karma*, the **Bhaiṣajyavastu* of the **Mūlasarvāstivādavinaya* gives a second story. In a previous life, the Buddha was a man of bad temper named Weilou. He loved a prostitute and bestowed upon her many nice cloths as presents prior to marriage. Later he discovered that she had left with another man, taking his presents. He killed her when he found her again, but he threw the knife stained with blood in front of a *pratyekabuddha* who was meditating at the foot of a tree. Thus, the *pratyekabuddha* was mistaken for the killer by the king's men. When Weilou saw him again, the *pratyekabuddha* was being arrested and taken to be killed. Regretful of his deeds, Weilou was surrounded and persecuted. As a result, the Buddha suffered in hell for a long time and the remaining effect of that *karma* was slander by others.

28 See J. Walters (1990) 'The Buddha's Bad Karma: A Problem in the History of Theravāda Buddhism', *Numen*, vol. XXXVII, fasc. 1, pp. 76–7.

29 T4, 190a–202a. This *sūtra* was translated by Dharmarakṣa in 303 CE. The Buddha's bad *karma* is found in the last part of the *sūtra*, 201a–202a.

30 T4, 163c–174b. The whole *sūtra* is devoted to an explanation of the ten bad *karmas* of the Buddha.

31 T24, the part on the bad *karma* is found in pages 95a–97a, the last part of the **Bhaiṣajyavastu*.

32 E. Lamotte (1988) *History of Indian Buddhism, from the Origins to the Śaka Era*, Louvain-la-Neuve: Université Catholique de Louvain, Institut Orientaliste, English translation by Sara Boin-Webb, p. 692.

33 The last verse in the Buddha's speech is incomplete as some lines are missing.
34 The text starts thus:

> Near the Anotatta Lake, on the delightful rocky ground, where various gems were sparkling and various sweet scents [were exuded] in the forest, the Lord of the World, surrounded by a huge community of monks, sitting down, then explained his own previous *karma*: 'Hear from me, O monks, the *karma* produced by me [and] the ripening of strands of *karma* in the Buddha himself.

Cited from Walters, 'The Buddha's Bad Karma', p. 76.
35 See ibid., pp. 76–7.
36 Cited from S. M. Cutler (1994) 'The Pāli Apadāna Collection', *Journal of the Pali Text Society*, vol. XX, pp. 14–15.
37 Some scholars think that the Mūlasarvāstivāda school may predate the Sarvāstivāda school, so they hesitate to say that the former is a sub-sect of the latter. However, the Chinese translation of the Buddhist *Tripiṭaka* shows that the term Mūlasarvāstivāda is not mentioned in early texts but only in Yijing's (the end of the seventh to the beginning of the eighth century) translations, while the term Sarvāstivāda is mentioned in Paramārtha's (mid-sixth century) translations. Therefore, we are probably not wrong in saying that the Mūlasarvāstivāda is derived from the Sarvāstivāda.
38 Walters, 'The Buddha's Bad Karma', pp. 77–9.
39 Ibid., p. 78. See E. B. Cowell and R. A. Neil, eds (1886) *The Divyāvadāna, A Collection of Early Buddhist Legends*, Cambridge: Cambridge University Press, p. 87 line 8; p. 150 line 24; p. 241 line 26.
40 Walters, 'The Buddha's Bad Karma', p. 78. Cowell and Neil, *Divyāvadāna*, p. 150: 'Anavatapte mahāsarasi śrāvakaih sārdham pūrvikā karmaplotir vyākrita bhavati.' Dr T. Skorupski has orally informed the present writer that this *karmaploti* in the *Divyāvadāna* is one of the ten inevitable actions of the Buddha.
41 Walters, 'The Buddha's Bad Karma', p. 78.
42 N. Dutt (1978a) *Mahāyāna Buddhism*, Delhi: Motilal Banarsidass, pp. 75–6.
43 T3, 932a.
44 T24, 78a–97a.
45 Each story starts with the phrase 'Thus [I] heard, the Buddha once sojourned at the Lake Anavatapta with five hundred *bhikṣus* who were all *arhats* with the six transcendental powers' and concludes with the phrase 'all delighted and happy to accept the Buddha's discourse'.
46 In the prose section of the *sūtra*, it is said that Pure-eye, the actor, killed a prostitute for her nice clothes and buried her body in the hut of a *pratyekabuddha*. Thus the *pratyekabuddha* was caught and suffered. On seeing the *pratyekabuddha*'s suffering, the actor took pity and rescued him. T4, 164c–165a.
47 The **Lokānuvartanasūtra* (T17, 773a–774c), which was translated by Indo-Scythian *śrāmaṇa* Lokakṣema between 178 and 189 CE, is the earliest Chinese translation among all the seven texts in which the bad *karma* of the Buddha is rejected. The Chinese translation is entirely in prose, but as Harrison points out, apart from the introduction and conclusion, ninety verses are clearly distinguishable. The Tibetan translation by Jinamitra, Dānaśīla and Ye shes sde around the beginning of the ninth century is entirely in verse, containing 113 four-line stanzas. The Tibetan translation displays certain differences from the Chinese version since the texts are separated by six hundred years. This text is very short and falls roughly into two parts, the first describing the person and life of

the Buddha, the second primarily dealing with his teaching. See P. Harrison (1982) 'Sanskrit Fragments of a Lokottaravādin Tradition', in L. A. Hercus, ed., *Indological and Buddhist Studies: Volume in Honour of Professor J. W. de Jong on his Sixtieth Birthday*, Canberra: Faculty of Asian Studies, pp. 211, 212.

48 The three incidents of bad *karma* are:

1 'The Prince sat at the foot of a tree in Jambudvīpa and from then on for six years, he suffered hardship. It is in conformity with the ways of the world that he makes such a show of suffering from hardship' (T17, 751c lines 14–15; this translation is mine).

2 'The Buddha's body has never suffered illness, yet he manifests illness, summons doctors and takes medicine. The giver of the medicine obtains immeasurable blessings. It is in conformity with the ways of the world that he makes such a show' (T17, 752a lines 12–13; the translation is taken from Harrison, 'Sanskrit Fragments', pp. 220–1).

3 'The blessings of the Buddha's merits are inexhaustible, and no one can surpass them. The Buddha enters the city for *piṇḍapāda*, and leaves with an empty *pātra*. It is in conformity with the ways of the world that he makes such a show' (T17, 752b lines 6–7; the translation is also taken from Harrison, 'Sanskrit Fragments', p. 222).

49 T17, 752c.
50 T17, 753a.
51 The similarities between the *Lokānuvartanasūtra* and the relevant part of the *Mahāvastu* of the Lokottaravāda were first discovered and demonstrated by Takahara Shinichi in his article '*Mahāvastu* ni mirareru fukutokuron', in *Fukaoka daigaku sanjūgoshūnen kinen ronbunshū, Jinbunhen*, 1969, pp. 117–41. Shizutani Masao commented upon it in his *Shoki daijobukkyo no seiritsu katei*, Kyoto, 1974, pp. 282, 315–18. See Harrison, 'Sanskrit Fragments', p. 213.
52 Cited from Harrison, 'Sanskrit Fragments', p. 227.
53 The relevant part of the text is quoted from Masuda, *Origin and Doctrines*, pp. 18–21.
54 Ibid., p. 19.
55 T17, 752a.
56 T17, 752a.
57 T17, 753b.
58 T17, 753b.
59 Masuda, *Origin and Doctrines*, p. 20.
60 T17, 752b.
61 T17, 752b.
62 T17, 753a.
63 Masuda, *Origin and Doctrines*, p. 20.
64 T17, 752a.
65 T17, 733c.
66 The three Chinese translations are: (1) T12, no. 345, translated by Dharmarakṣa in 285 CE; (2) T11, no. 310.38 translated by Nandi in 420 CE; (3) T12, no. 346, translated by Dānapāla in 1005 CE. See P. Harrison (1995a) 'Searching for the Origin of Mahāyāna: What Are We Looking for?', *The Eastern Buddhist*, vol. 18, no. 1, pp. 8–9. There is also an English translation of T11, no. 310.38 in Garma C. C. Chang, ed. (1983) *A Treasury of Mahāyāna Sūtras: Selections from the Mahāratnakūṭa Sūtra*, University Park, Pa.: University of Pennsylvania Press, pp. 427–68. According to P. Harrison there are also two Tibetan versions,

the first being a translation from the Chinese by Gos Chos grub (Chinese Wu Facheng), based on Dharmarakṣa's rendition entitled **Upāyakauśalyasūtra*. This is an independent work found in the Tibetan Kanjur. The second was translated from the Sanskrit by Dānaśīla, Karmavarman and Ye shes sde, with the same title as the first and found in the Tibetan version of the *Ratnakūṭa*. See Harrison, 'Searching for the Origin', 9. The first of these, Wu Facheng's version, was translated into English by M. Tatz as *The Skill in Means (Upāyakauśalya) Sūtra*, Delhi: Motilal Banarsidass, 1994.

67 T12, 165c lines 12–15. Nandi's translation is somewhat different:

> Good man, I have finished explaining and revealing my ingenuity. You should keep this a secret and not speak of it to lowly, inferior people who have few good roots. Why? Because even *śrāvakas* and *pratyekabuddhas* cannot comprehend this *sūtra*, much less can lowly and inferior, ordinary persons believe or understand it. Ordinary people cannot learn ingenuity, and so the *Sūtra of Ingenuity* is of no use to them; not a single ordinary person can accept or practise it. Only *Bodhisattvas* can learn and teach the doctrine of ingenuity.

From C. C. Chang, *A Treasury of Mahāyāne Sūtras.*

68 T12, 159c line 15, 162a line 16, 162b line 19.

69 Harrison, 'Sanskrit Fragments', p. 56.

70 T12, 156a–165c. Here the Chinese word *Huishang* means 'superior in wisdom'. The **Lokānuvartana* also begins with Mañjuśrī requesting the Buddha to expound *upāyakauśalya*. Mañjuśrī is a bodhisattva superior in wisdom. I suspect that the original Sanskrit text of Dharmarakṣa's translation is an outgrowth of and a further development of the **Lokānuvartanasūtra* because in both *sūtras*, Mañjuśrī and Huishang are bodhisattvas who request the Buddha to expound on *upāyakauśalya*.

71 T12, 163b.

72 T12, 165c.

73 The **Ratnakūṭasūtra*, T11, 154c–157a, and the **Mahāyānadaśadharmakasūtra* T11, 767b–769a.

74 T11, 154c. The translation is adapted from E. Lamotte (1976) *The Teachings of Vimalakīrti*, London: PTS, English translation by Sara Boin-Webb, p. 297.

75 Of the three Chinese translations of the **Tathāgatapratibimbapratiṣṭhānusaṃsāsūtra*, T16, no. 692 was translated under the Eastern Han dynasty 25–220 CE; T16, no. 693 under the Jin dynasty 317–420 CE; and T16, no. 694 by Devaprajñā in 691 CE. Only the last one mentions the bad *karma*s. Moreover, in the latter half of Devaprajñā's translation, the dialogue is mainly conducted between the Buddha and bodhisattva Maitreya concerning the merit of making Buddha images. However, in the middle of this dialogue, the *sūtra* mentions that a person doubted whether the Buddha did make images in the past and thus bad *karma* was introduced. These passages were most probably inserted into the text later when the bad *karmas* became an issue of debate. According to B. Nanjio (1989) *A Catalogue of the Chinese Translation of the Buddhist Tripiṭaka*, Delhi: Classics Indian Publications, p. 76, there is also a Tibetan translation of the *sūtra* similar to the first two Chinese translations.

76 The *sūtra* mentions seven of the problematic events that occurred in the life of Gautama Buddha: the Devadatta incident, the three months of eating barley, the Buddha's return with an empty bowl, the *khadira* thorn and three episodes of illness.

77 There is a controversy regarding the authorship of the MPPŚ. Western scholars such as Lamotte are of the opinion that Nāgārjuna is not the author while Yinshun disagrees. See *Dongfang zongjiao yanjiu*, Taiwan, 1990, no. 2, pp. 9–70.
78 T25, 121c. 若佛神力無量威德巍巍不可稱說，何以故受九罪報？
79 T25, the list of the bad *karma* of the Buddha is found in 121b–122b.
80 Yinshun (1994) *Chuqi Dacheng Fojian Zhi Qiyuan Yu Zhankai*, Taipei: Zhengwen Publication, p. 167.
81 This was pointed out to me by P. Harrison when he was at SOAS delivering a series of lectures on the *Sukhāvatīvyūha* in 1999.
82 T32, 37b–c.
83 An earlier version of this section was originally published in the *World Hongming Philosophical Quarterly*, vol. 2002, December, with the same title. Internet URL: www.whpq.org or www.whpq.net.
84 The MSA states that the Śrāvakayāna and the Mahāyāna are different in five ways: (1) the initiate's mind for enlightenment (*bodhi*); (2) the learning and teaching of the Dharma; (3) the skilful means; (4) the activity of converting and saving people; (5) the period of time required for enlightenment. The *śrāvakas* practise the first three aspects with the purpose of benefiting themselves, for the attainment of *nirvāṇa*. They do not make much effort to convert and save people so they do not have much merit. The period required for liberation is also short, namely three lifetimes. The Mahāyānists are quite different. They practise the first three aspects for the benefit of others, they spend their lives converting and working towards liberating individuals, thus acquiring great merit. The period required for liberation is very long, namely three *mahāsaṃkhyeya kalpas*. T31, 591b–c.
85 The MPPŚ states (T25, 121b–c):

> The Buddha had accumulated immeasurable merit during the countless *kalpas* and when all are considered, no human being is comparable. Great causes result in great rewards. Again, the Buddha, in countless lives, practised all kinds of austerities and made offerings to beings with his own head, eyes, marrow, brain, let alone country, wealth, wife and children. [He] had practised and completed all kinds of discipline (*śīla*), all kinds of forbearance (*kṣānti*), all kinds of energy (*vīrya*), all kinds of meditation (*dhyāna*) and pure, indestructible and inexhaustible wisdom (*prajñā*). It is due to the power of the reward from these actions that [the Buddha] had such marvellous attributes.

86 T1, 15c; D ii, 115.
87 Z. Yao (1996) *Yibu zonglun lun*, Taiwan: Foguang publication, p. 165.
88 T9, 42c. This translation, with some changes, has been taken from B. Watson (tr.) (1993) *The Lotus Sutra*, New York: Columbia University Press, p. 227.
89 E. Lamotte (tr.) (1998) *Śūraṅgamasamādhisūtra, the Concentration of Heroic Progress*, English translation by Sara Boin-Webb, London: Curzon Press, pp. 235–8.
90 T15, 645a. The translation is adapted from ibid., p. 238.
91 T9, 589c.
92 T16, 335c. There are three Chinese translations of this *sūtra*. T16, no. 663 was translated by Dharmarakṣa in the Northern Liang dynasty 397–439 CE. T16, no. 664 is a combination of three translations edited by Baogui: Dharmarakṣa's translation, Jñānagupta's translation in the Northern Zhou 557–581 CE and

Paramārtha's translation in 548–569 CE. The latter two translations are lost. T16, no. 665 was translated by Yijing in 700–712 CE.

93 T16, 335c–336b. 一切諸水，可知幾滴，無有能數，釋尊壽命。諸須彌山，可知斤兩，無有能量，釋尊壽命。

94 This is an indication that the followers of Hīnayāna schools opposed the idea of the eternal Buddha of the Mahāyānists.

95 T16, 794c–795a.

96 T25, 124b.

97 T25, 311c–312b. *Zhang* (丈) and *li* (里) are Chinese measurements, one *zhang* is 3.33 metres and one *li* is 500 metres.

98 The **Saddharmapuṇḍarīkasūtra* explains quite clearly why the life-span of Śākyamuni Buddha was short while asserting that the real life-span of the Buddha is immeasurable. It states,

> If the Buddha remains in the world for a long time, those persons with shallow virtue will fail to plant good roots but, living in poverty and lowliness, will become attached to the five desires and be caught in the net of deluded thoughts and imaginings. If they see that the Thus Come One is constantly in the world and never enters extinction, they will grow arrogant and selfish, or become discouraged and neglectful. They will fail to realize how difficult it is to encounter the Buddha and will not approach him with a respectful and reverent mind.

Watson, *The Lotus Sutra*, p. 227. The author of the MPPŚ may have consulted the *Saddharmapuṇḍarīka Sūtra* or have had this *sūtra* in mind.

99 T12, 390a. 迦葉復言：如來云何名曰常住？如佛言曰：如燈滅已，無有方所，如來亦爾，既滅度已，亦無方所。

100 T12, 382c–383a.

101 T12, 596a.

102 T12, 445c. 佛性即是如來，如來即是法，法即是常。

103 T12, 539b. 眾生佛性亦復如是，雖處五道受別異身，而是佛性常一無變。

104 Here the audience are the *dharmatākāya* bodhisattvas.

105 T25, 121c–122a.

106 T25, 131c.

107 T25, 274a.

108 T25, 278a–b.

109 T25, 303b.

110 T25, 313b.

111 T25, 683a.

112 T25, 747a.

113 The two-body theory in the *Vibhāṣā* refers to the *dharmakāya* and the *rūpakāya* while the MPPŚ uses the term *nirmāṇakāya* instead of *rūpakāya*. This is because the author of the MPPŚ considered Śākyamuni as a body of transformation only, but the Sarvāstivādins considered that the historical Buddha attained enlightenment in this life, so to them Śākyamuni was a *rūpakāya* and not a *nirmāṇakāya*.

114 T25, 303b.

115 T25, 274a. 佛法有二種：一者世諦，二者第一義諦，世諦故說三十二相，第一義諦故說無相。

116 T25, 274a. The sixteen active aspects of the Four Noble Truths (*ṣoḍāśa-ākāra*), which are sixteen ways of analysing the meaning of the Four Noble Truths, include four ways for each noble truth. The first noble truth is analysed as

(1) containing the meanings of impermanence (*anitya*); (2) unsatisfactoriness (*duḥkha*); (3) emptiness (*śūnya*); (4) no-self (*anātmaka*). The second noble truth contains the implications of (5) the cause of suffering (*hetu*); (6) gathering (*samudaya*); (7) continuation (*prabhava*); (8) conditions (*pratyaya*). The third noble truth implies (9) extinction of physical attachments (*nirodha*); (10) the calming of afflictions (*śānta*); (11) the sublimity of no discomfort (*praṇita*); (12) escape from all difficult circumstances (*nihsaraṇa*). Within the fourth noble truth are seen (13) the path to cessation (*mārga*); (14) accordance with the correct principle (*nyāya*); (15) activity leading to *nirvana* (*pratipatti*); (16) transcendence of life and death (*nairyāṇika*).

117 T25, 746b.

118 T25, 126b.

119 T25, 58c–59a.

120 T25, 121b–c.

121 T25, 340a.

122 Makransky, *Buddhahood Embodied*, pp. 54–5.

123 There are Chinese (T31, 589b–661c) and Tibetan translations of the MSA, and a Sanskrit version was found in Nepal and edited by the French scholar Sylvain Levi, who published it in 1907. (See Note 135.) The French translation by the same scholar was published in 1911. Since then many Japanese scholars have studied and translated it, e.g. U. Hakuju (1979) *A Study on the Mahāyānasūtrālaṁkāra*, Tokyo; K. Nobuchiyo (1984) *A Study on the Mahāyānasūtrālaṁkāra*, Tokyo; H. Noriaki's Japanese translation of the MSA with introduction, Tokyo, 1993.

124 T8, 455a. 我不復欲聞，是故說是皆非佛所說，餘外事耳。

125 E. Conze (1967) *Thirty Years of Buddhist Studies*, Oxford: Bruno Cassirer, p. 178: 'naitad buddhavacanaṃ kavi-kṛtaṃ kāvyam etat'.

126 T13, 907a–b. The Chinese scholar Yinshun takes these two quotations as textual evidence for the traditional dispute regarding whether the Mahāyāna is the teaching of the Buddha. Yinshun, *Chuqi Dacheng*, p. 1.

127 若四輩弟子得聞是經，言非正法，作如是說，是邪說，非如來說。(T10, 893c, 11–13); Cf. The *Mahāratnakūṭa Sūtra* (T11, 522b3–b21).

128 T12, 892c, 25. 言方等經皆是魔說，言摩訶衍者，是諸黠慧正法刺劍，諸佛世尊皆當無常而說常住。

129 T50, 190c. 不信大乘，謂摩訶衍非佛所說; cf. J. Takakusu (tr.) (1904) 'The Life of Vasubhandhu', *T'oung Pao Archive*, Series II, vol. V, p. 290.

130 T50, 189a. The translation is taken from Takakusu, 'The Life of Vasubhandhu', p. 279.

131 T31, 591a.

132 G. Nagao (1961) *An Index to Asaṅga's Mahāyānasaṃgraha, Part Two: Sanskrit–Tibetan–Chinese*, Tokyo: The International Institute for Buddhist Studies, p. 285. Nagao mentions twenty-eight sources cited in the *Mahāyānasūtrālaṃkāra*, twenty-one are given titles and seven are just mentioned as the *āgama*, *sūtra* or *yathoktam bhagavatā*.

133 The Chinese and Tibetan translations also have this sentence, but the Chinese translation omits the word 'bodhisattva': 'Here ends the *Mahāyānasūtrālaṃkāra* that was told when it was pure.' The Tibetan translation is: 'theg pa chen po mdo sde'I rgyan byan chub sems dpa' chen po rtogs pa rnam par byang bas bshad palas.' Cited from Shi Shanyin (1999) 'Dacheng Zuangyianjinglun Zhi Yianju', *Chu-Hwa Buddhist Journal*, vol. III, note 10.

134 See Takeuchi, 'Buddhakau', p. 170, Makransky, *Buddhahood Embodied*, p. 65.

135 Sylvain Levi, who found the Sanskrit text in Nepal, and edited and translated it into French, is of the opinion that both the text and the *bhāṣya* were composed by Asaṅga (*Asaṅga, Mahāyānasūtrālaṁkāra, Exposé la Doctrine du Grand Véhicule selon le Système Yogācāra*, Paris, E. Leroux, 1907). The reason for Levi's opinion is that Prabhākaramitra, who made the Chinese translation in 630–633 CE, is the first person to mention Asaṅga as the author of both the text and the *bhāṣya*. However, Xuanzang, nearly half a century later, stated that it was Maitreya who inspired Asaṅga to compose it while the Tibetan translation was made much later by the Indian Śākyasiṃha and the Tibetan dPal brcogs. (See Shi Shanyin, 'Dacheng Zuangyianjinglun Zhi Yianju', p. 24.) Moreover, one ought to consider the Chinese catalogue *Zhiyuanlu* (a general catalogue of the Dharmaratna or Buddhist sacred books collected in the Zhiyuan period, under the Yuan dynasty), compiled by *śrāmaṇa* Phagspa, an imperial adviser of the Yuan Dynasty, along with other learned monks with imperial patronage. This catalogue was published in 1287 CE, and both the text and the *bhāṣya* are attributed to Asaṅga.

The Japanese scholar Hakuju Ui is of the opinion that the text is by Maitreya and the *bhāṣya* by Vasubandhu as he argues that Maitreya was a historical figure who lived between 270 and 350 CE (H. Nakamura (1996) *Indian Buddhism: A Survey With Bibliographical Notes*, Delhi: Motilal Banarsidass, p. 256). Hakuju Ui thinks that Asaṅga, who heard it from Maitreya, taught it to Vasubandhu who in turn wrote the *bhāṣya*; therefore Asaṅga is neither the author nor the commentator. However, Hakuju Ui regards the *bhāṣya* as having been composed by Vasubandhu while he was staying with his brother Asaṅga. Erich Frauwallner is also of the same opinion as Hakuju Ui that the text is by Maitreya. He has also argued that had Asaṅga considered himself inspired in a vision by the bodhisattva Maitreya he would have written not philosophical treatises (*śāstra*) but rather *sūtras*. But since these three texts, the *Madhyāntavibhāga*, the *Dharmadharmatāvibhāga* and the MSA, are unitary philosophical works, and differ somewhat from works known to be by Asaṅga, this indicates an authorship by Maitreyanātha rather than by the bodhisattva Maitreya (P. Williams (1989) *Mahāyāna Buddhism: The Doctrinal Foundations*, London: Routledge, p. 81). But other scholars like Lamotte, Noriaki Hakamaya, Nobuchiyo Kotani and Takashi Yamaguchi think differently, believing that the text is by Asaṅga and the *bhāṣya* is by Vasubandhu.

136 Cited from Shi Shanyin, 'Dacheng', p. 24. Hakamaya regards Maitreya as a legendary person so he takes Asaṅga as the founder of Yogācāra. See his Japanese translation of the MSA, 1993, Tokyo, pp. 18f. Kotani, who made a comparative study of the language and considered both Asaṅga and Vasubandhu, asserts that Asaṅga composed the text and Vasubandhu the commentary. See his *A Study of the Mahāyānasūtrālaṁkāra* (in Japanese), Tokyo, 1984, pp. 10ff. Yamaguchi, on the basis of the first verse in the MSA, says that the texts were composed by Asaṅga with the supernatural power of the great Bodhisattva. See also Kotani's *Study*, p. 14.

137 Scholars like J. Takakusu (1905) 'On the Abhidharma Literature of the Sarvāstivādins', *Journal of the Pali Text Society*, pp. 67–146; E. Frauwallner (1951) *On the Date of the Buddhist Master of the Law Vasubandhu*, Rome: Istituto Italiano per il Medio ed Estremo Oriente, and other Japanese scholars have studied the dates of Asaṅga and Vasubandhu. The dates of Asaṅga are regarded as roughly 310–390 CE and the dates of Vasubandhu approximately 320–400 CE. See H. Nakamura, *Indian Buddhism*, pp. 264, 268.

138 *The Life of Vasubandhu* was translated into Chinese by Paramārtha, T50, 188b–c. This was again translated into English by Takakusu (1904) 'The Life of Vasubandhu'. J. Takakusu also made a study of the life and dates of Vasubandhu: 'A Study of Paramārtha's Life of Vasubandhu and the Date of Vasubandhu', *Journal of the Royal Asiatic Society*, 1905, pp. 33–53. Xuanzang also gives a brief account of the lives of Asaṅga and Vasubandhu in his *Datangxiyuji* ('Record of the Western Regions'), T51, 896b–897a.
139 The MSA itself quoted many Mahāyāna *sūtras* and *śāstras* which were already in existence.
140 E. Lamotte (1990) 'Dazhidulun De Zhuozhe Jiqi Fanyi', Chinese translation by Guo Zhongsheng, *Diguan*, vol. 62, p. 125. This Sarvāstivādin scholar is the same as the author of the MPPŚ, Nāgārjuna according to Chinese tradition. But the authorship of the MPPŚ is a controversy among scholars.
141 The MSA, T31, 591a–593a, and all three Chinese translations of the *Mahāyānasaṃgraha* (T31, 97a–b, 113b–c, 132c–133a), record: 'An interpretation of the scriptures such as this demonstrates that the truths of the Great Vehicle are the very words of the Buddha.' Cited from John P. Keenan's English translation of *The Summary of the Great Vehicle*, Los Angeles: Numata Center for Buddhist Translation and Research, 1992, p. 11.
142 Shih Hengching (1996) 'Dabanniepanjing de Foxinglun', *Journal of the Centre for Buddhist-Studies*, vol. 1, p. 35.
143 Ibid.
144 T50, 190c, Vasubandhu 'was versed in all the principles of the eighteen schools [of Buddhism] and thoroughly understood the Hīnayāna'. 法師既遍通十八部義，妙解小乘. Takakusu, 'A Study', p. 290.
145 T31, 606b.
146 T31, 372b–c.
147 In the MSA, the term *saṃbhogakāya* is translated in two ways: 'the body of food', which is a *literary* translation, and 'the body of enjoyment'. In the three Chinese translations of the *Mahāyānasaṃgraha* of Asaṅga, Buddhaśānta translated it as 'the reward body', Paramārtha 'the body of enjoyment' and Xuanzang 'the body of enjoyment'. In the three Chinese translations of the *Mahāyānasaṃgrahabhāṣya* of Vasubandhu, Gupta and Xingju translated it as 'the body of enjoyment', Paramārtha 'the body of transformation' and Xuanzang 'the body of enjoyment'. It is noticed that Paramārtha's translation is not consistent, but Xuanzang consistently translated it as 'the body of enjoyment'.
148 Makransky, *Buddhahood Embodied*, pp. 105–6.
149 T31, 606b.
150 M. Williams [1899] (1986) *A Sanskrit–English Dictionary*, Tokyo: Meicho Fukyu Kai, pp. 1152, 1178. Here *saṃbuddha* is translated as 'well perceived, perfectly known or understood'.
151 According to M. Williams, *A Sanskrit–English Dictionary*, p. 767, *bhoga* is derived from the verb *bhuj* meaning 'to eat'.
152 T26, 326a. 又受用身略有二種，一自受用，三無數劫修所成故，二他受用，為諸菩薩受法樂故。
153 T31, 57c–58a.

6 THE ORIGIN AND DEVELOPMENT OF THE *NIRMĀṆAKĀYA*

1 Some scholars like Teresina Rowell are of the opinion that the *nirmāṇakāya* originated from the idea of the magical power (*ṛddhi*) of the Buddha, by which

he could multiply himself as many times as sought. T. Rowell (1935) 'The Background and Early Use of the Buddhakṣetra Concept', *The Eastern Buddhist*, vol. VI, no. 4, p. 135.

2 D i, 77. M ii, 17–18.

3 Vsm. 342.

4 T1, 85c.

5 D i, 195. The belief in the three modes of personalities is pre-Buddhistic. It was a view commonly accepted in India. Poṭṭhapāda himself admitted this in the *sutta*. However, from the Buddhist point of view, these modes of existence are purely temporary. They are the fleeting union of qualities that temporarily comprise an unstable individuality. This was pointed out by T. W. Rhys Davids (1995) *Dialogues of the Buddha*, Oxford: PTS, in a footnote of his translation of the *sutta*.

6 Vsm. ii, 380.

7 The six kinds of direct knowledge are supernatural power, the divine ear, the ability to read the minds of others, the recollection of past lives, the divine eye and the extinction of all cankers. They are mentioned in the *Sāmaññaphalasutta*, D i, 77–8, *Ākankheyyasutta*, M i, 34, *Mahāvacchagottasutta*, M i, 494, *Mahāsakuludāyisutta*, M ii, 17, *Gopakamoggallānasutta*, M iii, 11–12.

8 According to the *Sāmaññaphalasutta*, the other seven types of magical power are as follows. (1) The meditator appears and disappears. (2) He goes unimpeded through walls, ramparts and mountains as if through space. (3) He dives in and out of the earth as if it were water. (4) He walks on water without sinking as if it were dry land. (5) Sitting cross-legged, he flies through the air like a winged bird. (6) With his hand he touches and strokes the sun and moon. (7) He exercises influence with his body that reaches as far as the Brahma worlds.

9 Vsm. 323–8.

10 T1, 86a; T2, 711a. This supernatural power is also mentioned in a similar way in an independent *sūtra* translated by An Shigao in the second century CE. This *sūtra* is a translation from the **Ekottarāgama*.

11 D i, 79.

12 The *Paṭisambhidāmagga*, 388.

13 D ii, 109.

14 T2, 802c.

15 T30, 493a–c.

16 T31, 810c.

17 T17, 753b.

18 T8, 473b.

19 The *Fangguang Banruojing*, translated by Mokṣala in 291 CE, T8, 113b–c.

20 The corresponding chapter in Śikṣānanda's translation of the **Avataṃsaka* is chapter thirty-seven entitled 'The Appearance of the Tathāgata'.

21 T10, 603c.

22 T9, 483c. 諸佛出世，安立眾生於智慧門，入真實義，顯現不可思議如來化身，普照無量無數不可思議諸佛世界及諸法界。

23 T9, 602a. 如來有大人相，名曰普照淨法輪雲... 出生無量如來化身。

24 T9, 726c.

25 T9, 483a, T10, 329c.

26 T9, 726c.

27 T9, 752a, 763c.

28 T9, 598c.

29 T9, 763c.

30 T24, 997c.

31 T25, 698b.

32 Lamotte (1992) 'Shi Chapin Zhong Pusa', *Diguan*, vol. 69, thinks that this *sūtra* is the 'Sūtra of Buddha's Ascension to the Trayastriṃsa Heaven to Preach the Dharma for his Mother's Sake' (T17, no. 815, 795b–c), translated by Dharmarakṣa in 270 CE. There is another translation of the same *sūtra* entitled the 'Sūtra on the Unlimited Changes of the Supernatural Footsteps' (T17, no. 816, 811b–812a), translated by Fa Qin in the Western Jin Dynasty 265–316 CE.
33 T25, 302b–c.
34 T9, 486c.
35 T9, 617a–c.
36 T16, 711a.
37 T16, 708b–c.
38 T30, 493b–c.
39 This translation is taken, with minor changes, from P. Griffiths, N. Hakamaya, J. P. Keenan and P. L. Swanson (1989) *The Realm of Awakening: A Translation and Study of the Tenth Chapter of Asaṅga's Mahāyānasaṃgraha*, New York: Oxford University Press, pp. 251–2.
40 This translation is taken, with minor changes, from ibid., p. 263.
41 T31, 269a–b.
42 T31, 129c, 149a.
43 T31, 810c–811a.
44 T31, 808c–809a.
45 T26, 325c.
46 T31, 58a.
47 T44, 820c.
48 T16, 362c.

7 THE ATTRIBUTES OF THE BUDDHA AND OTHER BUDDHAS IN EARLY AND MIDDLE MAHĀYĀNA *SŪTRAS*

1 Mahāyāna *sūtras* are extremely difficult to date as they are all attributed to the historical Buddha, Śākyamuni. However, we conventionally use the date of the Chinese translation as a working hypothesis.
2 According to the MPPŚ (T25, 309a), not only the Buddha has bodily light but gods, bodhisattvas and other beings also have it. The gods have bodily light because their minds are pure due to their practice of generosity and discipline. People who make offerings to *stupas*, Buddha images and monasteries with bright objects such as lamps, jewels, a mirror and so forth also have bodily light. Those who practise the concentration of visualizing Buddhas also have bodily light. Again, those who teach and liberate ignorant sentient beings have the light of wisdom and also bodily light. These are the causes for having bodily light.
3 D ii, 134:

> It is so, Ānanda. There are two occasions, Ānanda, when the skin of the Tathāgata appears exceedingly clear and radiant. Which are these two? The night, Ānanda, when the Tathāgata becomes fully enlightened in unsurpassed, supreme Enlightenment, and the night when the Tathāgata comes to his final passing away into the state of *nibbāna* in which no element of clinging remains. These, Ānanda, are the two occasions on which the skin of the Tathāgata appears exceedingly clear and radiant.

This translation is adapted from T. W. Rhys Davids (1995) *The Dialogues of the Buddha*, PTS, vol. II, Oxford: PTS, p. 146. The same saying is also found in the Chinese *Dīrghāgama*, T1, 19c, 佛告阿難：有二因緣，如來光色有殊於常，一者佛初得道，成無上正真覺時，二者臨欲滅度，捨於性命般涅槃時。阿難，以此二緣，光色殊常。The other three independent Chinese translations of the *Mahāparinirvāṇasūtra* also mention this: T1, 168b–c, 184a, 196b–c.

4 T25, 308c.

5 T25, 399b. According to Fazang (T35, 499c), there are four kinds of light: (1) the light of phenomena such as comets, cloud and stars; (2) the light of Dharma to illuminate the methods of practice; (3) the light of reason such as blue, yellow, red and white that is not subject to birth and death; (4) the light of non-obstruction, which is the first of three kinds of light that manifest without obstacles.

6 T25, 399c.

7 T25, 308c. After saying that the Buddha emitted light at different stages in his life, the MPPŚ states: 'Thus, this is the light of supernatural power as it is said in the *sūtras*.'

8 According to the **Mahāvibhāṣā*, (T27, 64a) light is considered as a kind of *rūpa* (form). There are twenty-one kinds of visible forms (*varṇa-rūpa*): (1) blue (*nīla*); (2) yellow (*pīta*); (3) red (*lohita*); (4) white (*avadāta*); (5) cloud (*abhra*); (6) smoke (*dhūma*); (7) dust (*rajas*); (8) fog (*mahikā*); (9) shadow (*chāyā*); (10) heat (*ātapa* is very difficult to render into English), for example the radiance of the sun; (11) light (*āloka*), such as the light of the moon, stars, lightning and jewels; (12) darkness (*andhakāra*); (13) length; (14) shortness; (15) squareness; (16) roundness; (17) height; (18) lowness; (19) rightness; (20) not rightness in position. Sometimes, (21) emptiness is added to make the number twenty-one. The light under discussion consists of *ātapa* (heat) and *āloka* (light). *Ātapa* means something which can emit both light and heat while *āloka* means something that reflects light and does not necessarily have heat, according to the *Vibhāṣā*.

9 T27, 506a.

10 T25, 311c.

11 T12, 343b.

12 T27, 506a–c.

13 T8, 44a.

14 T15, 655b.

15 T15, 654c.

16 T26, 131a.

17 There are two kinds of aid bestowed by the Buddha: the manifested or external aid bestowed by the Buddha (顯加) as the blessings and powers pertaining to this life, and the invisible aid bestowed by the Buddha (冥加) in the abandonment of negativities, increasing virtue, etc. Fazang explains that the Buddha bestows aid to people in three ways: (1) by word of mouth to bestow his eloquence; (2) by the mind to bestow his wisdom; (3) by the body to bestow his power. The first and third are the manifested aids and the second is invisible aid. See T35, 499c.

18 Chapter twenty-nine of the **Avataṃsaka* translated by Buddhabhadra is entitled the 'Ocean of Marks of the Tathāgata' and chapter thirty is on 'The Merit of Light of the Buddha's Minor Marks'. T9, 601a–606c.

19 T. Cleary (1985) *The Flower Ornament Scripture: A Translation of the Avataṃsaka Sūtra*, Boston and London: Shambhala, vol. II, p. 257.

20 T9, 605c.

21 T9, 605a–c.

22 T9, 2b. According to Dharmarakṣa's translation the Buddha emits rays of light from his face and mouth. T9, 63c.

23 T9, 63c. Dharmarakṣa's translation of the *Lotus Sutra* and T9, 2b, Kumārajīva's translation of the same sutra.
24 It is found in different versions of the *Prajñāpāramitāsūtras*: T8, 1b–c, 147b–c, 217b–c.
25 T25, 220b.
26 T9, 593b.
27 T26, 195b.
28 T35, 499c.
29 T25, 121c. 是法性身滿十方虛空無量無邊，色像端正，相好莊嚴，無量光明，無量音聲。
30 T25, 712b. 是中是法性身，佛身無量，無邊光明，說法音聲，遍滿十方國土。
31 T16, 711a.
32 T9, 593b.
33 T10, 264b.
34 T25, 126b.
35 T31, 223b.
36 T32, 639c.
37 T32, 154a.
38 T9, 599b.
39 T10, 492a.
40 T9, 540b.
41 T9, 436a–438a.
42 T30, 330a–b.
43 T31, 146a.
44 T36, 309c.
45 T31, 359b.
46 T31, 425a.
47 T31, 225b. The experiential wisdom (如量智), also called the conventional or discriminating wisdom, apprehends the function of the myriad phenomena. The undefiled, non-discriminating wisdom is also called the wisdom of principle (如理智) that understands things as they are. It is the wisdom of direct insight into the principle of reality.
48 T25, 303b–c. The **Buddhabhūmiśāstra* (T26, 298b) states that *śrāvakas* comprise the internal retinue, because *śrāvakas* are always with the Buddha and in their physical appearance they are also like the Buddha. The great bodhisattvas are the great retinue. Although the *śrāvakas* are in one assembly with the great bodhisattvas, the former cannot see the latter because of their own *karma*. However, they can see the *nirmāṇakāya* in the impure land.
49 T31, 606a–c.
50 The twelve accomplishments, according to the **Śatasāhasrikā Prajñāpāramitā*, are: (1) *Ananta-parigraha*; (2) *deva-nāga-yakṣa-gandharvāsura-garuḍa-kinnara-mahoraga-ruta-jñāna*; (3) *paripūrṇa-pratibhā-nirdeśa-jñāna*; (4) *garbhāvakrānti-sampat*; (5) *Kula-sampat*; (6) *jāti-sampat*; (7) *Gotra-sampat*; (8) *paricāra-sampat* (or *parivāra-sampat*); (9) *Janma-sampat*; (10) *abhikramaṇa-sampat*; (1) *bodhivṛkṣa-vūha-sampat*; (12) Sarva-guṇa-paripūri-sampat. See Hisao Inagaki (1963) 'The Adoption of the Buddha's Life Pattern in the Ten Bhūmi Systems', *Indogaku Bukkyōgaku Kenkyū*, vol. II, no. 2, pp. 792–7. According to the *Guangzanjing*, it is in the tenth *bhūmi* that a bodhisattva should fulfil twelve accomplishments and a bodhisattva in the tenth stage is already a Buddha. (See T8, 197a.) In other **Prajñāpāramitāsūtras*, it is in the ninth *bhūmi* that a bodhisattva fulfils the twelve accomplishments (T8, 27c, 257b–c.) Perhaps the *Guangzanjing* represents the early stage of development of the ten bodhisattva *bhūmis*.

51 Inagaki 'The Adoption of the Buddha's Life Pattern'.
52 《放光般若經》(T8, 72c) 十住菩薩摩訶薩當名之為如來。《光讚經》(T8, 197a) 第十菩薩摩訶薩者，即謂是佛。《摩訶般若波羅蜜經》(T8, 257c) 十地菩薩當知如佛。
53 T9, 111b.
54 T8, 259b. Kumārajīva's translation of the **Pañcaviṃśatisāhasrikā* says: 'What is the accomplishment of bodhisattva retinue? It is because of having only the bodhisattva-Mahāsattva retinue.' This means that great bodhisattvas in the ninth stage (*bhūmi*) have only the bodhisattva-Mahāsattva retinue. And this is the accomplishment of bodhisattva retinue.
55 T25, 303b–c.
56 T10, 503a–526c.
57 T9, 442a. 諸佛大眷屬，清淨菩薩眾，斯從十方來，跏趺正安坐。
58 T9, 422b–426c.
59 T35, 496c–497a.
60 T35, 495c.
61 T9, 631b; T10, 279a. T. Cleary, *The Flower Ornament Scripture*, translates the passage as follows:

> At that time, the World-Honoured One was in the country of Magadha, in the forest, in the shrine of universal light at the site of enlightenment, sitting on a lotus lion seat; he had completely fulfilled ineffable enlightenment, put an end to afflictions and views, and arrived at formless truth. Abiding in the abode of Buddhas, he had attained the equanimity of Buddhas and arrived at non-obstruction in the states of imperturbability. All his actions were unimpeded. He stood in the inconceivable and saw through all time. His body continually pervaded all lands; his knowledge always comprehended all things. He understood all activities. He exhausted all doubts. His knowledge was that sought by all enlightening beings. He had arrived at the non-dual ultimate perfection of Buddhahood and fully attained the equal liberation of the enlightened. He had realized the stage of impartiality of Buddhas, which is without extremes or middle, extending throughout the cosmos, equal to space.

62 T9, 631b; T10, 279a.
63 T16, 720c.
64 T35, 685b. The MS discusses these twenty-one qualities at T31, 121c–122a, 141c. These twenty-one qualities are different from the twenty-one qualities of the *dharmakāya* discussed in the tenth chapter of the MS.
65 The **Buddhabhūmisūtraśāstra*, T26, 296a–298b. According to Xuanzang's translation of the **Buddhabhūmisūtraśāstra*, the author is Bandhuprabha, while according to the Sanskrit text entitled **Buddhabhūmivyākhyāna*, it is composed by Śīlabhadra. See J. Makransky (1997) *Buddhahood Embodied: Sources of Controversy in India and Tibet*, New York: State University of New York Press, p. 452.
66 T35, 686b.
67 Paramārtha's translation of the MS, T31, 122a; Xuanzang's translation, T31, 141c.
68 T26, 296c.
69 These discussions are found at T31, 347a–348a, 409b–411b. The **Buddhabhūmisūtra*, T16, 720c.

70 T26, 296b.
71 T35, 420a.
72 The ten Buddha bodies and the ten Buddhas are mentioned in Buddhabhadra's translation of the **Avataṃsaka* at T9, 565b–c, 634c, and Śikṣānanda's translation at T10, 282a, 200a respectively. The ten Buddha bodies are also mentioned in the **Daśabhūmikasūtra* (T10, 522a) and the ten Buddhas in the **Buddhabhūmiśāstra* (T26, 327c).
73 T10, 648a.
74 The ten Buddhas are mentioned in Buddhabhadra's translation, T9, 663b, 634c, and Śikṣānanda's translation, T10, 282a, 308a. The **Buddhabhūmisūtraśāstra* (T26, 327c) also mentions the ten Buddhas with similar names. The *Fajijing* mentions ten Buddhas, but their names are different: the Buddha of habitual force, the Buddha of reward of action, the Buddha of concentration, the Buddha of the vow, the Buddha of mind, the Buddha of truth, the Buddha of equality, the Buddha of manifestation, the Buddha of offering and the Buddha of image.
75 The founding of the Huayan school is traditionally attributed to a series of five 'patriarchs' who were instrumental in developing its doctrines. They are: Dushun (杜順 557–640), the first patriarch; Zhiyan (智儼 602–668), the second; Fazang (法藏 643–712), the third; Chengguan (澄觀 738–839), the fourth; and Zongmi (宗密 780–841), the fifth. These men each played a significant and distinct role in the development of the philosophy of the school. Dushun is known to have been responsible for the establishment of Huayan studies as a distinct field; Zhiyan is thought to have established the basic doctrines of the sect; Fazang is thought to have rationalized the doctrine for greater acceptance by society; Chengguan and Zongmi are understood to have further developed and transformed the teachings. The school suffered severely during the purge of 841–845 CE, and never regained its former strength and vitality despite the appearance of several eminent Huayan scholars in the Sung dynasty. Cited from C. Muller, ed. (2001) *Digital Dictionaries of Buddhism*, available online, http://www.acmuller.net/ddb/.
76 T35, 424a–b; T45, 599c–600a.
77 T35, 904b.
78 T9, 429b.
79 T9, 565b–c. The ten kinds of bodies of the Tathāgata are also found in the **Daśabhūmikasūtra*, T10, 522a.
80 T45, 560a.
81 T10, 354c.
82 T36, 120c–121a.
83 T36, 120a, 705a. According to Chengguan, each body has a special mark or attribute (T36, 607a). The body of power has the quality of entering everywhere and benefiting all. The body of transformation has the quality of manifesting itself to all without thinking. The body of enlightenment has the quality of manifesting itself equally in accordance with needs. The body of wisdom has the quality of non-attachment and non-obstruction. The body of dharma has the quality of pervading the ten directions. The body of merit and virtues has the quality of benefiting sentient beings and adorning the Buddha lands. The body endowed with excellent physical attributes has the quality of non-birth and potential benefit. The body of the vow has the quality of adornment and the vow fulfilled. The body of preservation of the true teaching has the quality of infinite future. The body of mind has the quality of abiding.
84 T35, 505c.

85 T45, 362b–c.

86 T36, 143b. Chengguan is not consistent in his argument. In another part of the same commentary (T36, 31a) he says that the body of enlightenment, the body of the vow, the body of transformation, the body of preservation of the true teaching and the body of mind comprise the *nirmāṇakāya*. The body of power, the body of merit and virtues, and the body endowed with excellent qualities can be either the *saṃbhogakāya* or the *nirmāṇakāya*. The body of Dharma is the *dharmakāya* and the body of wisdom can be the three bodies.

87 D. T. Suzuki (1930) *Studies in the Laṅkāvatāra Sūtra*, London: George Routledge, chapter on the triple body of the Buddha, pp. 308–38.

88 Ibid., p. 319.

89 T16, 473a–b. 阿難，何者是菩提行處？三種道理，顯現三身，一者甚深道理，二者廣大道理，三者萬德道理。

90 The Chinese term *Weide* (威德) literally means power and virtue. The power is for crushing evil and the virtue is for increasing good.

91 T31, 606a–b.

92 H. Nakamura (1996) *Indian Buddhism: A Survey With Bibliographical Notes*, Delhi: Motilal Banarsidass, pp. 229–30. The other *sūtras* in the first periods are the **Tathāgatagarbhasūtra*, the *Buzengbujianjing*, the **Srīmālādevīsiṃhanādasūtra*, the Mahāyāna *Mahāparinirvāṇasūtra*, etc. which are considered by some Japanese scholars to be commentaries on the **Anuttarāśrayasūtra* J. Takasaki holds the opinion that the **Anuttarāśrayasūtra* is a composition based upon the **Ratnagotravibhāga*, with its contents reshaped into the style of a *sūtra* while keeping the stress on the *bodhi* aspects which form the ultimate basis. See J. Takasaki (1960) 'Structure of the *Anuttarāśrayasūtra* (Wu-shang-I-ching)', *Indogaku Bukkyōgaku Kenkyū*, vol. VIII, no. 2, p. 747.

93 Vasubandhu quoted once in his **Mahāyānasaṃgrahabhāśya*, T31, 259c, and four times in the **Buddhagotraśāstra*, T31, 801c, 806b (twice), 812a.

94 Cited from Nakamura, *Indian Buddhism*, p. 230, footnotes 12 and 14. Hakuju Ui discusses the composition of the **Anuttarāśrayasūtra* in his *Bukkyo Kyotenshi* ('History of Buddhist Scriptures'), Tokyo: Tosei Shuppar-sha, 1957, p. 143. D. Tokiwa discusses the *sūtra* in the *Bussho Kaisetsu Daijiten*, vol. X, p. 409.

95 Takasaki, 'Structure', p. 743.

96 The Sanskrit terms are given in Takasaki's articles on the **Anuttarāśrayasūtra*. See ibid., p. 747.

97 See Makransky, *Buddhahood Embodied*, p. 54.

98 P. Griffiths, N. Hakamaya, J. P. Keenan and P. L. Swanson (tr.) (1989) *The Realm of Awakening: A Translation and Study of the Tenth Chapter of Asaṅga's Mahāyānasaṃgraha*, New York: Oxford University Press, p. 170.

99 T16, 723b. 自性法受用，變化差別轉，如是淨法界，諸佛之所說。

100 T26, 325c.

101 In her dissertation 'The Background and Early Use of the Buddhaṣektra Concept', *The Eastern Buddhist*, vol. VI, no. 4, 1935, pp. 414–31, Teresina Rowell discusses many factors for the rise of the belief in the simultaneous existence of many Buddhas. She gives six reasons.

1 It is a natural corollary of the enlarging cosmology. For just as Śākyamuni is the Buddha in this Sahā world so there are other Buddhas in other universes.
2 As there are many contemporaneous bodhisattvas practising, so there are many Buddhas.

3 The Cakravartin ideal also serves as a model for juat as there are many Wheel Turning Monarchs in existence, so there are many Buddhas in existence simultaneously.
4 Since in Hinduism there are various chief gods who are believed to preside over various worlds or heavens, there was probably a necessity for Buddhists to produce similar heavens for Buddhas.
5 The rise of devotion (*bhakti*) in Buddhism also explains the ascendance of this belief that the Buddha or any Buddha must be somewhere in the universe to bring his followers to rebirth in his heaven.
6 The sixteen *arhats* who had been entrusted the *Saddharma* by the Buddha stayed out of *nirvāṇa* in different parts of the world in order to maintain and teach the Dharma until it becomes extinct. This reflects a significant stage in the evolution of local division of responsibility among those mandated to preach the Dharma, which points to the later assignment of future Buddhas to various areas of the universe destined to be their Buddha lands.

102 Jan Nattier (2000) 'The Realm of Akṣobhya: A Missing Piece in the History of Pure Land Buddhism', *Journal of International Buddhist Studies*, vol. 23, no. 1, pp. 89–90.
103 The idea is found in early Buddhism that there can never be two Buddhas in one world simultaneously.
104 The **Yogācārabhūmiśāstra*, T30, 499b–500b; the **Bodhisattvabhūmidharasūtra*, T30, 902a–b; the *Kośa*, T29, 64c–65a; the *Mahāyānasaṃgraha*, T31, 112a, 151b; the **Mahāyānasaṃgrahaśāstrabhāṣya*, T31, 266a–c, 319b, 378a–b; 447b–448c; the **Abhidharmanyāyānusāraśāstra*, T29, 423b; and the **Mahāyānāvatārakaśāstra*, T32, 43c.
105 All the quotations are from the so-called larger *Sukhāvatīvyūhasūtra* (T12, 301a–302b) translated by Zhiqian. These quotations are from the twenty-four vows which are thought to be earlier than the forty-eighty vows. The number shows the order of the vows in the *sūtra*.
106 T8, 458a. The *sūtra* also mentions that bodhisattvas, who have no doubts after listening to the **Prajñāpāramitāsūtra* and establishing firm faith in the Buddha's words, will be born in the land of Akṣobhya. The *Daoxingbanruojing* was translated in 179 CE, and the *Akṣobhyavyūha* in 186 CE or before.
107 Some scholars like P. Harrison think that the *Sukhāvatīvyūha* which is listed under the translations of Lokakṣema was probably translated by Dharmarakṣa, whose activity of translation (266–313) in China was fifty to a hundred years later than Lokakṣema's. If this is correct, it also supports the late origin of Amitābha. Cited from P. Harrison's public lectures at SOAS, October to December 1999.
108 Nattier, 'The Realm of Akṣobhya', pp. 101–2.
109 Yinshun (1994) *Chuqi Dacheng Fojian Zhi Qiyuan Yu Zhankai*, Taipei: Zhengwen Publication, pp. 475–7.
110 T11, 753c, 756a.
111 Ñāṇamoli (1995), *The Middle Length Discourse of the Buddha*, Boston: Wisdom Publication, p. 714.
112 T11, 752b.
113 T11, 755b.
114 T11, 762c.
115 See F. Kotatsu (1996) 'The Origin of the Pure Land', *The Eastern Buddhist*, vol. 29, no. 1, pp. 33–51.
116 T12, 344c–345b.

117 T2, 788c–789a.
118 T14, 420a.
119 T9, 405a–418a.
120 T9, 412a.
121 T9, 605c.
122 T9, 763c. The *sūtra* states that Mahāmāyā was the mother of Vairocana throughout his bodhisattva career because of the following vow: 'I will be his mother until his enlightenment.' This vow was made in the distant past when Vairocana was a Wheel Turning Monarch. The story goes thus: in the north of his capital there was a temple in which resided a bodhisattva who was about to attain enlightenment when Māra came with his army to destroy him. The Wheel Turning Monarch who had the mastery of magical power of a bodhisattva came and defeated Māra. The bodhisattva attained enlightenment. Upon seeing this, the guardian god of the temple, who became Mahāmāyā in the last life of Vairocana, thus made the above vow.
123 T24, 997c.
124 T8, 828a. 三賢十聖住果報，唯佛一人居淨土。
125 T10, 614b.
126 Buddhabhadra's translation, chapter two, 'The Vairocana Buddha'. T9, 405a–418a.
127 T10, 968b.
128 T31, 58b.
129 T45, 370b.
130 E. Lamotte (tr.) (1976) *The Teachings of Vimalakīrti*, London: PTS, pp. 275–84.
131 T45, 369b.
132 T45, 370b.
133 T45, 372a.
134 T31, 719c.
135 T24, 997c.
136 T26, 194a–c.
137 T30, 295a.
138 T31, 436a.
139 T45, 372a. The physical world of this Pure Land is described as endowed with various excellences (*sampad*) in both the **Avataṃsaka* and the **Buddhabhūmisūtra*. The *Mahāyānasaṃgraha* of Asaṅga translated by Xuanzang summarizes it into eighteen excellences of: (1) colour (*varṇa*); (2) shape (*saṃsthāna*); (3) dimension (*pramāṇa*); (4) realm (*deśa*); (5) cause (*hetu*); (6) fruit (*phala*); (7) sovereign (*adhipati*); (8) assistance (*pakṣa*); (9) entourage (*parivāra*); (10) support (*adhiṣṭhāna*); (11) activity (*karman*); (12) beneficence (*upakāra*); (13) fearlessness (*nirbhaya*); (14) beauty (*āspada*); (15) path (*mārga*); (16) vehicle (*yāna*); (17) door (*mukha*); (18) base (*ādhāra*) (T31, 151a). These eighteen excellences are also found in both Vasubandhu's and Asvabhāva's commentaries on the *Mahāyānasaṃgraha*, both of which were translated by Xuanzang (T31, 376c, 445a). However, they are not found in either Buddhaśanti's or Paramārtha's translations of the *Mahāyānasaṃgraha*, both dated earlier than Xuanzang's, nor are they found in Vasubandhu's commentary translated by Paramārtha. The Sanskrit *Mahāyānasaṃgraha* translated by Xuanzang was probably a revised version with some additions.
140 An earlier version of this section was originally published in the *World Hongming Philosophical Quarterly*, vol. 2002, September, under the title 'Is Amitābha a Sambhogkāya?'. Internet URL: www.whpq.org or www.whpq.net.

141 Takeuchi Shiyoukou (1983) 'Buddhakan no hensen', in Akira Hirakawa, ed., *Daijō Bukkyō*, Tokyo: Shunjusha, vol. I, pp. 168–9.
142 Mochizuki Shinkō thinks that according to master Tanluan (488–554) Amitābha was indeed a *sambhogkāya*. However, Tanluan never expressed this idea in his writings. See David Chappell (1977) 'Chinese Buddhist Interpretations of the Pure Lands', in Michael Saso and D. W. Chappell eds, *Buddhist and Taoist Studies*, Hawaii: The University Press of Hawaii, vol. I, p. 36.
143 T47, 5c. 《安樂集》：現在彌陀是報佛，極樂寶莊嚴國是報土。
144 T47, 5c–6a.
145 Chappell, 'Chinese Buddhist Interpretations', p. 37.
146 T47, 5c14. 然古舊相傳，皆云阿彌陀佛是化身，土亦是化土。
147 Chappell, 'Chinese Buddhist Interpretations', pp. 26–36.
148 T31, 606c.
149 T31, 129c, 149a.
150 The Chinese translations of T12, no. 361 and no. 362 list twenty-four vows, T12, no. 363 lists thirty-six, while T12, no. 360, no. 364, the Sanskrit as well as the Tibetan versions, describe forty-eight. However, the Chinese Buddhists in general believe in the forty-eight vows in their daily practice.
151 According to the *Vibhāṣā*, there are two Śākyamuni Buddhas. The present Śākyamuni Buddha, as a bodhisattva aeons ago, made his vows to become a Buddha in exactly the same way as the ancient Śākyamuni Buddha who became a Buddha when the life-span of people was around a hundred years. See T27, 891b–892a.
152 T25, 313b.
153 T9, 411c. 所謂有佛興世，色身示現，遍滿法界，或有短壽，或無量劫。
154 T25, 312a–b. 以是故知，諸佛壽命實皆無量，為度人故，現有長短。
155 T14, 554a. 諸佛如來功德平等，為化眾生故，而現佛土不同。
156 T14, 554a. The translation is taken with some changes from R. Thurman (1976) *Vimalakīrtinideśa-sutra*, Philadelphia: State University of Pennsylvania Press, p. 121.
157 'Alougen' is an early translation of the name Avalokiteśvara. See W. E. Soothhill *et al.*, eds, (1989) *A Dictionary of Chinese Buddhist Terms*, Taiwan: Fokuang Buddhist Publication, p. 399a.
158 T12, 291a. The passages quoted in T12, no. 361 and T12, no. 362 are the same but T12, no. 364 is different. 'After the *parinirvāṇa* of Amitābha, bodhisattva Avalokiteśvara will attain Buddhahood and take over the role of teaching to liberate humans as well as gods of the ten directions of the world by establishing them all in *nirvāṇa*.' T12, 336b lines 18–21. The **Karuṇapuṇḍarikasūtra* also mentions the same idea of the *parinirvāṇa* of Amitābha Buddha, T3, 186a.
159 T31, 606a–c.
160 T31, 606b.
161 T31, 372b–c. There are three Chinese translations of the *Mahāyānasaṃgrahabhāṣya* of Vasubandhu: (1) T31, no. 1595 translated by Paramārtha in 563 CE; (2) T31, no. 1596 translated by Dharmagupta in 590–616 CE; (3) T31, no. 1597 translated by Xuanzang in 647–649 CE. The English translation is taken with a few changes from Griffiths *et al.*, *The Realm of Awakening*, pp. 113–14.
162 T12, 307a–b. This is a long passage describing how after Amitābha proclaimed the *sūtra*, the listeners reached various stages of attainments.

SELECT BIBLIOGRAPHY

I Primary sources

1 Pāli texts

Aṅguttaranikāya, vols I & II ed. R. Morris, vols III–V ed. E. Hardy, Oxford: PTS, reprinted 1989, 1995.

Apadāna, vols I & II, ed. M. E. Lilly, Oxford: PTS, 1925, 1927.

Buddhavaṃsa and *Cariyāpiṭaka*, ed. N. A. Jayawickrama, Oxford: PTS, reprinted 1995.

Dhammapada, eds O. von Hinuber and K. R. Norman, Oxford: PTS, 1995.

Dhammapada aṭṭhakathā. English translation: *Buddhist Legends*, vols I–III, tr. Eugene Watson Burlingame, Cambridge, Massachusetts: Harvard University Press, 1921.

Dīghanikāya, vols I & II, eds. T. W. Davids and J. E. Carpenter, vol. III ed. J. E. Carpenter, Oxford: PTS, 1890–1911.

Kathāvatthu, vols I–II ed. A. C. Taylor, Oxford: PTS, reprinted 1979. *Points of Controversy*, tr. S. Z. Aung and Mrs C. A. F. Rhys Davids, Oxford: PTS, reprinted 1934.

Majjhimanikāya, vol. I ed. V. Trenckner, vols II & III ed. R. Chalmers, Oxford: PTS, reprinted 1993, 1994.

Manorathapūraṇi (*Aṅguttaranikāya* commentary), vols I–V eds M. Walleser and H. Kopp, Oxford: PTS, reprinted 1973–1977.

Milindapañha, vols I & II ed. V. Trenckner, Oxford: PTS, reprinted 1986.

Papañcasūdanī (*Majjhimanikāya* commentary), vols I–II eds J. H. Woods and D. Kosambi, 1922, 1979, vols III–V ed. I. B. Horner, 1933, 1937, 1938, Oxford: PTS.

Paṭisambhidāmagga, vols I–II ed. A. C. Taylor, Oxford: PTS, reprinted 1979. *The Path of Discrimination*, tr. Ñānamoli, Oxford: PTS, reprinted 1991.

Saṃyuttanikāya, vols I–V ed. L. Feer, Oxford: PTS, reprinted 1976–1991.

Sāratthapakāsinī (*Saṃyuttanikāya* commentary), vols I–III ed. F. L. Woodward, Oxford: PTS, 1932, 1937.

Sumaṅgalavilāsini (*Dīghanikāya* commentary), vol. I eds T. W. Rhys Davids and J. E. Carpenter, vols II & III ed. W. Stede, Oxford: PTS, reprinted 1968–1971.

Suttanipāta, eds Dines Andersen and Helmer Smith, Oxford: PTS, reprint 1990. English translation: *The Rhinoceros Horn and Other Early Buddhist Poems*, tr. K. R. Norman, Oxford: PTS, 1985; *The Suttanipāta*, tr. H. Saddhatissa, London: Curzon Press, 1985.

Theragāthā, ed. H. Oldenberg, and *Therīgāthā*, ed. R. Pischel, Oxford: PTS, reprinted 1990. English translation: *Elders' Verses*, vols I & II tr. K. R. Norman, Oxford: PTS, reprinted 1990, 1995.

Udāna, ed. P. Steinthal, Oxford: PTS, reprinted 1982. *The Udāna*, tr. P. Masefield, Oxford: PTS, 1994.

Vinayapiṭaka, vols I–VI ed. H. Oldenberg, Oxford: PTS, reprinted 1969–1995.

Visuddhimagga, vols I–II, ed. Mrs C. A. F. Rhys Davids, Oxford: PTS, reprinted 1975. *The Path of Purification*, tr. Ñyāṇamoli, Colombo: R. Semage, 1956.

2 Chinese texts and some with translations

**Abhidharma-āṣṭaskandha-śāstra* (阿毘曇八犍度論), T26, no. 1543, attrib. Kātyāyanīputra, tr. Dharmapriya, Saṅghadeva and Zhu Fonian, 383.

**Abhidharma-dharmaskandhapāda-śāstra* (阿毘達磨法蘊足論), T26, no. 1537, attrib. Śāriputra (Sanskrit version), Mahāmaudgalyāyana (Chinese version), tr. Xuanzang, 659.

**Abhidharma-hṛdaya-śāstra* (阿毘曇心論), T28, no. 1550, by Dharmaśrī, tr. Saṅghadeva and Huiyuan, 391.

**Abhidharma-jñānaprasthāna-śāstra* (阿毘達磨發智論), T26, no. 1544, attrib. Kātyāyanīputra, tr. Xuanzang, 657–660.

**Abhidharma-kośa-śāstra* (阿毘達磨俱舍論), T29, no. 1558, by Vasubandhu, tr. Xuanzang, 651.

**Abhidharma-kośavyākhyā-śāstra* (阿毘達磨俱舍釋論), T29, no. 1559, by Vasubandhu, tr. Paramārtha, 564–567. English translation: *Abhidharmakośabhāṣyam*, vols I–IV tr. Leo M. Pruden from Louis de la Vallée Poussin's French translation, Berkeley, California: Asian Humanity Press, 1990.

**Abhidharma-mahāvibhāṣā-śāstra*. There are three translations: *Vibhāṣāśāstra* (鞞婆沙論), T28, no. 1547, tr. Saṅghabhūti (or Saṅghabhadra?), Dharmanandin, Buddharakṣa, 383; *Abhidharmavibhāṣāśāstra* (阿毘達磨毘婆娑論), T28, no. 1546, tr. Buddhavarman, Daotai, 437–439; *Mahāvibhāṣāśāstra* (大毘婆沙論), T27, no. 1545, tr. Xuanzang, 656–659.

**Abhidharma-nyāyānusāra-śāstra* (阿毘達磨順正理論), T29, no. 1562, by Saṅghabhadra, tr. Xuanzang, 653–654.

**Abhidharma(piṭaka)prakaraṇaśāsana-śāstra* (阿毘達磨藏顯宗論), T29, no. 1563, by Saṅghabhadra, tr. Xuanzang, 651–652.

**Abhidharma-prakaraṇapāda-śāstra* (阿毘達磨品類足論), T26, no. 1542, attrib. Vasumitra, tr. Xuanzang, 659.

**Abhidharma-vijñānakāyapāda-śāstra* (阿毘達磨識身足論), T26, no. 1539, attrib. Devaśarman, tr. Xuanzang, 649.

**Abhiniṣkramaṇa-sūtra* (佛本行集經), T3, no. 190, tr. Jñānagupta, 587. English translation: *The Romantic Legend of Śākya Buddha, A Translation of the Chinese Version of the Abhiniṣkramaṇasūtra*, tr. Samuel Beal, London: Trübner, 1885 (original 1875).

**Ajātaśatrurāja-sūtra* (佛說阿闍世王經), T15, no. 626, tr. Lokakṣema, 25–220.

**Akṣobhyatathāgatasyavyūha-sūtra* (阿閦佛國經), T11, no. 313, tr. Lokakṣema, 186.

**Amitāyurbuddhadhyāna-sūtra* (佛說觀無量壽佛經), T12, no. 365, tr. Kālayasas, 424.

**Anuttarāśraya-sūtra* (佛說無上依經), T16, no. 669, tr. Paramārtha, 557.

*Āryavasumitrabodhisattvasaṅgīti-śāstra (尊婆須密菩薩所集論), T28, no. 1549, attrib. Vasumitra, tr. Saṅghabhadra (Saṅghabhūti?), Dharmanandin, Saṅghadeva and Zu Fonian.

Aṣṭasāhasrikā Prajñāpāramitā-sūtra. There are four Chinese translations: *Daoxingbanruojing* (道行般若經), T8, no. 224, tr. Lokakṣema, 179 (E. Conze translated the title of this *sūtra* as the *Prajñāpāramitā-sūtra of the Practice of the Way*); *Damingdujing* (大明度經), T8, no. 225, tr. Zhi Qian, 222–229 (E. Conze translated the title of this *sūtra* as the *Sūtra of Unlimited Great-brightness-crossing*); *Mohebanruochaojing* (摩訶般若鈔經), T8, no. 226, tr. Dharmapriya, 382 (E. Conze translated the title of this *sūtra* as the *Extract of the Prajñāpāramitā-sūtra*); the smaller *Prajñāpāramitāsūtra* (小品般若波羅蜜經), T8, no. 227, tr. Kumārajīva, 408.

*Atītapratyutpanna-hetuphala-sūtra (過去現在因果經) T3, no. 189, tr. Guṇabhadra, 420–479.

*Bhaiṣajyavastu of the *Mūlasarvāstivāda-vinaya* (根本說一切有部藥事), T24, no. 1448, tr. Yijing, 695–713.

*Bodhisattvabhūmidhara-sūtra (菩薩地持經), T30, no. 1581, tr. Dharmakṣena, 414–421.

*Brahmajāla-sūtra (梵網經), T24, no. 1484, said to be translated by Kumārajīva in 406. This is considered a Vinaya text of bodhisattvas.

*Buddhabhūmi-sūtra (佛說佛地經), T16, no. 680, tr. Xuanzang, 645.

*Buddhabhūmisūtra-śāstra (佛說佛地經論), T26, no. 1530, by Bandhuprabha, tr. Xuanzang, 649.

Buddhacarita (佛所行讚), T4, no. 192, by Aśvaghosa, tr. Dharmakṣena, 414–421.

*Buddhadhyānasamādhisāgara-sūtra (佛說觀佛三昧海經), T15, no. 643, tr. Buddhabhadra, 317–420.

*Buddhagotra-śāstra (佛性論), T31, no. 1610, by Vasubandhu, tr. Paramārtha, 557–569.

*Buddhasaṅgīti-sūtra (諸佛要集經), T17, no. 810, tr. Dharmarakṣa, 266–313.

*Buddhāvataṃsaka-mahāvaipulya-sūtra (大方廣佛華嚴經), T9, no. 278, tr. Buddhabhadra, 317–402; T10, no. 279, tr. Śīkṣānanda, 695–699; and T10, no. 293, tr. Prajñā, 796–798.

Buzengbujian-jing (佛說不增不減經 '*Sūtra* on Neither Increasing Nor Decreasing'), T16, no. 668, tr. Bodhiruci, 519–524.

*Caryāmārgabhūmi-sūtra (修行道地經), T15, no. 606, attrib. Saṅgharakṣa, tr. Dharmarakṣa, 284.

*Caryānidāna-sūtra (修行本起經), T3, no. 184, tr. Mahābala, together with Kang Menxiang, 197.

Chinese Electronic Tripiṭaka Series, Taisho Tripiṭaka vols 1–55 & 85, Taipei: Chinese Buddhist Electronic Text Association, 2002 (CD ROM).

Dachengfayuanyilinzhang (大乘法苑義林章), T45, no. 1861, by Kuiji, Tang dynasty 618–907.

Dachengxuan-lun (大乘玄論), T45, no. 1853, by Jizang, Sui dynasty 581–618.

Dafangbianfo-baoen-jing (大方便佛報恩經), T3, no. 156. The name of the translator is lost and it is registered in the list of *sūtras* translated under the Eastern Han dynasty 25–220.

Dafangguangfohuayanjing-shu (大方廣佛華嚴經疏), T35, no. 1735, by Chengguan, Tang dynasty 618–907.

Dafangguangfohuayanjing Suishuyanyichao (大方廣佛華嚴經隨疏演義鈔), T36, no. 1736, by Chengguan.

Dahuayanjingluece (大華嚴經略策), T36, no. 1737, by Chengguan.

**Daśabhāṇavāravinaya* (十誦律), T23, no. 1435, tr. Puṇyatara and Kumārajīva, 404. It is also entitled the *Sarvāstivāda-vinaya*.

**Daśabhūmika-sūtra* (十住經), T10, no. 286, tr. Kumārajīva, 384–417. (漸備一切智德經 *Jianbeiyiqiezhide-jing* '*Sūtra* on Making Gradually Complete All the Wisdom and Virtue'), T10, no. 285, tr. Dharmarakṣa, 265–316.

**Daśabhūmikasūtra-śāstra* (十住經論), T26, no. 1522, by Vasubandhu, tr. Bodhiruci, 508–511.

**Daśabhūmikavibhāṣā-śāstra* (十住毘婆沙論), T26, no. 1521, attrib. Nāgārjuna, tr. Kumārajīva, 405.

Datangxiyuji (大唐西域記), T51, no. 2087, by Xuanzang, 646.

**Dharmapadāvadāna-sūtra* (法句譬喻經), T4, no. 211, compiled by Dharmatrāta, tr. Faju and Fali in 290–306.

Dengmupusasuowensanmei-jing (等目菩薩所問三昧經 '*Sūtra* on a *Samādhi* asked by the Bodhisattva Samacakṣus'), T10, no. 288, tr. Dharmarakṣa, 256–316.

**Dharmaguptakavinaya* (四分律), T22, no. 1428, tr. Buddhayasas, 408–413.

**Dharmasaṃghītisūtra* (佛說法集經), T17, no. 761, tr. Bodhiruci, 515.

**Dharmasaṃgrahanāmasaṅkhyasūtra* (法集名數經), T17, no. 764, tr. Dānapāla, 980–989.

**Dhyānaniṣṭhitasamādhi-sūtra* (坐禪三昧經), T15, no. 614, by Saṅgharakṣa, tr. Kumārajīva, 402.

**Dīrghāgama* (長阿含經), T1, no. 1, tr. Buddhayaśas and Zhu Fonian, 412–413.

Dushipin-jing (度世品經 '*Sūtra* of the Chapter on Going across the World'), T10, no. 292, tr. Dharmarakṣa, 265–316.

**Ekottarāgama* (增一阿含經), T2, no. 125, tr. Saṅghadeva, 317–420.

Huayanjing-neizhangmendengzakongmu (華嚴經內章門等雜孔目), T45, no. 1870, by Zhiyan, Tang dynasty 618–907.

Huayanjing-tanxuanji (花嚴經探玄記), T35, no. 1733, by Fazang, Tang dynasty 618–907.

Huayanjing-wenda (華嚴經問答), T45, no. 1873, by Fazang.

Huayanjing-wenyigangmu (花嚴經文義綱目), T35, no. 1734, by Fazang.

Huayanyuyi (華嚴遊意), T35, no. 1731, by Jizang.

Jingguangming Zuishengwangjing Shu (金光明最勝王經疏), T39, no. 1788, by Hui Zhao, 695–714.

**Jñānamudrāsamādhi-sūtra* (佛說慧印三昧經), T15, no. 632, tr. Zhi Qian.

**Karuṇāpuṇḍarīka-sūtra* (悲華經), T3, no. 157, tr. Dharmakṣena of the Northern Liang dynasty, 397–439.

**Kāruṇikārājā-prajñāpāramitā-sūtra* (仁王般若波羅蜜經 '*Prajñāpāramitāsūtra* on a Benevolent King who Protects his Country'), T8, no. 245, tr. Kumārajīva, 401–417.

**Kumāra-kuśalaphala-nidāna-sūtra* (太子瑞應本起經), T3, no. 185, tr. Zhi Qian, 222–228.

Laṅkāvatāra-sūtra. There are three translations: (入楞伽經), T16, no. 671, tr. Bodhiruci, 486–534; *Mahāyānalaṅkāvatāra-sūtra* (大乘入楞伽經), T16, no. 672, tr. Sikṣānanda, 700–704; *Laṅkāvatāra-sūtra* (楞伽阿跋多羅寶經), T16, no. 670, tr. Gunabhadra, 443.

Lokānuvartana-sūtra (佛說內藏百寶經), T17, no. 807, tr. Lokakṣema, 179.
**Madhyamāgama* (中阿含經), T1, no. 26, tr. Gautama Saṅghadeva, 397–398.
**Madhyametyukta-sūtra* (中本起經), T4, no. 196, tr. Dharmaphala together with Kang Menxiang, 207.
**Mahālaṅkāra-sūtra-śāstra*(大莊嚴經論),T4,no.201,attrib.Aśvaghoṣa,tr.Kumārajīva, 405.
Mahāparinirvāṇa-sūtra (大般涅槃經), T12, no. 374, tr. Dharmakṣena, 423.
Mahāparinirvāṇa-sūtra (佛說大般泥洹經), T12, no. 376, tr. Faxian, 400–420.
**Mahāprajñāpāramitā-śāstra* (大智度論), T25, no. 1509, attrib. Nāgārjuna, tr. Kumārajīva, 402–405. French translation: *Le Traité de la Grande Vertu de Sagesse de Nāgārjuna*, tr. E. Lamotte, vols I–V, Louvain: Bureaux Du Museon, 1944.
**Mahāprajñāpāramitā-sūtra* (大般若波羅蜜多經), T5, T6, T7, no. 220, tr. Xuanzang, 659.
**Mahāsatyanirgranthaputra-vyākaraṇa-sūtra* (大薩遮尼乾子所說經), T9, no. 272, tr. Bodhiruci, 519.
**Mahāvaipulya-tathāgatagarbha-sūtra* (大方等如來藏經), T16, no. 666, tr. Buddhabhadra, 317–420; T16, no. 667, tr. Amoghavajra, Tang dynasty 618–907.
**Mahāyānābhidharmasaṃyuktasaṅgīti-śāstra* (大乘阿毗達磨雜集論), T31, no. 1606, by Sthiramati, tr. Xuanzang, 646.
**Mahāyānadaśadharmaka-sūtra* (大寶積經・大乘十法會), T11, no. 310.9, tr. Buddhaśanti, 386–534 and (佛說大乘十法經) T11, no. 314, tr. Saṅghapāla, 502–557.
**Mahāyānadharmadhātvaviśeṣatā-śāstra* (大乘法界無差別論), T31, no. 1626, by Sthiramati, tr. Devaprajña, 691.
**Mahāyānamahākaruṇāpuṇḍarīka-sūtra* (大乘大悲分陀利經), T3, no. 158. The name of the translator is lost and it is registered in the list of *sūtras* translated under the Qin dynasty 350–431.
Mahāyānasaṃgraha of Asaṅga. Chinese translations: (攝大乘論), T31, no. 1592, tr. Buddhaśānti(?), 531; (攝大乘論), T31, no. 1593, tr. Paramārtha, 563; (攝大乘論本), T31, no. 1594, tr. Xuanzang, 648–649.
**Mahāyānasaṃgrahabhāṣya* of Vasubandhu. Chinese translations: (攝大乘論釋), T31, no. 1595, tr. Paramārtha, 563; (攝大乘論釋論), T31, no. 1596, tr. Dharmagupta and Xingju, 590–616; (攝大乘論釋), T31, no. 1597, tr. Xuanzang, 647–649.
**Mahāyānasaṃgrahabhāṣya* (攝大乘論釋), T31, no. 1598, by Asvabhāva, tr. Xuanzang, 647–649.
Mahāyānasūtrālaṃkāra (大乘莊嚴經論), T31, no. 1604, attrib. Asaṅga, tr. Prabhākaraṇamitra, 630–633.
**Mahāyānāvatāraka-śāstra* (入大乘論), T32, no. 1634, by Sthiramati, tr. Daotai, 397–439.
**Maitreya-paripṛcchā-sūtra* (彌勒菩薩所問本願經) T12, no. 349, tr. Dharmarakṣa, 265–361.
**Maitreya-vyākaraṇa-sūtra*. Chinese translations: (佛說彌勒下生成佛經) T14, no. 454, tr. Kumārajīva, 384–417; (佛說彌勒下生成佛經) T14, no. 455, tr. Yijing, 701; (佛說彌勒來時經) T14, no. 457. The name of the translator is lost and it is registered in the list of *sutras* translated under the Eastern Jin Dynasty 317–420.
**Mañjuśrībuddhakṣetraguṇavyūha-sūtra* (文殊師利佛土嚴淨經), T11, no. 318, tr. Dharmarakṣa, 290; (大聖文殊師利菩薩佛刹功德莊嚴經), T11, no. 319, tr. Amoghavajra, 771; (文殊師利授記會), T11, no. 310.15, tr. Śīkṣānanda, 695–704.

Mañjuśrīparinirvāṇa-sūtra (佛說文殊師利般涅槃經), T14, no. 463, tr. Nie Daozhen, 280–312.

Mañjuśrīparipṛcchā-sūtra (大乘百福相經), T16, no. 661, tr. Divākara, 683.

Mūkakumāra-sūtra (佛說無言童子經), T13, no. 401, tr. Dharmarakṣa, 265–316.

Mūlajāta-hṛdayabhūmi-dhyāna-sūtra (大乘本生心地觀經), T3, no. 159, tr. Prajñā and others, 785–810.

Mūlasarvāstivādavinaya (根本說一切有部毘奈耶), T23, no. 1442, tr. Yijing, 695–713.

Nāgasena Bhikṣu Sūtra (那先比丘經), T32, nos. 1670a and 1670b. The translators of both versions are lost, so they are registered under the Jin dynasty (317–420).

Pañcadharmacaryā-sūtra (阿毘曇五法行經), T28, no. 1557, tr. An Shigao, 148–170.

Pañcaśatasthavirāvadāna-sūtra (佛五百弟子自說本起經), T4, no. 199, tr. Dharmarakṣa, 303.

Pañcavastuka-śāstra (薩婆多宗五事論), T28, no. 1556, tr. Facheng, Tang dynasty 618–907.

Pañcavastukavibhāṣā-śāstra (五事毘婆沙論), T28, no. 1555, attrib. Dharmatrātā, tr. Xuanzang, 663.

Pañcaviṃśatisāhasrikā Prajñāpāramitā-sūtra. Chinese translation: (放光般若經), T8, no. 221, tr. Mokṣala, 291; (光讚經), T8, no. 222, tr. Dharmarakṣa, 286; (摩訶般若波羅蜜經), T8, no. 223, tr. Kumārajīva, 403–404.

Prakaraṇapāda-śāstra (眾事分阿毘曇論), T26, no. 1541, attrib. Vasumitra, tr. Guṇabhadra, Bodhiyaśas, 435–443.

Pratyutpanna-buddhasammuhkāvasthitā-samādhi-sūtra (般舟三昧經), T13, no. 418, tr. Lokakṣema, Eastern Han dynasty 25–220.

Pūrṇamukhāvadāna-śātaka (撰集百緣經), T4, no. 200, tr. Zhi Qian, 223–253.

Pusaxingwushiyuansheng-jing (菩薩行五十緣身經) ['*Sūtra* spoken by the Buddha on (the characteristic marks on) his person as (the result of) fifty causes of the practice of bodhisattva'], T17, no. 812, tr. Dharmarakṣa, 265–316.

Ratnagotravibhāga-Mahāyānottaratantra-śāstra and *Vyākhyā* (究竟一乘寶性論), T31, no. 1611, author unknown, tr. Ratnamati, 508.

Rulaixingxian-jing (如來興顯經 '*Sūtra* Spoken by the Buddha on the Manifestation of the Tathāgata), T10, no. 291, tr. Dharmarakṣa, 265–316.

Saddharmapuṇḍarīka-sūtra. Chinese translations: (正法華經), T9, no. 263, tr. Dharmarakṣa, 265–316; (妙法蓮華經), T9, no. 262, tr. Kumārajīva, 384–417; and (添品妙法蓮華經), T9, no. 264, tr. Jñānagupta and Dharmagupta, 601.

Samadatta-mahārāja-sūtra (眾許摩訶帝經), T3, no. 191, tr. Faxian, 982–1001.

Samantaprabhāsa-sūtra (普曜經), T3, no. 186, tr. Dharmarakṣa, 308. A translation of the *Lalitavistara*.

Samayabhedavyūhacakra by Vasumitra. Chinese translations: (異部宗輪論), T49, no. 2031, tr. Xuanzang, 662; (十八部論), T49, no. 2032, tr. Paramārtha; (部執異論), T49, no. 2033, tr. Paramārtha, 557–569.

Saṃghabhedavastu of the *Mūlasarvāstivāda-vinaya* (根本說一切有部破僧事), T24, no. 1450, tr. Yijing, 710.

Saṃyuktābhidharmahṛdaya-śāstra (雜阿毘曇心論), T28, no. 1552, by Dharmatrātā, tr. Saṅghavarman, Baoyun, 434.

Saṃyuktāgama (雜阿含經). There are two translations: T2, no. 99, tr. Guṇabhadra, 435–553; and (別譯雜阿含經), T2, no. 100. The name of the translator is lost and the date of the translation is between 350–431.

**Sandhinirmocana-sūtra*. There are two translations: (深密解脱經), T16, no. 675, tr. Bodhiruci, 386–534; (解深密經), T16, no. 676, tr. Xuanzang, 645.

**Sarva-buddha-mahā-rahasya-upāya-kauśālya-jñānottara-bodhisattva-paripṛcchā-parivarta-nāma-mahāyāna-sūtra*. There are three Chinese translations: (大寶積經・大乘方便會) T11, no. 310.38, tr. Nandi; (慧上菩薩問大善權經), T12, no. 345, tr. Dharmarakṣa, 265–316; and (佛說大方廣善權方便經), T12, no. 346, tr. Dānapāla, 980–1000.

**Sarvadharmaratnottara(-artha)-saṅgīti-śāstra* (集諸法寶最上義論), T32, no. 1638, attrib. Bodhisattva Sumuni(?) (善寂菩薩造), tr. Dānapāla, 980–1000.

**Satyasiddhi-śāstra* (成實論), T32, no. 1646, by Harivarman, tr. Kumārajīva, 417–418.

Shimoheyan-lun (釋摩訶衍論 'An Exposition of the Mahāyāna'), T32, no. 1668, attrib. Nāgārjuna, tr. Vadimata? (筏提摩多), 384–417.

Shizhuduanjie-jing (十住斷結經), T10, no. 966, tr. Zhu Fonian, 384–417.

**Śrīmālādevīsiṃhanāda-sūtra* (勝鬘師子吼一乘大方便方廣經), T12, no. 353, tr. Guṇabhadra, 420–479. *Śrīmālādevī* (勝鬘夫人會), T11, no. 310.48, tr. Bodhiruci, Tang dynasty, 618–907.

**Sucintidevaputra-sūtra* (須真天子經), T15, no. 588, tr. Dharmarakṣa, 266.

Sukhāvatīvyūha-sūtra. Larger Version (佛說阿彌陀三耶三佛薩樓佛檀過度人道經), T12, no. 362, tr. Zhi Qian, 220–280; (佛說大阿彌陀經), T12, no. 364, collected by Wang Rixiu, 1160–1162; Smaller Version (佛說阿彌陀經), T12, no. 366, tr. Kumārajīva, 402.

**Sumati-sūtra* (佛說三摩竭經), T2, no. 129, tr. Zhu Luyan, of the Wu dynasty, 222–280.

**Śūraṃgamasamādhi-sūtra* (佛說首楞嚴三昧經), T15, no. 642, tr. Kumārajīva, 402–412.

**Sūryajiḥmīkaraṇaprabhāsamādhi-sūtra* (佛說超日三昧經), T15, no. 638, tr. Nian Chenyuan, 265–316.

**Suvarṇaprabhāsa-sūtra* (金光明經), T16, no. 663, tr. Dharmakṣena, 397–439.

Suvarṇaprabhāsottamarāja-sūtra (金光明最勝王經), T16, no. 665, tr. Yijing, 695–713.

**Tathāgatamahākāruṇikanirdeṣa-sūtra* (大哀經), T13, no. 398, tr. Dharmarakṣa, 265–316.

**Tathāgatapratibimbapratiṣṭhānuśaṃsā-sūtra* (佛說大乘造像功德經), T16, no. 694, tr. Devaprajñā, 691.

**Vaipulyamahāvyūha-sūtra* (方廣大莊嚴經), T3, no. 187, tr. Divākara, 683. This is another translation of the *Lalitavistara*.

**Vijñāptimātratāsiddhi-śāstra* (成唯識論), T31, no. 1585, by Dharmapāla and nine others, tr. Xuanzang, 659. English translation: *Ch'eng wei-shih lun*, tr. Wei Tat, Hong Kong: Ch'eng wei-shih lun Publication Committee, 1973. French Translation: *Vijñaptimātratāsiddhi: la Siddhi de Hiuan-Tsang*, vols I & II, tr. Louis de La Vallée Poussin, Paris: Librairie Orientaliste Paul Guenther, 1929.

**Vimalakīrtinirdeśa-sūtra*. Chinese translations: (佛說維摩詰經), T14, no. 474, tr. Zhi Qian, 220–280; (維摩詰所說經), T14, no. 475, tr. Kumarājīva, 406; (佛說無垢稱經), T14, no. 476, tr. Xuanzang.

Xingqixingjing (佛說興起行經 *Nidānacaryā-sūtra*?), T4, no. 197, tr. Kang Menxiang, 194–199.

Yizu-jing (佛說義足經 '*Sūtra* on the Sufficiency of Truth'), T4, no. 198, tr. Zhi Qian, 222–280.
* *Yogācārabhūmi-śāstra* (瑜伽師地論), T30, no. 1579, attrib. Maitreya, tr. Xuanzang, 654.

II Secondary sources

Akanuma C. (1921) 'The Buddha', *The Eastern Buddhist*, vol. 1, pp. 47–60.
—— (1922) 'The Triple Body of the Buddha', *The Eastern Buddhist*, vol. 2, pp. 1–29.
—— (1958) *The Comparative Catalogue of Chinese Āgamas and Pāli Nikāyas*, Tokyo: Hajinkaku-Shobo.
An Yang-Gyu (1998) 'Buddhology in the *Mahāparinibbāna Suttanta* and Its Commentary, with an Annotated Translation of Buddhaghosa's Commentary', unpublished Ph.D. thesis, University of Oxford.
Bareau, A. (1969) 'The Superhuman Personality of the Buddha and Its Symbolism in the *Mahāparinirvāṇasūtra* of the Dharmaguptaka', in J. M. Kitagawa and C. H. Long, eds, *Myths and Symbols: Studies in Honor of Mircea Eliade*, pp. 9–22.
—— (1980) 'The Place of the Buddha Gautama in the Buddhist Religion During the Region of Aśoka', in S. Balasooriya, ed., *Buddhist Studies in Honour of Walpola Rahula*, London: Fraser, pp. 1–9.
Beal, S. (tr.) (1884) *Si-yu-ki, Buddhist Records of the Western world*, 2 vols, London: Trübner.
Chang, Garma C. C. (tr.) (1983) *A Treasury of Mahāyāna Sūtras: Selections From the Mahāratnakūṭa Sūtra*, University Park: The Buddhist Association of the United States, Pennsylvania State University Press.
Chappell, D. W. (1977) 'Chinese Buddhist Interpretations of the Pure Lands', in M. Saso and D. W. Chappell, eds, *Buddhist and Taoist Studies*, vol. I, Hawaii: The University Press of Hawaii, pp. 23–53.
Ch'en, K. S. K. [1964] (1972) *Buddhism in China: A Historical Survey*, Princeton: Princeton University Press.
Cleary, T. (tr.) (1985) *The Flower Ornament Scripture: A Translation of the Avataṃsaka Sūtra*, Boston and London: Shambhala. (This is a translation made from Śīkṣānanda's version.)
Committee of Foguangshan Buddhist Order, ed. (2000) *Foguang Buddhist Dictionary*, 2nd edn, Taiwan: Foguang Culture Corporation (CD ROM).
Conze, E. (1960) *The Prajñāpāramitā Literature*, s-Gravenhage: Mouton.
—— (1967) *Thirty Years of Buddhist Studies*, Oxford: Bruno Cassirer.
—— [1958] (1970) (tr.) *Aṣṭasāhasrikā Prajñāpāramitā-sūtra*, Calcutta: The Asian Society.
Cutler, S. M. (1994) 'The Pāli Apadāna Collection', *Journal of the Pali Text Society*, vol. XX, pp. 1–42.
Dayal, H. (1932) *The Bodhisattva Doctrine in Buddhist Sanskrit Literature*, London: Routledge & Kegan Paul.
Dutt, N. (1925) *Early History of the Spread of Buddhism and Buddhist Schools*, London: Luzac.
—— (1930) *Aspects of Mahāyāna Buddhism and Its Relation to Hīnayāna*, London: Luzac.
—— (1937) 'Doctrines of the Mahāsāṃghika School of Buddhism', *Indian Historical Quarterly*, 13, pp. 549–580, 14, pp. 110–113.

—— (1978a) *Mahāyāna Buddhism*, Delhi: Motilal Banarsidass.

—— (1978b) *Buddhist Sects in India*, Delhi: Motilal Banarsidass.

Edgerton, F. [1953] (1985) *Buddhist Hybrid Sanskrit Grammar and Dictionary*, 2 vols, Kyoto: Rinsen Book Co.

Endo, T. (1997) *Buddha in Theravāda Buddhism: A Study of the Concept of Buddha in the Pāli Commentaries*, Colombo: The Buddhist Culture Center.

Eliade, M., ed. (1987) *The Encyclopaedia of Religion*, New York: Macmillan; London: Collier Macmillan.

Fausböll, V. (1881) *The Suttanipāta: A Collections of Discourses*, vol. X, Part II of *The Sacred Books of the East*, Oxford: Clarendon Press.

Frauwallner, E. (1951) *On the Date of the Buddhist Master of the Law Vasubandhu*, Rome: Istituto Italiano per il Medio ed Estremo Oriente.

Gokhale, B. G. (1994) *New Light on Early Buddhism*, London: Sangam Books.

Gombrich, R. F. (1980) 'The Significance of Former Buddhas in the Theravādin Tradition', in S. Balasooriya, ed., *Buddhist Studies in Honour of Walpola Rahula*, London: Fraser, pp. 62–72.

—— (1987–1988) 'Recovering the Buddha's Message', in T. Skorupski, ed., *The Buddhist Forum*, vol. I, London, pp. 5–23.

—— (1992) 'Why Six Former Buddhas?', *The Journal of Oriental Research*, vols LVI–LXII, pp. 326–30.

—— [1988] (1994a) *Theravada Buddhism: A Social History from Ancient Benares to Modern Colombo*, London: Routledge & Kegan Paul.

—— (1994b) 'The Buddha and Jains: A Reply to Professor Bronkhorst', *Asiatische Studien*, vol. XLVIII, no. 4, pp. 1069–96.

—— (1996) *How Buddhism Began*, London: Athlone, London & Atlantic Highlands.

Gomez, L. (1987a) 'Mahāsāṃghika', in M. Eliade, ed., *The Encyclopedia of Religion*, vol. 9, pp. 120–2.

—— (1987b) 'Sarvāstivāda', in M. Eliade, ed., *The Encyclopedia of Religion*, vol. 13, pp. 75–80.

Gomez, L. O. and Silk, J. A., eds (1989) *Studies in the Literature of the Great Vehicle: Three Mahāyāna Buddhist Texts*, Michigan: Collegiate Institute for the Study of Buddhist Literature and Center for South and Southeast Asian Studies, the University of Michigan.

Griffiths, P., Hakamaya, N., Keenan, J. P. and Swanson, P. L. (tr.) (1989) *The Realm of Awakening: A Translation and Study of the Tenth Chapter of Asaṅga's Mahāyānasaṃgraha*, New York: Oxford University Press.

Guang Xing (1994) '*Nāgasena Bhikṣu Sūtra*: An Annotated Translation and Study', unpublished M.Phil. thesis, University of Kelaniya.

Habito, R. (1978) 'The Development of the Buddha-body Theory', *Shūkyō Kenkyū*, vol. L2-2, no. 237, pp. 1–22.

Hare, E. M. (tr.) (1995) *The Book of the Gradual Sayings*, vols III & IV, Oxford: PTS, reprinted.

Harrison, P. (1982) 'Sanskrit Fragments of a Lokottaravādin Tradition', in L. A. Hercus, ed., *Indological and Buddhist Studies: Volume in Honour of Professor J. W. de Jong on his Sixtieth Birthday* (Canberra: Faculty of Asian Studies), pp. 211–34.

—— (1987) 'Who Gets to Ride in the Great Vehicle? Self Image and Identity Among the Followers of the Early Mahāyāna', *Journal of the International Association of Buddhist Studies*, vol. 10, no. 1, pp. 67–89.

—— (1992) 'Is the Dharma-kāya the Real Phantom Body of the Buddha?', *Journal of the International Association of Buddhist Studies*, vol. 15, no. 1, pp. 44–94.

—— (1993) 'The Earliest Chinese Translations of Mahāyāna Buddhist Sūtras: Some Notes on the Works of Lokakṣema', *Buddhist Studies Review*, vol. 10, no. 2, pp. 135–77.

—— (1995a) 'Searching for the Origin of Mahāyāna: What Are We Looking for?', *The Eastern Buddhist*, vol. 18, no. 1, pp. 48–69.

—— (1995b) 'Some Reflections on the Personality of the Buddha', *The Otani Gakuho*, vol. LXXIV, no. 4, March, pp. 1–29.

Hastings, J. with the assistance of John A. Selble and other scholars (eds) (1908–1926) *Encyclopaedia of Religion and Ethics*, Edinburgh: T. & T. Clark.

Hirakawa, A. (1963) 'The Rise of Mahāyāna Buddhism and Its Relationship to the Worship of Stūpa', *Memoirs of the Research Department of the Toyo Bunko*, 22, pp. 57–106.

—— (1965) 'Development of the Various Bhūmis, Especially of the Common Ten Bhūmis', *Indogaku Bukkyōgaku Kenkyū*, vol. XIII, no. 2, March, pp. 290–310.

Horner, I. B. (tr.) (1963) *Milinda's Questions*, vols I & II, London: Luzac.

—— (tr.) (1992–1993) *The Book of the Discipline*, vols I–VI, Oxford: PTS, reprint.

Inagaki, H. (1963) 'The Adoption of the Buddha's Life Pattern in the Ten Bhūmi Systems', *Indogaku Bukkyōgaku Kenkyū*, vol. 11, no. 2, March, pp. 792–7.

Jaini, H. S. (1958) 'Buddha's Prolongation of Life', *Bulletin of the School of Oriental and African Studies*, vol. 21, pp. 546–52.

Jones, J. J. (tr.) (1956) *Mahāvastu, Translated from the Buddhist Sanskrit*, vols I–III, London: Luzac.

Kajiyama, Y. (1985) 'Stūpa, the Mother of Buddhas and Dharma-body', in A. K. Warder, ed., *New Paths in Buddhist Research*, Durham, North Carolina: The Acorn Press, pp. 9–16.

—— ed. [1983] (1989) *Banruo Sixiang* 般若思想 (The Thought of Prajñā), Chinese translation by Xu Yangzu, Taipei: Faer Publication.

Kawamura, K. (1972) 'Sūtras Quoted in the *Mahāparinirvāṇa Sūtra*', *Indogaku Bukkyōgaku Kenkyū*, vol. XX, no. 2, pp. 54–9.

—— (1990) 'The Conditions for Obtaining the Eternal Dharma-body in the *Mahāparinirvāṇa Sūtra*', *Indogaku Bukkyōgaku Kenkyū*, vol. XXXVIII, no. 2, pp. 292–8.

Keenan, J. P. (tr.) (1992) *The Summary of the Great Vehicle by Bodhisattva Asaṅga*, Los Angeles: California: Numata Center for Buddhist Translation and Research. (This is a translation made from Paramārtha's translation of a Chinese version.)

—— (tr.) (2000) *The Scripture on the Explication of Underlying Meaning*, Berkeley, California: Numata Center for Buddhist Translation and Research.

Koei, A. (1964) 'Trikāya', *Shūkyō Kenkyū*, vol. 37, no. 4 (Nr. 179), March, pp. 27–57.

Kotatsu, F. (1958) 'An Aspect of the Buddhas, Found in the Early Buddhist Scriptures, with Reference to the Present-Other Worlds Buddhas', *Indogaku Bukkyōgaku Kenkyū*, vol. VI, no. 2, March, pp. 64–73.

Kritzer, R. (1992) '*Pratītyasamutpāda* in the *Daśabhūmikasūtra*', *Indogaku Bukkyōgaku Kenkyū*, vol. XL, no. 2, pp. 1067–72.

Kumataro, K. (1958) 'Ten Stages of Bodhisattva', *Indogaku Bukkyōgaku Kenkyū*, vol. VI, no. 2, March, pp. 186–9.

Lamotte, E. (1957) 'Khuddakanikāya and Kṣudrakapiṭaka', *East and West*, Year VII, no. 4, pp. 341–8.
—— (tr.) (1976) *The Teachings of Vimalakīrti*, London: PTS. English translation by Sara Boin-Webb.
—— (1985) 'The Assessment of Textual Interpretation in Buddhism', *Buddhist Studies Review*, vol. 2, no. 1, pp. 5–24.
—— (1988) *History of Indian Buddhism, from the Origins to the Śaka Era*, Louvain-la-Neuve: Université Catholique de Louvain Institut Orientaliste. English translation by Sara Boin-Webb. (French original 1958).
—— (1990) 'Dazhidulun De Zhuozhe Jiqi Fanyi', 大智度論之作者及其翻譯 ('The Authorship and the Translation of the *Mahāprajñāpāramitāśāstra*'). Chinese translation by Guo Zhongsheng, *Diguan*, vol. 62, pp. 97–179.
—— (tr.) (1992) 'Shi Chupinzhong Pusa' 釋初品中菩薩 ('On the Bodhisattva of the First Chapter of the *Mahāprajñāpāramitāśāstra*'). Chinese translation by Guo Zhongsheng, *Diguan*, vol. 69, pp. 5–106.
—— (tr.) (1998) *Śūraṅgamasamādhisūtra, the Concentration of Heroic Progress*. English translation by Sara Boin-Webb, London: Curzon Press. (French original 1965.)
Lancaster, L. (1968) 'The Chinese Translation of the *Aṣṭasāhasrikā-Prajñāpāramitāśūtra* Attributed to Chih Ch'ien', *Monumenta Serica*, 28, pp. 246–57.
—— (1975) 'The Oldest Mahāyāna Sūtra: Its Significance for the Study of Buddhist Development', *The Eastern Buddhist* (new series), vol. 8, no. 1, pp. 30–41.
—— (ed.) (1977) *Prajñāpāramitā and Related Systems: Studies in Honour of Edward Conze*, Berkeley: Buddhist Studies Series.
La Vallée Poussin, L. (1906) 'Studies in Buddhist Dogma: The Three Bodies of the Buddha (Trikāya)', *Journal of the Royal Asiatic Society of Great Britain and Ireland*, pp. 943–77.
Makransky, J. (1997) *Buddhahood Embodied: Sources of Controversy in India and Tibet*, New York: State University of New York Press.
Malalasekera, G. P., ed. (1937) *Dictionary of Pāli Proper Names*, vols I–II, London: John Murray.
—— ed. (1961) *Encyclopedia of Buddhism*, vol. I, Sri Lanka: Government of Sri Lanka.
—— ed. (1966) *Encyclopedia of Buddhism*, vol. II, Sri Lanka: Government of Sri Lanka.
—— ed. (1971) *Encyclopedia of Buddhism*, vol. III, Sri Lanka: Government of Sri Lanka.
Masuda, J. (tr.) (1922) *Origin and Doctrines of Early Indian Buddhist Schools, Asia Major*, vol. II, fascicle I, Leipzig: Verlag Asia Major.
Misra, G. S. P. (1972) *The Age of Vinaya: A Historical and Cultural Study*, New Delhi: Munshiram Manoharlal.
Mitomo, R. (1988) 'The Buddhas of the Ten Directions and the Sixteen Princes', *Indogaku Bukkyogaku Kenkyu*, vol. XXXVI, no. 2, pp. 785–92.
Muller, C. and others, eds (1999–2002) *Digital Dictionaries of Buddhism*, available online, http://www.acmuller.net/ddb/.
Nagao, G., ed. (1961) *An Index to Asaṅga's Mahāyānasaṃgraha, Part Two: Sanskrit-Tibetan-Chinese*, Tokyo: International Institute for Buddhist Studies.

—— (1973) 'On the Theory of Buddha-body (Buddhakāya)', *The Eastern Buddhist*, vol. 6, no. 1, pp. 25–53.
Nagata, M. (1973) 'Nāgārjuna's View on Buddhakāya', *Indogaku Bukkyōgaku Kenkyū*, vol. XXII, no. 1, pp. 369–72.
Nakamura, H. [1977] (1987) *Gotama Buddha*, Los Angeles and Tokyo: Buddhist Books International.
—— (1996) *Indian Buddhism: a Survey with Bibliographical Notes*, Delhi: Motilal Banarsidass Publishers. (Original Japanese edition 1980.)
Ñāṇamoli, Bhikkhu (tr.) (1995) *The Middle Length Discourse of the Buddha*, Boston: Wisdom Publication.
—— [1972] (1998) *The Life of the Buddha, according to the Pāli Canon*, Sri Lanka: Kandy Buddhist Publication Society.
Nanjio, B. (tr.) [1882] (1989) *A Catalogue of the Chinese Translation of the Buddhist Tripiṭaka*, Delhi: Classics Indian Publications.
Narain, A. K., ed. (1980) *Studies in the History of Buddhism*, Delhi: B. R. Publishing Corporation.
Nattier, J. (2000) 'The Realm of Akṣobhya: a Missing Piece in the History of Pure Land Buddhism', *Journal of the International Association of Buddhist Studies*, vol. 23, no. 1, pp. 71–102.
Naughton, A. (1991) 'Buddhist Omniscience', *The Eastern Buddhist*, vol. 24, no. 1, pp. 28–51.
Nishio, K. (1938) 'A Study of Many Buddhas in the Present Period', *Bukkyō Kenkyū*, vol. 2, no. 4, pp. 142–56.
Pachow, W. (1986) 'A Hermeneutical Approach to the Supernatural Phenomena in Buddhist History', *Chinese Culture*, vol. XXVII, no. 1, pp. 15–36, no. 2, pp. 73–100.
Paul, D. Y. (1982) 'The Life and Times of Paramārtha (499–569)', *Journal of the International Association of Buddhist Studies*, vol. 5, no. 1, pp. 37–69.
Rahula, Walpola (1974) 'Buddha', *Encyclopaedia Britannica*, fifteenth edition, Chicago and London: Encyclopaedia Britannica.
—— (1985) *What the Buddha Taught*, London: Gordon Fraser.
Raymond, B. W. (1970) 'Historical Criticism of a Buddhist Scripture: The *Mahāparinibbāna Sutta*', *Journal of The American Academy of Religion*, vol. XXXVIII, no. 2, pp. 156–67.
Ren Jiyu 任繼愈, ed. [1985] (1997) *Zhongguo Fojiao Shi* 中國佛教史 ('History of Chinese Buddhism'), vols I, II & III, Beijing: Chinese Academy of Social Sciences. (Original 1985.)
Reynolds, F. E. (1977) 'The Several Bodies of the Buddha: Reflections on the Neglected Aspects of Theravāda Tradition', *History of Religions*, 16, I, pp. 374–89.
Reynolds, F. and Charles, H. (1987) 'Buddha', *The Encyclopedia of Religion*, New York: Macmillan; London: Collier Macmillan, vol. 2, pp. 319–322.
Rhys Davids, C. A. F. (tr.) (1913) *Psalms of the Early Buddhists*, vols I & II, Oxford: PTS.
Rhys Davids, C. A. F. and Woodward, F. L. (tr.) (1993–1995) *The Book of Kindred Sayings*, vols I–V, Oxford: PTS, reprint.
Rhys Davids, T. W. (tr.) (1890) *The Questions of the King Milinda*, in *Sacred Books of the East*, vols 35 & 36, Oxford: Clarendon Press.
—— (tr.) [1899] (1995) *The Dialogues of the Buddha*, vols I–III, Oxford: PTS.

Rockhill, W. W. (tr.) (1884) *The Life of the Buddha and the Early History of His Order*, London: Trübner.

Rowell, T. (1934) 'The Background and Early Use of the Buddhakṣetra Concept', *The Eastern Buddhist*, vol. VI, no. 3, pp. 199–246. Introduction and Chapter I.

—— (1935) 'The Background and Early Use of the Buddhakṣetra Concept', *The Eastern Buddhist*, vol. VI, no. 4, pp. 379–431. Chapters II and III.

—— (1937) 'The Background and Early Use of the Buddhakṣetra Concept', *The Eastern Buddhist*, vol. VII, no. 2, pp. 131–76. Chapter IV and Appendixes.

Schopen, G. (1991) 'Monks and the Relic Cult in the *Mahāparinibbāna Sutta*: An Old Misunderstanding in Regard to Monastic Buddhism', in G. Schopen and K. Shinohara, eds, *From Benaras to Beijing: Essays on Buddhism and Chinese Religion in Honour of Jan Yun-Hua*, London: Mosaic Press, pp. 187–201.

—— (ed.) (1997) *Bones, Stones and Buddhist Monks*, Honolulu, Hawaii: University of Hawaii Press.

Shih Hengching 釋恆清 (1996) 'Dabanniepanjing de Foxinglun' 大般涅槃經的佛性論 ('The Theory of the Buddhadhātu in the *Mahāparinirvāṇasūtra*'), *Journal of the Center for Buddhist Studies*, vol. I, pp. 31–88.

Shih Shanyin 釋善因 (1999) 'Dacheng Zuangyianjinglun Zhi Yianju' 大乘莊嚴經論之研究 ('A Study on the *Mahāyānasūtrālaṃkāra*'), *Chu-Hwa Buddhist Journal*, vol. III, pp. 19–41.

Shimoda, M. (1997) *A Study of the Mahāparinirvāṇasūtra with a Focus on the Methodology of the Study of Mahāyāna Sūtras*, Tokyo: Shunjū-sha.

Skorupski, T., ed. (1990) *Buddhist Forum*, vol. I, London: SOAS.

—— ed. (1997) *Buddhist Forum*, vol. V, London: SOAS.

Snellgrove, D. L. (1973a) 'Śākyamuni's Final Nirvāṇa', *Bulletin of the School of Oriental and African Studies*, vol. 36, pp. 399–411.

—— (1973b) 'In Search of the Historical Buddha', *South Asian Review*, 7, pp. 151–7.

Soothhill, W. E., Hodous, L. and Shik Sheng-kang, eds (1989) *A Dictionary of Chinese Buddhist Terms*, Taiwan: Fokuang Buddhist Publication.

Suzuki, D. T. (1907) *Outlines of Mahāyāna Buddhism*, London: Luzac.

—— (1930) *Studies in the Laṅkāvatāra Sūtra*, London: George Routledge.

—— (tr.) (1932) *The Laṅkāvatāra Sūtra, A Mahāyāna Text*, London: George Routledge.

Takakusu, J. (tr.) (1904) 'The Life of Vasubandhu by Paramārtha (AD 499–569)', *T'oung Pao Archive*, Series II, vol. V, pp. 269–296, 620.

—— (1904–1905) 'On the Abhidharma Literature of the Sarvāstivādins', *Journal of the Pali Text Society*, pp. 67–146.

—— (1905) 'A Study of Paramārtha's Life of Vasubandhu and the Date of Vasubandhu', *Journal of the Royal Asiatic Society*, pp. 33–53.

Takasaki, J. (1960) 'Structure of the *Anuttarāśrayasūtra* (Wu-shang-I-ching)', *Indogaku Bukkyōgaku Kenkyū*, vol. VIII, no. 2, pp. 748–41.

—— (1966) 'Dharmatā, Dharmadhātu, Dharmakāya and Buddhadhātu', *Indogaku Bukkyōgaku Kenkyū*, vol. XIV, no. 2, pp. 903–19.

—— (1974) *Formation of the Tathāgatagarbha Theory: A Study on the Historical Background of the Tathagatagarbha Theory of Mahāyāna Buddhism Based upon the Scriptures Preceding the Ratnagotravibhāga*, Tokyo: Shunjusha.

Takeuchi, S. (1983) 'Buddhakan no hensen', in A. Hirakawa, ed., *Daijō Bukkyō*, vol. I, Tokyo: Shunjusha, pp. 166–70.

Tamaki, K. (1982) 'Prajñāpāramitā and Śūnyatā in the *Aṣṭasāhasrikā*', *Indogaku Bukkyōgaku Kenkyū*, vol. XXXI, no. 1, pp. 93–8.

Tang Yongtong 湯用彤 [1938] (1997) *Han Wei Liajin Nanbeichao Fojiao Shi* 漢魏兩晉南北朝佛教史 ('History of Buddhism During the Han, Wei, North and South Dynasties'), Beijing: Beijing University Press.

Thurman, R. A. F. (tr.) (1976) *Vimalakīrtinirdeśa-sūtra*, University Park: Pennsylvania State University Press.

Walters, J. (1990) 'The Buddha's Bad Karma: A Problem in the History of Theravāda Buddhism', *Numen*, vol. XXXVII, fasc. 1, pp. 70–95.

Warder, A. K. (1956) 'On the Relationship Between Early Buddhism and Other Contemporary Systems', *Bulletin of the School of Oriental and African Studies*, 18, pp. 43–63.

—— (ed.) (1985) *New Paths in Buddhist Research*, Durham, North Carolina: Acorn Press.

—— [1970] (1997) *Indian Buddhism*, Delhi: Motilal Banarsidass.

Warren, H. C. (1909) *Buddhism in Translation*, Cambridge, Massachusetts: Harvard University.

Watson, B. (tr.) (1993) *The Lotus Sutra*, New York: Columbia University Press.

Willemen, C., Dessein, B. and Cox, C. (1998) *Sarvāstivāda Buddhist Scholasticism*, Leiden, New York and Cologue: Brill.

Williams, M., ed. [1899] (1986) *A Sanskrit–English Dictionary*, Tokyo: Meicho Fukyu Kai.

Williams, P. (1989) *Mahāyāna Buddhism: The Doctrinal Foundations*, London: Routledge.

Winternitz, M. (1988) *History of Indian Literature*, vol. II. English translation by S. Sarma. Delhi: Motilal Banarsidass.

Woodward, F. L. (tr.) (1995) *The Book of the Gradual Sayings*, vols I, II & V, Oxford: PTS, reprinted.

Yao, Z, ed. (1996) *Yibu zonglun lun* (異部宗輪論 *Samayabhedavyūhacakra*), Taiwan: Foguang Publication.

Yinshun 印順 (1968) *Shuoyiqieyoubu De Lunshu Yu Lunshi Zi Yanju* 說一切有部為主的論書與論師之研究 ('A Study on the Treatises and Masters of the Sarvāstivāda'), Taipei: Zhengwen Publication.

—— (1988) *Hua Yu Ji* 華雨集, vol. III, Taipei: Zhengwen Publication.

—— (1990) 'Dazhidulun Zi Zhuozhe Jiqi Fanyi' 大智度論之作者及其翻譯 ('The Authorship and the Translation of the *Mahāprajñāpāramitāśāstra*'), *Dongfang Zongjiao Yanjiu* ('Journal of Oriental Religions'), vol. 2, Taipei: The Dongfang Zhongjiao Yejun Publication, pp. 9–70.

—— (1991) *Yuanshi Fojian Shengdian Zhi Jicheng* 原始佛教聖典之集成 ('The Compilation of the Primitive Buddhist Canon'), Taipei: Zhengwen Publication.

—— [1921] (1992) *Rulaizang Zhi Yianju* 如來藏之研究 ('A Study on the Tathāgatagarbha'), Taipei: Zhengwen Publication.

—— [1981] (1994) *Chuqi Dacheng Fojian Zhi Qiyuan Yu Zhankai* 初期大乘佛教之起源與展開 ('The Origin and Development of Early Mahāyāna Buddhism'), Taipei: Zhengwen Publication.

Yoshioka, R. (1963) 'The *Sukhāvatīvyūha Sūtra* and Lokottaravāda', *Indogaku Bukkyōgaku Kenkyū*, vol. XI, no. 1, pp. 136–7.

Zurcher, E. [1959] (1972) *The Buddhist Conquest of China: The Spread and Adaptation of Buddhism in Early Medieval China*, 2 vols, Leiden: E. J. Brill.

INDEX

An environmentally friendly book printed and bound in England by www.printondemand-worldwide.com

PEFC Certified

This product is from sustainably managed forests and controlled sources

PEFC

PEFC/16-33-415

www.pefc.org

Mixed Sources

Product group from well-managed forests, and other controlled sources

FSC

www.fsc.org Cert no. TT-COC-002641

© 1996 Forest Stewardship Council

This book is made entirely of chain-of-custody materials

#0252 - 211211 - C0 - 234/156/14 - PB